Cahiers du Cinéma

Harvard Film Studies

Cahiers du Cinéma

1960–1968: New Wave, New Cinema, Reevaluating Hollywood

Edited by
Jim Hillier

Harvard University Press
Cambridge, Massachusetts
1986

Library of Congress Cataloging-in-Publication Data

Cahiers du cinéma, the 1960s.
  Bibliography: p.
  Includes index.
    1. Moving-pictures—Philosophy. 2. Moving-pictures—
France. 3. Moving-pictures—United States. I. Hillier,
Jim. II. Cahiers du cinéma.
PN1995.C295 1986   791.43'01   86–14235

ISBN 0–674–09062–4

Contents

Contents

Part Two American Cinema: Celebration

Part Three American Cinema: Revaluation

Part Four Towards a New Cinema/New Criticism

Contents

Preface

When a four-volume anthology of material from *Cahiers du Cinéma* was first discussed, it was intended that each volume should be self-contained and coherent in its own terms, should seek to be representative of the period covered, should contain largely material not readily available before in English translation, should be relevant to contemporary film education and film culture, should be accessible to the non-specialist reader, and should be pleasurable. It was only after working for several years on the first two volumes that I realized how tall this order was, but I hope that at least some of these original requirements have been met.

My main function as editor, and the one that has taken most time, has been to sift through twenty years' output of *Cahiers* (nine years and over a hundred issues for this second volume) for the tiny selection of material – just thirty-nine items in this case – which would make sense of the journal's interests and importance at the time and still be relevant to readers coming to it more than twenty years later. Needless to say, this has not been easy.

As editor I have seen my main task as placing *Cahiers* in context, rather than imposing my own views about it (though my views should be clear enough) or offering a radical critique from today's perspective of the ideological position or positions which *Cahiers* enshrined. I have felt it particularly important to plan the volumes as a guide, a resource, a base for further work and further reading, as well as self-contained books. It is with this in mind that the volumes include appendices which list other material from *Cahiers* during the relevant periods available in English translation, as a means of significantly extending the necessarily limited scope of these volumes themselves. My introductions and often (intentionally) profuse footnotes aim to point readers backwards, forwards and sideways to earlier, later and parallel developments in *Cahiers* as well as to contemporaneous and later developments in critical and theoretical writing in Britain and the USA. In part I have wanted to point, through these references, to some of the work in which a critique of *Cahiers* has taken place, both within *Cahiers* – clear enough at the end of this volume, and to be elaborated more clearly in the forthcoming Volume 3, covering the period 1969–1972 – and elsewhere.

My general introduction, '*Cahiers du Cinéma* in the 1960s', tries to sketch out the context for the whole volume. Whereas the introductions to each section aim to discuss some of the major threads and implications in the material comprising the individual section, the general introduction tries to place the contents of the whole volume within a broader perspective as well as to offer an additional range of references from *Cahiers*.

The sectional organization of the volume is not ideal but it does represent, I believe, some important structures of thinking in *Cahiers* in the period. In other words, I have tried to organize the volume along some of the primary conceptual lines on which *Cahiers* made sense of cinema in the 1960s. Material is arranged chronologically within each section, but my introductory discussions of each section do not strictly follow the order of the articles which follow. Inevitably, as in Volume 1, there is some artificiality in the sectional organization and material needs to be read and related in a variety of ways – within each section or area of cinema but also in the context of writing and thinking in other sections. The material on French cinema, for example, needs to be read alongside what was being written about new cinema, which needs to be read alongside what was being written about American cinema, and so on. Some of the inter-relationships are pointed to in my introductions and annotation.

Intentionally, the sectional organization of the volume closely relates to the organization of Volume 1. The prominence given in this volume to, for example, Jean-Luc Godard, François Truffaut, Eric Rohmer and Jacques Rivette as critics and as film-makers, to American cinema and particularly Hawks, Hitchcock and Ray, and to questions of realism, authorship and *mise en scène* represents a conscious desire to select material which relates directly back to Volume 1. My introductions and annotation, again, try to point to some of these relationships.

A note on translations

Translation always poses problems about accurate rendition, especially when, as in this case, several different translators are involved and when some of the original writing is quite difficult. It would be wrong to pretend that we have not experienced occasionally quite severe problems of translation. There are a number of points where we have had difficulty in grasping the precise sense of the original and others where, despite such a grasp, the right translation has been difficult to find.

The French terms *auteur* and *mise en scène* have entered critical discussion in English, but *auteur* in particular did not always have some of the meanings currently attached to it. We have usually retained *auteur* when 'author' would have been a direct translation and *mise en scène* where 'direction' might have been a suitable rendering, but we have tried to be sensitive to the varying usage of the terms.

Les Cahiers du Cinéma (literally, 'Cinema Notebooks') are plural, but we have preferred to refer to *Cahiers* – the normal abbreviation used – as if in the singular.

In the period 1951–1969 *Cahiers* was an almost wholly male preserve, marked at times by considerable misogyny. Only two items in the two volumes involve a woman critic – Sylvie Pierre – and both are from 1968. Accordingly, it seemed appropriate to maintain 'he', 'him' and 'his' to mark this sexual inequality. Similarly, we have kept 'American' where 'US' is strictly correct, since this was the way *Cahiers* was thinking in the 1950s and 1960s.

Notes and references

All notes are the editor's except where specifically designated as authors' or translators' notes.

A number of books referred to in notes with some frequency are given in abbreviated form in references. Full details can be found in the section 'Books Frequently Cited in the Text', on pp. xiii–xiv.

Acknowledgments

We are indebted to *Cahiers du Cinéma* for the agreement to produce these volumes of anthology from their material.

In addition, the editor and publishers acknowledge permission to reprint the following material:

Chapter 4, translated by Tom Milne, is reprinted (in extract) from *Godard on Godard*, edited by Jean Narboni and Tom Milne (© Martin Secker and Warburg, 1972).

Chapter 38, translated by Amy Gateff, is reprinted (in extract) from *Rivette: Texts and Interviews*, edited by Jonathan Rosenbaum (© British Film Institute, 1977).

As I said in Volume 1, my principal personal debts are – as any teacher's must be – to my students, past and present, in various contexts over the last twenty years, and especially at British Film Institute Summer Schools, in University of London/BFI extra-mural classes, at Bulmershe College of Higher Education and, briefly, at Eastern Michigan University. Those students' ideas, their answers and their questions, have always been the most vital sources of stimulation. But I have also had the good fortune, over the last fifteen years, to have worked with exceptionally stimulating colleagues and, one way or another, I owe a great deal to a wide range of colleagues and their work. I have in mind particularly BFI Education, including summer schools and extra-mural classes (Charlotte Brunsdon, Ed Buscombe, Jim Cook, Richard Dyer, Christine Geraghty, Christine Gledhill, Sylvia Harvey, Geoff Hurd, Jim Kitses, Alan Lovell, Terry Lovell, David Lusted, Colin McArthur, Nicky North, Sam Rohdie, Tom Ryall, Philip Simpson, John Stewart, the late Paddy Whannel, Christopher Williams, Peter Wollen); the Film and Drama Division at Bulmershe College of Higher Education (Stuart Cosgrove, Steve Lacey, Pete Mathers, Laura Mulvey, Peter Muschamp, Doug Pye, Mike Stevenson, Tom Wild); the editorial board of *Movie* (Charles Barr, Andrew Britton, Ian Cameron, V. F. Perkins, Doug Pye, Michael Walker, Robin Wood). Several valued friends have housed me and *Cahiers* in congenial and even productive surroundings away from home and thanks on this score are due to Leslie Meyer, Karen Brumer, Lucy Stewart. BFI Library Services, one of the finest such resources in the world, is essential to many books, and this volume is no exception: my thanks to Gillian Hartnoll and her staff. My editors at the BFI, Angela Martin and, more recently, David Wilson, have been exceptionally patient, indulgent, understanding. Behroze Gandhy was central to my life while I worked on *Cahiers*: her support was vital to me, and I thank her. Similarly, the love and support of my children, Amy and Joachim, has been fundamental: this volume is for them, in the hope that cinema can be for them what it has been, and is, for me, both a source of pleasure and a form of knowledge.

Books Frequently Cited in the Text

Abbreviated forms and full bibliographical details

Bazin, *What is Cinema? Vol. 1*

Bazin, André, *What is Cinema? Volume 1* (Essays selected and translated by Hugh Gray, foreword by Jean Renoir), Berkeley, University of California Press, 1967; selected from Bazin, *Qu'est-ce que le cinéma? tome 1: Ontologie et langage* and *tome 2: Le Cinéma et les autres arts*, Paris, Editions du Cerf, 1958, 1959.

Bazin, *What is Cinema? Vol. 2*

Bazin, André, *What is Cinema? Volume 2* (Essays selected and translated by Hugh Gray, foreword by François Truffaut), Berkeley, University of California Press, 1971; selected from Bazin, *Qu'est-ce que le cinéma? tome 3: Cinéma et sociologie* and *tome 4: Une esthétique de la réalité: le néo-réalisme*, Paris, Editions du Cerf, 1961, 1962.

Brecht, *Brecht on Theatre*

Bertolt Brecht, *Brecht on Theatre: The Development of an Aesthetic* (edited and translated by John Willett), New York, Hill & Wang, 1964.

Cameron, *Movie Reader*

Cameron, Ian (ed.), *Movie Reader*, London, November Books; New York, Praeger, 1972.

Caughie, *Theories of Authorship*

Caughie, John (ed.), *Theories of Authorship*, London, Routledge & Kegan Paul, 1981 (BFI Readers in Film Studies series).

Godard on Godard

Godard, Jean-Luc, *Godard on Godard: Critical Writings by Jean-Luc Godard* (edited by Jean Narboni and Tom Milne, with an introduction by Richard Roud), London, Secker & Warburg; New York, Viking, 1972 (Cinema Two series); originally published as *Jean-Luc Godard par Jean-Luc Godard*, Paris, Editions Pierre Belfond, 1968.

Graham, *New Wave*

Graham, Peter (ed.), *The New Wave* (Critical landmarks selected by Peter

xiii

Graham), London, Secker & Warburg; New York, Doubleday, 1968 (Cinema One series).

Nichols, *Movies and Methods*

Nichols, Bill (ed.), *Movies and Methods: An Anthology*, Berkeley, University of California Press, 1976.

Screen Reader 1

Screen Reader 1: Cinema/Ideology/Politics, London, Society for Education in Film and Television, 1977.

Williams, *Realism and the Cinema*

Williams, Christopher (ed.), *Realism and the Cinema*, London, Routledge & Kegan Paul, 1980 (BFI Readers in Film Studies series).

Throughout this volume, '**Volume 1**' refers to:

Hillier, Jim (ed.), *Cahiers du Cinéma: The 1950s — Neo-Realism, Hollywood, New Wave*, Cambridge, Massachusetts, Harvard University Press; London, Routledge & Kegan Paul, 1985.

Cahiers du Cinéma

Introduction: *Cahiers du Cinéma* in the 1960s

1959–60 marked the international triumph not of *Cahiers du Cinéma* but of the *nouvelle vague*, or 'new wave', as Jean-Luc Godard's *A bout de souffle*, François Truffaut's *Tirez sur le pianiste*, Claude Chabrol's *Les Bonnes femmes*, Louis Malle's *Zazie dans le métro*, Jacques Demy's *Lola*, and other films, followed the success of *Les 400 coups*, *Les Cousins* and *Hiroshima mon amour*. Through most of the 1960s, and into the 1970s – less so today, although habits of thinking die hard – Paris was seen internationally as a kind of world film capital. But, and to a significant extent, that reputation was also built upon a sense that French *criticism*, and not only French cinema, led the world in having something new to say. The prestige of the *nouvelle vague* films conferred status, or at the very least intense interest, on the critical stance of *Cahiers*, even though many *nouvelle vague* films were made by directors not associated with the magazine (Alain Resnais, Agnès Varda, Jacques Demy, Louis Malle, for instance), and even though *Cahiers* was by no means the only source of critical interest. *Positif*, for example, the main rival to *Cahiers*, was a very interesting, very polemical film journal at this time (although a good deal of its polemic was in fact provoked by and aimed at *Cahiers* and the *Cahiers* directors in the *nouvelle vague*). *Positif* simply had the misfortune, in terms of international recognition and attention, of not producing, at a particular moment, new French film directors making successful feature film debuts.

Richard Roud, in *Sight and Sound*, made the connection between the international success of the *nouvelle vague* and interest in *Cahiers* criticism absolutely explicit. Commenting on the contents of the *Cahiers* ten best films of the year, he says:

> I wonder how many English critics would have included Hitchcock's *Vertigo*, Samuel Fuller's *Run of the Arrow*, Douglas Sirk's *A Time to Love and a Time to Die*, or Nicholas Ray's *Wind Across the Everglades*. One's first reaction might be to conclude that these men must be very foolish. And indeed, until a year

1

or two ago, one might have got away with it. But today it would be difficult, I think, to maintain that film-makers like Alain Resnais, François Truffaut, Claude Chabrol, Jean-Luc Godard, Pierre Kast and Jean-Pierre Melville are fools . . . if one admits, as one must, that some of them have made remarkable and even great films, then rather than throwing up one's hands in the air or dismissing them all as mad, one should try to see why and how their judgments of American films differ so substantially from ours.[1]

Certainly, the contents of serious British and American film journals in the period from 1959 into the early 1960s bear vivid witness to the debate which French criticism and French cinema generated and to the critical questioning – sometimes outrage and soul-searching – they provoked.[2]

What were the central critical issues which *Cahiers* was forcing, or helping to force, out into debate? As I tried to characterize the main focus of criticism in *Cahiers* at the end of the 1950s in my introduction to Volume 1 in this series,[3] it had to do centrally with ideas of authorship, in the *politique des auteurs* (which passed more generally into British and American criticism in the 1960s as 'the *auteur* theory'[4]). But increasingly towards the end of the 1950s the *politique des auteurs* was underpinned by ideas about *mise en scène* and the specificity of cinema. Whereas ideas about authorship were relatively easily admitted, at some level at least, into general critical writing or, more precisely, relatively easily extended into areas of popular cinema, the ideas about *mise en scène* proved more problematic (and, partly in consequence, opened up, ultimately, more important critical-theoretical issues). Issues about style, about form, content and meaning, and hence about the task of the critic and the specific nature of cinema as an art form or medium – 'Style is not just an embellishment; it is the method by which meaning is expressed', as Ian Cameron, V. F. Perkins and Mark Shivas put it in Britain[5] – are centrally addressed by many of the articles translated in this volume, most directly and most characteristically for the period perhaps in Fereydoun Hoveyda's 1960 articles, 'Nicholas Ray's Reply: *Party Girl*' and 'Sunspots'.[6] These issues are discussed more fully in the Introduction to Part II, 'The Apotheosis of *mise en scène*'.

In the 1961 special issue of *Cahiers* on criticism, Jacques Rivette's contributions usefully summarized and clarified the *Cahiers* position (in so far as there was *a* position) at this time on both authorship and *mise en scène*:

It is more interesting to look in *Mabuse* – which in my view is not the greatest Lang film – for what is personal in it and for the possible evolution of the film-maker, than to look for what might be least bad in the latest film by Boisrond. So, it's clear that the *politique des auteurs* simply says: we'll talk about Fritz Lang, who is someone worth talking about, and not Boisrond, who is nothing. That doesn't mean we're saying: all Fritz Lang's films are masterpieces. That would become an error. In the same way, when you extend the *politique des auteurs* to people like Minnelli or ten other American film-makers, it becomes an aberration, because it is clear that Minnelli is a talented 'director' but has never been and never will be an *auteur*. When you talk about Minnelli the first thing to do is talk about the screenplay, because he always subordinates his talent to something else. Whereas when you talk about Fritz Lang, the first thing is to talk about Fritz Lang, then about the screenplay. . . .

I find it crazy to say that in a film on the one hand there's the content and on the other hand the technique. It's beyond my imagination. We have often been accused of defending in *Cahiers mise en scène* in a pure state. It's not true. What we tried to say, on the contrary, is that a film is a whole. There's not content on the one hand and technique on the other, there's 'expression' and, if the film succeeds, this expression forms a whole.[7]

In discussion of authorship and *mise en scène*, as in Hoveyda's articles and Rivette's comments here, American cinema tends to become the primary focus of debate, but American cinema was not necessarily the most important for *Cahiers*, as has too often been supposed. *French* cinema was always, in effect, the main point of reference, if only because *Cahiers* critics saw themselves as future – and, by now, actual – *French* film-makers. Hence, no doubt, the enhanced intensity of some of the pieces relating to French cinema in this volume: these were very *immediate*, concrete issues for *Cahiers*. Italian and other European cinema was in general evidently much closer to what *Cahiers* critics might aspire to make themselves than American cinema was. But, as Richard Roud recognized in *Sight and Sound*,[8] and as Andrew Sarris confirmed a little later in *Film Culture*,[9] critically American cinema came to be the central focus for debates about both authorship and *mise en scène*. There were two main, and linked, reasons for this. First, it had become a critical commonplace – and *Cahiers*, with its highly developed taste for polemics, was very often in the business of challenging critical commonplaces – that the industrialized, commercial nature of Hollywood necessarily militated in the extreme against 'personal expression'. It was in this light that debates about authorship and the expression of the 'personal' they implied were most fierce, and most crucial, in the area of American cinema. Second, American cinema best exemplified 'classical' film language, the whole body of conventions which constitute the illusionist aesthetic, that narrative cinema which, essentially, Bazin validated, and which is so expertly characterized by V. F. Perkins in *Film as Film*:[10] it was this cinema which formed the main analytical basis for debates about *mise en scène*.

If there is a popular view of *Cahiers* in the 1960s, it is probably a rather fuzzy one, with *Cahiers* having little clear identity other than generally continuing with its 1950s positions, with their main 1950s advocates progressively abandoning criticism for film-making. Then, in the late 1960s, the events of May 1968 supposedly turned the values of *Cahiers* – along with many French social, political and cultural values more generally – on their heads. Certainly, in the early 1960s it did sometimes look as if both the French cinema and criticism which *Cahiers* had struggled for in the 1950s had been won or, at least, as far as criticism was concerned, placed firmly on the agenda. It seemed so to some of the contestants: in

3

their 1962 interviews, Truffaut thought that 'the kind of cinema I used to champion is now with us',[11] and Godard argued that *Cahiers* was going downhill 'due chiefly to the fact that there is no longer any position to defend. . . . Now that everyone is agreed, there isn't so much to say. The thing that made *Cahiers* was its position in the front line of battle'.[12]

Yet a look at the contents of *Cahiers* in 1960–1 as represented in this volume reveals a very different picture, with very little sense of stability or consensus of values and interests. It may be true that, say, Jean Douchet's article on Hitchcock[13] represents, in some ways, continuity with 1950s *Cahiers*, or that Hoveyda's 'Nicholas Ray's Reply: *Party Girl*' and 'Sunspots' centre on Ray and American cinema and *mise en scène*. But if they do represent continuity they do so in ways which also imply the beginning of a re-thinking of earlier ideas about authorship: new forms of analysis, new problems, are being addressed. And Michel Mourlet's 'In Defence of Violence' and 'The Beauty of Knowledge'[14] – indeed the MacMahonist stance in general – problematize in a particularly intense way certain conceptions of cinema and of *mise en scène* and their ideological allegiances which had been generated by *Cahiers* itself.[15] And if American cinema persists as the basis for such articles, alongside them are articles on the radically different French cinemas of Godard, of Resnais, of Rouch,[16] all representing breaks with 'classical' narrative cinema, all different versions of modernism, all very much pointing in new formal and ideological directions. At the same time, the 1960 special issue of *Cahiers* devoted to Bertolt Brecht, and particularly Bernard Dort's 'Towards a Brechtian Criticism of Cinema',[17] poses a very direct challenge to most of the values – formal and ideological – that *Cahiers* had stood for in the 1950s, as well as to much that was represented by *nouvelle vague* cinema itself. Yet a different version of Brecht provides an explicit reference point for, for instance, André S. Labarthe's article on *Les Bonnes femmes*[18] and Jean Douchet's and Michel Mourlet's articles on Losey's work.[19]

Clearly, contradictions abounded here. In a sense, of course, contradictions had always abounded in *Cahiers*, as Volume 1 of this series made clear. *Cahiers* could defend Hollywood as a *system*, but necessarily elevated film-makers within that system to *individual* artists with *auteur* status; it could defend genre as a body of conventions – though it rarely did so with much conviction – yet *auteurs* necessarily transcended those conventions. Only a *conscious* raising of questions about the nature of cinema as a popular art form could begin to reconcile such positions, but these were questions rarely addressed directly or seriously by anyone except Bazin.[20] Part of the 'productivity' of *Cahiers* in the 1950s and 1960s, however, is that they did 'raise', indirectly, such questions, precisely through the contradictions. At the beginning of the 1960s, the central contradiction had to do with the enshrinement of *mise en scène* above all else – 'everything is in the *mise en scène*', as Hoveyda puts it in 'Sunspots' – and the general repression of the ideological and economic implications of American cinema. It is in this perspective that we can see 1960–1 as a critically difficult, but productive, period for *Cahiers*, one of perhaps several important turning points in the 1960s. Hoveyda, of course, in 'Self-Criticism',[21] pointing forward to new critical-theoretical concerns (just as he does at the end of '*Cinéma vérité*, or Fantastic Realism',[22] written at the same time), makes it very explicit – interestingly, in the same issue devoted to criticism in which Rivette, as we saw earlier, re-states the *auteur* principle and the centrality of *mise en scène*: 'the *politique des auteurs* has had its day: it was merely a staging-post on the road to a new criticism'.

John Caughie is surely correct, writing with the advantage of hindsight in 1981, when he claims that the 'challenge to the concept of the author as source and centre of the text – as that which criticism must reveal in the text – has been decisive in contemporary criticism and aesthetic theory'.[23] Twenty years before, it cannot have seemed so: in terms of cinema and cinema criticism, the opposite must have seemed true. As yet, in 1961, only in very confused ways does Hoveyda see a different way forward, a way not seen much more clearly by the time of the 1965 editorial discussion 'Twenty Years On: American Cinema and the *politique des auteurs*'.[24] We need to acknowledge the important place in the development of film criticism and theory occupied by the *politique* as elaborated and practised in *Cahiers*, and we need to understand the controversies it generated, and why those controversies are of continuing interest today.

As Caughie points out, on the one hand *auteur* criticism represented simply the installation in cinema of 'the romantic artist, individual and self-expressive', already known from other art fields.[25] On the other hand, as he puts it, '*Cahiers*'s function in the history of film criticism appears as a shaking loose of established modes. Not necessarily progressive in itself, *Cahiers* seemed to enable progress. In so far as there was a "critical revolution" it was a revolution within bourgeois film criticism, which made other critical revolutions possible and necessary'.[26]

How was this? Again, Caughie:

> In the first place, the shift which *auteurism* effected was a shift in the way in which films were conceived and grasped within film criticism. The personality of the director, and the consistency within his films, were not, like the explicit subject matter which tended to preoccupy established criticism, simply there as a 'given'. They had to be sought out, discovered, by a process of analysis and attention to a number of films.[27]

Or, as Geoffrey Nowell-Smith put it, 'It was in establishing what the film said, rather than reasons for liking or disliking it, that authorship criticism validated itself as an approach'.[28] It was in this process of discovery, establishment, analysis that the concept of *mise en scène* became inextricable from the idea of authorship. Caughie again, on the context of American cinema:

> Given the conditions of production in which subject matter and script are likely to be in the control of the studio, style at least has the possibility of

being under the control of the director, and it is here that his personality may be the most legible. *Mise en scène* has a transformative effect. It is with the *mise en scène* that the *auteur* transforms the material which has been given to him; so it is in the *mise en scène* – in the disposition of the scene, in the camera movement, in the camera placement, in the movement from shot to shot – that the *auteur* writes his individuality into the film.[29]

Ultimately, it is this attention to *mise en scène*, to those discourses specific to the cinema, which provokes quite different directions in film criticism and theory. Caughie is certainly right, from the point of view of *Cahiers* at least, to concentrate his documents under 'auteurism' in the 1951–61 period. The *auteur* principle is still very alive in *Cahiers* throughout the 1960s, as much of this volume makes clear, but it is so with a different critical edge, as a principle or concept always in question.

As we have seen, American cinema was central to the *politique des auteurs* and hence to the concept of *mise en scène*. The 1960s represent a significant shift away from American cinema, or rather from *Hollywood* cinema, and a major re-direction of critical interest and investment in 'new cinema'. Already in the early 1960s there were clear signs of a struggle within *Cahiers* between allegiance to American cinema and certain forms of 'new cinema'. The work of Michelangelo Antonioni, for instance, set against American cinema, was one source of polarization. Writing from the Cannes festival in 1960, for example, Jean Domarchi praised the perfection of Vincente Minnelli's *Home from the Hill* while dismissing *L'Avventura* as an irritating, pretentious 'annex of literature'.[30] Contrarily, on its opening in France, Jacques Doniol-Valcroze argued that *L'Avventura* (along with *Hiroshima mon amour*) inaugurated the 'new cinema'.[31] Similarly, the 1962 Cannes festival finds Jean Douchet praising Otto Preminger's *Advise and Consent* while attacking *L'Eclisse* as 'a monstrosity . . . the height of artifice, trickery',[32] leaving it to André S. Labarthe to recognize the modernity and grandeur, if not perfection, of *L'Eclisse* as 'not a film, but a series of notes, the blueprint of a work to come – unless it reveals the impossibility for a work to see the light of day'.[33]

Doniol-Valcroze defined this particular terrain of battle very succinctly when forced to defend Alain Robbe-Grillet's *L'Immortelle* in the pages of *Cahiers*.[34] Arguing for the film primarily as an attempt to expel reality as a referent for film, in favour of the film's own reality, Doniol placed special importance on its attempt to provide 'the first cinematographic equivalent of "mental time", a time perpetually in the present'.[35] But Doniol's main point, and attack, was a more general one:

Robbe-Grillet often explains that modern art is in a phase in which each work is a searching which ends by destroying itself, and that that is why Rivette's *Paris nous appartient* is the most significant and most resolutely modern work of the new cinema. If only those at *Cahiers* would reflect a little, instead of pinning photos of Sylvie Vartan[36] to the walls while affirming that Hawks's cinema 'at the level of man' is once and for all the be-all and end-all of the seventh art (I've nothing against Hawks, who is one of the greatest film-makers in contemporary cinema but whose work cannot be used as a defining limit), they would perceive perhaps that it is not a question of liking or disliking *L'Immortelle*, nor of knowing if one is bored or entertained, but rather of appreciating the new paths being opened up.[37]

In so far as a 'new cinema' is seen here to be emerging by Labarthe and Doniol-Valcroze – and equally, from a different perspective, by Domarchi and Douchet – it is one defined mainly in formal terms (though Bernard Dort, in 'Towards a Brechtian Criticism of Cinema', proposes a very different approach to Antonioni, for instance). This 'new cinema' is new or modern primarily because it breaks with traditional modes of story-telling.[38] In this sense 'new cinema' could be seen as coincident with the *nouvelle vague*, much of which was undoubtedly conventional and bourgeois in thematic terms but often innovative formally. When he writes about the 'modernity' of *Les Bonnes femmes* Labarthe[39] has in mind primarily the style of its *mise en scène*; although, of course, this 'vision' implies a world view it is, as Bernard Dort argues,[40] still very much a bourgeois world view. And it is the formal aspects of the narrative organiz-ation of *L'Année dernière à Marienbad* which for Labarthe[41] constitute its modernism.

Alongside this growing interest in formal innovation, American films were tending to please *Cahiers* less. Jean-André Fieschi's review of Preminger's 1963 film *The Cardinal* evokes some of the unease which mainstream American cinema had begun to generate. Even a Preminger has become infected, in Fieschi's phrase, by 'the virus of seductiveness', his *mise en scène* now mechanical. Fieschi points very clearly to the necessarily 'oppositional' status of the only cinema *Cahiers* could now admire:

> there is not a single major recent work which is not *first and foremost* in opposition to its audience, and the past year bears witness to this fact by the richness of the misunderstood films it has offered us – *Muriel, Les Carabiniers, Le Procès de Jeanne d'Arc, The Exterminating Angel*, even *Adieu Philippine*. . . . It may be that the broken engagement with the audience will be made up some day, but it will not be made up with compromise and *flattery*, at the cost of the works themselves.[42]

It is striking that although V. F. Perkins in *Film as Film* uses several examples from *The Cardinal* to make points about effective *mise en scène* (although the phrase *mise en scène* is one he studiously avoids using), the same concept of audience 'flattery' as a debilitating feature of post-1960s American cinema enters Perkins's contribution to the 1975 *Movie* editorial discussion of contemporary Hollywood.[43]

The general tone of despondency at much of the output of Hollywood had already marked the 1963 *Cahiers* editorial discussion 'Questions about American Cinema'.[44] The tone here is symptomatic, as the former critical 'young Turks' of the 1950s, most of them now *nouvelle vague* film-makers and perhaps somewhat 'old guard' critics – Chabrol, Doniol-Valcroze, Godard, Kast, Moullet, Rivette and Truffaut – recognize that American cinema is no longer what it was. Just as Fieschi's remarks on *The Cardinal* make a striking contrast with, say, Rivette's account of the intelligence and economy of Preminger's *mise en scène* in *Angel Face*,[45] so the guarded nostalgia and disappointment of the 1963 discussion contrasts sharply with the unbridled enthusiasm for American cinema manifest throughout the Christmas 1955 special issue.[46]

The crisis in attitudes towards American cinema was exacerbated, and partly caused, by the situation of American cinema at this time. In the late 1950s and early 1960s a number of major Hollywood directors, and ones much admired by *Cahiers*, were reaching or maintaining a certain peak: Hawks, Hitchcock, Ford, Ray, Sirk, Preminger, Minnelli, Cukor, Boetticher, Anthony Mann, Brooks, Aldrich, Fuller, Losey (though Losey, having been blacklisted in the early 1950s, was working in Britain). American cinema seemed in good health. But the early to mid-1960s soon began to reveal a very different picture. Welles had returned to the US to make *Touch of Evil* in 1958, but was to make no more American films; Lang's 1956 *Beyond a Reasonable Doubt* turned out to be his last American picture, and his career anywhere was virtually over; after *Imitation of Life*, in 1959, Sirk left both the cinema and the US. McCarey, Borzage, King Vidor, Chaplin, Walsh, Sternberg were all effectively at the end of their active careers. The output of Cukor and Minnelli declined in both quantity and quality. Fittingly enough, given the '*hitchcocko-hawksien*' label often applied to the 'young Turks' of criticism in the 1950s, Hawks and Hitchcock, probably the two most important of the older generation of film-makers – those who had begun their careers in the silent era – for *Cahiers* in the 1950s,[47] survived both the 1960s and *Cahiers*'s revaluation of American cinema most successfully. Nicholas Ray, the crucial figure for *Cahiers* in the 1950s among the younger generation of American film-makers,[48] is now seen to have worked best in conditions of studio-based constraint, his individuality becoming lost in 'super-productions' like *King of Kings* (1961) and *55 Days at Peking* (1963); this was a fate shared by others of his generation, like Mankiewicz (*Cleopatra*), Anthony Mann (*The Fall of the Roman Empire*), Aldrich (*Sodom and Gomorrah*) and even Brooks (*Lord Jim*). Preminger, long involved in and habituated to independent production, seemed to work best in large-scale productions, like *Exodus* and *Advise and Consent* – until *The Cardinal*, anyway. It became clear, in fact, despite several newer American directors who interested *Cahiers* a great deal – pre-eminently Jerry Lewis and Arthur Penn – that American cinema as a whole was undergoing significant, and in some ways decisive, changes: the 'studio system' had passed definitively, and there was perceived a lack of direction, and a confused sense of what the mass audience – in so far as a *mass* audience still existed – wanted.

At the same time, as Fieschi's comments on *The Cardinal* make clear – and the same conclusion had already significantly informed the 1963 discussion around Resnais's *Muriel*[49] – no longer could American cinema be considered except in relationship to the 'new cinema' which, implicitly or explicitly, challenged it. And, as the 'Questions about American Cinema' discussion begins to acknowledge, this relationship between Hollywood and 'new cinema' must be understood not just in terms of forms, but also in terms of economics, of power. Thus, the concern for 'new cinema' which began as a concern primarily with new *forms* – the break with traditional story-telling represented in different ways by *Hiroshima mon amour*,[50] by Godard, by Rouch and *cinéma vérité*, by Antonioni – began to become, and increasingly explicitly, an intensely *political* concern. In effect, what happened to *Cahiers* through the 1960s – and not just in 1968 – can best be described as 'politicization'.

In this process of politicization Brecht and all that Brecht's work embodied was a decisive influence. As George Lellis has put it, 'Brecht has been a pivotal figure in the change in *Cahiers du Cinéma* from Platonist, Catholic, idealist writing about film to a Marxist, materialist approach'.[51] In terms of the 1950s and 1960s we might characterize the former approach by, for example, Bazin's work on film language and neo-realism[52] or Amédée Ayfre's 'Neo-Realism and Phenomenology'[53] or Eric Rohmer's 'The Cardinal Virtues of CinemaScope';[54] and the latter by, say, the 1968 editorials in this volume or the 1969 editorial by Jean-Louis Comolli and Jean Narboni, 'Cinema/Ideology/Criticism',[55] Brechtian in both its critique of 'realist' representation and its consciousness of what Brecht called the 'apparatus' or 'public entertainment machine', the social and economic conditions in which art is socially produced.[56] As Bernard Dort makes clear in his 1960 essay 'Towards a Brechtian Criticism of Cinema', any Brechtian approach to cinema criticism had to put the political at its centre, and such a project necessarily challenged positions and assumptions which *Cahiers* held dear. In the same Brecht special issue Louis Marcorelles (unlike Dort, a regular *Cahiers* contributor, though one whose interests were often at a tangent to those of the major figures on the journal) spelled this out, challenging *Cahiers* tendencies in a very direct way. Marcorelles called for

an interrogation of the economic structures in which the so-called seventh art is suffocating, the refusal to play the capitalist game and the refusal of the *Paris Match*-style success myth. It would mean being responsible for one's acts, seeking lucidity [. . . .] It would mean, finally, our critics, above all our young critics, deciding to come down from that planet of so-called 'pure cinema' and look at the world around them, helping to transform it a little. It would mean not being content with idealist speculations about the genius of directors – above all American directors – with no control over their actions and subordinate to the necessities of commerce alone. Nature has decided that we should live right in the middle of this scientific century to which Brecht wanted to give an art worthy of its ambitions. The cinema will or will not be the prodigious recorder of the contradictions of modern man.[57]

In the editorial to the Brecht issue, the first in a number of key editorials through the 1960s, *Cahiers* partly recognizes the nature of the challenge while not, perhaps, seeing its full implications. Looking back on it, it is a remarkable document, poised very precisely between past, established achievements and future changes. Devoting a whole issue to a non-cinema subject obviously demanded comment: 'Is Brecht a *Cahiers auteur*?' No, is the reply, if cinema must be modern only in the Brechtian sense,

> No, if it is true that a 'Brechtian criticism of cinema' undertakes to destroy pretty much all the objects of our past and present passions: *auteurs*, works, and approaches to those works and those *auteurs* [. . . .] But if we distrust a cinema seeking in its neighbour [theatre] its only inspiration, we do not condemn our art all the same to an isolation which, though fruitful in the past, is today sterile. We think that, henceforth, points of convergence with rival disciplines are not only necessary, but desirable.[58]

The editorial's cautious but prophetic engagement with Brecht's ideas and all they represent requires some comment. If the early 1960s interest in *Cahiers* in 'new cinema' was primarily a formal interest, this was also true of much of its early interest in Brecht. To a significant extent *Cahiers* came to its interest in Brecht via the figure of Joseph Losey, who had worked with Brecht and whose cinema was at this time exemplary for many *Cahiers* critics. Symbolically, and paradoxically, the front cover of the Brecht special issue carried a photograph from the Berliner Ensemble's production of *Mother Courage*, while the back cover carried an advertisement for the MacMahon cinema (as was usual at this time) and its presentation of Losey's *The Sleeping Tiger* (though for this issue the traditional yellow cover had been replaced by a red one). It is in the figure and work of Losey that two apparently opposed tendencies of *Cahiers* in this period came together – the reactionary tendencies of Michel Mourlet and the MacMahonists and the potential for progressive ideas represented by Brecht. George Lellis suggests that an explanation for the conjunction of influences is to be found in the phenomenological approach of Bazin and others, very much underpinning the broad perspective of Mourlet and the MacMahonists, which saw film as the art of physical relationships between actors and setting,[59] and the Brechtian preference for external, and externalized, action and gesture over introspective psychology.[60] Losey's account of Brecht in his article in the Brecht special issue[61] – and, essentially, the dominant account of Brecht in Britain at this time[62] – is an important key to understanding this first wave of influence of Brecht on *Cahiers*, since Losey effectively depoliticizes Brecht's theory and practice, making available to criticism certain almost abstract techniques. Commenting on a quotation from Galileo tacked up over Brecht's desk in New York, Losey says he 'took it to mean to Brecht not that the truth was absolute, but that it was precise – there is a right and wrong way, no more and no less than necessary, exactness of observation, economy of means of communication'.[63] Such comments, rather than anything more political, significantly inform the use *Cahiers* makes at this time of Brecht, particularly in discussing Losey's work.[64]

It is very much the same depoliticized Brecht that we can see at work in some *nouvelle vague* films of the period. Godard is explicit about it when, in the 1962 interview, he refers to *Vivre sa vie* as being formally Brechtian: he made it, he says 'in tableaux to emphasize the theatrical, Brechtian side'. This kind of assimilation of Brecht by the *nouvelle vague* was much attacked by critics on *Positif*, whose relationship to Brecht, as one would expect from a left-wing, anti-clerical journal, was much clearer, and more clearly political at this time than that of *Cahiers*. Robert Benayoun's general condemnation of the *Cahiers* critics-turned-film-makers on the basis that they 'refuse to commit themselves, they escape into formalism',[65] is amplified in Gérard Gozlan's attack on Rivette's *Paris nous appartient*:

Rivette is making a fool of us and of himself when he sees himself already evolving towards a Brechtian manner. . . . The Brechtian spectacle defines the how and why of the situation it describes, it is an effort to reveal the true organization of society and expose its contradictions. It requires a demon-stration, a 'dismantling', to make the spectator grasp this. Its purpose is radically different from that of Rivette: Brecht is never ambiguous. That is why not only conservatives but 'liberals' hate him . . . using realism and 'up-to-dateness' as a pretext, the artist has no right to give us a chaotic portrayal of a chaotic period – he should try rather to fathom it; we are not ashamed to state and state again that *Paris nous appartient*, like *A bout de souffle*, lures fools into taking it seriously.[66]

Losey's Brecht was not, however, the only Brecht which *Cahiers* was beginning to become conscious of, as the articles in the Brecht issue by Dort and Marcorelles make clear. Dort, in particular, had been closely associated with Roland Barthes as co-editors on *Théâtre Populaire*, and that journal had been an ardent supporter of the Berliner Ensemble's first performances in Paris in 1954 and did a great deal to make Brecht's theatre and ideas gain wide currency in France during the 1950s and beyond. From a very early point, Barthes's perception of Brecht's importance was very different from the dominant perceptions of Brecht in Britain. In its own special issue on Brecht, in January–February 1955, Barthes's editorial for *Théâtre Populaire*, 'The Brechtian Revolution', made this perception very clear:

Whatever our final evaluation of Brecht, we must at least indicate the coinci-dence of his thought with the great progressive themes of our time: that the evils men suffer are in their own hands – in other words, that the world can be changed; that art can and must intervene in history; that it must contribute to the same goal as the sciences, with which it is united; that we must have an art of explanation and no longer merely an art of expression; that the theatre must participate in history by revealing its movement; that the techniques of the stage are themselves 'committed'; that, finally, there is no such thing as an 'essence' of eternal art, but that each society must invent the art which will be responsible for its own deliverance.[67]

In an important 1956 essay, 'The Tasks of Brechtian Criticism', Barthes pointed to the exemplary status of 'Brechtian criticism', 'by definition extensive with the problematics of our time',[68] and to the need for it to analyse at the level of sociology, ideology, semiology and morality. On Brecht and semiology, Barthes says:

Semiology is the study of signs and significations. I do not want to engage here in a discussion of this science, which was formulated some forty years ago by the linguist Saussure and which is generally accused of formalism. Without letting ourselves be intimidated by the words, we might say that Brechtian dramaturgy, the theory of *Episierung*, of alienation, and the entire practice of the Berliner Ensemble with regard to sets and costumes, propose an explicit semiological problem. For what Brechtian dramaturgy postulates is that, today at least, the responsibility of a dramatic art is not so much to express reality as to signify it. Hence there must be a certain distance between signified and signifier: revolutionary art must admit a certain arbitrary nature of signs, it must acknowledge a certain 'formalism', in the sense that it must treat form according to an appropriate method, which is the semiological method.[69]

The ideas being elaborated by Barthes here significantly inform his writing on Brecht in the 1950s,[70] and Barthes's *Critical Essays* as a whole, covering the period 1953–63, chart in an illuminating way the coming together of a range of influences, disciplines and art practices in a new kind of political critical practice – Lévi-Strauss and structuralism, Alain Robbe-Grillet, Michel Butor and the *nouveau roman* or new novel, as well as Brecht. These are sources of thinking and of critical methodology which we begin to see exerting a clear influence on *Cahiers* writing in the early 1960s, in, for example, Fereydoun Hoveyda's '*Cinéma vérité*, or fantastic realism' and 'Self-Criticism', contributing to the 'new criticism' whose advent Hoveyda himself was proclaiming.

The 1960 special issue of *Cahiers* on Brecht opened the magazine up to the possibility of discussing disciplines other than cinema. At the same time as new concepts and new names from other disciplines began to enter *Cahiers* critical writing, so *Cahiers* also went on the offensive, went out to bring new areas into the magazine. As a direct development of its interest in Brecht, for example, *Cahiers* interviewed in 1962 theatre director Roger Planchon, best known for his attempt to establish a genuinely popular theatre, much influenced by Brecht's ideas and practice, with his Théâtre de la Cité de Villeurbanne, in Lyons.[71] But it was not until 1963 that *Cahiers* embarked on a series of interviews with what it called 'certain outstanding witnesses of contemporary culture'.[72] Appropriately, given his pivotal place in developments in cultural criticism at this time, Barthes was the first 'witness' interviewed, in the interview translated in this volume,[73] followed by composer Pierre Boulez[74] and then by anthropologist Claude Lévi-Strauss.[75] It seems that *Cahiers* had also wanted to interview Jean-Paul Sartre around this time: Godard in 1966 records that 'Sartre has once again refused an interview with *Cahiers*'.[76] The results of the Boulez and Lévi-Strauss interviews proved less interesting or useful than those of the Barthes interview (and perhaps this is why the interview project was not extended): Boulez's comments remain very music-specific, although his 'modernity within classicism' position must have found a good deal of sympathy in *Cahiers*; Lévi-Strauss determinedly favours unselfconscious American popular cinema, spectacle, and shows a good deal of hostility to much 'modernism', even while recognizing the need for conventions to be broken. But the impulse behind the project was clear enough, and equally clear, in the interviews themselves, was a sense that 'modernism', new cinema and new criticism and 'theory' were becoming urgent issues for *Cahiers*.

This much was signalled by another important editorial, in July 1963, which announced that an editorial board was taking over from the single main editor.[77] This change was presented in the editorial as simply an organizational one but it seems to have marked, in reality, the ousting of Eric Rohmer, chief editor since Bazin's death in November 1958, and his replacement as chief editorial influence by Jacques Rivette in the period 1963–5. Rivette's period of editorial influence represents a very conscious attempt to extend the cultural base of *Cahiers*, an impulse that was not just Rivette's but which reflected thinking in *Cahiers* more generally. The editorial assured readers that *Cahiers* was 'not changing its line or orientation' but, as if to challenge Godard's claim that *Cahiers* was no longer 'in the front line of battle',[78] it concluded: 'it seemed to us that as well as continuing to fulfil its original role as an organ of culture and information, it was necessary to become once again an instrument of struggle'.[79]

Struggle for what, then? Essentially for a politicized concept of cinema, in all its manifestations, but particularly for a 'new cinema' and, equally and necessarily complementary, a new, politicized concept of criticism: it is effectively this struggle which this volume tries to trace and record. *Cahiers* had already begun to be very interested in the work of individual new film-makers from Canada or Latin America or Poland, but it was only in 1965 that much attempt was made to make any broader, more international sense of 'new cinema' as a specific phenomenon.[80] From 1966 onwards, discussion of new cinema becomes perhaps the most consistent and persistent feature of *Cahiers*.[81] Jean-Louis Comolli, after 1965 the dominant editorial voice (along with Jean Narboni and Jean-André Fieschi), offered in March 1966 another highly significant editorial-manifesto, laying out the ground for the idea of a 'new cinema'. Comolli argued that in the wake of the *nouvelle vague* what had changed irrevocably was less the 'art' of cinema than 'a certain conception of the entertainment industry', in other words that conditions of work, economic structures, technical requirements, had changed more than aesthetic values. As a result, more films were being made outside of the traditional market and were finding audiences. Comolli's statement came in an issue which focussed on new cinema in Brazil ('cinema nôvo') and Quebec.[82] As Comolli pointed out, these cinemas had in common not only their novelty, nor even the fact that they came from countries with little tradition of film production, but also 'each finds itself at the sharp point of a struggle which is not only artistic but which involves a society, a morality, a civilization: cinemas of revolution'. And, since these films were difficult for many people to see, *Cahiers* had 'chosen to be part of the struggle' by helping to get such films shown.[83]

Given such changes in the status and function of cinema, what was the task of criticism? A year and a half later – and the intervening period must be read in terms of the already sharply more militant tone – Comolli answers:

> Certainly, no longer should it be Olympian, lofty and detached, braiding together crowns and interpretations; no longer, either, should it be oracular, Pythian, making the dead speak. Rather, it must be compromised and implicated up to the neck in work being done now, criticism which finishes off the dying on the field of battle, no longer criticism which rifles the pockets of corpses; criticism as a result of which cinema is more dangerous, more effective, more present. . . . Criticism must therefore not only go down into the arena, but it must fight and debate there with every available means – writing, thinking and – less noble and perhaps more useful – action.[84]

It is, of course, somewhat distorting to focus, as I have done here, on developments in intellectual life in France and on *Cahiers*, since these points of focus did not, and could not, exist in isolation. For example, the currents affecting *Cahiers* in the 1960s inevitably also affected a magazine like *Positif*, the other single most important film journal in France. The effects were different because the roots of *Positif* were in different soil. Their interest in Brecht, for example, was more 'natural' to them since they had always been more leftist, and there is not the 'discovery' of Brecht that one feels in *Cahiers*. Similarly more natural was the growing interest in Cuban cinema, Brazilian 'cinema nôvo' and the whole new cinema phenomenon in film-makers such as Jancsó, Makavejev, Skolimowski, Bertolucci, Bellochio, all figures as central for *Positif* as they were for *Cahiers*. The political stance of *Positif* significantly affected its attitude to the French *nouvelle vague*: as we have seen, violent in its opposition to the film-makers of the *Cahiers* group, whose films they found not only incompetent technically but also morally and politically at best uncommitted, at worst reactionary, but lavish in their praise of the 'Left Bank' group of Resnais, Varda and others. Most striking is the difference – and not only in the 1960s – in their attitudes to American cinema, attitudes stemming from two different sources: on the one hand, the inheritance – still very much alive – from surrealism, and on the other, the commitment to left-liberal politics. Thus, from the former came a consistent interest in the horror movie and the 'fantastic' in general (Sternberg and Corman, for example), in certain kinds of crazy comedy (especially Tashlin and Jerry Lewis) and in eroticism and the star phenomenon (particularly women stars like Marilyn Monroe, Kim Novak, Louise Brooks, but also, for instance, Brigitte Bardot, an interest pursued with much of the implicit misogyny of the early surrealists). And from the latter, a consistent interest in liberal, humanist film-makers like Huston, Brooks, Penn, a rehabilitated Kazan. Very few of these concerns and interests were not equally evident in *Cahiers*, but the perspective was often rather different. Something of the duality of interests (if not schizophrenia) in *Positif* may be suggested by its June–July 1968 issue: editorial comments on the Langlois affair and the Estates-General of the French Cinema,[85] followed by a – doubtless long-planned – 'Lexicon of Eroticism in the Cinema'. . . .

Taking a broader perspective in a different sense, it is clear that the disenchantment of *Cahiers* with American cinema cannot be separated off from more significant political and economic developments in the US during the 1960s. This was a period heavily marked by economic and military expansion by the US, Vietnam being the most obvious instance, of course, but also in the spread of transnational conglomerates, an activity specially relevant to the media industries, including film-making; and the *nouvelle vague* film-makers had now some more practical experience of the effects of these developments.[86] In the face of such activity, the liberal or socially critical image of the US sustained by much American cinema, despite the Cold War, and despite the House UnAmerican Activities Committee, became increasingly discredited. This was a period marked by growing anti-Americanism among many European intellectuals.

Despite growing anti-Americanism, despite the radical revaluation of American cinema, and despite the commitment to new cinema, American cinema was not in any sense 'dropped' by *Cahiers*. But, as this volume makes clear, there was a need both to talk about a *different* American cinema – experimental and often political film-makers like Peter Emmanuel Goldman, Shirley Clarke, Juleen Compton, Robert Kramer and, represented in this volume, John Cassavetes[87] – and to re-think the Hollywood *auteurs* as well as to re-read and re-position works of the past. At the same time as Comolli was committing *Cahiers* to new cinema,[88] he was also, in 'Notes on the New Spectator',[89] arguing that the American *auteurs* whom *Cahiers* had championed – 'Hawks, Hitchcock, Lang, Ford, Fuller, DeMille, Sternberg, Preminger, Ray, etc.' – were, and always had been, in tension with the system of 'closed-circuit cinema' characteristic of Hollywood, always productive of active spectators rather than passive consumers.[90]

As we have seen, a number of the *auteurs* admired by *Cahiers* were reaching the ends of their careers and their later or last films, sometimes apparently contradicting or contrasting sharply with earlier work, tended to pose certain difficulties of reading. This was sometimes related to the nature of 'super-productions' – 'the vast machines in which Hollywood places its hopes for survival', as Comolli called them in his review of Ray's *55 Days at Peking*[91] – and was often to do with questions about the conscious intentions of the *auteurs*. The tendency – fully exemplified in this volume by Comolli's 'The Ironical Howard Hawks' and Narboni's 'Against the Clock: *Red Line 7000*'[92] – was often to treat the late works as being about the *auteur*'s whole *oeuvre* and, by extension, about the cinema itself. Thus, just as *Man's Favorite Sport* prompts Comolli to ask 'Who is H.H.?', so *Cheyenne Autumn* prompted him to ask 'Who is Ford?',[93] while *55 Days at Peking* 'elicts from us nothing more than some reflections on the "status" of the artist, and on the logic of the choice which Ray has been constrained to make between his life and his art'.[94] Such works had been generally dismissed as aberrant, or simply as bad. *Cahiers* needed to make sense of them in *auteur* terms at the same time as it questioned conventional *auteur* principles and marked the works off from more typical Hollywood products. Thus, for example, Comolli on *Cheyenne Autumn* continues:

> Who is Ford? After ten films we already begin to talk about an author. After thirty, we talk about him a lot. But past a hundred, how can we still talk about what the author is? What 'thematic' can we derive when the repetition more than a hundred times over of the *same* themes, situations, relationships, roles, must clearly have led to an infinite diversity of nuances or, on the contrary, to a whittling away until the friction of one against the other has reduced them all to nothing? Depending on the point of view, Ford seems rich and confused, or perfunctory and narrow.[95]

As well as the re-reading of Hawks represented in this volume, Hitchcock – the other half of the *hitchcocko-hawksien* epithet from the 1950s – was also subjected to a different kind of reading consonant with the newer critical concerns of the later 1960s, however much it may have grown equally out of earlier accounts like Jean Douchet's 1960 'Hitch and his Audience'.[96] *Torn Curtain*, for example, comes to be seen – whether consciously intended as such or not – as a play with convention, in other words as being about the cinema. Thus, Sylvain Godet: 'At the start, Hitchcock shows us his cards, refusing the facility of a plot that would rest solely on the identity of the characters, choosing and assuming his actors with their mythologies. . . . Within the framework of these well-defined types, Hitchcock interests himself only in variations and modulations.'[97] Or, even more explicitly, Comolli on the same film: 'Spectator and hero are both involved . . . in a systematic discovery of the powers of cinematographic language, a veritable lesson in reading, with its exercises, its codes to decipher.'[98]

American cinema became, in a sense, 'cracked apart' critically – its codes or conventions of representation and narrative deconstructed, its ideological work analysed, its mode of production emphasized – at the

16

same time as it was, as a production system, in many ways itself 'cracking apart'. The critical work of cracking apart did not take place only in the form of written criticism. New cinema was a vital *critical practice*, addressing itself to established forms as well as to established modes of production. The *nouvelle vague* had been, certainly, an important development in this process, even if it had not set out to be. Ian Cameron, in his introduction to *Second Wave* (studies of Dusan Makavejev, Jerzy Skolimowski, Nagisa Oshima, Ruy Guerra, Glauber Rocha, Gilles Groulx, Jean-Pierre Lefèbvre, Jean-Marie Straub) makes the point succinctly:

> the New Wave of 1958–60 and the *cinéma-vérité* developments of 1962–63 left behind more than a group of new directors to be assimilated into the fabric of the industry and a heap of apparatus which was to be God's gift to television reportage. Both were stages on the cinema's route towards a financially and aesthetically viable means of survival: an alternative, that is, to the sort of film-making that, wherever it takes place, is still best conjured up by the word Hollywood. . . .
>
> In the wake of the New Wave, and provoked to a large extent by the experience of the films themselves, has come more formal discussion about the cinema than there has been since the abortive theorizing of the 'twenties. This process undermined many of the preconceptions about film which had been accepted equally by the 'commercial' and 'art' cinemas. Here the key figure has been Godard. . . . The New Wave has provided not so much the inspiration for the films described in this book – many of them were made before their directors had seen films by Godard and the rest – but has created the pre-conditions for their acceptance.[99]

As Cameron says, Godard was the key figure. And in many ways the politicization of Godard – Brecht's influence expanding on him after the formal Brechtianism of films like *Vivre sa vie* and becoming more pervasive and more deeply understood in its politics in films like *Deux ou trois choses que je sais d'elle* and *La Chinoise* – parallels the politicization of *Cahiers*.

Despite the early 1960s emphasis on formal innovation, there were at the same time the beginnings of a sense of the *politics* of a new cinema, a politics of form as well as of content. Luc Moullet, back in 1960 in his article 'Jean-Luc Godard', already recognized some of this, a sense of the different directions which the *nouvelle vague* would take, when he contrasted the Godard of *A bout de souffle* with Truffaut: 'where Truffaut applies himself to the task of making our own civilization fit a classical framework, Godard – more honestly – seeks a rationale for our age from within itself'.[100] Similarly, the 1963 discussion 'The Misfortunes of *Muriel*'[101] and Jean-André Fieschi's 'Neo-neo-realism: *Banditi a Orgosolo*',[102] also from 1963, offer clear evidence of the changes in critical thinking, the developing politicization of criticism, taking place. From a very different perspective – also crucial for any consideration of what happened to the *nouvelle vague* and what it represented over the decade – Rohmer's 1965 interview, 'The Old and the New', and Truffaut's 1967 interview[103] offer clear evidence of a *resistance* to precisely these developments in *Cahiers*. There is a very real discordance and tension between Rohmer's and Truffaut's readings of the meanings of the *nouvelle vague* and, for example, Comolli's determination, in his 'Polemic: Lelouch, or the Clear Conscience',[104] to distinguish Lelouch's work from what, for him, the *nouvelle vague* represented. It is a tension and discordance even clearer, perhaps, between the Rohmer and Truffaut interviews on the one hand, and the 1967 interview with Godard ('Struggling on Two Fronts') and the 1968 interview with Rivette ('Time Overflowing'[105]) on the other. By 1968 it was Godard and Rivette, of the ex-*Cahiers* faction of the *nouvelle vague*, who best represented in their work what had happened to critical writing in *Cahiers* in the 1960s. Godard's interview, in particular, bears eloquent testimony to the process of politicization which had taken place, and Godard's 'Manifesto' in the press-book for *La Chinoise*, August 1967, can serve as a kind of summary of where Godard and *Cahiers* were situating themselves as May 1968 drew closer:

> Fifty years after the October Revolution, the American industry rules cinema the world over. There is nothing much to add to this statement of fact. Except that on our own modest level we too should provoke two or three Vietnams in the bosom of the vast Hollywood-Cinecittà-Mosfilm-Pinewood-etc. empire, and, both economically and aesthetically, struggling on two fronts as it were, create cinemas which are national, free, brotherly, comradely and bonded in friendship.[106]

Notes

1 Richard Roud, 'The French Line', *Sight and Sound*, vol. 29, no. 4, Autumn 1960, p. 167.
2 Much of the debate in Britain was generated by critics Ian Cameron, Mark Shivas, V. F. Perkins, Paul Mayersberg, Robin Wood and Charles Barr at Oxford and Cambridge in the pages of *Oxford Opinion* and *Granta* in 1959–60. Before these critics came together to form, or write for, *Movie*, in 1962, their ideas had already been taken up and challenged in other journals. See, for example: Dai Vaughan, 'Towards a Theory', *Definition*, no. 1, February 1960; Penelope Houston, 'The Critical Issue', and Richard Roud, 'The French Line', *Sight and Sound*, vol. 29, no. 4, Autumn 1960; 'Attack on Film Criticism': (1) Ian Cameron, 'All Together Now', (2) Ian Jarvie, 'Preface to Film Criticism', *Film*, no. 25, September–October 1960; Ian Cameron, V. F. Perkins, Mark Shivas, 'Commitment in Films' (letter), *The Spectator*, 14 October 1960; Editorial, and Penelope Houston, 'Enthusiasm, for What?', Robin Wood, 'New Criticism?', *Definition*, no. 3, 1960; Peter John Dyer, 'Counter Attack', *Film*, no. 26, November–December 1960; Dai Vaughan, Philip Riley, 'Letters from the Trenches', *Film*, no. 27, January–February 1961; Ian Cameron, 'What's the Use?', Peter Armitage, 'Free Criticism', Ian Jarvie, 'Comeback', *Film*, no. 28, March 1961; Ian Cameron, 'Films, Directors and Critics', *Movie* 2, 1962 (reprinted in Cameron, *Movie Reader*). Extracts from some of these

articles are available from the Education Department of the British Film Institute in a duplicated document compiled by Jim Cook, 'The Critical Debate'.

The debate in Britain overlapped with the debate in the US, but began with a response to *Cahiers* then centred very much on the mediation of *Cahiers* in the work of American critic Andrew Sarris. See, for example: Andrew Sarris, 'The Director's Game', *Film Culture*, no. 22–3, Summer 1961; Ernest Callenbach, 'Editor's Notebook: "Turn On! Turn On!"', *Film Quarterly*, vol. 16, no. 3, Spring 1962; Andrew Sarris, 'Notes on the *Auteur* Theory in 1962', *Film Culture*, no. 27, Winter 1962–3 (reprinted in John Stuart Katz, *Perspectives on the Study of Film*, Boston, Little Brown, 1971; in P. Adams Sitney, *Film Culture Reader*, New York, Praeger, 1970, published as *Film Culture*, London, Secker & Warburg, 1971; in Gerald Mast and Marshall Cohen, *Film Theory and Criticism*, New York, Oxford University Press, 1974; extracts in Caughie, *Theories of Authorship*); Andrew Sarris, 'The American Cinema', *Film Culture*, no. 28, Spring 1963 (this, together with the ideas in 'Notes on the *Auteur* Theory in 1962', formed the basis of Sarris's book, *The American Cinema*, New York, E. P. Dutton, 1968); Pauline Kael, 'Circles and Squares', *Film Quarterly*, vol. 16, no. 3, Spring 1963 (reprinted in Pauline Kael, *I Lost it at the Movies*, Boston, Little, Brown, 1965; London, Jonathan Cape, 1966; extracts reprinted in Mast and Cohen, *op. cit.*); Andrew Sarris, 'The *auteur* theory and the perils of Pauline', *Film Quarterly*, vol. 16, no. 4, Summer 1963; 'Controversy and Correspondence': Ernest Callenbach, 'The *Auteur* Policy'; Ian Cameron, Mark Shivas, Paul Mayersberg, V. F. Perkins, '*Movie* vs. Kael'; Pauline Kael, 'Criticism and Kids' Games', *Film Quarterly*, vol. 17, no. 1, Fall 1963.

3 Volume 1, pp. 1–14.

4 For the transformation of the *politique des auteurs* into the '*auteur* theory', see Ch. 20, note 2.

5 Cameron, Perkins, Shivas, 'Commitment in Films', *op. cit.*

6 Chs 11 and 13 in this volume.

7 Jacques Rivette in Morvan Lebesque, Pierre Marcabru, Jacques Rivette, Eric Rohmer, Georges Sadoul, 'La Critique: Débat', *Cahiers* 126, December 1961, pp. 18, 16.

8 Roud, 'The French Line', *op. cit.*

9 Sarris, 'Notes on the *Auteur* Theory in 1962', *op. cit.*

10 V. F. Perkins, *Film as Film*, Harmondsworth, Penguin Books, 1972.

11 'Entretien avec François Truffaut', *Cahiers* 138, December 1962, translated (extracts) as 'Interview with François Truffaut' in Graham, *The New Wave*, p. 91.

12 'Entretien avec Jean-Luc Godard', *Cahiers* 138, December 1962, translated as 'Interview' in *Godard on Godard*, reprinted (extracts) as Jean-Luc Godard, 'From Critic to Film-Maker: Godard in Interview', Ch. 4 in this volume.

13 Ch. 15 in this volume.

14 Chs 12 and 14 in this volume.

15 See Introduction to Part II, 'The Apotheosis of *mise en scène*', for further discussion of the 'MacMahonist' tendencies.

16 Chs 1, 3, 5 and 24 in this volume.

17 Ch. 23 in this volume.

18 Ch. 2 in this volume.

19 Chs 14 and 16 in this volume.

20 See, for example, André Bazin, 'De la politique des auteurs', *Cahiers* 70, April

1957, translated as 'On the *politique des auteurs*', Chapter 31 in Volume 1; 'Beauté d'un western', *Cahiers* 55, January 1956 (on *The Man from Laramie*), translated as 'Beauty of a Western', Chapter 22 in Volume 1; 'Un western exemplaire', *Cahiers* 74, August–September 1957 (on *Seven Men from Now*), translated as 'An Exemplary Western', Chapter 23 in Volume 1. See also 'Evolution du Western', *Cahiers* 54, Christmas 1955, translated as 'Evolution of the Western' in Bazin, *What is Cinema? Vol. 2*, reprinted in Nichols, *Movies and Methods*.

21 Ch. 25 in this volume.
22 Ch. 24 in this volume.
23 Caughie, *Theories of Authorship*, p. 1.
24 Ch. 20 in this volume.
25 Caughie, *op. cit.*, p. 10.
26 Ibid., p. 38.
27 Ibid., p. 11.
28 Geoffrey Nowell-Smith, 'Introduction' to 'New Hollywood Cinema', *Film Reader* 1, Evanston, Illinois, 1975, p. 58.
29 Caughie, *op. cit.*, pp. 12–13.
30 Jean Domarchi, 'Cannes 1960', *Cahiers* 108, June 1960, pp. 39–41.
31 Jacques Doniol-Valcroze, 'Le Facteur rhésus et le nouveau cinéma', *Cahiers* 113, November 1960, pp. 47–9, translated as 'The RH Factor and the New Cinema' in *New York Film Bulletin*, series 2, no. 5 (31); also translated in *Cahiers du Cinéma in English*, no. 2 (1966).
32 Jean Douchet (and Luc Moullet), 'Cannes 1962', *Cahiers* 132, June 1962, pp. 23–4, 30.
33 André S. Labarthe, 'Promethée enchaînée', *Cahiers* 136, October 1962, pp. 52–5. It is worth noting that *L'Eclisse* (along with other films, like Godard's *Vivre sa vie*) provoked considerable disagreements among the *Movie* critics in Britain: see Ian Cameron, Paul Mayersberg, V. F. Perkins, Mark Shivas, '*Movie* Differences: a discussion', *Movie* 8, April 1983, reprinted in Cameron, *Movie Reader*.
34 'Forced' because, as the film's main actor, it was hardly appropriate for him to defend it, but no one else on *Cahiers* would do so.
35 Jacques Doniol-Valcroze, 'Istanbul nous appartient', *Cahiers* 143, May 1963, p. 55.
36 Sylvie Vartan, young, blonde female singer, very popular at this time.
37 Doniol-Valcroze, *op. cit.*, p. 56.
38 This 'modern cinema' was not necessarily 'new'. Characteristically, for example, writing on Carl Dreyer's *Gertrud* in *Cahiers* 164, March 1965, Michel Delahaye proposes Dreyer as the 'crux of modern cinema', linking Dreyer not only to Godard and Straub, but also to Hitchcock, Mizoguchi and Bresson. On the 'modernity' of Dreyer, cf. Noël Burch and Jorge Dana, 'Propositions', *Afterimage* 5, Spring 1974.
39 Ch. 2 in this volume.
40 Ch. 23 in this volume.
41 Ch. 3 in this volume.
42 Jean-André Fieschi, 'Schisme', *Cahiers* 154, April 1964, p. 65.
43 Ian Cameron, Jim Hillier, V. F. Perkins, Michael Walker, Robin Wood, 'The Return of *Movie*', *Movie* 20, Spring 1975.
44 Ch. 17 in this volume.

45 Jacques Rivette, 'L'Essentiel', *Cahiers* 32, February 1954, translated as 'The Essential', Ch. 17 in Volume 1.

46 A number of articles from this issue, *Cahiers* 54, Christmas 1955, are translated in Volume 1: Eric Rohmer, 'Redécouvrir l'Amérique', translated as 'Rediscovering America', Ch. 7; Jacques Rivette, 'Notes sur une révolution', translated as 'Notes on a Revolution', Ch. 8; Claude Chabrol, 'Evolution du film policier', translated as 'Evolution of the Thriller', Ch. 21. For André Bazin's 'Evolution du western', in the same issue, see note 20 above.

47 See, for example, in Volume 1, Jacques Rivette, 'Génie de Howard Hawks', *Cahiers* 23, May 1953, translated as 'The Genius of Howard Hawks', Ch. 16 (reprinted from Joseph McBride, *Focus on Howard Hawks*, Englewood Cliffs, N.J., Prentice-Hall, 1972; also reprinted in Leo Braudy and Morris Dickstein, *Great Film Directors*, New York, Oxford University Press, 1978), and Claude Chabrol, 'Les Choses sérieuses', *Cahiers* 46, April 1955, translated as 'Serious Things', Ch. 18. Cf. material on Hitchcock in *Godard on Godard*, François Truffaut, *The Films in my Life*, New York, Simon & Schuster, 1978; London, Allen Lane, 1980, and Eric Rohmer and Claude Chabrol, *Hitchcock* (Paris, 1957), translated as *Hitchcock, The First Forty Four Films*, New York, Ungar, 1979.

48 See, for example, in Volume 1, 'Dossier on Nicholas Ray': Jacques Rivette, 'De l'invention', *Cahiers* 27, October 1953 (on *The Lusty Men*), translated as 'On Imagination', Ch. 10; François Truffaut, 'L'Admirable certitude', *Cahiers* 46, April 1955 (on *Johnny Guitar*), translated as 'A Wonderful Certainty', Ch. 11; Eric Rohmer, 'Ajax, ou le Cid?', *Cahiers* 59, May 1956 (on *Rebel Without a Cause*), translated as 'Ajax, or the Cid?', Ch. 12; Jean-Luc Godard, 'Rien que le cinéma', *Cahiers* 68, February 1957 (on *Hot Blood*), translated as 'Nothing but Cinema', Ch. 13 (reprinted from *Godard on Godard*); Jean-Luc Godard, 'Au-delà des étoiles', *Cahiers* 79, January 1958 (on *Bitter Victory*), translated as 'Beyond the Stars', Ch. 14 (reprinted from *Godard on Godard*); Charles Bitsch, 'Entretien avec Nicholas Ray', *Cahiers* 89, November 1958, translated as 'Interview with Nicholas Ray', Ch. 15.

49 Ch. 5 in this volume.

50 See the discussion between Jean Domarchi, Jacques Doniol-Valcroze, Jean-Luc Godard, Pierre Kast, Jacques Rivette, Eric Rohmer, 'Hiroshima, notre amour', *Cahiers* 97, July 1959, translated as Ch. 6 in Volume 1.

51 George Lellis, 'Brecht and *Cahiers du Cinéma*', in Betty Nance Weber and Hubert Heinen, *Bertolt Brecht: Political Theory and Literary Practice*, Manchester, Manchester University Press, 1980, p. 129.

52 For Bazin's work on film language, see this volume, Ch. 3, note 2. Bazin's main work on neo-realism is collected in Bazin, *What is Cinema? Vol. 2*, to which can be added his brief note on *Umberto D*, translated as Ch. 24 in Volume 1.

53 Amédée Ayfre, 'Neo-Réalisme et Phénoménologie', *Cahiers* 17, November 1952, translated as 'Neo-Realism and Phenomenology', Ch. 25 in Volume 1.

54 Eric Rohmer, 'Vertus cardinales du CinémaScope', *Cahiers* 31, January 1954, translated as 'The Cardinal Virtues of CinemaScope', Ch. 36 in Volume 1.

55 Jean-Louis Comolli and Jean Narboni, 'Cinéma/Idéologie/Critique I', *Cahiers* 216, October 1969, translated as 'Cinema/Ideology/Criticism' in *Screen*, vol. 12, no. 1, Spring 1971, reprinted in *Screen Reader 1* and Nichols, *Movies and Methods*.

56 Bertolt Brecht, 'The Modern Theatre is the Epic Theatre' in Brecht, *Brecht on Theatre*.
57 Louis Marcorelles, 'D'un art moderne', *Cahiers* 114, December 1960, p. 53.
58 *Cahiers* 114, December 1960, p. 2.
59 Jacques Joly, in a review of Minnelli's *Home from the Hill*, asked, in fact, 'What is *mise en scène*, if not precisely the confrontation of a character and a setting?', 'La Montagne de verre', *Cahiers* 121, July 1961, p. 53.
60 Lellis, *op. cit.*, pp. 131–2.
61 Joseph Losey, 'L'oeil du maître', *Cahiers* 114, December 1960, translated as 'The Innocent Eye' in *Encore*, March 1961, reprinted in Charles Marowitz, Tom Milne, Owen Hale, *The Encore Reader*, London, Methuen, 1965 (republished as *New Theatre Voices of the Fifties and Sixties*).
62 See also, for example, George Devine, 'The Berliner Ensemble', *Encore*, April 1956, reprinted in Marowitz, Milne and Hale, *op. cit.* We should remember that Brecht's writings in *Brecht on Theatre* were not widely available in English until 1964 and, more generally, that contemporary understandings of Brecht owe a good deal to the context of post-1968 debates on the politics of culture.
63 Losey, 'The Innocent Eye', *The Encore Reader*, p. 206.
64 See, for example, Michel Mourlet, 'Beauté de la connaissance', *Cahiers* 111, September 1960, translated as 'The Beauty of Knowledge', Ch. 14 in this volume, and Jean Douchet, 'Un Art de laboratoire', *Cahiers* 117, March 1961, translated as 'A Laboratory Art', Ch. 16 in this volume.
65 Robert Benayoun, 'Le Roi est nu', *Positif* 46, June 1962, translated as 'The King is Naked' in Graham, *The New Wave*, p. 172.
66 Gérard Gozlan, 'Les délices de l'ambiguïté (Eloge d'André Bazin)', *Positif* 47, July 1962, translated as 'In Praise of André Bazin', in Graham, *The New Wave*, pp. 125–6, 128.
67 *Théâtre Populaire*, January–February 1955, translated as 'The Brechtian Revolution' in Roland Barthes, *Critical Essays*, Evanston, Illinois, Northwestern University Press, 1972, p. 38.
68 'The Tasks of Brechtian Criticism', in Barthes, *op. cit.*, p. 71.
69 Ibid., pp. 74–5. Cf. Barthes's comments in his 1963 interview, Ch. 28 in this volume.
70 See also, in Barthes, *op. cit.*, for example, 'Mother Courage Blind', 'The Diseases of Costume', 'On Brecht's *Mother*'.
71 Claude Gauteur, 'Entretien avec Roger Planchon', *Cahiers* 129, March 1962.
72 *Cahiers* 147, September 1963, p. 21, preface to the interview with Roland Barthes.
73 Ch. 28 in this volume.
74 Jacques Rivette and François Weyergans, 'Entretien avec Pierre Boulez', *Cahiers* 152, February 1964. Boulez, born 1925, was probably the leading contemporary composer, pianist and conductor in France, central to developments in *musique concrète* and in serial music.
75 Michel Delahaye and Jacques Rivette, 'Entretien avec Claude Lévi-Strauss', *Cahiers* 156, June 1964. The work of Lévi-Strauss, born 1908, in anthropology became extremely important over a much wider field in the development of structural or structuralist critical methodology. Lévi-Strauss's main works before 1964 were translated as *Structural Anthropology*, Harmondsworth, Penguin, 1972 (originally published Paris, 1958), collecting papers from the period 1944–57; *The Elementary Structures of Kinship* (1949), London, Eyre and

Spottiswoode, 1969; *Tristes Tropiques* (1955), New York, Russell, 1967; *Totemism* (1963), Harmondsworth, Penguin, 1969. Lévi-Strauss's place in the development of structuralism is charted in Barthes's *Critical Essays* (see, for example, the 1963 essay 'The Structuralist Activity'). For a contemporary discussion of Lévi-Strauss's influence, see, for example, Rosalind Coward and John Ellis, *Language and Materialism*, London, Routledge & Kegan Paul, 1977.

76 Godard continues: 'Why must image and sound be always so scorned by the powerful of this world?', Jean-Luc Godard, 'Trois milles heures de cinéma', *Cahiers* 184, November 1966, translated as '3000 Hours of Cinema' in *Cahiers du Cinéma in English*, no. 10, May 1967, extracts from which are reprinted in Toby Mussman, *Jean-Luc Godard*, New York, E. P. Dutton, 1968, pp. 294–5.

77 The 'Comité de Rédaction' consisted of: Jean Domarchi, Jean Douchet, Jean-Luc Godard, Fereydoun Hoveyda, Pierre Kast, Léonard Keigel, André S. Labarthe, Dossia Mage, Claude Makovski, Louis Marcorelles, Luc Moullet, Jacques Rivette, Eric Rohmer, François Truffaut. The committee gives the impression of more continuity with the 1950s than was really the case. One effect of the success of the *nouvelle vague*, of course, was to deprive *Cahiers* of several of its major contributors in the 1950s. Chabrol almost completely ceases to be a contributor; Truffaut and Doniol-Valcroze remain faithful – a fidelity crucial to the survival of *Cahiers* after financial crises in 1963–4 and 1969 – though Truffaut contributes almost exclusively as a film-maker; this was equally true of Godard, though Godard's contributions retained a more fierce critical edge. Godard, Truffaut, Doniol and Kast all remained closely involved with the *Cahiers* editorial committee and Rivette (who was not involved in film production between *Paris nous appartient* and beginning work on *La Religieuse* in 1965) in this period as well as continuing their film-making activities.

78 See note 11, above.

79 Editorial, *Cahiers* 145, July 1963, p. 1.

80 See, particularly, Luc Moullet, 'Contingent 65 1 A', *Cahiers* 166–7, May–June 1965.

81 There is a certain irony in the fact that *Cahiers* had been bought by fashionable publisher Daniel Filipacchi in 1964, when the reputation and circulation of *Cahiers* was very high – circulation reaching its peak of about 13,000 in 1964–9. Filipacchi changed the look of *Cahiers* from the relatively austere but much loved yellow and black and white cover which had survived since 1951 (when it was inherited from *La Revue de Cinéma*) to a larger, more glossy and more colourful format just at the time when the magazine's direction was already shifting away clearly towards both a cinema and a criticism less popular in appeal. In the aftermath of May 1968 and the extreme politicization and theorization of *Cahiers*, Filipacchi wanted to get rid of *Cahiers* and it was bought back from him.

82 Some of the perspectives implied in the choice of Brazil and Quebec are taken up in, for example, Michael Chanan, *25 Years of the New Latin-American Cinema*, London, British Film Institute/Channel 4, 1983, which collects important manifesto texts by Fernando Birri, Glauber Rocha, Fernando Solanas and Octavio Getino, Julio García Espinosa, Jorge Sanjines; and, for Quebec, in Susan Barrowclough, *Jean-Pierre Lefèbvre: The Quebec Connection*, London, British Film Institute, 1981, which documents the context of Quebec cinema in general as well as focussing on the work of Lefèbvre.

83 Jean-Louis Comolli, 'Situation du nouveau cinéma, I', *Cahiers* 176, March 1965, p. 5.
84 Jean-Louis Comolli, 'Pourquoi? Où? Comment? Quand?' ('Why? Where? How? When?'), *Cahiers* 195, November 1967, p. 38.
85 Cf. Chs 34 and 35 in this volume.
86 For general accounts of 'media imperialism' in the 1960s and beyond see, for example, Herbert I. Schiller, *Mass Communications and American Empire*, New York, Kelley, 1970, or Jeremy Tunstall, *The Media are American*, London, Constable, 1977. On the film industry within this general context see, particularly, Thomas H. Guback, *The International Film Industry*, Bloomington, Indiana University Press, 1969, and Guback's article 'Hollywood's International Market' in Tino Balio, *The American Film Industry*, Madison, Wisconsin, University of Wisconsin Press, 1976.
87 Ch. 39 in this volume.
88 See note 83 above.
89 Ch. 21 in this volume.
90 This was the beginning of an elaboration which became enshrined in the celebrated 'category E' of Comolli and Narboni's 1969 editorial 'Cinema/Ideology/Criticism' (see note 55 above) – 'films which seem at first sight to belong firmly within the ideology and to be completely under its sway, but which turn out to be so only in an ambiguous manner'.
91 Jean-Louis Comolli, 'Divorce absolu', *Cahiers* 146, August 1963.
92 Chs 18 and 22 in this volume.
93 Jean-Louis Comolli, 'Signes de piste', *Cahiers* 164, March 1965, translated as 'Signposts on the trail' in Caughie, *Theories of Authorship*, p. 114.
94 Comolli, 'Divorce absolu'.
95 Comolli, 'Signposts on the trail', pp. 114–15. Cf. Jean Narboni, 'La preuve par huit', *Cahiers* 182, September 1966, translated as 'Casting out the eights: John Ford's *Seven Women*' in Caughie, *Theories of Authorship*.
96 Ch. 15 in this volume.
97 Sylvain Godet, 'Angoisse derrière la vitre', *Cahiers* 186, January 1967, translated as 'Anxiety Behind the Window Pane' in *Cahiers du Cinéma in English*, no. 10, May 1967, p. 55.
98 Jean-Louis Comolli, 'Le Rideau soulevé, retombé', *Cahiers* 186, January 1967, translated as 'The Curtain Lifted, Fallen Again' in *Cahiers du Cinéma in English*, no. 10, May 1967, p. 52.
99 Ian Cameron, 'Introduction', in Cameron, *Second Wave*, London, Studio Vista, 1970, p. 5.
100 Luc Moullet, 'Jean-Luc Godard', Ch. 1 in this volume.
101 Ch. 5 in this volume.
102 Ch. 27 in this volume.
103 Chs 7 and 10 in this volume.
104 Ch. 9 in this volume.
105 Chs 31 and 38 in this volume.
106 Translated in *Godard on Godard*, p. 243.

Part One

New Wave/French Cinema

Introduction: Re-thinking and Re-making French Cinema

Given the long history of polemics in *Cahiers* for a new French cinema,[1] and given also the international acclaim for the early *nouvelle vague* films in 1958–60, surprisingly little about the new French cinema then appeared in the pages of *Cahiers* in the early 1960s. The editorial in the 1962 *nouvelle vague* special issue explained the point in these terms:

> We are reproached for not talking about young French cinema. That cinema is not only dear to us, but close to us too, and there is always something indecent in talking about oneself. We find ourselves unable either to judge this *nouvelle vague* for which we did rather more than facilitate the birth with the requisite objectivity or even to consider it with sufficient distance.
>
> Yet, on the other hand, our magazine cannot allow itself to ignore the existence of a *fact* already being promoted as historical fact. So let's silence our scruples, at least this once. Since it is difficult for us to place ourselves outside the *nouvelle vague*, let's remain inside it. This perspective is rather special, but it is productive. Lacking the truth, let's give *our* truth: people will take it for what it is worth, but we believe it is a truth which people should not be indifferent to knowing.[2]

Part of that truth was a growing disenchantment with both the system of distribution and exhibition (and, later, production too) and with the critical habits of the French press,[3] blamed equally for what was to be perceived as a continuing 'Crisis of French Cinema', as a 1965 special issue was subtitled.[4] This 1965 issue contained a section called 'Bitter Victories', devoted to important films which had been misunderstood or undervalued and which had failed to find an audience,[5] very much the kind of incomprehension or lack of clarity which André S. Labarthe complains of in the reception of Chabrol's *Les Bonnes femmes*. In his 1967 interview, François Truffaut makes the same general point about the press, while Jean-Luc Godard, in his 1962 interview, may have felt that there was 'no longer any position to defend' and that *Cahiers* was no longer 'in the front line

27

of battle' but was nevertheless soon to find himself replying, in the pages of *Cahiers*, to virulent attacks on *Les Carabiniers*.[6]

In a sense, at the same moment as the *nouvelle vague* 'triumphed' it also began to recognize its problems and the differences between its film-makers. The interviews with Godard, Truffaut and Chabrol in the 1962 special issue[7] showed very clearly the developing differences in perspective within the *Cahiers* group of film-makers, differences which became much more open during the 1960s, as Jacques Rivette and Eric Rohmer became more active and established as directors and as paths diverged more widely. One aspect of this is that Godard and Rivette realized increasingly that the *nouvelle vague* – or their own conception and development of it – was not going to be the new 'popular' French cinema. While, ultimately, Truffaut, Chabrol and Rohmer could be said to have achieved some kind of serious 'popular' success, Godard and Rivette came to understand that their new cinema would be 'oppositional', avant-garde, almost necessarily condemned to marginalization and misunderstanding by the press and by the general public.[8]

In reality, these divergences should not be surprising, since the *nouvelle vague* never professed a concerted body of doctrine or saw itself as a 'movement' in any precise way, with manifestos and the like. One looks in vain in the 1965 Rohmer interview and the 1967 Truffaut interview translated here for much retrospective illumination on what, for them, was 'new' in the *nouvelle vague*. For Rohmer the greatest innovation was 'making films cheaply', while Truffaut is explicit that there was no aesthetic programme: for him the *nouvelle vague* meant 'to make a first film with a reasonably personal theme before you were 35' and 'simply an attempt to rediscover a certain independence which was lost somewhere around 1924'.

How was the *nouvelle vague* perceived in *Cahiers* earlier in the decade? When Luc Moullet calls *A bout de souffle* 'most representative' he has in mind its spontaneity in the observation of character, for example, and its fully personal, 'authorial' nature: 'a film is not written or shot during the six months or so allotted to it, but during the thirty or forty years which precede its conception'. When Labarthe claims *Les Bonnes femmes* as the 'high point of the new French cinema' he does so on the basis of the purity of its *mise en scène*, the 'objectivity' of the way it looks at the world.[9]

Such observations are useful, but the originality of the *nouvelle vague* was to be found elsewhere, in other aspects of the work of Godard, in the work of Alain Resnais, and in Jean Rouch's experiments in *cinéma vérité*.[10] In Volume 1, I argued[11] that in 1959 the critical reception in *Cahiers* of Truffaut's *Les 400 coups*[12] marked the triumph of André Bazin's conservative aesthetic of realism, especially as elaborated around neo-realist films like *Paisà* and *Bicycle Thieves*,[13] while Resnais's *Hiroshima mon amour* enforced recognition on the part of *Cahiers* of more modernist tendencies in narrative cinema, owing something to developments in literature but in many ways moving beyond them.[14] Labarthe's short but striking essay here on Resnais's *L'Année dernière à Marienbad* signals again the engagement with modernist developments but also skilfully combines the tendencies represented by *Les 400 coups* and *Hiroshima* by relating them to Bazin's thesis that both the photographic realism of deep focus in film-makers like Wyler and Welles[15] and the realism of episodic, elliptical narrative organization to be found in Italian neo-realism predicated a more active spectator. In this view *Marienbad* becomes, interestingly if surprisingly, the ultimate development of neo-realism in that it insists upon the active, critical spectator – a conception of the spectator crucial to the development of a wider conception of 'new cinema' during the 1960s.

During the 1960s Resnais's work proved a consistent focus for debate in *Cahiers*. In the editorial discussion of *Muriel* here there is a very clear sense that Resnais is perceived as being very different from the *Cahiers* group in the *nouvelle vague* and as being in the vanguard of developments in 'modern' cinema in a way that the *Cahiers* group was not: the literary reputations of Marguerite Duras, Alain Robbe-Grillet and Jean Cayrol, screenwriters of *Hiroshima*, *Marienbad* and *Muriel* respectively, and all exponents of the *nouveau roman*,[16] was important here. Despite its considerable interest in relation to *Muriel* itself the discussion comes to centre on more general issues, particularly the differences between French and European cinema and American cinema. There is a great deal of continuity with *Cahiers* critical writing of the 1950s as well as some important new positions. Rivette, for example, is very clear, from the perspective of the *nouvelle vague*, on why French and other European cinema was so different from the 'classical' American cinema, and even from the work of figures like Renoir and Rossellini. Importantly, it also becomes a discussion fundamentally about 'realism': how to define social reality, the relationship between the individual and society, and how to render that social reality in cinema. Back in 1957 a *Cahiers* editorial discussion[17] had complained that French cinema failed to represent contemporary French social reality, while the strength of American cinema (and equally of Italian cinema) was taken to be precisely its social context. Now, as more politicized ways of thinking begin to gain ground, as American cinema is seen to be changing and its classical period perhaps ending, as new forms of narrative emerge in film-makers like Resnais, Godard, Rouch and in 'new cinema' in general, the relationship between classical narrative and the representation of heroism and of social reality as an organic or coherent whole began to be clearer.[18]

As the listings in both 'Twenty Years of French Cinema: the Best French Films Since the Liberation' and the *Cahiers* Annual Best Films Lists 1960–81[19] make clear, Godard's work was undoubtedly the most important for the development of both 'new cinema' and *Cahiers* itself. With only Godard's short films and *A bout de souffle* to go on (although, importantly, he refers to Godard's critical writings also), Luc Moullet in 1960 was more sensitive to what was to become characteristic of Godard than to what was 'representative of the *nouvelle vague'*. Moullet's emphasis on Godard's dialectical play with opposites (thought and speech, sound and image), on his use of narrative disruption and the 'image of disorder' it produces (in contrast to the 'highly structured' work of Resnais) is prophetic in relation to Godard's work – and the work it inspired – as it will develop in the 1960s: 'Godard observes reality scrupulously, while at the same time he tries to reconstitute it by means of flagrant artifice'. In his 1962 interview Godard himself already articulates very clearly the sense of constructing a new, different cinema on the ruins of the old cinema: he is very clear that classical Hollywood no longer existed. He wants to 'take a conventional story and remake, but differently, everything the cinema had been'. The idea of 'returning to zero' is one which recurs frequently in *Cahiers* critical writing in the 1960s.[20]

Not surprisingly Godard was the former critic turned film-maker most consistently featured in *Cahiers* in the 1960s, but the journal frequently turned to other former contributors and editors for interviews, although very often these became less interviews than discussions, and as much about cinema as about an individual *oeuvre*: Truffaut, Rohmer and Rivette, as well as Godard, are represented here by such interview-discussions. By 1965, the date of the Rohmer interview, *Cahiers* was already embracing many of the formal and political concerns associated with Godard's work and new cinema in general, and opposing more classical illusionist conventions. Attempts were made to preserve Truffaut for a certain version of modernism,[21] but the politicization of *Cahiers* put its critics at some distance from the conservative ideas – aesthetic and political – of Rohmer.[22] Both Truffaut and Rohmer espouse relatively traditional conceptions of narrative cinema and make clear how keenly they feel the operation of a kind of 'terrorism' which would have them embrace certain ideas of both modernism and leftism. Rohmer's comment that one should not 'be afraid of not being modern . . . you have to know how to go against the trend at times too' resumes the essential position of both of them as the politicization of *Cahiers* gathers momentum.

It was not, however, out of loyalty or nostalgia for past relationships with *Cahiers* that the newer editors remained interested in someone like Rohmer, even when the relationship between Rohmer and *Cahiers* could only be described as openly hostile.[23] It was also because Rohmer and Truffaut had ideas about cinema, ideas fiercely defended in discussion and fiercely exemplified in their work, work always responsible, individual and personal, and work not concerned with being fashionable. These were important qualities, and ones strongly associated with the *nouvelle vague*. They were precisely the qualities which Jean-Louis Comolli is unable to find in Claude Lelouch's film, *Un Homme et une femme*, even though Truffaut includes Lelouch in his (unhelpfully broad) definition of the *nouvelle vague*: 'Lelouch shoots with a hand-held camera and without a carefully planned script: if he isn't part of the *nouvelle vague*, then it doesn't exist'.

Cahiers had adopted the practice of writing about films they liked rather than films they did not like, and in this sense Comolli's attack on Lelouch was not typical. However, as we have seen, after the first triumphs of the *nouvelle vague* many important films by new French directors had met with critical incomprehension and commercial failure. From the mid-1960s the French cinema championed by *Cahiers* became increasingly less 'commercial'.[24] It was important, then, in 1966 to confront the enormous international success of *Un Homme et une femme* and, more particularly, its popular designation as a *nouvelle vague* film. In Comolli's argument what the film lacked was the 'rigour and morality' which would be characteristic of, say, a Rohmer film. Interestingly, given Truffaut's emphasis in his interview on decision-making as fundamental to the process of film direction, Comolli argues precisely, in his cancer metaphor, that Lelouch's film represents an *in*ability to make decisions, an easy accommodation with the spectator. *Un Homme et une femme*, he argues, manifests certain external formal mannerisms often associated with the *nouvelle vague* – episodic and elliptical narrative, improvisation, freedom of camera movement, location shooting, and so on – while completely failing to comprehend the relationship between form and meaning which had been central to the concept of *mise en scène* as practised in *Cahiers*.

As well as being concerned with the present and future of cinema, and especially its own French cinema, *Cahiers* had always been concerned also with re-assessing films and film-makers of the past, a process significantly sustained by the programming of Henri Langlois at the Cinémathèque Française. In itself such re-assessment is the common currency of serious film journals. If it was somewhat special in the case of *Cahiers* it was because this concern with the past was always very much directed towards contemporary practice. Eric Rohmer prefaced an interview with Henri Langlois with: 'For the cinema to have a future, its past could not be allowed to die. . . . Can you imagine a budding musician who was unable to listen to the works of Bach or Beethoven, a young writer who was unable to read the works of the past by going to a library? So by what right is the budding film-maker (or film critic) denied the same rights?'[25] Typically more dialectically and more politically, Godard spoke of 'the revolution that might be effected in the aesthetic of moving pictures by this new vision of its historicity',[26] while Rivette claimed that the 'Cinémathèque Française is both the Louvre and the Museum of Modern Art of film as they should be, and not as they are. . . . One could see there successively at 6.30 p.m. Griffith's *Broken Blossoms* and at 8.30 Andy Warhol's *The Chelsea Girls*. And it was fabulous precisely because one could see Griffith and Warhol together on the same night. Because it was then that one realized that there are not two or three kinds of cinema, there is only one cinema. It was the perpetual interaction of the present and the past of the cinema that was so exciting'.[27]

Thus, when Labarthe writes here about Marcel Pagnol it is very natural for him to refer, for comparison or contrast, to the contemporary practices of Godard, Rohmer, Eustache, Resnais, Bresson. This process of placing history in the present and bringing contemporary concerns to bear on the past, the process of 're-reading history' as Jean-André Fieschi puts it, became crucial to *Cahiers* as it developed in the 1960s and 1970s:

> The advent of a generation of film-makers conscious of their *heritage* is at last writing the History we were waiting for. The finest *critical* text on Murnau's *Tartuffe* is called *Nicht versöhnt* (*Not Reconciled*); the best exegesis of Feuillade's *Les Vampires* is called *L'Année dernière à Marienbad*; and the keys for understanding the open forms of Mack Sennett are to be found today in *Weekend* and *Les Carabiniers*.[28]

It is appropriate to end this introduction to *Cahiers* 1960s writing on French cinema with a further recognition of the continuing debt which the journal owed to the work of André Bazin, who had died late in 1958, just before the explosion of the *nouvelle vague*. Labarthe's essay on Pagnol naturally draws on Bazin's earlier essay on Pagnol[29] but, more fundamentally, both this and his earlier essay on *Marienbad* are founded on Bazin's theses about realism and the evolution of film language.[30] In the same issue with Labarthe's Pagnol essay – a special issue devoted to Sacha Guitry and Pagnol – the major article on Guitry by Jacques Bontemps[31] also takes a strikingly Bazinian line on film history. Rohmer's closeness to Bazin's thinking – his ideas having developed often at the same time as Bazin's – is very clear in his interview. Manifestly, however, as the call in *Cahiers* for a new, politicized, anti-illusionist, materialist cinema becomes more strident and more urgent, Bazin's aesthetic of realism becomes an aesthetic less to elaborate and extend than, ever productive, an aesthetic to challenge and reject.

Notes

1 Going right back to François Truffaut, 'Une Certaine Tendance du cinéma français', *Cahiers* 31, January 1954, translated as 'A Certain Tendency of the French Cinema' in Nichols, *Movies and Methods*.

2 *Cahiers* 138, December 1962, p. 1.

3 See particularly '3 Points d'économie: éléments pour un dossier' in *Cahiers* 138.

4 *Cahiers* 161–2, January 1965.

5 'Amères victoires' (the title of the article being borrowed from Nicholas Ray's 1957 film), *Cahiers* 161–2, comprised *Le Testament du Dr Cordelier* (Jean Renoir, 1961), *Le Signe du Lion* (Eric Rohmer, 1962), *Le Rendez-vous de minuit* (Roger Leenhardt, 1962), *Les Honneurs de la guerre* (Jean Dewever, 1961), *Adieu Philippine* (Jacques Rozier, 1963), *Muriel* (Alain Resnais, 1963), *Les Carabiniers* (Jean-Luc Godard, 1963), *Cyrano et d'Artagnan* (Abel Gance, 1963), *Paris nous appartient* (Jacques Rivette, 1960), *Les Godelureaux* (Claude Chabrol, 1960).

6 Jean-Luc Godard, 'Feu sur *Les Carabiniers*', *Cahiers* 146, August 1963, translated as 'Taking Pot Shots at the Riflemen' in *New York Film Bulletin*, no. 46, reprinted in Toby Mussman, *Jean-Luc Godard*, New York, E. P. Dutton, 1968; translated as '*Les Carabiniers* under Fire' in *Godard on Godard*.

7 *Cahiers* 138, December 1962. The interview with Godard is translated in *Godard*

on *Godard*, from which extracts are reprinted in this volume; the interview with Truffaut is translated in Graham, *The New Wave*.

8 See, for example, the 1967 interview with Jean-Luc Godard and the 1968 interview with Jacques Rivette in Part Four of this volume, Chs 31 and 38 respectively.

9 Labarthe's review needs to be read alongside the other 1960 material in this volume, particularly Jean Douchet's and Michel Mourlet's work on Joseph Losey, Chs 14 and 16.

10 See my Introduction to Part IV of this volume, 'Re-thinking the Function of Cinema and Criticism', and Fereydoun Hoveyda, '*Cinéma vérité*, or Fantastic Realism', Ch. 24.

11 'Introduction' to Part I, French Cinema, Volume 1, pp. 24–6.

12 See particularly Fereydoun Hoveyda, 'La Première Personne du pluriel', *Cahiers* 97, July 1959, translated as 'The First Person Plural', Ch. 5 in Volume 1.

13 Bazin's main writings on neo-realism are collected in André Bazin, *What is Cinema? Vol. 2*.

14 See particularly Jean Domarchi, Jacques Doniol-Valcroze, Jean-Luc Godard, Pierre Kast, Jacques Rivette, Eric Rohmer, 'Hiroshima, notre amour', *Cahiers* 97, July 1959, extracts translated as 'Hiroshima, notre amour', Ch. 6 in Volume 1.

15 For Bazin's work on film language see Ch. 3, note 1, in this volume.

16 The *nouveau roman* or 'new novel' is an important focus in the critical writing of Roland Barthes in the late 1950s and early 1960s, collected in Barthes, *Critical Essays*, Evanston, Illinois, Northwestern University Press, 1972. For a later evaluation of the importance of the new novel, see Stephen Heath, *The Nouveau Roman*, London, Elek, 1972.

17 André Bazin, Jacques Doniol-Valcroze, Roger Leenhardt, Jacques Rivette, Eric Rohmer, 'Six personnages en quête d'auteurs: débat sur le cinéma français', *Cahiers* 71, May 1957, extracts translated as 'Six Characters in Search of *auteurs*: A Discussion about the French Cinema', Ch. 2 in Volume 1.

18 Thomas Elsaesser develops some of these points in an important later article, 'Notes on the Unmotivated Hero: The Pathos of Failure – American Films in the 1970s', *Monogram*, no. 6, October 1975.

19 See Appendix 1.

20 See, as one example among many, Michel Delahaye, 'Jean-Luc Godard ou l'enfance de l'art', *Cahiers* 179, June 1966, translated as 'Jean-Luc Godard and the Childhood of Art' in *Cahiers du Cinéma in English*, no. 10, May 1967.

21 See, for example, Jean-André Fieschi's review of *La Peau douce* in *Cahiers* 157, July 1964, or Jean-Louis Comolli, 'Au coeur des paradoxes', *Cahiers* 190, May 1967.

22 The ideas embodied in the Rohmer interview-discussion were already well developed in Rohmer's earlier critical work in the 1950s (see note 1 to Ch. 7, the interview with Rohmer) and from articles such as 'Le Goût de la beauté', *Cahiers* 121, July 1961. Rohmer used the title of this article for a collection of his criticism of the 1940s and 1950s, *Le Goût de la beauté*, Paris, Cahiers du Cinéma/Editions de l'Etoile, distributed by Editions du Seuil, 1983.

23 See Pascal Bonitzer, Jean-Louis Comolli, Serge Daney, Jean Narboni, 'Nouvel entretien avec Eric Rohmer', *Cahiers* 219, April 1970, translated in extracts in Williams, *Realism and the Cinema*, pp. 244–53. As Williams comments, 'What is

remarkable about the discussion is that the interlocutors agree about nothing at all' (p. 244).

24 See, for example, the brief editorial, 'Zéro de conduite', introducing an issue devoted to 'four French film-makers' – Jacques Rivette, Jean-Daniel Pollet, Philippe Garrel, Marc'O, *Cahiers* 204, September 1968.

25 'Entretien avec Henri Langlois', *Cahiers* 135, September 1962, quoted in Richard Roud, *A Passion for Films: Henri Langlois and the Cinémathèque Française*, London, Secker and Warburg; New York, Viking Press, 1983, p. 65.

26 Jean-Luc Godard, 'Speech Delivered at the Cinémathèque Française on the occasion of the Louis Lumière Retrospective in January 1966: Thanks to Henri Langlois', *Le Nouvel Observateur*, 12 January 1966, translated in *Godard on Godard*, pp. 234–7.

27 Jacques Rivette, quoted in Roud, *op. cit.*, p. xxvii.

28 Jean-André Fieschi, 'Billet: Relire l'Histoire', *Cahiers* 198, February 1968, p. 5.

29 See Ch. 8, note 3.

30 For Bazin's theses on the evolution of film language, see Ch. 3, note 2.

31 Jacques Bontemps, 'Une gravité enjouée', *Cahiers* 173, December 1965.

1 | Luc Moullet: 'Jean-Luc Godard'

('Jean-Luc Godard', *Cahiers du Cinéma* 106, April 1960)

In the four months between the sneak preview and the first public showing of *A bout de souffle*, on 16 March 1960, Jean-Luc Godard's film has managed to acquire a notoriety never before achieved, I think, by any film prior to its release. The reasons for this notoriety are the Prix Jean Vigo, and the appearance of a record, a novel which is a distant relation of the film and an unfaithful rendering of it, and in particular press reviews indicative of a passion as strong – and unprecedented – in its panegyric as in its destructiveness.

Of all the films now being made by the newcomers to French cinema, *A bout de souffle* is not the best, since *Les 400 coups* has a head start on it; it is not the most striking – we have *Hiroshima mon amour* for that. But it is the most representative.

This point about the type of film it is means that *A bout de souffle* will be a great deal more successful than other films by young directors. It is the first film to be released in cinemas whose audience is essentially made up of 'the public at large', the 'average public' which is untouched by snobbishness. This is the fulfilment of what for ten years has been the new generation's most cherished desire: to make films not just for the art-house audience, but films which will be successful on the magic screens of the Gaumont-Palace, the Midi-Minuit, the Normandie, Radio City Music Hall, Balzac-Helder-Scala-Vivienne. *A bout de souffle* is not dedicated to Joseph Burstyn, or even to Warner Bros. or Fox, but to Monogram Pictures, the Allied Artists of yesteryear. In other words, it is a homage to American cinema at its most commercial – to which we shall return.

Jean-Luc Godard was born on 3 December 1930 in Paris. He studied in Nyon and then in Paris, where he gained a certificate in ethnology. Hence his passion for Rouch and his desire to become the Rouch of France. *A bout de souffle* is a little 'Moi, un Blanc',[1] or the story of two perfect fools.

During his first year at the Sorbonne (the preliminary year when, as is well known, students have nothing to do), he discovered the cinema,

35

thanks to the Ciné-Club du Quartier Latin, true source of today's new generation. Between 1950 and 1952 he wrote seven or eight articles in the Bulletin of the Ciné-Club ('Cinema is the art of lofty sentiments'), the *Gazette du Cinéma* (where he wrote one of the first pieces on Mankiewicz),[2] and *Cahiers du Cinéma* ('Defence and illustration of classical construction'),[3] which in general are eccentric and mediocre, accurate at odd moments and incomprehensible most of the time. Godard himself did not think them of any great importance since he nearly always signed them with a pseudonym, such as Hans Lucas. He broke with his family, sowed his wild oats, then did his little world tour – to the two Americas, that is – before returning to Switzerland where he worked as a labourer on the huge Grande-Dixence dam, to whose construction he dedicated his first short film, *Opération béton* (1954), which he financed with what he had saved from his pay. This is an honest documentary, straightforward and with no frills, if one disregards the very Malraux-like commentary: all his life Godard was to show himself to be a great admirer of the author of *Les Conquérants* (1933). In this first effort we can already see the principle which governs Godard's work and personality: that of alternation – after Malraux, Montherlant. An introverted ethnologist, scrutinizing the slightest gesture or look of other people, but without revealing what he is thinking behind the mask of thick dark glasses which he always wears, Godard is a disquieting personality precisely because he appears to be totally indifferent to what in reality affects him more than anyone.

This continuous displacement, maintained at times with a complacency which we would be wrong to fault since it gives us him in his best mood, explains why Godard is also the most extrovert of film-makers. The most important thing for an individual is not what he knows or what he is, but what he does not know and is not. Without denying himself, indeed to enrich himself, the individual tries to be what he is not. This is the theme that Chabrol, a friend of Godard, examines with varying success through the opposition of two characters. If Godard is a great director, it is because his natural reserve and esotericism, characteristic of his early writing, have pushed him towards a necessary, intentional and artificial extroversion which is much more significant than the same quality in those most effervescent of directors, Renoir and Rossellini. So Godard jumps from the Ciné-Club du Quartier Latin to the Incas, from the Sorbonne to manual labour. We love only the opposite of what we are.

Godard will sometimes do what he likes but is not, sometimes what he does not like but is. He will sometimes take lessons from Preminger and Hawks, and at other times do precisely the opposite: *A bout de souffle* comprising a synthesis of these two tendencies. So, after the openly conventional *Opération béton* came the very personal *Une femme coquette* (1955), a variation on the theme of everyday life in the streets of Geneva and on that fascination with cars which comes directly from *Viaggio in Italia* (Rossellini, 1953) and *Angel Face* (Preminger, 1952). But how inferior is the pupil to his masters, with his childish and pretentious esotericism!

There's no sense at all in this, no direction to this mediocre attempt at film-making. This same confusion can be found in Godard's later contributions to *Cahiers du Cinéma* (1956–7).[4] Then, after the production of *La sonate à Kreutzer* (Eric Rohmer, 1956) and a brief appearance in *Le coup du berger* (Jacques Rivette, 1956), the break comes with *Tous les garçons s'appellent Patrick* (1957), which Godard prefers because it is slighter than his later short films, because it respects the rules of traditional comedy, because it is less like him, and because it was a big public success.

> In the Luxembourg Gardens, Patrick meets Charlotte, makes a pass at her, and asks her out for the evening. Five minutes later he meets Véronique, who only the audience knows is Charlotte's room-mate: same story. The girls exchange many a secret about their admirer, whom they suddenly see embracing a third girl.

This sparkling little film works well because of the precision of its construction, the vivacity and originality of its dialogue, and the humour of its variously rehearsed effects in the two pick-up scenes. And in particular because of the remarkably engaging spontaneity of the two women when they are together in their tiny apartment, portrayed with an authenticity hitherto unknown in French cinema. There was Becker and Renoir, of course, but the girl they pictured was the pre-war girl, not the girl of today. And what grace there is in these heroines, much more so here than in *Une femme coquette*. The spareness of the artificial effect created by a superb piece of editing (Godard, who worked as a professional editor on other directors' films around 1956–7, does not make unmatched cuts unless they are intentional and, as here, knows how to edit within the rules of editing, something a Richard Quine or a Denys de la Patellière might well envy him for)[5] – this spareness chimes in very well with the naturally artificial grace of these little flirts. As with Cocteau, in the highest artifice there is realism and, especially, poetry.

For the second time the pendulum had swung towards the commercial, and this – together with his work for a weekly paper (*Arts*, from 1957 to 1959)[6] which hardly sanctioned esotericism – helped him to clarify his thoughts: from then on the articles he published in *Cahiers du Cinéma* were both very comprehensible and very personal. The article devoted to *Bitter Victory* (*Cahiers* no. 79)[7] is without any doubt the finest evocation of the work of Nicholas Ray.

Then another complete change with *Charlotte et son Jules* (1958), Godard's best short film and one of the most personal ever made. Just a few set-ups in a single apartment, shot in one day for 550,000 old francs. No one has done better for less.

> Charlotte gets out of her current lover's car (Gérard Blain) and goes up to her ex-lover's room (Jean-Paul Belmondo). He greets her with a display of just about every attitude a man can show towards a woman: wily, paternal,

condescending, he soon turns to pleading. Charlotte, who hasn't uttered a word, says to him, 'I forgot my toothbrush', and leaves.

No one before has articulated this comprehensive and dizzily spinning evolution of the ideas and feelings which are so much part of Godard, or in so concise a manner – twelve minutes, the time it takes to smoke a quarter of a cigar. We have here two remarkable actors, the artificial spontaneity which in Godard's previous film was that much more pronounced, and in particular, rounding off this astounding physical and moral whirligig, the hero's splendid soliloquy. With a comedy, Godard can express his own ideas through the medium of his characters. If these ideas seem likely to shock people, he gets round that by making the character articulating them appear comic. This is how in *Charlotte*, as in *A bout de souffle*, he can deal with the most serious problems which people have to face without losing his lightness of touch, and frequently finds an answer to them with exceptional elegance and understanding. What is so admirable is that his intellectuals manage to say very serious things so very naturally, without being pompous or boring. No one before Godard has been capable of giving concrete expression to a language which has always seemed very abstract – which accounts for our surprise and our laughter. As a film critic, Godard has a feeling for the verbal expression and likes to spin out his sentences, with a rhythm tuned to the easy pace of multiple clauses which allow only a moment or two for breath before their eight or ten syllable ending: a style which allows him to write a line, as an exercise, which carries us with no disruption or discontinuity from Père-Lachaise to Kilimanjaro, from Camus to Truffaut. This is the best possible dialogue, and for an actor the easiest, most natural and most fluent. Like all Godard films, *Charlotte* was post-synchronized; and since Belmondo was no longer available after the filming, Godard devised a way of dubbing his hero himself by carefully ensuring that he did not speak until a moment after Belmondo had opened his mouth. This has the effect of accentuating the element of fantasy in the text, while at the same time marking the gap between what the character says and what he is thinking. This character already shares some of his creator's characteristics – at once admiring, sceptical and disenchanted as far as women are concerned – thereby revealing in himself Godard's own double nature, a detachment that is both real and feigned. Like that of von Sternberg in *The Saga of Anatahan* or Cocteau in *Le Testament d'Orphée*, Godard's narration is superb: they are all directors who, by lending their own voice to the film, give it as it were a new physical rationale. The very soul of the director is heard in counterpoint. Godard's naturalness, at once nonchalant and resolute, as well as the way he has of lowering his voice for each effect, is testimony to a perfect harmony between film and film-maker, and testimony to his sincerity.

Audiences as well as nit-picking critics have cried horror in the face of so revolutionary a concept of film dialogue, a concept which also regenerates the art of cinema. On the same pretext of amateurism – a ludicrous notion given that the films are so dissimilar – both *Charlotte et son Jules* and *Tous les garçons s'appellent Patrick* were turned down by the selection committee of the Tours festival. If *Tous les garçons s'appellent Patrick* was applauded when it was released, while its companion piece *Un témoin dans la ville*[8] was hissed down, *Charlotte et son Jules* was jeered by people who just a few minutes later were to applaud *L'Eau à la bouche*.[9] It's a pity that the film's technical flaws, even though turned to good effect, should cause such a stir in the audience; to like *Charlotte et son Jules* you don't need to know that Godard himself dubbed the film. In fact, this derision stems from the snobbishness of those critics and people in the audience who insist on letting everyone else know that they recognize the technical tricks, though what they ignore is that the voice-gap is so obvious it can only be intentional.

Also in 1958, Truffaut shot *Une histoire d'eau*, the story of two young people who flee the suburbs and their floods to discover Paris and love. Despite one or two amusing touches, the shots he took were uneditable. Truffaut handed over to Godard, who filmed some linking shots, cut it all together, wrote a commentary, and in the end saved the film. How? By accentuating the film's disjunctiveness so as to give it the style of a natural ballet. First by means of syncopated, chopped up editing – there was just not enough material – of the kind he admired so much in *The Wrong Man* (Hitchcock, 1956) and *Kiss Me Deadly* (Aldrich, 1954), which he used on his own account in *Une femme coquette*, and which he was subsequently to employ with devastating success; and secondly by means of the endlessly serpentine commentary, reminiscent of the immensely long sentences of his most recent critical articles. Even more than in *Charlotte*, the text overlays the image. Puns and word plays accumulate, to an extent that the audience loses its bearings, can't keep up with Godard's hallucinating improvisation, and can only pick up snatches here and there. We should not forget that Godard made these two films in the wake of his admiration for *The Quiet American* (Mankiewicz, 1957),[10] which partly inspired in him this renewal through dialogue and the penchant for constructing a film like a swirling current which ends in a fall.

The spirit of Resnais is here too, each gag arising out of a close relationship between shot, editing and commentary but with the additional qualities of grace, humour and insouciance. Out of an amiable, harmless little story Godard made a frenzied poem. This is one of the high peaks of the art of cinema, reaching on the level of film synthesis what in *Charlotte* Godard had reached only on the level of subject and dialogue.

Then, after several scripts written for other directors and a remarkable performance in *Le Signe du Lion* (Eric Rohmer, 1959), Godard made *A bout de souffle*.

A bout de souffle began as an outline written by Truffaut, which Truffaut himself and Molinaro wanted to adapt. Godard chose it . . . because he didn't like it. 'I think it's a good system,' Truffaut commented in *Radio-*

Télévision-Cinéma. 'Working freely on a project, but one to which you feel close enough to be drawn to it. This gives you enough distance to judge the work and cut down its weaknesses, and at the same time you're sensitized to it.' Godard originally wanted to make a film about death and heroes obsessed with death. But being too lazy to write a script before starting to shoot, he let himself be guided by inspiration, relying on just a few lines of direction. In fact, the theme was reduced to just the occasional, though brilliant, notation.

A bout de souffle was shot in four weeks (17 August–15 September 1959), on location (interiors and exteriors), without sound, in Paris and Marseille, and for 45 million old francs – the minimum possible when you consider that the producer had to pay a celebrated international star like Jean Seberg. The camera was almost always hand-held by the cameraman himself, at one moment hidden inside a hand-cart steered by Godard so as to get passers-by into the shot.

> Michel Poiccard, anarchist car thief, kills the motorcycle cop who is chasing him. In Paris, he looks up his American girlfriend, Patricia Franchini, and becomes her lover again. He persuades her to leave for Italy with him. But the police discover the identity of the killer and track him down. Patricia gives Michel away and he is casually shot down by the police.

A perfect theme for a thriller. Godard originally wanted to make a commercial film within the rules of the genre. But in the end, partly out of laziness and partly because he likes to take risks, he decided to dispense with all the elements of the genre except plot and physical action. He was not trying to uncover the hidden soul of the genre's conventions, as did Hawks and all the great Americans and as he himself tried to do in *Tous les garçons s'appellent Patrick*. Godard preferred the straight French approach to the American double game. He is not discreet; he paints his characters' psychological quirks in black and white. This is no longer the uniquely interior depth much vaunted over the previous five years by the young absolutists of *Cahiers du Cinéma*, but a depth which is both interior and exterior, and by that token anti-commercial. What I mean is that Godard finds his expression in his dialogue as well, since *A bout de souffle* – like *Hiroshima* but on a more serious level – is a dialogue between two lovers a little lost amid the problems of their time. This ambivalence in *A bout de souffle* will ensure a twofold success with audiences: the Champs-Elysées snobs will be gratified in their own way, and the mass audiences who thrive on action and gags will be sufficiently entertained to forget about the occasionally difficult esoteric element in certain sequences. For audiences to like a film doesn't mean that they have to like it for the whole ninety minutes (producers afraid of upsetting audiences should never cut a few shots out of their films: they should either leave them as they are or remake them from scratch). Twenty or so strong elements are enough to keep audiences involved.

What's new about *A bout de souffle*? To begin with, the way the characters are conceived. Godard never uses a particularly precise line in the way he sketches his characters; instead, he follows – consciously – a series of contradictory directions. Godard is an instinctive creator, and rather than logic *per se* (which he was happy enough to follow in his first, tentative efforts, but which he is now too lazy to follow – and I don't think it interests him), he follows the logic of his instinct. He explains this in *Charlotte et son Jules*:

> I seem to be saying something,
> But that's not so; but then that's not so either.
> From the mere fact that I say a phrase,
> There's necessarily a connection with what comes before it.
> Don't be bewildered,
> It's Cartesian logic.
> But yes,
> I'm deliberately speaking as in the theatre.

A film is not written or shot during the six months or so allotted to it, but during the thirty or forty years which precede its conception. The film-maker, as soon as he types out the first letter of his script on his typewriter, only needs to know how to let himself go, how to let himself get absorbed in a passive task. He only needs to be himself at each moment. This is why Godard doesn't always know why a certain character does this or that. But he only needs to think about it for a moment, and he always finds out why. Given a certain kind of behaviour, even contradictory behaviour, there's no doubt that one can always explain it. But with Godard it's different: everything comes together, chiefly because of the accumulation of little details, for the simple reason that Godard has thought of everything in a natural way, by standing in for his subject. The psychology – freer, invisible almost – is consequently more effective.

Our two heroes possess a moral attitude hitherto unknown in the cinema. The erosion of Christianity since the end of the last century – which Godard, being of Protestant origin, is very conscious of – has left people free to choose between the Christian concept of a shared human existence and the modern deification of the individual. Both notions have their good points, and our heroes oscillate between one and the other, feeling a little lost. This is why the film is stamped with the seal of the greatest of philosophical schools, the sophists.

A bout de souffle is an attempt to go beyond sophism; as with Euripides, to adapt sophism to reality, from which can emerge happiness. Belmondo had already said to Charlotte:

> I'm not cross with you, yes I am cross with you,
> No, I'm not cross with you, or rather yes,
> I am cross with you. I don't know,

41

It's funny, I don't know.
I'm cross with you for not being cross with you.

And Patricia says:

I don't know if I'm free because I'm unhappy, or if I'm unhappy because I'm free.

It's partly because she loves Michel that Patricia informs on him, and it's partly because of a liking for originality and for having the last word that Michel wants to give himself up to the police: the changing attitudes of our times can sometimes produce a complete inversion of conventional psychology, turning it into its exact opposite. One result of this perpetual to and fro movement is the lure of the *mise en scène*, commonly encountered in all great films since their authors are also their directors. Fascinated by their dizzy behaviour, our heroes detach themselves from their own selves and *play* with these selves to see what effect this will produce. In the last shot, by a supreme irony, as Michel dies he makes one of his favourite comic faces, to which Patricia responds. An ending which is at once optimistic and harrowing – harrowing because comedy intrudes into the heart of tragedy.

Critics have already pointed to the differences in the way the man and the woman behave; differences which were admirably highlighted by Jean Domarchi's article in last month's issue.[11] Patricia is a little American intellectual who doesn't have much idea of what she wants and who ends up by informing against the man she loves. Like Charlotte, she is a much less sympathetic personality than the man, who is sparkling, quick-witted and with an astonishing lucidity in among a fair amount of tomfoolery. Should we see a misogynist in Godard? No, because this misogyny is external, confined by the subject matter. It reflects the contradiction which is at the root of a man's real love for a woman – an admiration combined with a certain amused contempt for the kind which, in the encounter of reason and taste, prefers man to woman. Those who say they want their films to be 'the work of a man who loves women, who says so, and who proves it' are in fact misogynists, because they tip the balance in favour of women in the way they choose their subject, and because they hire the country's most attractive actresses and then don't direct them or direct them badly: they don't know how to reveal their qualities. Once again this alternation between what one is and what one would like to be: 'I am not what I am', as Shakespeare said. Whereas the association of Godard and Seberg proved to be a magnificent one, doubtless because there is in Seberg that dialectic to which Godard is so drawn. By affecting a masculine appearance in the way she lives and with her boyish hairstyle, she is all the more feminine. It's well known, of course, that a woman is much sexier in trousers and with her hair cut short, since this lets her purge her femininity of its superficial aspects.

But one's respect for Patricia increases when she telephones the police. This is an act of courage. She resolves in the end to extricate herself from the awful quagmire in which she is trapped. But like all acts of courage it is a facile solution, and Michel bitterly reproaches her for it. He takes full responsibility for what he is; he plays the game, doesn't like Faulkner or half measures, and goes right to the heart of his constant dilemma. But he plays the game too well: his death is the natural sanction demanded at one and the same time by logic, by the audience and by morality. He has gone too far, wanting to set himself apart from the world and its objects in order to dominate them.

It's here that we see how Godard, while literally sticking close to his hero, at the same time very slightly detaches himself, thanks to his other personality, that of the objective, pitiless, entomological film-maker. Godard both is and is not Michel, being neither a killer nor dead – quite the opposite in fact. Why this slight superiority of the author over his character, which bothers me a little? Because Michel is only Godard's virtual double. He makes real what Godard thinks. A good illustration of this difference is provided by the scene where Michel goes out into the Paris streets and lifts up women's skirts. *A bout de souffle* has been criticized for having an essentially psychoanalytical rationale. Certainly it's with the cinema that psychoanalysis begins or ends; but when the film-maker is aware of the idiosyncrasies of his mind and of their vanity, they can become a source of beauty. *A bout de souffle* is an attempt at liberation through film: Godard is not – is no longer – Michel because he made *A bout de souffle* and Michel did not.

We may note that the form of the film wholly reflects the behaviour of its hero, and indeed of the heroine. Better, she justifies this behaviour. Michel, and Patricia even more so, are overtaken by the disordered times we live in, the continual moral and physical changes and developments that are uniquely of our era. They are victims of this disorder, and the film is therefore a point of view on disorder, both within and without. Like *Hiroshima* and *Les 400 coups*, it is an attempt – more or less successful – to overcome this disorder: less successful, as it happens, since if it were successful the disorder would no longer exist. To make a film on disorder whose structure is not itself imbued with disorder seems to me the surest condemnation of that film. What I admire in *Les 400 coups* is that throughout the film, thanks to Truffaut's detachment and, particularly in the final sequence, to the harmonious working out of the plot, disorder is resolved by order; and also that Truffaut is here at one and the same time a young man and an old man of seventy. Yet there is a little more natural mischief in this than openness; the artist is only one person at the time he is making the film, and any development at the centre of the work is necessarily an assumed one, either in its origin or in its conclusion. Godard's superiority to Truffaut, then, lies in the fact that where Truffaut applies himself to the task of making our own civilization fit a classical framework, Godard – more honestly – seeks a rationale for our age from within itself.

In art, according to some people, value is order and disorder is its opposite. I don't agree, since the essence of art is that it has no laws; even public esteem is a myth which it is sometimes convenient to scotch. As always with Godard, the *mise en scène* creates this image of disorder in two different voices: first, by naturalness, freedom, the risks of invention. Godard takes from life everything he finds there, without selecting; or, more precisely, he selects everything he sees and sees only what he wants to see. He omits nothing, and tries simply to reveal the meaning of everything he sees and everything that goes through his head. Continuous, natural breaks in tone create this image of disorder. And one shouldn't be at all surprised if, during a love scene, there is a sudden transition from Faulkner to Jean de Létraz.[12] Similarly, when Godard makes a play on words, it's either a good one or a very bad one, in which case we laugh at his intentional mediocrity. What Godard reveals is the profound unity which comes out of this disorder, this permanent external diversity. It's been said that the film is not structured and that neither it nor its characters evolve, except in the last quarter of an hour and then only slightly. But that's because Godard is against the idea of evolution, just like Resnais, who reaches the same conclusion by the totally different method of a work which is highly structured. This notion is in the air: the camera is a mirror taken along a road, but there is no road left. Like *Hiroshima*, *A bout de souffle* could have lasted two hours, and it did last effectively two hours on the first cut. The remarkable *Time Without Pity* (Joseph Losey, 1957) shows evidence of a very precise construction and of a constant forward movement, but how arbitrary this seems. Godard, on the other hand, follows a higher order, that of nature, the order in which things appear to his eye and his mind. As he said above: 'From the mere fact that I say a phrase, there's necessarily a connection with what comes before it.'

The film is a series of sketches, interludes which are at first sight unconnected, like the interview with the writer. But the mere fact that they exist gives these episodes a profound relationship with one another, as with all life's phenomena. The interview with Parvulesco sets out clearly the main problems our lovers have to solve. Like *Astrophel and Stella* (Sir Philip Sidney, 1581), *A bout de souffle* is formed out of little separate circles which, by the end of the sequence or the sonnet, turn out to be linked by an identical cone at a common point – Stella in Sidney, Patricia or something else in Godard.

The nature of the effect, so long as there is an effect in the shot, is immaterial. This is what realism is about. Hence the preponderance of little ideas, gags. Godard has been taken to task for his accumulation of private jokes which are only understood by cinephiles or Parisians. They won't be understood by a general audience, but that won't bother them because with a few exceptions they won't notice them. It's true that they will miss a lot. But the fact is that many great works of art are by nature esoteric, starting with Aristophanes, who is unintelligible without footnotes. A work has a greater chance of attaining immortality the more precise and comprehensive its definition of a time and place. Even the classical directors indulged in these private jokes (Griffith as much as Autant-Lara), and we usually miss them because they no longer mean anything to us. The scene where Michel looks at Patricia through a rolled up poster and kisses her is a homage to an unreleased film by a minor American director. It's not necessary to know the film to enjoy the effect, though it's less successful than in the original.

Godard can be more legitimately taken to task for the ideas that don't work. Lighting the lamps on the Champs-Elysées has no point at all.

And what purpose is served by the titles which loudly proclaim the fundamental differences between the French language and the American language, this Apollinaire film with dialogue by Boetticher, the absence of credits? Original, amusing, but no more than that.

This is not too irritating, though, because one detail follows fast on another and there is no time to notice that one of them doesn't work.

Whereas in a Doniol-Valcroze or a Chabrol film (*A bout de souffle*, incidentally, is the best contribution to cinema by a man in tortoise-shell spectacles) one notices how much less frequent, and less good, the effects are.

What I've just said is incorrect, and I apologize for it. Because the unique thing about Godard is that everything you can say about him will always be right (at the same time as doing what he says, he also sticks to his principle: 'I always do the opposite of what I say,' he admitted to Michel Leblanc in the December 1959 issue of *L'Etrave*). No critical comment on Godard can be wrong, but it will always accumulate errors of omission, for which I will be fiercely taken to task by Godard. For film truth, as a reflection of life, is ambiguous, in contrast to the truth of words. In *L'Express* (23 December 1959), Godard let us into his secret: 'I must admit, I have a certain difficulty with writing. I write: "It's a nice day. The train enters the station," and I spend hours asking myself why I couldn't just as well have written the opposite: "The train enters the station. It's a nice day" or "It's raining". With films, it's easier. Simultaneously it's a nice day and the train enters the station. There's an inevitability about it. That's where you have to go.'

Which explains both the appeal of criticism for Godard and his aversion to it, as something which allows him to clarify the disorder he perceives. Periods of disorder and advance, like the eighteenth century and the twentieth century, as opposed to periods of greater stability and creation, like the seventeenth and nineteenth centuries, in which certain people of genius stand out, witness the triumph of self-reflexion, the striving towards synthesis (hence the multiple references in *A bout de souffle* to painting, cinema and literature). These periods are essentially marked by the work of critics (neither Racine nor Molière really practised criticism, as opposed to Voltaire and Diderot who did little else) with a natural gift for synthesis. And to talk of synthesis is to talk of the considerable importance of editing. Today we have a whole range of creator-critics and editors and no one has a clear lead over the others. Of the new generation, there is no single name which *can* be separated from the rest. If *A bout de souffle* is better than *Hiroshima*, that is because Godard had seen and written about *Hiroshima* before he started his own film; not because Godard is better than Resnais. So if you want to become very famous today, don't go into the creative arts, go into politics. The young French cinema is the work of very different personalities, but it is also partly a collective work. There are some who go a little further, others who go a little less far; the difference is quantitative.

But I'm wrong about this, since Godard achieves this *tour de force* of being, on his own terms, both very like Rossellini, as we have seen, and not like Rossellini at all. Which is why one often thinks of Resnais. Godard observes reality scrupulously, while at the same time he tries to reconstitute it by means of flagrant artifice. All new directors, from fear of the risks of film-making, have a tendency to plan their films carefully and to make grand stylistic flourishes. In *Charlotte et son Jules*, for instance, we saw decor being used as scientifically as in a Lang film. This explains the editing style of *A bout de souffle*, where flash shots are skilfully interwoven with very long takes. Just as the characters' behaviour reflects a series of false moral connections, the film itself is a suite of false connections. Only how beautiful, how delightful these false connections are! In fact, though, this is precisely what is least new in the film: the simple and systematic expression of the theme by means of construction, editing and choice of angles. There's nothing especially clever about tilting the camera every time a character is prostrate. Aldrich, Berthomieu[13] and Clément have done it all their lives, and it rarely works. Nevertheless, there is method in it when, in the same travelling shot, we jump from Seberg and Belmondo on the Champs-Elysées to Belmondo and Seberg on the same Champs-Elysées passing by the shadows of De Gaulle and Eisenhower in procession. The implication is that the only thing that matters is oneself, not the external political and social world – and by trimming the shots in which the generals appear the censors have reduced them to mere entities, ridiculous puppets. The implication also is that what will remain of our age is *A bout de souffle*, and not De Gaulle or Eisenhower, like all statesmen pitiful if inevitable tinpot figures. There is method also when, in a very different way from *Vertigo* (Hitchcock, 1957) and *Les Cousins* (Chabrol, 1958), the great Coutard's camera rolls and rolls and rolls, always in tempo with the mind of the protagonist. This has a precise meaning. It is a very classical expression of modern behaviour.

But what gives *A bout de souffle* a slight superiority over that other formal film, *Hiroshima*, is that with Godard spontaneity transcends form (which completes and consolidates it), whereas with Resnais spontaneity is involved only in the direction of the actors. Another aspect of Godard's superiority is that he is dealing with something that is concrete, whereas recollection, forgetting, memory, time are not concrete things; they are things which have no existence, and like Christian doctrine or communism are not subjects serious enough to be treated by a language as profound as that of the screen. The fact that *Hiroshima* is not suited to a *concrete* evocation of these problems is nevertheless fascinating, in that it helps to give expression to something which is very different.

Godard could not perhaps steel himself to represent the disorder of our times in a clear-cut way or head-on; and so relied on the facility of technique to help him out. There is no conflict between point of view and what is shown, as there is with Truffaut; but that may be the price you pay for perfect sincerity. Although in my view *A bout de souffle* would have been no less inspired if it had been deprived of this artifice.

In fact, I think *Hiroshima* proved that it was necessary to resort to certain devices in order to reproduce a vision of the contemporary world, where both physically and morally our field of vision is conditioned by a great deal of artifice. Cinema which looks at the world from above ends up by being obsolete. Where Resnais half succeeds, and his imitators – fashion-followers like Pollet (the excellent *La Ligne de mire*, 1959), unthinking directors like Hanoun (*Le Huitième jour*, 1959) or Molinaro (*Une Fille pour l'été*, 1959) – fail lamentably, Godard succeeds in getting us to accept that this modern universe, as metallic and threatening as science-fiction, superbly represented by Jean Seberg (who may be less 'alive' than she is in Preminger's films but is more lunar in the cracked surface of her being), is a universe of wonderment and great beauty. Godard is a man who lives with the times, as is demonstrated by the respect he has for those emblems of a specifically modern civilization such as cars or the comic-strips of *France-Soir*.[14] The real civilization of our times is not that reactionary civilization of the right, incarnated by *L'Express*[15] or the plays of Sartre and characterized by its denial of what is and by its morose intellectualism; the real civilization is the revolutionary civilization of the left, as represented by, among other things, those celebrated comic-strips.

This is why it would be wrong to compare Godard with Rousseau on the theory that they are the greatest French-Swiss artists. If Jean-Jacques offers us nature in opposition to the artefact, Jean-Luc reclaims modern civilization, the city and the artefact, with a hundred per cent interest. Following the American tradition (in the best sense of that phrase) of Whitman, Sandburg, Vidor and even Hawks, he accomplishes art's highest mission: he reconciles man with his own time, with the world which so many constipated pen-pushers – who are frequently not best placed to judge, knowing nothing else – take for a world in crisis, a world which crucifies man. As if man were no longer capable of self-revelation in a world which seems to torment him. For Godard, the twentieth century is not an enormous affront to the mind of the creator; it is enough to know how to see and admire. The strength and beauty of his *mise en scène*, whose realization can offer no other image than that of serenity and optimism, enables us to discover the profound grace of a world which at first sight seems terrifying; and it does this through a poetry of false connections and of doom.

Translated by David Wilson

Notes

1 The reference is to anthropologist-film-maker Jean Rouch's first feature-length film, *Moi, un Noir* (1957). Until 1960 and *Chronique d'un été*, which focussed on a group of Parisians, Rouch's work had been wholly concerned with Black Africa. For details of Rouch's work, see Mick Eaton, *Anthropology-Reality-Cinema: The Films of Jean Rouch*, London, British Film Institute, 1979.

2 'Joseph Mankiewicz', *Gazette du Cinéma* 2, June 1950, translated in *Godard on Godard*, pp. 13–16. Other Godard articles from the *Gazette* also appear in this book.

3 'Défense et illustration du découpage classique', *Cahiers* 15, September 1952, translated as 'Defence and Illustration of Classical Construction' in *Godard on Godard*, pp. 26–30.

4 Godard's contributions to *Cahiers* are translated in *Godard on Godard*: see Appendix 2, Volume 1, and Appendix 2, this volume.

5 Richard Quine, mainstream American film director, b. 1920, active especially in the 1950s and 1960s; Quine's *Pushover* (1954) has been taken to be an influence on Godard's *A bout de souffle* (see interview with Godard translated in *Godard on Godard*, p. 175). Denys de la Patellière, French mainstream director, b. 1921, feature films since 1955.

6 Godard's contributions to *Arts* are translated in *Godard on Godard*.

7 'Au-delà des étoiles', *Cahiers* 79, January 1958, translated as 'Beyond the Stars' in *Godard on Godard* and reprinted in Volume 1, Ch. 14.

8 Directed by Edouard Molinaro, 1959, with Lino Ventura.

9 Directed by Jacques Doniol-Valcroze, 1960.

10 Godard's review of *The Quiet American* appeared in *Arts* 679, 22 July 1958, translated in *Godard on Godard*, pp. 81–4.

11 Jean Domarchi, 'Peines d'amour perdues', *Cahiers* 105, March 1960.

12 Jean de Létraz, popular French comic playwright.

13 André de Berthomieu, 1903–60, prolific commercial French film director.

14 *France-Soir*, Paris evening newspaper.

15 *L'Express*, French liberal weekly news magazine, modelled on *Time* and *Newsweek*.

2 | André S. Labarthe: 'The Purest Vision: *Les Bonnes Femmes*'

('Le plus pur regard', *Cahiers du Cinéma* 108, June 1960)

Generally speaking, Chabrol's latest film has had a mixed reception from the critics to say the least. While few may have hated it outright it is interesting to note that those who liked either the whole film or parts of it – from, say, Pierre Marcabru to René Cortade and Claude Choublier – were hard put to find the easy (or uneasy) justifications one might have expected. So much so that one has to ask if *Les Bonnes femmes* has been properly understood. It's as if those who did recognize it as Chabrol's best film, the one in which he himself goes 'to the limit' (Choublier), were themselves unable to carry their arguments through to the end. It's a pity for instance that Pierre Marcabru, whose reservations outweigh his praise by far, failed to work his analysis out fully: each of his statements about the film ultimately comes out right or wrong depending on whether it is applied to one element or the film as a whole; each provides ammunition for condemning the film, whereas were it to be developed and related back to the particular moment it characterizes, it might actually pass to the pro side. These statements set the tone which has marked virtually the whole critical response to the film. If I may quote briefly: 'If I weren't afraid of raising a smile I would say that the characters lack a soul. . . . There's a certain way of looking down on them from above, a fear of being compromised with them, a way of keeping a distance, a guardedness. . . . After *Le Beau Serge* one had hopes of better things. This is a director who refuses to show his hand. And he doesn't have much to say.' But the truth is not so simple, as we shall see.

It will by now be clear, I think, that I regard Chabrol's last film as not just his masterpiece, but the high point of the new French cinema as a whole. I have no wish to offend the keenest supporters of *A bout de souffle* – I flatter myself I can count myself among them – but is Godard's film really the crowning point of the new wave, as people have claimed? It is certainly an *auteur* film, but then is it really those film-makers who are *auteurs* first and foremost that take a language forward? I would say rather that they benefit from its advances without determining them, or only in small measure. *A bout de souffle* is a Godard film *before* it is a modern film, whereas *Les Bonnes femmes* is clearly a modern film. Which, to put it simply, means that Godard uses the cinema, while Chabrol serves it. Chabrol may 'have nothing to say', but after all it isn't necessarily the message which determines the call to make films; it can also be the plain and pressing need to apply a way of looking, a vision.

In Chabrol, the *mise en scène* is quite simply the exercising of that vision: with him, the greatest mastery is quite simply the exercise of a clearer vision. Chabrol's whole career can be summed up in the history of the purification of that vision, and if *Les Bonnes femmes* is his best film it is because the vision is here at its clearest. In this particular case the exercise of an ascetic discipline on the form is taken so far and Chabrol's vision is so purified of anything extraneous to it that the *mise en scène* comes to constitute a pure category, by which I mean an *a priori condition* of the profession of film-maker. It is in this sense that *Les Bonnes femmes* needs to be seen as the culmination of something, in the manner of *Le Déjeuner sur l'herbe*. (In any case, Chabrol surely comes closer than anyone to the *auteur* of *Le Testament du Docteur Cordelier*.[1]) *Les Bonnes femmes*, like *Le Déjeuner sur l'herbe*, takes cinema definitively into a new era, the era of realism, synthesism, objectivity, call it what you will: an era in which objective reality is dialectically founded by the *mise en scène*.

To recognize this function of the *mise en scène* is to recognize that the accusations of vulgarity levelled at *Les Bonnes femmes* must inevitably collapse. *French Cancan* incurred similar reproaches which Renoir has been brushing off ever since. The misunderstanding arises out of a recurrent confusion between two ideas of a distinctly different order. Today, *Les Bonnes femmes* is the focus of that confusion. 'After *Le Beau Serge* one had hopes of better things,' writes Marcabru. True, if one judges films by the yardstick of traditional cinema. But that cinema is precisely what Chabrol as film critic and then director has never ceased to censure. If on the contrary you agree that the new cinema is in the process of emancipating itself, then you have to agree that every one of Chabrol's films has marked a stage in that emancipation. So why the cries of treachery today, when Chabrol emerges on the dark side of the moon? It makes one wonder whether it isn't those who most eagerly supported Chabrol's early efforts who aren't the cinema's worst betrayers.

If, however, it is acknowledged that Chabrol is today directing a clearer look at reality, the reproach against him will no longer be vulgarity, but the choice of theme. Let me recapitulate the argument. The merit of *Le Beau Serge* was that it was somehow enmeshed in the web of Chabrol's biography; and behind the mechanics of *Les Cousins* it was still possible to discern a certain complicity between the *auteur* and his characters. In a word, Chabrol knew what he was on about! *A Double Tour* was the cut-off point. The brilliance of the *mise en scène*, it was said, could not conceal the impassiveness of the *auteur* who was already beginning to 'look down' on his characters, to 'keep his distance' and to be 'on guard'. As far as I remember, only Louis Marcorelles saw what Chabrol's uncompromising distance on the theme was a response to – the need for objectivity. Even those who had applauded Chabrol's gift for 'entomological' observation in the first two films drew back when it came to recognizing the best sample of that particular talent. And yet, though Chabrol's development is characterized by an increasingly ascetic formal discipline and an ever more categorical conception of *mise en scène*, there should not be any hesitation about saying that his first films were *ill-served* by the autobiographical nature of their themes – dust in the film-maker's eye. Being, as one may well imagine, so close to his themes, how could Chabrol fail to load his characters with the feelings they inspired in him, how could he avoid embellishing them with features that reflected his own emotional interest in them? With *Les Bonnes femmes* it is that reflection which he has succeeded in eliminating more or less completely. That's what Marcabru, in his way, interprets as 'an *auteur* who refuses to show his hand'. But choosing a subject diametrically opposed to one's personal preoccupations does not necessarily mean evading responsibility for one's art. Quite the contrary, it means committing oneself rather more and giving a surer foundation to the function of the *mise en scène*. Chabrol's taste for what he calls 'minor themes' has no other significance but that. Moreover, that is what makes *Les Bonnes femmes* not just Chabrol's best film, but also the film in which his scriptwriter, Gégauff, plays the biggest part. Or rather, because this is Chabrol's best film it is *above all* a film by Gégauff; for surely it is to the degree that Gégauff is author of the plot that Chabrol's eye is that much less contaminated by it.

What we have therefore is Gégauff laying out to the clear eye of the film-maker a small world, chosen by him, the small world of ordinary women. We have him bringing them alive, animating them with an existence of their own, inventing a self-contained destiny for them. On all this Chabrol fixes his lens – his microscope? – through which he observes these strange creatures: four ordinary women, all speaking with the muted tones of Bernadette Lafont, all living the same life, made up of the same gestures and threaded through with the same obsessions. He examines them with curiosity, Pierre Kast would say with the eye of a zoologist discovering a colony of Martians. The look is in principle not complimentary, but nor is it ill-disposed – objectivity has its price. *Les Bonnes femmes* is before all else an encounter between two worlds.

This little world, seen not from some superior, suspicious or contemptuous level as has been suggested, but from a distance, will inevitably seem denuded of any significance. But a word of caution – that does not mean that it is of no significance to itself. It indicates the eye of a film-maker striving for freedom from preconceptions. The study of human behaviour is in nature no different from the study of animal behaviour: the only difference is the object of study. Hence the long scenes at the swimming pool and especially at the Jardin des Plantes where the camera lens, with a stamp collector's impassivity, juxtaposes animal noises with the laughter of the women. For it is not just the gestures and behaviour of the women which strike us as absurd; so does their language, whose formal characteristics we grasp before we catch the meaning. Language itself is turned into an object, one might even say reified.

Cinema has not accustomed us to this kind of objectivity. We were used to following a film by catching links in meaning: if such and such a character made such and such a gesture we grasped the significance (the ins and outs of everything) *at once*; if they spoke, we went *directly* to what the words meant, even if in passing we noted the tone of voice, the charm of a gesture. *Les Bonnes femmes* robs us of that comfortable habit of going from the meaning to the form. You might say that *Les Bonnes femmes* is the first film not to be, *on principle*, a film 'with a message'.

The whole of the first part of *Les Bonnes femmes* supports that principled refusal. The danger is of course that the film rests at that and becomes just a way of turning circles around an object which may never yield up the smallest fragment of its mysteries. The danger is that the *auteurs* may shut their characters up in their glass case once and for all, and emerge at best into some kind of hopeless misanthropy. That, as we know, has been the sharpest criticism levelled at Chabrol since his second film: acquiescence in the sordid, contempt for his characters – the end of the road could only be fascism. But it seems to me that a closer analysis of the films does not lead to that conclusion. I will admit that a certain amount of masochism enters into the first part of *Les Bonnes femmes*, since we are after all in some way a part of the world we are shown. Chabrol and Gégauff's intention is to make it grate savagely – that is clear enough from the music. On this level I accept Marcabru's point that 'the characters have no soul', but only on condition that this is recognized to be a partial truth and therefore a counter-truth, in short a productive error, if one accepts Marx's statement that 'the false is a moment in the true'. Marcabru's judgment signals another danger which lay in wait for Chabrol, and that is the risk of introducing the human element merely in order to ensure its presence.

Marcabru's assertion is in the end a counter-truth because what impartial observation finally opens on to is precisely the soul of the characters – and I *don't* mind raising a smile. Because too, the grating tone of the early images is finally dissipated to make room for the blossoming of a profound sense of humanity, what I would call a kind of tenderness. Little by little the absurd pantomime, the frightful choruses of 'resounding inanity', by dint of being repeated and multiplied, organize themselves and in the end take on a sense – by that I mean not just a direction, but a meaning. The path mapped out by the film is itself the road to this gradual discovery. The humanity is born out of the spectacle alone; that is, solely from the ascetic discipline exercised on the *mise en scène*. It is no longer, as was always the case before, laid on from the outside, a veneer applied by the *auteur* to his characters, smuggled in via the detour of a 'major theme'.

To avoid begging the question in this way, a film-maker can never take too many precautions. Chabrol more so than anyone else. We have looked at two such precautions, which are moreover correlative: the *mise en scène* constituted as a pure category, and the choice of a 'minor theme'. This is where the role of Ernest comes in, the mysterious character who dogs the women throughout the film up to the moment of his own intervention. Ernest is Chabrol's answer to the claim that it is effectively impossible to observe impassively and innocently matters of which one is by definition a part. In Ernest is embodied, condensed and projected all the subjectivity the *auteur* had to shed in order to create a pure vision. Ernest's function is thus twofold: to render problematic the relation between the observer and the object observed, and to exorcize the last traces of subjectivity by plunging it into objectivity. In that way the essential ambiguity which defines the artist is sustained: neither totally innocent nor totally guilty, he remains witness to an acute and fundamental anguish.

Translated by Diana Matias

Note

1 *Le Déjeuner sur l'herbe* (1959) and *Le Testament du Dr Cordelier* (1961), at that time Jean Renoir's latest films; *Le Testament*, made for television, was not officially released until 1961.

3 | André S. Labarthe: 'Marienbad Year Zero'

('Marienbad année zéro', *Cahiers du Cinéma* 123, September 1961)

There will be no lack of people ready to stress *Marienbad*'s exceptional nature and I have no intention of competing with them. I would rather take a step in the opposite direction. Alain Resnais's most recent film is a film with a historical place. It was made in particular conditions and was undoubtedly based on accumulated experience. It fits of necessity into the final phase of an evolutionary development in cinema, or an idea of that development. For that reason I will begin by saying that *Marienbad* is the last of the great neo-realist films.

You will recall Bazin's analysis of narrative art in the Italian neo-realist cinema, *Paisà* in particular.[1] That was fifteen years ago. Neo-realism was as yet the future of cinema. It was to bring about the first significant revolution in film art, without which the works we love today would not be quite what they are.

Essentially, neo-realism replaced the classic scenario and its theatrically-based arrangement of scenes by an *open-ended* scenario, which was consequently closer to the experience we have of reality. The neo-realist film presents a sequence of fragments bound by no apparent logic and separated from each other by gaps, the gaps and fragments representing upstrokes and downstrokes on a canvas which bears no relation to the close-woven fabric from which the cinema had hitherto drawn its sharpest effects.

The notable result of all this is that the new conception of cinema entailed a new way of looking at film. The passive spectator was succeeded by an active spectator who converted the discontinuous narrative threads into a coherent continuity, just as he would do in everyday life. From that point the film no longer *functioned* without him.

This revolution in narrative method – as Bazin also showed[2] – joined the revolution represented by *Citizen Kane* and *The Magnificent Ambersons*, although by a different route. *Kane*, like *Paisà*, also turned its back on the finished view of the scenario and *mise en scène*. They no longer offered

54

predigested material ready for absorption. On the contrary, they present the spectator with raw material (even if it has in fact been heavily worked on) from which he may extract his *own* film. In short, the meaning of the film is no longer imposed on the spectator but has to be constructed by him from the *basis* provided by the elements of the film. As in everyday life again, the meaning of events is only ever a hypothesis, and if images constitute a language[3] it is a language which lacks signification.

In this perspective it at once becomes clear how Resnais's films, and *Marienbad* especially, fit naturally into the groove dug by neo-realism. The same gaps in the script, the same ambiguity in the events, the same effort demanded of the spectator. Some will object, with apparent justification, that at least it is possible to make out scenes between the gaps in *Paisà*. But can we be sure of this? Are we not prey to self-deception? Is it not rather the case that the spectacle of *Paisà* presents us with fragments of reality we have already appropriated to ourselves? If 'to represent' means slicing reality off from its past and its future in order to turn it into pure event, then even at the level of news film the project is an equivocal one. The proof is in the wide range of meanings instantly attached to an incident whether read about in the columns of the evening paper or seen in a newsreel. This shows how far we are incapable of looking at (I won't even say understanding) an incident without interpreting it and without our look adding to the event to form an amalgam, a mixture which by nature belongs as much to the documentary image as it does to the fiction with which we envelop it. All this boils down to saying that you cannot read reality as you might a novel, you read *into* it.

Traditional cinema had managed to do away with any possibility of ambiguity by building into every scene and shot what the spectator was *meant* to think of it: i.e. its meaning. Taken to its extreme, this kind of cinema did not need the spectator since he was already included in the film. The novelty of the films of Welles and the great neo-realists was to demand expressly the participation of the spectator. It is in this sense that we need to talk of phenomenology here: the spectator's look is as much creator of the film as is the intention of its makers.

By comparison with Welles or Rossellini, the originality of the films of Resnais and Robbe-Grillet is to have systematized this discovery. In *Kane* and *Paisà* the gaps in the narrative were in some sense tolerated; they were necessary because they were inevitable. But Resnais and Robbe-Grillet have turned those gaps into the actual theme of *Marienbad*. To such an extent that the film seems like a surface from which rise enigmatic images whose only palpable certainty is that they are part of the same film. In this sense *Marienbad* is a documentary, but a documentary of a special kind – the spectator does not know what is being documented. In short, Resnais and Robbe-Grillet have put together some documentary records, pilot images so to speak, leaving it to the spectator to convert them into a fiction which gives them a meaning. The first man to confront the nature of the world must have had the same difficulty in understanding it – ordering it. Faced with *Marienbad*, one is tempted to cry, like Valéry: 'It's as if the world were scarcely older than the art of creating the world!'

It is curious that no one has remarked on the fact that none of the craftsmen of neo-realism – not Visconti, Rossellini, De Sica, or even Fellini – resorted to the device of recalling the past. Welles himself abandoned it after his first film. It is as if the whole great effort towards more realism in general, with which the history of neo-realism merges, inevitably culminated in the elimination of anything which might disrupt the chronology of events. Since in the last analysis the justification of cinema was history, historical chronology had to be sustained. In that perspective the flashback of course seemed like the ultimate kind of fraud, an inadmissible recourse. Once it is allowed that the end result of the neo-realist aesthetic could be a film like the one Zavattini dreamed about, a precise and exhaustive record of ninety minutes in a man's life,[4] the dishonesty of the flashback can no longer be in doubt.

Things are not so simple in reality. As we have seen, in traditional cinema any gap or lack in the narrative was considered a fault, and the absolute aim of an *auteur*, scriptwriter as well as director, was to eliminate the gaps and present the film as a solid, unflawed block. The flashback therefore answered that same concern. Its only purpose was to fill in the remaining gaps, to weld the story to its immediate antecedents.

But what about *Kane*, you will say? And *Lola Montès*? And *Hiroshima*? There precisely lies the genius of Welles, Ophuls and Resnais. They used the classic device for ends diametrically opposed to those it had hitherto served: in *Kane*, *Lola Montès* and *Hiroshima* the function of the flashback is no longer to efface the discontinuity of the narrative. I would even go so far as to say the opposite. Of course the old function still persisted under the new: the flashback still served the story. It was still the sign of a desire to inject meaning since it was linked to a chronology. In *Marienbad* that sign disappears in turn. From this point the chronology of a story can only be what the most immediate 'essentialist' assumption makes it; to say that the film ends after three or four hundred shots is to give a meaning to a film which could flow on like a river into the sea from something that might be the beginning to something that could be the end. In *Marienbad* there is no end to anything. 'The End' coming up on the screen does not in itself bring to a close a story which might have worked itself out in time. In short, time (chronology) does not exist outside the way things are looked at, which is why *Marienbad* has a double need of the spectator if it is to constitute itself as a story. If this film exists, it is as an object – like the blots of the Rorschach test.

Put briefly, any scene in *Marienbad*, at whatever level of reality the consciousness of the spectator situates it, shares the same realism as those around it. If I may once again take up the parallel with the mode of the traditional narrative, I would say that usually the spectator is asked to *adjust* to the various shots in a film (just as the eye adjusts to moving from one object to another further away in the field of vision). *Marienbad*, however, presents itself to the spectator as a two-dimensional object whose parts are all situated on the same level of realism. There is no *objective* difference between a shot of the past and a shot of the present. It is the spectator who structures the film and establishes the differences of reality which give the object (the film) its perspective, in three, four or five dimensions, say.

To sum up, Resnais and Robbe-Grillet are doing in cinema what certain abstract artists have long been doing: they are offering not a story, but a sequence of images belonging to the same level of realism which is the film, and it is the spectator who introduces the depth. For the true successor of the figurative painter is not the abstract artist, but the spectator looking at the abstract painting. There is therefore less difference between Delacroix and Nicolas de Staël. Painting has changed its *function*. The task of the painter is no longer to paint a subject, but to make a canvas. So it is with cinema. The work of the film-maker is no longer to tell a story, but simply to make a film in which the spectator will discover a story. The true successor of the traditional film-maker is not Resnais or Robbe-Grillet, but the spectator of *Marienbad*.

Translated by Diana Matias

Notes

1 André Bazin, 'Le réalisme cinématographique et l'école italienne de la Libération', published in *Esprit*, January 1948, translated as 'An Aesthetic of Reality: Cinematic Realism and the Italian School of the Liberation' in Bazin, *What is Cinema? Vol. 2*.

2 André Bazin's theses about deep focus, or composition in depth, and realism were developed particularly in his essays 'William Wyler, ou le janséniste de la mise en scène', originally published in *La Revue du Cinéma* 11, March 1948, translated as 'William Wyler, or the Jansenist of *mise en scène*' in Williams, *Realism and the Cinema*, pp. 36–52, and 'L'Evolution du langage cinématographique', first published as a single essay in Bazin, *Qu'est-ce que le cinéma? tome 1: Ontologie et langage* (Paris, Editions du Cerf, 1958), translated as 'The Evolution of the Language of Cinema' in Bazin, *What is Cinema? Vol. 1* (reprinted in Gerald Mast and Marshall Cohen, *Film Theory and Criticism*, New York, Oxford University Press, 1974) and as 'The Evolution of Film Language' in Graham, *The New Wave*.

3 'But it is beginning to be clear that nothing could be more certain. Does anyone still believe in a "cinematic grammar"?' (Author's note). The 1960s were, of course, an intense period for work on 'film language': Christian Metz's 'Le Cinéma: langue ou langage?' (translated as 'The Cinema: Language or Language System?') was published in 1964; his 'A propos de l'impression de la réalité au cinéma' (translated as 'On the Impression of Reality in the Cinema') was published in *Cahiers* 166–7, May–June 1965; these essays, and later ones on semiology and narrative in cinema, were collected in Metz's *Essais sur la signification au cinéma*, Paris, Editions Klincksieck, 1971, translated as *Film Language: A Semiotics of the Cinema*, New York, Oxford University Press, 1974.

4 Cesare Zavattini's ideas are usefully represented in his article 'Some Ideas on

the Cinema', translated in *Sight and Sound*, October 1953, reprinted in Richard Dyer MacCann, *Film: A Montage of Theories*, New York, E. P. Dutton, 1966; a different version has been translated as 'A Thesis on Neo-Realism' in David Overbey, *Springtime in Italy: A Reader on Neo-Realism*, London, Talisman Books, 1978.

4 | Jean-Luc Godard: 'From Critic to Film-Maker': Godard in interview (extracts)[1]

('Entretien', *Cahiers du Cinéma* 138, December 1962)

Cahiers: Jean-Luc Godard, you came to the cinema by way of criticism. What do you owe to this background?

Godard: All of us at *Cahiers* thought of ourselves as future directors. Frequenting ciné-clubs and the Cinémathèque was already a way of thinking cinema and thinking about cinema. Writing was already a way of making films, for the difference between writing and directing is quantitative not qualitative. The only complete hundred-per-cent critic was André Bazin. The others – Sadoul, Balazs or Pasinetti[2] – are historians or sociologists, not critics.

As a critic, I thought of myself as a film-maker. Today I still think of myself as a critic, and in a sense I am, more than ever before. Instead of writing criticism, I make a film, but the critical dimension is subsumed. I think of myself as an essayist, producing essays in novel form or novels in essay form: only instead of writing, I film them. Were the cinema to disappear, I would simply accept the inevitable and turn to television; were television to disappear, I would revert to pencil and paper. For there is a clear continuity between all forms of expression. It's all one. The important thing is to approach it from the side which suits you best.

I also think there is no reason why one should not be a director without being a critic first. It so happens that for us things came about the way I described, but this isn't a rule. In any case, Rivette and Rohmer made 16 mm films. But if criticism was a first rung on the ladder, it was not simply a means. People say we made use of criticism. No. We were thinking cinema and at a certain moment we felt the need to extend that thought.

Criticism taught us to admire both Rouch and Eisenstein. From it we learned not to deny one aspect of the cinema in favour of another. From it we also learned to make films from a certain perspective, and to know that if something has already been done there is no point in doing it again. A young author writing today knows that Molière and Shakespeare exist. We were the first directors to know that Griffith exists. Even Carné, Delluc and René Clair, when they made their first films, had no real critical or historical background. Even Renoir had very little; but then of course *he* had genius.

Cahiers: Only a fraction of the *nouvelle vague* have this sort of cultural equipment.

Godard: Yes, the *Cahiers* group, but for me this fraction is the whole thing. There's the *Cahiers* group (along with Uncle Astruc, Kast and – a little apart – Leenhardt), to which should be added what one might call the Left Bank group:[3] Resnais, Varda, Marker. And there is Demy. They had their own cultural background. But that's about the lot. The *Cahiers* group were the nucleus.

People say we can no longer write about our colleagues. Obviously it becomes difficult having a coffee with someone if that afternoon you have to write that he's made a silly film. But the thing that has always distinguished *Cahiers* from the rest is our principle of laudatory criticism: if you like a film, you write about it; if you don't like it, don't bother with tearing it to pieces. One need only stick to this principle. So, even if one makes films oneself, one can still say that so-and-so's film is brilliant – *Adieu Philippine*,[4] for instance. Personally I prefer to say so elsewhere than in *Cahiers*, because the important thing is to lead the profession round to a new way of thinking about the cinema. If I have the money, I prefer to pay for a page in a trade paper to talk about *Adieu Philippine*. There are people better qualified than me to talk about it in *Cahiers*.

Cahiers: Your critical attitude seems to contradict the idea of improvisation which is attached to your name.

Godard: I improvise, certainly, but with material which goes a long way back. Over the years you accumulate things and then suddenly you use them in what you're doing. My first shorts were prepared very carefully and shot very quickly. *A bout de souffle* began this way. I had written the first scene (Jean Seberg on the Champs-Elysées), and for the rest I had a pile of notes for each scene. I said to myself, this is terrible. I stopped everything. Then I thought: in a single day, if one knows how to go about it, one should be able to complete a dozen takes. Only instead of planning ahead, I shall invent at the last minute. If you know where you're going it ought to be possible. This isn't improvisation but last-minute focusing. Obviously, you must have an overall plan and stick to it; you can modify up to a point, but when shooting begins it should change as little as possible, otherwise it's catastrophic.

I read in *Sight and Sound* that I improvised Actors' Studio fashion, with actors to whom one says 'You are so-and-so; take it from there.' But Belmondo never invented his own dialogue. It was written. But the actors didn't learn it: the film was shot silent, and I cued the lines.

Cahiers: When you began the film, what did it mean to you?

Godard: Our first films were all *films de cinéphile* – the work of film enthusi-asts. One can make use of what one has already seen in the cinema to make deliberate references. This was true of me in particular. I thought in terms of purely cinematographic attitudes. For some shots I referred to scenes I remembered from Preminger, Cukor, etc. And the character played by Jean Seberg was a continuation of her role in *Bonjour tristesse*. I could have taken the last shot of Preminger's film and started after dissolving to a title, 'Three Years Later'. This is much the same sort of thing as my taste for quotation, which I still retain. Why should we be reproached for it? People in life quote as they please, so we have the right to quote as we please. Therefore I show people quoting, merely making sure that they quote what pleases me. In the notes I make of anything that might be of use for a film, I will add a quote from Dosto-evsky if I like it. Why not? If you want to say something, there is only one solution: say it.

Moreover, *A bout de souffle* was the sort of film where anything goes: that was what it was all about. Anything people did could be integrated in the film. As a matter of fact, this was my starting-point. I said to myself: we have already had Bresson, we have just had *Hiroshima*, a certain kind of cinema has just drawn to a close, maybe ended, so let's add the finishing touch, let's show that anything goes. What I wanted was to take a conventional story and remake, but differently, everything the cinema had done. I also wanted to give the feeling that the tech-niques of film-making had just been discovered or experienced for the first time. The iris-in showed that one could return to the cinema's sources; the dissolve appeared, just once, as though it had just been invented. If I used no other processes, this was in reaction against a certain kind of film-making; but it should not be made a rule. There are films in which they are necessary; and sometimes they should be used more frequently. There is a story about Decoin[5] going to see his editor at Billancourt[6] and saying: 'I have just seen *A bout de souffle*; from now on, continuity shots are out.'

[. . .]

As I make low-budget films, I can ask the producer for a five-week schedule, knowing there will be two weeks of actual shooting. *Vivre sa vie* took four weeks, but shooting stopped during the whole second week. The big difficulty is that I need people who can be at my disposal the whole time. Sometimes they have to wait a whole day before I can tell them what I want them to do. I have to ask them not to leave the location in case we start shooting again. Of course they don't like it. That's why I always try to see that people who work with me are well paid. Actors don't like it for a different reason: an actor likes to feel he's in control of his character, even if it isn't true, and with me they rarely do. The terrible thing is that in the cinema it is so difficult to do what a painter does quite naturally: he stops, steps back, gets discouraged, starts again, changes something. He can please himself.

But this method is not valid for everyone. There are two main groups of directors. On one side, with Eisenstein and Hitchcock, are those who prepare their films as fully as possible. They know what they want, it's all in their heads, and they put it down on paper. The shooting is merely practical application – constructing something as similar as possible to what was imagined. Resnais is one of them; so is Demy. The others, people like Rouch, don't know exactly what they are going to do, and search for it. The film is the search. They know they are going to arrive somewhere – and they have the means to do it – but where exactly? The first make circular films; the others, films in a straight line. Renoir is one of the few who do both at the same time, and this is his charm.

Rossellini is something else again. He alone has an exact vision of the totality of things. So he films them in the only way possible. Nobody else can film one of Rossellini's scenarios – one would have to ask questions which he himself never asks. His vision of the world is so exact that his way of seeing detail, formal or otherwise, is too. With him, a shot is beautiful because it is right; with most others, a shot becomes right because it is beautiful. They try to construct something wonderful, and if in fact it becomes so, one can see that there were reasons for doing it. Rossellini does something he had a reason for doing in the first place. It's beautiful because it is.

Beauty – the splendour of truth – has two poles. There are directors who seek the truth, which, if they find it, will necessarily be beautiful; others seek beauty, which, if they find it, will also be true. One finds these two poles in documentary and fiction. Some directors start from documentary and create fiction – like Flaherty, who eventually made very carefully constructed films. Others start from fiction and create documentary: Eisenstein, starting in montage, ended by making *Que Viva Mexico!*

The cinema is the only art which, as Cocteau says (in *Orphée*, I believe), 'films death at work'. Whoever one films is growing older and will die. So one is filming a moment of death at work. Painting is static: the cinema is interesting because it seizes life and the mortal side of life.

Cahiers: From which pole do you start?

Godard: From documentary, I think, in order to give it the truth of fiction. That is why I have always worked with good professional actors. Without them, my films would not be as good.

I am also interested in the theatrical aspect. Already in *Le Petit soldat*, where I was trying to discover the concrete, I noticed that the closer I came to the concrete, the closer I came to the theatre. *Vivre sa vie* is very concrete, and at the same time very theatrical. I would like to film a play by Sacha Guitry; I'd like to film *Six Characters in Search of an Author* to show through cinema what theatre is. By being realistic one discovers the theatre, and by being theatrical. . . . These are the boxes of *Le Carrosse d'or*: behind the theatre there is life, and behind life, the theatre.

I started from the imaginary and discovered reality; but behind reality, there is again imagination.

Cinema, Truffaut said, is spectacle – Méliès – and research – Lumière. If I analyse myself today, I see that I have always wanted, basically, to do research in the form of a spectacle. The documentary side is: a man in a particular situation. The spectacle comes when one makes this man a gangster or a secret agent. In *Une Femme est une femme* the spectacle comes from the fact that the woman is an actress; in *Vivre sa vie*, a prostitute.

Producers say 'Godard talks about anything he pleases, Joyce, metaphysics or painting, but he always has his commercial side.' I don't feel this at all: I see not two things, but one.

[. . .]

The *nouvelle vague*, in fact, may be defined in part by this new relationship between fiction and reality, as well as through nostalgic regret for a cinema which no longer exists. When we were at last able to make films, we could no longer make the kind of films which had made us want to make films. The dream of the *nouvelle vague* – which will never come about – is to make *Spartacus* in Hollywood on a ten million dollar budget. It doesn't bother me having to make small, inexpensive films, but people like Demy don't like it a bit.

Everyone has always thought the *nouvelle vague* stood for small budgets against big ones, but it isn't so: simply for good films of any kind against bad ones. But small budgets proved to be the only way we could make films. Certainly some films are all the better for being made cheaply; but then think of the films that are all the better because money has been spent on them.

Cahiers: Suppose you had been asked to make *Vivre sa vie* on a hundred million franc budget?

Godard: I would never have accepted. What good would it have done the film? The only advantage would have been that I could have paid people more for working for me. In the same way, I refuse to make a film for a hundred million when I would need four hundred. People are beginning to offer me expensive films: 'Don't waste your time on those trifles. Come and adapt this book, make a real film, with so-and-so as star. We'll give you three hundred million.' Trouble is, it would take four hundred.

Certainly it's pleasant working American super-production style, shooting one set-up per day – especially as this is precisely how I work anyway. Like me, they take time off to think, only there it's done in the front office. So many lights and armchairs for stars have to be moved when setting up a scene that the director has nothing else to do but think during the removals. But there they have other problems: as soon as a film costs three or four hundred million, it becomes a producer's film, and he won't give you your head. Even if the film is made knowing it will lose money (as Bronston made *El Cid* and *55 Days at Peking* with money blocked in Spain), the producer watches you, because he doesn't want to lose his money any old how.

Actually, it is only in France that the producer recognizes – in principle, at least – the idea of an *auteur*. (Hitchcock is an exception: when other directors were finally getting their names in lights, *he* got a picture of himself.) Even the best Italian producers consider the director to be an employee. The difference is that the Italian industry is pretty worthless, whereas the Americans are pretty good – less so, perhaps, since the disappearance of the studio system, but until then they were the best in the world. American scriptwriters, too, simply dwarf even the better French writers. Ben Hecht is the best scriptwriter I have ever seen. In his book *The Producer*, it is extraordinary to see how Richard Brooks manages to construct a very fine, coherent script based on the Red Sea story which had been suggested to him. The Americans, who are much more stupid when it comes to analysis, instinctively bring off very complex scripts. They also have a gift for the kind of simplicity which brings depth – in a little Western like *Ride the High Country*, for instance. If one tries to do something like that in France, one looks like an intellectual.

The Americans are real and natural. But this attitude means something over there. We in France must find something that means something – find the French attitude as they have found the American attitude. To do so, one must begin by talking about things one knows. We have been accused of talking about certain subjects only, but we talk about things we know, looking for something which reflects us. Before us, the only person who really tried to see France was Jacques Becker, and he did so by filming fashion houses and gangsters. The others never filmed reality. All those reproaches aimed at us should have been directed against them, because their cinema was completely unreal. They were completely cut off: the cinema was one thing, life another. They didn't live their cinema. I once saw Delannoy[7] going into the Billancourt studios, briefcase in hand: you would have sworn he was going into an insurance office.

Cahiers: So we come back to the idea of departmentalizing.

Godard: France is made up of departments. But in any means of expression everything is connected and all means of expression are connected. And life itself is one of them. For me, making films and not making films are not two different ways of life. Filming should be a part of living, something normal and natural. Making films hasn't changed my life very much, because I made them before by writing criticism, and if I had to return to criticism, it would be a way of going on making films. It is true that things are different depending on whether you do or do not like preparing your films. If you need to prepare, then you have to prepare very carefully, and the danger is that the cinema may become detached and exclusive.

The only interesting film Clouzot has made is one in which he was seeking, improvising, experimenting, one in which he lived something: *Le Mystère Picasso*. Clément and the rest never live their cinema. It is a separate compartment, itself divided into compartments.

In France, as I have already said, one can't mix genres. In America, a thriller can also be political and include gags. Because it is American, this is acceptable here at a pinch, but try the same thing with things French, and they howl. This is why a French thriller never tells you anything about France. Of course this mental departmentalizing also corresponds to a departmentalization of social truths.

One mustn't mix the genres, but one mustn't mix people either. They must be kept separate. It's very difficult for someone who wants to mix things and different social milieux.

The *nouvelle vague* was honest in that it did well what it knew instead of doing badly what it didn't know or mixing up everything it knew. Talk about the workers? I would be glad to, but I don't know them well enough. I would love to film Vailland's *325,000 francs*, but it's a difficult subject and I'd be afraid to. What are they waiting for, the people who *do* know? The first time I heard a workman speak in the cinema was in *Chronique d'un été*. Rouch apart, none of the people who have done films about workers have had any talent. Naturally their workmen were phoney.

Nowadays, it is true, there are fewer complaints, because people have realized that we are beginning to deal with other things besides wild parties. Only Vadim has done nothing else, and nobody reproaches him for it. Vadim is the dregs. He has betrayed everything he could betray, himself included. It's the betrayal of the hireling. Today, for the powers-that-be, he is perfectly integrated morally and economically, and that is why people like him. He has the support of the Government because he is very right-thinking: in the area of eroticism and family entertainment he has no equal. The public loves it: Vadim is easy to take. And this is why he is inexcusable: he gives people the impression that they are getting Shakespeare when he offers them *Confidential* and *True Romance*. They say, 'You mean that's Shakespeare? But it's wonderful – why weren't we told before?'

I don't believe one can know one is doing something stupid or harmful and still go on doing it. Vadim probably isn't aware of what he is doing, and thinks he is making good films. At the beginning, when he was spontaneous and sincere, he wasn't aware either: he just happened to be there at the right moment. The fact that he was there at the right moment, when everyone else was lagging behind, gave the impression that he was out in front. Since then he has been marking time, while everyone else came up to date. So now he is lagging. Being also very resourceful by nature, he followed the track beaten by those directors who were ambitious and up-and-coming during the Occupation; he has taken their place exactly – and they were already beginning to date twenty years ago. It all happened like the ministerial changes under the Fourth Republic. He carried on the craft.

Having a craft is something which has always been important in France. Before the war, the film director was not comparable to a musician or a writer, but to a carpenter, a craftsman. It so happened that among the craftsmen there were artists like Renoir and Ophuls. Today the director is considered as an artist, but most of them are still craftsmen. They work in the cinema as one does in a skilled trade. Craftsmanship does exist, but not as they see it. Carné is a craftsman, and his craft makes him make bad films. To begin with, when he was creating his craft, he made brilliant films: now he creates no longer. Today Chabrol has more craft than Carné, and his craft serves for exploration. It is a worthy craft.

Cahiers: Does the *nouvelle vague* – in criticism and in film-making – have in common this will to explore?

Godard: We have many things in common. Of course I am different from Rivette, Rohmer or Truffaut, but in general we share the same ideas about the cinema, we like more or less the same novels, paintings and films. We have more things in common than not, and the differences are big about small things, small about big things. Even if they weren't, the fact that we were all critics accustomed us to seeing affinities rather than differences.

We don't all make the same films, of course, but the more so-called 'normal' films I see, the more I am struck by the difference between them and our own. It must be a big difference, because I usually tend to see the affinities between things. Before the war, there was a difference between, for instance, Duvivier's *La Belle équipe* and Renoir's *La Bête humaine*, but only one of quality. Whereas now, there is a real difference in kind between our films and those of Verneuil, Delannoy, Duvivier or Carné.

Much the same is true of criticism: *Cahiers* has kept a style of its own, but this hasn't prevented it from going downhill. Why? Whose fault is it? I think it is due chiefly to the fact that there is no longer any position to defend. There used always to be something to say. Now that everyone is agreed, there isn't so much to say. The thing that made *Cahiers* was its position in the front line of battle.

There were two kinds of values: true and false. *Cahiers* came along saying that the true were false and the false were true. Today there is neither true nor false, and everything has become much more difficult. The *Cahiers* critics were commandos. Today they are an army in peace-time, going out on manoeuvres from time to time. I think this is a passing phase. For the moment, as with all armies in peacetime, *Cahiers* is divided into clans, but this happens with all critics, particularly young ones. It has reached the same stage as Protestantism did when it divided into an incredible number of sects and chapels. Directors' names are bandied about because everyone has his own favourite and is necessarily obliged to detest everyone else's.

Other things baffle me too. *Cahiers* is enormously influential abroad. But – and everyone agrees about this – when one goes abroad one meets people who say, 'Do you really think Freda[8] is important?' It was difficult enough getting them to see that people like Ray and Aldrich had genius, but when they find interviews with directors like Ulmer, they give up. I am for the *politique des auteurs*, but not just anybody. Opening the door to absolutely everyone is very dangerous. Inflation threatens.

The important thing is not to *have* to discover someone. Leave the smart game of finding new names to *L'Express*.[9] The important thing is to know how to distinguish between the talented and the untalented, and if possible to define the talent, to analyse it. There are very few who try.

Of course, everything has become very difficult for critics now, and we also had many of the same faults *Cahiers* now suffers from. But at least we have in common that we are searching: those who do not seek will not long delude, for things always become clear in the end.

Translated by Tom Milne

Notes

1 Extracts only are reprinted here: the whole interview is translated in *Godard on Godard*, pp. 171–96.

2 Sadoul, Balazs, Pasinetti: film historians, critics and theorists. Georges Sadoul, French, 1904–1962; Béla Balazs, Hungarian, 1884–1949; Francesco Pasinetti, Italian, 1911–1941.

3 'The Left Bank group': So-called not only because they lived on the Left Bank in Paris, but because their cultural background (literature, politics, and the plastic arts) was very different from that of the film-oriented *Cahiers du Cinéma* group, comprising Godard, Truffaut, Chabrol, Rivette, Rohmer, and Doniol-Valcroze. (Translator's note.)

4 *Adieu Philippine* (1963), first feature by Jacques Rozier.

5 The veteran director Henri Decoin, whose films – e.g., *Les Inconnus dans la maison* (with Raimu, 1942), *La Vérité sur Bébé Donge* (with Gabin, 1951) – are competently made but reveal no individual personality. (Translator's note.)

6 Billancourt, French film studios, on the outskirts of Paris.

7 Jean Delannoy, veteran French film director, b. 1908, directing features since the mid-1930s; Delannoy very much represented the 'cinéma de papa' and was accordingly much attacked by *Cahiers* in the 1950s and early 1960s.

8 Riccardo Freda, an Italian director who brought an excellent sense of visual style to what were essentially exploitation pictures – horror films, muscle-man epics, swashbuckling adventures. As in the case of Edgar Ulmer, the enthusiasts from *Cahiers du Cinéma* tended to overpraise Freda's talent – unless misled by his habit of signing his pictures with an English pseudonym into writing him off completely, as they did with his delightfully outlandish horror film, *L'Orribile Segreto del Dottor Hichcock* (1962). (Translator's note.)

9 *L'Express*, French liberal weekly news magazine, modelled on *Time* and *Newsweek*.

5 | Jean-Louis Comolli, Jean Domarchi, Jean-André Fieschi, Pierre Kast, André S. Labarthe, Claude Ollier, Jacques Rivette, François Weyergans: 'The Misfortunes of *Muriel*'

('Les Malheurs de *Muriel*, *Cahiers du Cinéma* 149, November 1963)

A few of Cahiers's *collaborators were recorded discussing* Muriel *on tape – feeling free, as usual, to wander off the topic (to come back to it by a different route perhaps).*

Pierre Kast: If you're asking what Resnais is trying to do, I'd say it's to show a particular reality in a completely new light. He wants to force the spectator to confront an image of himself which he sees as true, but at the same time monstrously untrue because he's never thought of seeing himself that way. So on that level it's about a profound challenge to all the logical systems people use today to analyse the world outside. Obviously, if you choose a certain kind of language to describe the plot of *Muriel* you come up with an outline very similar to a story in *Elle* or *Marie-Claire*;[1] but that's precisely what's being challenged. In other words the film forces people to face up to their own experience with the same horror that can suddenly grab them in relation to the world outside – the monstrous reality in which they live and which they usually take for granted. Essentially, Resnais's intention is to open their eyes. He wants to tell them: take a look at yourselves, this is what you really are.

Claude Ollier: What's interesting about Resnais actually is the way he chooses characters from what's supposed to be the world of the mediocre in moral and psychological terms. But 'mediocre' begs a lot of questions. In my view, the choice of supposedly third-rate characters is an essential condition of the way Resnais's film functions; I mean, the choice of characters whose psychological and intellectual world is pretty colourless, who have no exceptional ambitions, whose emotional range is more or less average. In psychological terms it's the world of the commonplace and I believe that that's absolutely indispensable to the *auteur*'s intentions, that it couldn't be otherwise. It's as true of *Hiroshima* as it is of *Muriel* and *Marienbad* and I can see an amazing continuity between Resnais's three feature films. You could draw a parallel with the same kind of necessary (but not sufficient) condition of the contemporary novel; there the main characters are chosen from categories that up till now you would have classed as mediocre. The same criticism has been made of *The Birds*. Most of the critics said they were immensely bored by everything that led up to the fantastic moment when our feathered friends attack, that the three or four characters involved were ordinary, that their world was of no psychological or intellectual interest whatever. But that was an essential element of Hitchcock's intention. The more banal and average the world, the more Hitchcock's intention, or Resnais's here, comes across and is worked out.

Kast: In other words, by pleading the exception, he would have ended up justifying the rule; so he set out to be as ordinary as possible in order to keep absolutely within the general rule.

Ollier: In my view Resnais's aim is not primarily description of the psychologico-ethical kind, nor is he aiming at an exposition, description and resolution of conflicts. What it is is simply a pretext for revealing new logical structures; Kast put it well – it's a fundamental challenge, investigation and exploration. And for an exploration of this kind, the only thing to do is to take people whose psychological world is as simple as possible. The 'women's magazine' objection holds no water at all, I think; quite the contrary – that's how it has to be. Just as Robbe-Grillet's main characters are very simple, average people. In an enterprise of this kind, the thing to avoid is the exceptional.

But to get back to *Muriel*, the film is remarkably linear at first and then you gradually realize that its line is being more and more cut by obliques and curves with a frequency which reaches gale-force in the end. But for all that, the linear narrative continues perfectly chronologically, the scenes still follow one another, but in a more and more discontinuous way, the ellipses getting wider and wider. Finally, after an hour or so, you realize that the film has a different kind of movement, what you might call its 'deep' movement, which becomes fully clear at the end – a kind of spiral or circle opening further and further out so that the whole film seems to be basically centrifugal with everything projected to the outside. My main feeling watching it was pretty soon a rising anxiety, panic even, just what I felt watching *Marienbad*. It made me wonder at the time if *Muriel* wasn't the new version of *Marienbad*, *Marienbad* in a historical context. I still think of *Marienbad* as a completely spatial thing, nothing to do with recall or imagination, but an exploration of a spatial labyrinth. So *Muriel* seemed to me like the new edition of *Marienbad* – its 'expanded' sequel if you like, a *Marienbad* suddenly plunged into history. I think it's possible to analyse the different elements from this standpoint: space, time, characters, dialogue, as a function of the analogy I've just drawn. For example, the general movement of *Marienbad* is centripetal. The elements all circle more and more

69

tightly around a centre which is the centre of the labyrinth – the hotel and the park. That space is actually presented as labyrinthine; you knew there was a centre that had to be reached and in the end you reached it, but having got there you had to leave and, if you like, immediately start from square one again; and the representation of the film could begin again and again indefinitely.

In *Muriel* it's the same thing in reverse – the spiral works towards the outside. It's curious the way the characters multiply towards the end of the film, they nearly all have their doubles, triples even; lots of people make a sudden appearance and they're all very speedily projected outside the apartment, outside the town almost. In the end one last person arrives, and leaves, and the apartment is left empty. So on the one hand you have the space of *Marienbad* where things move by closing the circle towards a more or less clearly defined centre, and on the other you have *Muriel* with the apartment and the town as constants, two spaces separated by wide glass windows and unfinished doors, a whole shaky, temporary, unstable world from which the characters are abruptly ejected, and at great speed towards the end. That's why I had the same feeling of disorientation, and dislocation – stronger even than in *Marienbad* because, in my view, the more things are apparently 'realistic' the greater the sense of anxiety and strangeness. In *Marienbad* you could tell yourself ultimately – it's a nightmare, it's all very beautiful, but that's it. While in *Muriel* you have Boulogne-sur-Mer, the France of lower middle-class Europe in all the colours of today's world, and it's the same nightmare.

André S. Labarthe: It's true that the film starts out apparently as a straight line which then pulls you into a kind of circular movement. As far as the final tracking shot is concerned you could almost say that the movement of the film ends up by drawing the camera with it. But I wouldn't say that the characters appear suddenly . . .

Ollier: It would be truer to say they appear surreptitiously . . .

Labarthe: Yes, that's it. Seeing the film again, what struck me really was that I discovered characters at some point earlier than I had seen them on the first viewing. For instance, I hadn't noticed the first appearance of Ernest, standing in the shadows in front of a lighted window. So for me, the whole of my first viewing of the film went on with my having failed to pick up the arrival of the character, as if the one thing missing from his arrival was my attention, as if the arrival were just a transition from a shadow zone to light. Which confirms for me the way I saw the shots: at first as the arbitrary elements in a narrative and then as the 'deep' substance of the film.

Jacques Rivette: The thing that strikes you when you see the film again is that it has an extremely logical and mathematical construction, just like a thriller. But it doesn't tell you about one investigation, there are two or three or more, all overlapping. Contrary to what your first impression may be, there is not a single shot that isn't there because it has to be;

from the moment of the opening shots what you are given is just clues, every shot is a clue – in other words it's both the imprint left by an action and what the action entails, its mystery. The motive of the investigation or investigations is never revealed, any more than the end of the film provides solutions, or at least a resolution. Each shot is a clue exposed, but for its own sake. And it is the actual accumulation of these clues, the momentum they generate, which is absorbed into the dynamic structure and roundabout movement of the film, or rather what creates it. The clues seem to multiply of their own accord. As for the few shots which remain unexplained or rather unsubstantiated on second viewing, they are also clues, or become clues – to the unknowable (or irrational, aberrant) element which is at the bottom of any act, whether explained or not.

Labarthe: But what about the man with the goat for example?

Ollier: He's a repatriate from Australia, someone transplanted, a stranger to this place; just like the young man repatriated from Algeria; and just as Alphonse leaves for Belgium and thereby becomes an expatriate. No one is on home ground; everyone is looking for his plausible situation, a place he can live in. No one finds it and everyone leaves. This is a film which constantly creates emptiness around itself, and at the same time it seems to be on fire, starting with the film shot in Algeria perhaps; it's as if the film stock was in flames and shooting sparks in all directions, which is the direct opposite (or the same thing) as *Marienbad* where all these things converge. The impression you get is that the film has gone up in flames, as the town once did and as Algeria is doing now.

Jean-Louis Comolli: I agree with what's been said about *Muriel* being like a thriller. But I don't agree that there is no object to the investigation. There is, on the contrary, a very specific object involved and you'd be wrong to look for it outside the film. It would be a mistake to imagine that Resnais is trying to present a picture of the outside world, in whatever style, or even that he is interested in the outside world or in extrapolating some new logical system from it. . . . An investigation is under way all right, but it's turned on himself and what he ends up by discovering is himself. He is executing a self-portrait using the characters he interposes and disguised situations. So the pointers he gives, which are simply traces of Resnais himself, serve a purpose for him as much as for us.

Labarthe: That's right. Because these characters are in the end all to some extent Resnais's fantasy of himself.

Comolli: All the characters in the film are Resnais. They're all possible aspects of Resnais, whether past or present, and all of them are denied or dreaded by him to a greater or lesser extent. Bernard, for example, shooting film out in the streets – there's every chance that Resnais has done that. It's a way of coping with the past and going beyond it.

François Weyergans: Rather than clues, they're bits of evidence. Resnais

71

accumulates proof on proof as testimony against the splinter of dishonesty he has in himself.

Labarthe: But at the same time without your being able to say, in the face of a given clue, that it relates to this or that precise thing. Without your being able to say what it's a clue to. What it's really a clue to in fact is first of all the momentum of the film that envelops it.

Comolli: The nature of the clue is that it only explains itself when the motive is revealed, totally. It draws its meaning from the whole, whereas the whole is not always illuminated by the clues.

Jean Domarchi: For my part, if you'll allow me to approach the film from a different angle, what interests me in cinema today is the organic whole. By that I mean that, given that cinema is a collective art, and given that it needs thousands of spectators to survive, what's interesting is seeing how far it marries up with those conditions, how far there may be an equivalence between cinema and the idea of cinema, cinema as a popular art and the mass audience to which it is addressed. What cinema needs to reflect is the organic whole – in precisely the way that all the great American films reflected American society and everything that determined it. I have no sense of that in Resnais. If *Muriel* is truly, as has been claimed, a committed film, and if it's at the same time a profoundly personal film, an autobiography, then I'm forced to call it a failure because in terms of committed cinema it does not aim at the organic whole, i.e. the whole of a society viewed through a particular situation; and in terms of Resnais's autobiography, it reveals only a pure particularity which fails to relate to the universal. The desire for absolute particularity, absolute difference, is part of every work of art. But absolute difference in a work of art is only interesting if it is linked to its denial, i.e. to identity and the universal. But in *Muriel* the absolutely individual is only linked to pure individuality, denial is linked to pure denial. The series of negations never relate back to any concrete universal or to any negative within a positive. Whereas in Resnais's literary counterpart, Don Passos, for example, or Queneau, I can see reference back to the universal. But if you stay with Resnais, in the realm of absolute individuality, you have negation of the work of art itself, since art, it seems to me, always has to relate to the universal or to a form of universality in which people can recognize themselves. I don't recognize myself in the particular individuals presented by Resnais. You can't find the universal element in any given particular there. But perhaps that's the fault of France. Perhaps there's nothing to say about France as it is today, perhaps it's because there aren't any problems in France any more . . .

Ollier: But that would be extraordinary, wouldn't it . . .?

Domarchi: Well then, there's a total lack of equivalence between France and cinema.

Ollier: At this very moment *France Soir* and *Europe 1*[2] are carrying out a survey ('What is a Frenchman?'). And everyone approached just gives the optimistic, comfortable, peaceful version of their lives. There's been no despairing response, no tragic reaction. *Muriel* seems to me the indispensable complement of that survey; it's the shadowy, desperate side, people plunged in total dereliction and feeling completely lost.

Jean-André Fieschi: Someone mentioned thrillers, and *The Birds* was referred to. I think too that we have all noticed the film's links with Hitchcock in general (his silhouette appears next to a menu displayed in a restaurant window) and to *Vertigo* in particular (a few clues there too, like the chopping down of the tree filmed by Bernard, etc.). So we have a thriller, but a thriller where the enigma is the intention of the film itself and not its resolution. (It's worth noting that *The Birds* is also Hitchcock's first film where the tension isn't aimed at solving a mystery, but at elaborating and developing it.) The analogy doesn't stop there. It also relates to the actual way the mystery is treated: the first part of *The Birds*, which is banal, everyday and simple in its use of *signs*, is a preparation for the appearance of the fantastic element. The first part is therefore not fantastic itself but rather, looked at retrospectively, it's oneiric. *Muriel* is to me the equivalent of the first hour of *The Birds* expanded into a full-length film; the dreamlike quality, the sense of anxiety, the muted sense of terror, here also grow out of an accumulation of everyday details but taken to the point of exasperation. In the final shots it becomes almost physically unbearable – you actually long for some catastrophe to set you free. The final tracking shot, which again picks out the aggressiveness of the setting, fulfils that expectation and opens on to another anxiety and a different kind of fear. What you have here is a kind of exemplary chain-reaction reflecting the mechanism of the film – a musical structure whose extreme particularity is all that makes possible any link with universality, in the sense that you might say a personal diary has universal significance.

Kast: In fact the film moves from the particular to the universal in a very rigorous way; the everyday world is made to swing gently into a world beyond all forms of realism, be it neo-realism or socialist realism, which allows for a brutal introduction of contradiction and drama, just as fantasy is brought into Hitchcock's films. There is an absolute parallelism in the construction of the two films: on the psychological level it makes possible a transition from the particular to the general, and on the level of the way the film works, from the everyday to a transcendence of the everyday.

Comolli: I don't believe there's any transition from the particular to the general in the film because I don't think there's a fraction of the particular in the film. Domarchi would be correct if the film did move from the particular to the general, but I don't believe anything in *Muriel* is presented as particular. Neither the film nor the people it shows belong to the order of the particular. From the start we're dealing with the general, with a fable almost. In fact at no moment is anything *described* as particular or as likely to become so. *Muriel* is not a descriptive film, which is why realism is a pseudo-problem as far as this film is concerned. Even at the extreme, the problems and mannerisms of the characters don't count, for all that they exist and are powerfully presented. The essential thing is always what drives them. This is a film created out of that kind of drive and restraint, repulsions and attractions. Characters are defined and brought to life by just their physical behaviour, their way of walking, moving, entering the shot. And that's what brings *Muriel* close to American cinema, Preminger especially. Characters are reduced to their drives, their appearance, their emotions and impulses, and it's in that sense that the film seems to me to relate to a universality because what counts is not whether or not we are like the characters we see, but that we can share on a purely affective and almost responsive level in their emotions, impulses and instincts.

Labarthe: *Muriel* can be defined as movement; but the first tracking shot Resnais made of a Van Gogh painting[3] already summed up all the movement of *Muriel*.

Ollier: In any case, the film more than stands up to being tested and proved against 'realism' at every level. But that's not the essential thing. As far as I am concerned, I wouldn't mind if it were completely 'unrealist'.

Comolli: What we get is the realism of saturation – a world we are saturated with and don't see any more, given to us not in the way we might perhaps be capable of seeing it, but in the way we *absorb* it.

Domarchi: For my part, just as with painting, I am on the side of classicism in the broadest sense of the term, which goes from Piero della Francesca to Delacroix, and against impressionism which I consider to be regressive. And as far as cinema is concerned, I am for the classicism of the American cinema and against the impressionism of modern cinema (and not just French); for me that's a denial of cinema. Obviously it's possible to consider cinema from a dialectical point of view as a series of moments which reinforce or destroy each other, and accept the totality of its manifestations. But that way of approaching it seems to me difficult to accept.

Labarthe: But it's Domarchi's way of approaching it that seems unacceptable to me. Do we have the right to say that there is some essence of cinema which precedes its existence? In my view you can't argue like that. To the extent that it's necessary to refer to an essence at all, the cinema being made today makes its own contribution towards enlightening us as to what that essence is, but it does so by placing it in a sense in the future. In other words, it's by looking back to the origins that you can see how any film of any merit can be regarded as a kind of preface to the cinema of the future. As Nietzsche said, no doubt thinking of Hitchcock, 'Prophetic bird, its eyes turned towards the past'.

Domarchi: My reply to that would be that there has to be some measure of coincidence between cinema and society. That's basically why there is a profound link between American and Russian cinema. I am struck when I re-see Dovzhenko's *Poem of the Sea* for instance, by its links with Griffith. Those people made an epic cinema because the whole of society was always part of the project. While in European cinema, Bergman, Antonioni, Resnais, etc., society is always somewhere in the wings.

Rivette: The very fact of relegating society to the wings is an excellent definition of European cinema (at least part of it). But isn't it European society itself which forces film-makers to relegate it to the wings, or at least to bracket it off – since the only relation the individual can have to society today (in most European societies and for most individuals) is an external one? No Frenchman, Italian, or Swede can feel linked to the society of which in spite of himself he is a part in the way that a Russian or an American feels linked to his. To act or talk as if that were not so would be dishonest, and it's precisely Resnais's strength, the strength of Bergman and Antonioni too, that they express that truth, or include it in what they express. The only thing you can reproach them with is being, as film-makers, too French, too Italian, or too Swedish. But to do anything else can only end up as imposture. Witness Melville or Lizzani, for example, and the way they try artificially to acclimatize to a European context the myths of American cinema or socialist realism, neither of which correspond to anything in *our* circumstances.

Domarchi: But this is where we get to the heart of the problem. Speaking for myself, I am absolutely convinced that there is an incompatibility between Europe and cinema.

Rivette: No, between Europe and the particular cinema you like. But I think there's compatibility between Europe and another kind of cinema – it may not move you but it exists nevertheless, and precisely as the image of what is particular in contemporary European society.

Domarchi: When I say that cinema should express the totality, what I am saying goes beyond any question of realism or 'unrealism', fantasy or everyday reality. As far as you're concerned no equivalence ever exists between cinema and society and that's a purely personal point of view. When I watch films by Bergman and Antonioni, which I actually like, I always think to myself: these films affect you because you're a French petit bourgeois and in some way you're incapable (because you are what you are) of getting beyond the European petit bourgeoisie and a problem-free Europe. Whereas Americans and Russians are lucky enough to live with immense problems, which are beyond them individually and which force them, whether intelligent or not, perceptive or not, artists or not, to be great film-makers.

Comolli: But Domarchi, all you're doing is chasing your own tail. The real problem is not whether there is some significant equation to be drawn between cinema and society, cinema and Europe, but whether there is any such correspondence between society and the individual in Europe. And because in Europe there has for a long time been a lack of any correspondence between society and the individual, that has given rise to a particular artistic tradition. It has produced a cinema which deals

75

solely with that dislocation, and as a result also deals with the whole, since it deals with society in its relation to the individual.

Rivette: I also believe that European cinema expresses its totality just as much as the Russian and American cinemas do, to the extent that it accepts being, effectively, totally and profoundly, that inward-looking cinema which we have just briefly defined: a cinema where the relations of the individual and society, instead of being relations of exchange and integration, are relations not so much of opposition as of doubt – divorce would be too strong a word – doubt and suspicion. Films made by European film-makers properly so-called are based on that notion of doubt. But there are two ways of envisaging it. If the doubt is presented as a rejection (which is precisely the main criticism to be brought against the inferior imitators of both Bergman and Antonioni) then the films can only be negative. But the doubt is enriched and thereby (once more) encompasses a totality only when it is anxious, when it also doubts itself, when the doubt itself is open to doubt, when it is a doubt which is consciously aiming to go beyond doubt and which honestly, anxiously and intensely puts doubt to the test, only failing because it bumps up against an external *reality*, against the inertia of the real, the dense wall of concrete things. But it's a doubt which never gets tired of questioning that reality, attacking it constantly from new angles, and which makes an honest attempt to understand it, integrate it and join it. The totality of the social and individual is only ever grasped and sustained (grasped and sustained, that is, in the face of dangers that are always part and parcel of the process) by confronting that very question – and it's a question without any answer, which is how we answer it.

Domarchi: Then, Rivette, I'll allow myself a philosophical detour to throw some light on the debate, via Hegel's *Phenomenology of Mind*. There he describes ethical substance, i.e. the ancient city, the Greek city. In his commentary on Greek tragedy and on *Antigone* in particular, he shows that tragedy exists purely because in the beginning there is perfect correspondence between the citizen as part of the universal order and the private individual; hence the possibility of a dislocation, of drama, when someone tries to oppose that harmony: Creon and Antigone. Tragedy only appears within society when there is equivalence between the individual as an element of the particular and the individual as an element of the general. It's from the moment when there is a shift between the two, between the particular and the general, between Antigone and Creon, at the point where Antigone comes to represent the modern world against the old world, that there is tragedy. In the modern world, on the other hand, where everyone takes refuge in their individuality, tragedy is no longer possible because each person is expressing his own individuality for himself alone. You are quite right to speak of doubt, but that doubt is the expression of our individual isolation as Europeans of the 1960s, living within that individuality and nourishing ourselves from it without ever connecting up with the universal, with society. That's why tragedy has disappeared from Europe and why it has been taken up by American cinema and Russian cinema, which revive the antagonism between the individual and the universal, and revive ethical substance at the level of the structures of modern society.

Rivette: Revive . . . I would say, revived. What strikes me, on the contrary, is the point to which the American and Russian cinemas, which we have all loved, are the cinemas of the past, precisely because American and Russian societies are going to find themselves increasingly confronted by the problems which European societies have faced for some fifty to a hundred years. You can see the first evidence of that already (it's not very pretty, but that's not the point – it's there); like it or not, the cinemas of Russia and America are condemned to evolve towards bastard forms of European cinema, before they have any chance of rediscovering an individuality. And, like it or not, that European cinema, in spite of itself and without even seeking to do so, is at the moment historically in the avant-garde – I don't like the word much; let's say it is emerging as the pathfinder of world cinema.

Domarchi: But in a regressive way, an avant-garde in the form of a regression. Just as modern art is regressive by comparison with Greek tragedy.

Rivette: If we have to be Hegelian about this, let's try to do it properly (even if this means no longer being so at all). Is it possible to say in advance whether an evolution experienced as necessary is regressive or not? I think one has to follow it through, to try within that evolution itself (which may objectively have its regressive aspects) to perceive and accentuate, if that's still possible, its non-regressive aspects, those which have any hope of a future – and you always risk betting on the wrong thing, but that's life.

Domarchi: What interests me and what I should like to find again in France is a tragic world, not individual, but collective – the tragedy of the collective through an individual situation.

Fieschi: The collective tragedy as expressed through individual lives is exactly right as a definition of *Muriel*.

Domarchi: Well, poor tragedy then! . . . Can I tell you a story on the subject? It's taken from a letter by Haydn. Haydn goes to visit Hegel; I quote, 'I saw Hegel, that man of wood – he was translating the *Niebelungen* into Greek in order to appreciate its flavour better.'

Labarthe: Well, you told that one of your own free will. . . .

Comolli: Domarchi seems to believe that European cinema lacks the 'tragic dimension' . . . That's a view I would strongly oppose. We do have a European tragic cinema, a European cinema which goes further than doubt. It's the only one that interests me. Much more than Bergman or Antonioni, it's Renoir and Rossellini: their greatness is that their films always have something which breaks through the doubt and that thing is art, the achievement of art, whether you like it or not. The rest is failure and only failure – not a philosophy of failure, but a failure of creativity.

Domarchi: All I'm asking for is the rediscovery of antagonisms and oppositions, valid not just for France but for modern Europe. If I may quote Rossellini: 'Why are there never any heroes in contemporary European cinema?' That's the greatest criticism you could make of the whole of European cinema. Because Rossellini, in a way, is pursuing some kind of nostalgia for American cinema; in a certain sense, he too wants to rediscover heroism within the structures of modern Europe. What appals me is that I don't find that heroism anywhere in European cinema.

Rivette: When you see Rossellini's films you realize that even he hasn't ever shown heroes. He's shown characters attracted by heroism (and that's not the same thing), but unable to carry heroism through to the point where it leads to any purposeful action; or else he has shown heroes of the past like Garibaldi, the combatants of *Paisà* (already in the past) or, in a certain sense, Francis of Assisi. . . . In *Europe 51* Bergman is proof itself that heroism is absurd and contradictory in modern society (one may regret it, and one does, but that's the way things are) because on the one hand her real activities are insignificant, cancelled out completely, and on the other hand she's put behind bars. Heroism creates a scandal but a useless one (Joan of Arc was a useful scandal). No form of heroism in the classical sense or in the American sense is possible in the European society of our day. Even Rossellini, whatever his intention may have been, had to demonstrate that fact. . . . The first of the moderns, Baudelaire, produced the first definition of European cinema: it's a matter of 'showing the heroism of modern life'. But that's something that doesn't strike you at first glance. It's the life of Baudelaire himself, for example, a subject much closer to the themes of Bergman or Antonioni than those of Ford or Dovzhenko. There is at the moment an attempt to shed the Baudelairian kind of modernity, as Roland Barthes has pertinently noted. We are witnessing attempts by all kinds of people in all fields of art to go beyond the definition of modernity we have lived with for the last hundred years, and in my view *Muriel* is a major step in the attempt to transcend it. If you ask me why I say that, it's because in *Muriel* failure 'is not always a certainty'. *Muriel* is one of the first European films in which failure is not somehow sensed as inevitable, which, on the contrary, has a sense of the *possible*, an opening on to the future in all its forms. Failure does come in the end (although within the chronology of the film it's possible to imagine an out-there, beyond the film, which is free of failure), but I feel that there is, on the same level and in the same ambiguous way, hope. Just as there is at the end of *L'Eclisse*, a film much misunderstood from this point of view: the end is abyss and vertigo, but over a suddenly revealed plenitude of cosmic proportions, not over a void.

Domarchi: Now there you're falling back into existentialism, and I mean

Jaspers[4] in particular. His is a philosophy of failure, the shattered mirror, as he calls it.

Rivette: But *Muriel* is not the moment when the mirror shatters, it's the moment when one moves on from this broken mirror and tries to put it back together again, in a *different* way.

Comolli: You could say that the cinema has already gone further, that it's already moved beyond the attempt to transcend doubt, but that we just haven't noticed. Renoir and Rossellini both situate themselves somewhere *after* the point when the shattered mirror is repaired, at the point where people are beginning to look at their reflections again. That's the starting point of their cinema. Resnais is, understandably, just taking his first steps, at the very beginning of the process of appropriation and affirmation; these are his first hesitant sentences.

Rivette: I think that's a process everyone has to go through for themselves.

Comolli: Of course, cinema is this constant process of beginning again. That's why I think it is possible to talk about an 'essence' of cinema, and about a greater or lesser purity of that essence, to the extent that the new start is more or less true to itself.

Domarchi: Yes, but Renoir, before Resnais, had started the process. Renoir's cinema has a profound optimism about it . . .

Comolli: For all that, Renoir's cinema is deeply tragic. You said that European cinema doesn't offer heroes and isn't tragic. It isn't heroes who make tragedy, it's tragedy that makes heroes. In Renoir's films, and even in Rossellini's, the characters are heroes because the films, at their deepest and most secret level, are tragedies. Think of *La Règle du jeu* and *Toni*. And *Stromboli* or *Viaggio in Italia*. . . .

Rivette: Unfortunately I don't think that the example is quite accurate because Renoir, like Rossellini, is *in spite of himself* located in an 'earlier' world. Whereas the world of Resnais, like that of Antonioni, is the world of *after* Hiroshima in every sense: all Resnais's films are 'post-Hiroshima' (by force of circumstances).

Weyergans: That makes me think of something René Char[5] said, and this was already after *Hiroshima mon amour*: 'the atom bomb exploded in the nineteenth century'. That's the reason why today we have to shed a modernity which is already quite old, but without repudiating it. And this is where *Muriel* takes its rightful place. Resnais offers for preliminary examination what at first glance are the outward appearances and assurances of what we conventionally call 'modern', but behind those appearances he sets up another language which takes over the end of the film completely, just at the point when you feel the essential meaning of the film is disappearing, getting buried.

Comolli: What separates Resnais and Renoir is not a difference of worlds but a difference of genius. Renoir's latest films are also post-Hiroshima and they go much further than Resnais. *Le Déjeuner sur l'herbe* and *Le Caporal épinglé* completely renew and surpass the modernity which we agree is outdated and against which Resnais is struggling. In a sense,

Resnais and Antonioni are attacking the pseudo-problems of modernity, to the extent that the real problems of art and life today are both posed and resolved by Renoir in those two films.

Labarthe: It's possible to take up that basically paradoxical position time and time again. . . .

Comolli: It's because we are of today that we can't see, understand, or explain that today.

Rivette: Certainly, one can only rediscover that classicism by retracing the route for oneself; everyone has to take the classical route for himself. I'm afraid it's impossible, unfortunately, to try to skimp the process, just because somebody has already done it, impossible to want to take up the cinema subjectively at the point at which Renoir left it objectively in *Le Déjeuner sur l'herbe,* just as it's impossible to want to take up music at the point where Beethoven left it in his last quartets. Everyone has to start out from his own world, the strictly contemporary world in which he has no choice but to live and make his own way, and to discover at the end of the road that he has rediscovered what all great artists discovered in the end. But to refuse to pass by that road, over the actual hazards offered by the terrain one is faced with and which make the stages of one's own journey different from the 'classics' (and they only became classics afterwards, after completing the course themselves), can in the last analysis only make for a false classicism and a false modernism.

Comolli: Which defines an important idea – the idea of tradition in art. Art is the bottomless vessel of the Danaides (if you'll allow me the image) which has to be constantly refilled but whose initial shape persists and always imposes itself on the water, should the water fail to remember it . . .

Rivette: But it is of no help to us that an American cinema exists, that *Le Déjeuner sur l'herbe* exists and that the work of Bach and Beethoven exists (I mean of course in the sense of examples and guides) . . . because we have to act as if they didn't exist and then perhaps we may discover the proof of it for ourselves.

Comolli: I agree with the word 'act'. But it's a commonplace to say that literature, painting, cinema, etc., the whole of art, influence our life and change or direct it at possibly the deepest and most essential level. Which is why it's not useless, far from it, that Renoir or Rossellini exist; because we share life with them and on that basis it's possible for us to act.

Rivette: But knowing them with a knowledge which is at the same time a forgetting. I mean, knowing them, too, only in the context of doubt, putting them, too, in question, if only to be able to see them at last in their own true light.

Comolli: There is no real knowledge which is not at the same time doubt . . .

Labarthe: And so Blanchot[6] brings us back to *Muriel.*

Translated by Diana Matias

Notes

1 *Elle*, *Marie-Claire*: French weekly magazines aimed at women.
2 *France-Soir*, *Europe 1*: Paris evening newspaper, and a radio service.
3 The reference is to Resnais's short film *Van Gogh* (1948).
4 Karl Jaspers, German philosopher, 1883–1969, founding father, with Martin Heidegger, of the philosophy of existence, which formed the basis of existentialism.
5 René Char, b. 1907, modern French poet.
6 Maurice Blanchot, French literary critic, contemporary of Roland Barthes and, like Barthes, a contributor to journals like *Tel Quel* and *Critique*.

6 | *Cahiers du Cinéma*: 'Twenty Years of French Cinema: the Best French Films since the Liberation'

('Vingt ans de cinéma français: palmarès', *Cahiers du Cinéma* 164, March 1965)

1 *Pickpocket* (Robert Bresson, 1959)
2 *Lola Montès* (Max Ophüls, 1955)
3 *Le Carrosse d'or* (Jean Renoir, 1953)
4 *Le Testament d'Orphée* (Jean Cocteau, 1960)
5 *Le Testament du Dr Cordelier* (Jean Renoir, 1961)
6 *Les Carabiniers* (Jean-Luc Godard, 1963)
7 *Hiroshima mon amour* (Alain Resnais, 1959)
  Le Plaisir (Max Ophüls, 1952)
9 *Muriel* (Alain Resnais, 1963)
10 *Adieu Philippine* (Jacques Rozier, 1963)
11 *A bout de souffle* (Jean-Luc Godard, 1960)
12 *La Pyramide humaine* (Jean Rouch, 1959)
13 *Eléna et les hommes* (Jean Renoir, 1956)
14 *Les Bonnes femmes* (Claude Chabrol, 1960)
15 *Casque d'or* (Jacques Becker, 1952)
16 *La Poison* (Sacha Guitry, 1951)
17 *Lola* (Jacques Demy, 1961)
18 *Procès de Jeanne d'Arc* (Robert Bresson, 1963)
19 *Une femme est une femme* (Jean-Luc Godard, 1961)
20 *Le Petit soldat* (Jean-Luc Godard, 1960)
21 *Orphée* (Jean Cocteau, 1950)
22 *Le Mépris* (Jean-Luc Godard, 1963)
23 *Le Caporal épinglé* (Jean Renoir, 1962)
24 *La Vie d'un honnête homme* (Sacha Guitry, 1953)
25 *Les Enfants du paradis* (Marcel Carné, 1945)
  Les Godelureaux (Claude Chabrol, 1961)
27 *Jules et Jim* (François Truffaut, 1962)
28 *Paris nous appartient* (Jacques Rivette, 1960)
29 *Vivre sa vie* (Jean-Luc Godard, 1962)
30 *Les Dames du Bois de Boulogne* (Robert Bresson, 1945)

31 *Moi, un Noir* (Jean Rouch, 1959)
32 *Bande à part* (Jean-Luc Godard, 1964)
   Le Signe du Lion (Eric Rohmer, 1959)
34 *Le Journal d'un curé de campagne* (Robert Bresson, 1951)
35 *Les Enfants terribles* (Jean-Pierre Melville, 1950)
   Les 400 coups (François Truffaut, 1959)
   Tirez sur le pianiste (François Truffaut, 1960)
38 *Les Dernières vacances* (Roger Leenhardt, 1948)
39 *Nuit et brouillard* (Alain Resnais, 1956)
40 *Le Déjeuner sur l'herbe* (Jean Renoir, 1959)

7 | Eric Rohmer: 'The Old and the New': Rohmer in interview with Jean-Claude Biette, Jacques Bontemps, Jean-Louis Comolli (extracts)

('L'Ancien et le nouveau: entretien avec Eric Rohmer', *Cahiers du Cinéma* 172, November 1965)

For a long time now we have wanted to talk to Eric Rohmer the film director. But for us at Cahiers *that could only mean giving him back the floor. Though silenced when he abandoned one form of 'writing' for another, his voice has never ceased to guide us. For in giving up the 'marble'[1] of* Cahiers *hasn't he given us on celluloid some of his finest critiques? Following our round-table discussion earlier in this issue[2] and our conversation with Jean-Luc Godard last month,[3] the discussion below also needs to be read in the same way – as a clarification of our own critical positions, with the stress on the continuity of a* Cahiers *line to which (in its best aspects) Eric Rohmer and Jacques Rivette gave both solid direction and flexibility (greater than has sometimes been thought). The title we have given to this interview echoes that concern. It is also intended to suggest – by joining the old and the new not as a simple addition but for the light they shed on each other – that modern cinema in the person of one of its best exponents can recognize its place in the domain established by Griffith, just as criticism could not be really new without going back to Maurice Schérer[4] for the secret of such innovation. Following on from the essay by Pier Paolo Pasolini ('The Cinema of Poetry', in our last issue[5]), this discussion with the champion of a 'prose cinema' takes an initial theoretical turn.*

Eric Rohmer: I admire Pasolini for being able to write things like that while still making films. I am very interested in the question of cinematographic language, even if I'm not sure whether it's a real problem or a pseudo-problem, and even if I know that it risks distracting you from actual creative work. Because the question is so abstract it requires you to take a position *vis-à-vis* cinema which is neither that of the *auteur* nor that of the spectator. It rules out the pleasure you get from watching a film. Having said that, I am with Pasolini on the fact that cinematographic language is actually a style. There's no such thing as cinematographic grammar. What there is is a rhetoric which is moreover in one sense extremely weak and in another extremely unstable.

Cahiers: The other equally interesting thing about Pasolini's viewpoint is his distinction between two stages of cinema: a classical age and a modern age, the difference between the two being in round terms that for a long time the *auteur*, or the *metteur en scène*, put all his skill into effacing the signs of his intervention, into hiding himself behind his 'work', while increasingly now he makes his presence evident. . . .

Rohmer: On that point I am not in the least in agreement with Pasolini. I don't believe at all that modern cinema is necessarily a cinema in which you have to be aware of the camera's presence.[6] It so happens that at the moment there are plenty of films where you are aware of the camera, and so there were in earlier days. But I don't believe that the distinction between modern and classical cinema can lie in that statement. I don't think that modern cinema is a 'cinema of poetry' and that the old cinema was no more than a prose or narrative cinema. For me there is a modern form of the prose and 'romance' cinema in which poetry is present although it was not directly intended. It comes in as an extra without being expressly solicited. I am not sure that I can make myself clear on this point because it would mean making judgments about the films of my contemporaries and that I won't do. In any case, it seems to me that *Cahiers* on the one hand and the critics on the other tend to be too much concerned with cinema which makes one aware of the camera and the *auteur* – which doesn't make it the *only* kind of *auteur* cinema there is – at the expense of another kind of cinema, the narrative cinema, which is immediately regarded as classical whereas in my view it is no more classical than any other kind of cinema. Pasolini cites Godard and Antonioni. You could also cite Resnais and Varda. They are film-makers of a very different kind, but from a certain viewpoint it's possible to lump them together.

As for those who are, I won't say my preference, but who seem to me to be closer to what I myself am trying to do, who are they? They are film-makers in whose films you are aware of the camera, but that isn't the essential thing; it's the thing that is filmed that has more of an autonomous existence. In other words they are interested in a world which is not a cinematographic world from the very beginning. For them, cinema is less an end than a means, while with Resnais, Godard or Antonioni you get the sense that the cinema is contemplating itself, that the people filmed exist only inside the film, or inside cinema in general. For them, cinema is a way of revealing people to us, making us familiar with them, whereas for the 'moderns' cinema is more a means of making the cinema reveal itself.

The film-makers I am talking about are film-makers who have made only a few films and I can't claim that they won't change and go over to the other side. I am taking their films as they are now, and moreover not so much the films as a whole as certain moments in them; particular passages of *Adieu Philippine*,[7] for example, especially the wasp scene, or the film to which you gave qualified approval but which I like very much, Alain Jessua's *La Vie à l'envers*. Or the best aspects of Chabrol, because of course Chabrol has his cinephile side too, though I find that a mystificatory element of his work which to me does not seem to go very deep. Chabrol's characters are interesting independently of the fact of being filmed. So there's a cinema which does not project itself to the forefront but offers us situations and characters, whereas in the other kind of cinema characters and situations seem to me less interesting because before all else they are defining a concept of cinema.

[. . .]

In the films I have cited the characters are not a pretext for anything. But that doesn't prove anything. I'm speaking for myself, and I'm saying that I feel more affinity with certain film-makers despite everything that separates me from them on other levels. I have the impression that my interest is turning more and more in that direction and I must insist on the modernity of it. A cinema where the camera is invisible can be a modern cinema. What I would like to make is cinema where the camera is *completely* invisible. You can always make the camera less visible. There is (still) work to be done in this field.

'Modern' is in any case a rather compromised term. You ought not to set out to be modern; if you deserve it, you are. And neither should you be afraid of not being modern. It mustn't become an obsession.

Cahiers: For us the demand for modernity has polemical value: the modern film-makers are all those – including film-makers of long standing like Renoir – who have not only brought their worlds into being but at the same time have always redefined the cinema in relation to themselves, who have turned it in a new direction.

Rohmer: What direction is that? The remarkable thing in cinema is that you can do everything, whereas in music or painting there are taboos, prohibitions. In music you have to choose whether you are going to be before twelve-tone music or after it. But in cinema, while you do of course have to choose to be before or after the talkie, the choice is dictated by the technology alone. Every time people tried to champion a new technical possibility they were right and their attitude was justified by history. Inversely, every time someone has tried to defend a purely aesthetic position, even where it seemed to be linked to technical innovations, however intelligent the defence they were always mistaken. Take Bazin. The most debatable part of his position is precisely his defence of a new cinema founded on deep focus.[8] That didn't stand up at all. The same goes for the question of a cinema which was to be purely realist. So too for a purely 'poetic' cinema; or a cinema like Resnais's where chronology disappears and the subjective and objective are merged into one. Doors are opened, but they don't lead anywhere. These innovations are doomed to die without issue. It has never been possible to lay down the law on the direction cinema might be about to take. Every time people thought it was moving in a particular direction, in fact it went completely the opposite way.

The best and most real thing about the *nouvelle vague* is the contribution it has made on the technical level, both to filming and production. The fact of making films cheaply is something that's here to stay, one can't go back on that.

Cahiers: Shouldn't we add to the list of productive innovations technical developments of a more general kind, like that of the narrative for instance. It underwent numerous variations, was fixed in a number of conventional forms during the reign of Hollywood, and now is reacting against those conventions. Isn't chronology, for example, a technique in the same way as the mounted camera or the shot-reverse shot, and as a technique, can't it be replaced by new forms?

Rohmer: I approve of the shot-reverse shot and I approve of chronology. I am not saying that you have to always use the shot-reverse shot or that you have to respect chronology. [. . .] I think that it's by respecting chronological order that you will go furthest and be most modern. That's a purely personal opinion and I have no way of proving it. But the experiments that have been made in the direction of a non-chronological cinema prove that it is of little interest. You may have noted moreover that the majority of the film-makers I've cited follow a chronological order. Even Godard hasn't so far made anything genuinely non-chronological.

Cahiers: It's not so much in terms of chronology that narrative technique is developing today. It's more the way the story is taken forward, the way the plot is constructed, which is undergoing the biggest upheavals: there are more ellipses, or rather, certain things long considered essential are passed over in favour of bringing other things to the forefront.
. . .

Rohmer: There I agree with you. I mean, what used to be shown is no longer shown now, and what is shown now used not to be shown. But for that the poetic cinema is not the most appropriate; it seems to me that poetic cinema is more traditionalist than the other kind as far as ellipses are concerned because it seeks to show the high points of the action above all. Poetic cinema often consists of bravura moments. It's in the cinema which seeks to be prosaic rather than poetic that you will find an attempt to break the traditional narrative mode, but the method is devious rather than spectacular and it doesn't borrow some of the techniques of the novel. I stand firm on that point. I believe one should not transpose the methods of the novelist into cinema. The thing has to be spontaneous, it has to come to the film-maker as an answer to the actual needs of his form of expression, quite innocently and without any other reference. . . .

Cahiers: Let's take the case of Bresson . . .

Rohmer: But I don't know what category to put Bresson in. You could very well say that he is above categories, but I'm not sure. At the moment I would tend to put him into that of poetic rather than narrative cinema. He is a film-maker in whose work you sense the presence of the camera, even through its absence, if I may put it that way. The camera is effaced but the effacement itself indicates that it could be there. In Bresson, you have an enormous sense of the film-maker's presence. I think that what interests him is *the way things are shown* but not the way *particular* things are shown. In other words the cinema is largely an end to him, and not a means.

[. . .]

Cahiers: A cinema which is turned towards the world and does not take itself as the object is a good description of American cinema in the terms you defended it in *Cahiers*.

Rohmer: I don't think I can actually argue the point. I'd almost be prepared to say that I couldn't tell you whether a film was American or not. At one time I liked American cinema very much, but the American thing interests me less now. When I say that it's possible to have a modern cinema which isn't necessarily a reflection on cinema, it doesn't follow that it has to be a naive cinema. I'm making a distinction between two kinds of cinema, one which takes itself for object and end, and one which takes the world for its object and its means. But I am quite capable of thinking about cinema as a means and I have a great many ideas on the subject. The Americans are very naive. I mean, they never wrote or reflected on cinema, whether as means or end. If you questioned them, almost all of them (with the possible exception of Hawks, who had certain ideas on cinema as a means, though they were very simple ideas) had thought about cinema as a technique, or else about the world as an object, and that's it. But we can think about the cinema as both a means and an end. It seems to shock you that I say cinema is a means and not an end.

Cahiers: No, not at all.

Rohmer: I notice that critics often admire some of the films I've cited but are at a bit of a loss about what to say about them, whereas whenever a film takes cinema as its object it's possible to talk about it, and talk about it they do, at length. When they're not doing that, they say things I find even more banal and conventional, and in the end they more or less see it as a good classical film, which is not what it is to me.

Cahiers: If a lot of films today seem more complex and more abstract, that may be because the world they claim to describe itself seems more complex and abstract, more indefinable. It may be that the world can't be reduced to a linear scenario.

Rohmer: I don't agree. You're going to tell me I'm a reactionary and not just a classicist. As far as I am concerned the world doesn't change, at least not much. The world is always the world, neither more confused or clearer. What changes is art, ways of approaching the world.

[. . .]

Cahiers: To what extent has making films modified your ideas on cinema?

Rohmer: You might say that I've gone the opposite way to the ideas I had. I even wonder if I ever had ideas. If you think about it, it's Bazin who had ideas, while what we had was tastes. Bazin's ideas are all good, but his tastes are very debatable. Bazin's judgments have not been confirmed by posterity – that's to say, he didn't really establish one great film-maker. He liked certain film-makers who are great, but I don't think what he said about them really established them. Whereas we didn't say much of any importance on the theory of cinema, all we did was to elaborate Bazin's ideas. On the other hand, I think we established good values, and those who came after us confirmed our tastes: we have established the reputations of film-makers who've lasted and I think will last. I've come round to going against my theories (if I ever had any). What were they? The long take, camera continuity in preference to editing. These theories, such as they are, were for the most part taken from Bazin and Leenhardt. Leenhardt defined them in an article called 'Down with Ford, Long Live Wyler',[9] in which he said that modern cinema was a cinema not of images and editing, but of camera shots and camera continuity. But the films I have made have everything to do with editing. Up till now, editing has been the most important part of my films. In an extreme case, I could absent myself from the shooting, but I'd have to be there at the editing. Besides, during shooting I'm increasingly interested in framing and photography rather than the shot itself. I believe in the shot less than I used to.

There's another idea that was common to everyone of my generation and that has to do with directing actors. I used to think that it was the most important thing in cinema and I was always a bit apprehensive in that area. Now I regard the directing of actors as a pseudo-problem, it doesn't exist, there's no reason to worry, it's the simplest thing there is about filming. So my concerns are the exact opposite of what they were once, but that seems to me quite natural.

Cahiers: Maybe your tastes in terms of cinema are more in tune with what you do in practice than they are with your theories. . . . What are your cinematic reference points?

Rohmer: There are none. If I had them I'd be paralysed. I admire people who can say: 'I asked myself what Hitchcock would have done in my place.' Personally, not only do I not ask myself that, I don't even see how I could possibly ask it because I have no idea what Hitchcock does. When I watch a film I'm not thinking about the technique it employs at all, and I'd be incapable of plagiarizing a film. I remember what happens, there are interesting moments, a face with an expression that's memorably different. As for the way it's shown, I don't see it on first viewing, nor even on second or third, and it doesn't interest me. When I shoot something, I think about the thing I'm showing. If I wanted to show this chair, it would pose problems for me and I might have to feel my way, but the fact that Hitchcock or Renoir or Rossellini or Murnau have filmed a chair is no help to me. [. . .] From that point of view I am fairly opposed to most of the *Cahiers* people who, as distinct from me, love cinematic cross-references.

Cahiers: And of whom you could say – they've said it themselves – that their criticism is their first film. It's not the same with you.

Rohmer: I don't think so. I made some little amateur films while I was writing. I think all of us at *Cahiers* very quickly began, if not filming, because we didn't have the means, at least wanting to make films. Our criticism had a vested interest. We aren't critics who've gone on to make films, but film-makers who started out by doing a bit of film criticism.

When I'm filming I reflect on the story, the theme, the way the characters are created. But the cinematic technique, the means used, are dictated to me by my wish to show something. In other words if I work with short takes rather than long it's because the short take is the more interesting for what I am trying to show. If it so happened that I could only show it in long takes, that's what I'd opt for. I certainly don't have any form decided *a priori*.

[. . .]

More and more when I go to a gallery and look at a painting I look at what's been painted, and that gives me as great a knowledge of painting as if I'd given my considered attention to the brush stroke of the painter. When I did my TV programme on La Bruyère[10] I went to the Louvre just to find out how they made glass in the seventeenth century. But I saw in those paintings things I wouldn't ever have seen if I hadn't been looking at them solely from the point of view of glass. I was not trying to distinguish between the different painters, nor was I trying to judge their colour and technique. Nevertheless, the exercise gave me a much broader notion of painting. Taking it from there I would say that cinema, just because it may seem slightly reactionary in relation to the other arts, slightly anecdotal, can introduce you to a much broader knowledge of things.[11]

[. . .]

Cahiers: But isn't cinema – as an art of images, sounds and words – impure by definition?

Rohmer: It's a mistake to think of the purity of cinema in terms of just one of its aspects. It's just as silly to consider the cinema pure simply because it consists of images, as it is to consider it pure simply because it consists of sound. The image is no more pure than sound or anything else, but I believe that a purity specific to cinema can emerge within the union of its different aspects. What I would call impure is that particular way of envisaging cinema which means that it fails to reveal its own specific potential, so that instead of tracing a route exclusively its own it sets out along the paths of the other arts. I'm especially irritated by a cinema which aims too much at plasticity of form because the inspiration is the fine-art conception of plasticity. Similarly, cinema is a dramatic art, but it shouldn't as such take its inspiration from the theatre. It is also a literary art, but its merits ought not to lie exclusively in the script and

90

the dialogue. The close union of speech and image creates a purely cinematographic style. On the other hand, making actors say things which could be assigned to a commentary begins to smack of the theatrical. I find it much less cinematographic to make someone say something which informs the spectator on some point than to have it said by a commentary. It's less artificial. The use of subtitles in silent cinema posed an analogous problem. They too freed the image of one function, that of signifying. The image is not meant to signify, but to show. Its role is not to say that someone is something but to show his way of being it, which is infinitely more difficult. There already exists an excellent tool for the work of signifying and that's the spoken language. We ought to make use of it. If you use images to express what can be said in a couple of words, it's wasted effort.

Cahiers: But showing is also signifying. . . .

Rohmer: That's right. In showing, you are signifying, but you ought not to signify without showing. Signification should only come in as something extra. Our purpose is to show. Signification has to be envisaged at a stylistic, not a grammatical level, or otherwise at a metaphorical level, using the term in a wider sense. The symbolist cinema is the worst of all. You see retrograde films from time to time in which the image is trying to play the exact role of the word or phrase. That's gone completely out of fashion now, don't let's dwell on it.

Cahiers: You have in your time defended Bergman, so one must assume that you do not subscribe to the criticisms some have made of him as being a 'literary' film-maker and using only 'symbols'. . . .

Rohmer: I haven't changed my opinion. I am not going back on my critical work. I still defend those I've defended, just as I still attack those I used to attack. So I still think what I always thought of Bergman. I like him very much. In any case, I don't have any *a priori* position. So, even with the subjective cinema I've just objected to, it may well turn out that some really powerful film-maker will make me accept it.

Cahiers: Are you therefore still absolutely loyal to the *politique des auteurs*?

Rohmer: Yes, I haven't changed.

Cahiers: Do you still believe in *mise en scène*?

Rohmer: It's possible to assert, as does Godard, that *mise en scène* doesn't exist. But if you regard *mise en scène* as the art of cinema, if it's the cinematic process as such, then denying its existence comes down to denying that cinema is an art and the film-maker an artist. On the other hand if you regard *mise en scène* as a technique which is in the end close to the theatrical technique, or what the theatre profession calls 'directing', the act of 'realizing', a performance art, then it's very possible to claim that it doesn't exist. But if I personally hold to the term *mise en scène*, it's because I understand it not as 'directing', but as conception – the art of conceiving a film. That conception is then realized by the crew at your disposal which includes a cameraman, an editor, and so on. It is no doubt possible to do without a cameraman or an editor, but it is

91

also quite possible to rely on them and still remain the *metteur en scène*. That's why denying *mise en scène* as it is of course understood by *Cahiers* comes down to denying cinema. I don't believe that the best dialogue in the world can of itself make a good film. And yet the *mise en scène* may be so much a part of it that it makes work on the set unnecessary. That doesn't mean that the *mise en scène* doesn't exist, it means that in that particular case the scenario was already the *mise en scène*. And while it is true that one may not have to be present at the shooting, it's also true that *mise en scène* may happen at the editing stage.

Cahiers: In your articles, especially the earliest ones, you took up a position which was not just aesthetic, but political as well.

Rohmer: Yes, and conservative, too. I now regret it. Politics are useless. Or rather, they did not serve my cause well. But the situation wasn't the same in 1950. Read *L'Écran Français*[12] again: American cinema was condemned en bloc. In order to denounce the imposture of the left you had to weight the balance to the right, to correct one excess with another. But for nearly ten years now in France, criticism has thrown politics to the wind. That's what makes it the best criticism in the world. That said, there's nothing to stop a critic or a film-maker from having his own convictions. At the moment I'm quite indifferent to politics – at least in the narrow sense – but I haven't changed. I don't know if I'm on the right politically, but in any case what's certain is that *I am not on the left*. That's right, why should I be left-wing? For what reason? What's to compel me? I'm free to choose, aren't I? Well, people aren't free. Nowadays you have to make your act of faith with the left, and then you can do anything. [. . .]

And then, just because you're a writer, a painter or a film-maker, why should it follow that your views on the government of society are more correct than the views of those responsible for catering for its needs rather than, like us, for its pleasures? Every time an artist meddles in politics, instead of contributing what one has the right to expect, that is, a view of things that's calmer, broader and more conciliatory, he entrenches himself in the most narrow, bigoted and extreme kinds of attitudes. He urges prison, massacre, destruction, he ignores forgiveness, tolerance and respect for the adversary. That's normal. Plato said it: he who is born to exalt man's passions can be only a poor governor of men.

Cahiers: Do you think then that a film-maker should be indifferent to his times?

Rohmer: No, not at all. Quite the reverse. I'd even say that he can and must be committed, but not politically in the narrow, traditional sense of the term. What does art give people? Pleasure. The artist should be committed to the organization of that pleasure, and since we're told we are entering an age of leisure, perhaps he will be able to discover for himself an important, exciting role that is completely worthy of him. [. . .]

Faced with the way the modern world is going, the film-maker is opting out of his responsibilities, which is deplorable in a way that disinterest in politics is not. Every one of them tries to evade responsibility and doesn't seem in the least affected by the infinite banality, infinite vulgarity – there are exceptions, I will admit – of the press, radio, television and cinema which does, it's true, serve them as a foil. It's a good thing to be 'trendy' sometimes. But you have to know how to go against the trend at times too. Art is not a reflection of the times, it's the precursor. You shouldn't go along with popular taste, you should be in advance of it. You have to remain deaf to statistics and graphs. You have above all to distrust publicity like the plague, even the most intelligent kind. Publicity is the disease number one of cinema. It falsifies everything, it makes a mess of everything, even the pleasure of the spectator and the judgment of the critics. You have to refuse to play the game. You're going to say that that's not possible, or that the only way out is to make amateur films. All right, that's what I'm doing, more or less.

Translated by Diana Matias

Notes

1 The word used here is 'marbre' which in French, as well as meaning marble, is also the technical term for the bed of a printing press. The use of 'marble' and 'celluloid' here refers directly to a series of important articles by Rohmer in *Cahiers du Cinéma* in 1955, 'Le Celluloïd et le marbre': 'I: Le Bandit philosophe', *Cahiers* 44, February 1955, 'II: Le Siècle des peintres', *Cahiers* 49, July 1955, 'III: De la métaphore', *Cahiers* 51, October 1955, 'IV: Beau comme la musique', *Cahiers* 52, November 1955, 'V: Architecture d'apocalypse', *Cahiers* 53, December 1955. Extracts from this series (parts II and III) are translated in Williams, *Realism and the Cinema*. Rohmer's articles, in which he tries to establish the relationship of film to the other arts and adumbrates a realist theory of film, are discussed by Colin Crisp in 'The Ideology of Realism: Eric Rohmer – "Celluloid and Marble" and *My Night with Maud*', *Australian Journal of Screen Theory* 2, 1977.
2 'Vingt ans après: le cinéma américain et la politique des auteurs', translated as 'Twenty Years On: A Discussion about the American Cinema and the *politique des auteurs*', Ch. 20 in this volume.
3 'Parlons de *Pierrot*: nouvel entretien avec Jean-Luc Godard', *Cahiers* 171, October 1965, translated as 'Let's Talk about *Pierrot*' in *Godard on Godard*, also in Jean-Luc Godard, *Pierrot le fou*, London, Lorrimer Publishing, 1969.
4 Until 1954 Rohmer signed his critical writings with his real name, Maurice Schérer.
5 Pier Paolo Pasolini, 'Le Cinéma de poésie', *Cahiers* 171, October 1965, originally given as a paper at the first Festival of New Cinema, Pesaro, Italy, June 1965, translated as 'Pier Paolo Pasolini at Pesaro: The Cinema of Poetry', *Cahiers du Cinéma in English* 6, December 1966, reprinted as 'The Cinema of Poetry' in Nichols, *Movies and Methods*.
6 Pasolini had written, with film-makers such as Antonioni, Bertolucci and

Godard in mind, of certain tendencies of modern cinema: 'The primordial characteristic of these indications of a tradition of the cinema of poetry consists in a phenomenon which technicians define normally and tritely as "making the camera felt". In sum, the maxim of wise film-makers in force up till the '60s – "Never let the camera's presence be felt" – has been replaced by its opposite', Pasolini in Nichols, *Movies and Methods*, p. 556.

7 *Adieu Philippine* (1963), first feature by Jacques Rozier, a commercial failure but in many ways a key film in critical discussion in *Cahiers* of the *nouvelle vague*.

8 See Labarthe, 'Marienbad Year Zero', Ch. 3, note 2, in this volume.

9 Roger Leenhardt, 'A bas Ford, vive Wyler', *L'Ecran Français* 146, 13 April 1948 (see note 12 below).

10 *Les Caractères de la Bruyère*, one of a number of short programmes made by Rohmer for schools television in the period 1964–6.

11 Rohmer's arguments here draw significantly on his earlier writings, such as the 'Celluloid and Marble' series (see note 1, above), and are particularly close to the positions in 'Le Goût de la beauté', *Cahiers* 121, July 1961, where he argues, for example, for the 'modernity' of Otto Preminger's *Exodus* in its ability to make us forget human intervention in art and concentrate on the natural beauty of the depicted world.

12 *L'Ecran Français*, French film journal begun in 1943, during the Occupation and Resistance, and sponsored by engaged film-makers and the Communist Party. A vital arena of debate about aesthetics and politics, especially in relation to American cinema, throughout the 1940s. Alexandre Astruc and Roger Leenhardt wrote for it and André Bazin was among its most important critics, breaking with it in the late 1940s as its increasingly conventional Marxist line, particularly against American cinema as a whole, became more pronounced and when it became fully subsidized by the Communist Party. *L'Ecran Français* is crucial to an understanding of later developments in film criticism in France in the 1950s. The complexities of the period and of the journal's place within it are documented in Olivier Barrot, *L'Ecran Français, 1943–1953, histoire d'un journal et d'une époque*, Paris, Editions Les Editeurs Français Réunis, 1979, and are usefully discussed by Dudley Andrew in 'Bazin before *Cahiers*: Cinematic Politics in Postwar France', *Cinéaste*, vol. XII, no. 1, 1982. Much of Bazin's writing of the war and post-war period, particularly for *L'Ecran Français*, is collected in André Bazin, *French Cinema of the Occupation and Resistance: The Birth of a Critical Aesthetic*, New York, Oxford University Press, 1981, and André Bazin, *The Cinema of Cruelty*, New York, Seaver Books, 1982.

8 | André S. Labarthe: 'Pagnol'

('Pagnol entre centre et absence', *Cahiers du Cinéma* 173, December 1965)

'We have to come to an agreement about the term *"maudit"*[1] as it is used with regard to cinema', wrote Jean Cocteau at the beginning of the Biarritz Festival manifesto in 1949.[2] And to distinguish between two kinds of curse, one of which, borrowed from Mallarmé, was directly applicable to Biarritz: a work will be *maudit* if it 'sets out to contradict a fashion even if it's an extreme fashion'. At Biarritz, a *film maudit* was one that hadn't found its audience, i.e. that hadn't *yet* found it. In other words, it wasn't enough for a film to be considered avant-garde, this avant-garde had to be a *cinematic* one; and cinema, as Bazin explained a few pages further on, was 'the product of a clearly defined industry whose fundamental law couldn't possibly be called into question – *to obtain in one way or another the approval of the audience*' (my italics). The Biarritz Festival set out purely and simply to give a chance to films that hadn't yet met with this approval (*Cronaca di un amore*, *Les Dames du Bois de Boulogne*) since, as Bazin also noted, 'all films are born with equal rights'.

But there is another form of curse of which Cocteau was also perfectly well aware: 'Make no mistake about it, a film doesn't have to be a failure. A success based on a misapprehension can send people off on the wrong track. Thus Chaplin's films – truly Kafkaesque dramas – weren't seen that way, etc.'

The curse which hangs over Pagnol's films is of this order. You could say that their popularity has up till now hidden their great novelty. Besides that, the overblown pronouncements of the author haven't simply alienated those who don't like his films, they have had the strange effect – probably the exact opposite of what Pagnol anticipated – of putting off commentators, critics and theorists who thought the case had been heard and decided (in short that this was just filmed theatre) and haven't bothered to take the matter any further.

Now that the argument has cooled off, it is at last possible to examine

95

both Pagnol's films and his theoretical positions perfectly calmly and to restore them to their rightful place.

To borrow the title of the only sensible article on his films, it seems to me that the Pagnol question[3] illustrates one of the great paradoxes in the disruption that resulted from the transition from an art of the image to a talking cinema: it was often the people who were the least competent on a technical level who were the best able to grasp the meaning of the revolution that was taking place, as if their ignorance of the rules had, instead of undermining their position, guaranteed their freedom, making it possible for them to be straightforward and sincere, in short giving them that freshness of invention that we now admire so much.

We have to remember that the professionals remained terribly suspicious of this new art for a very long time. But these suspicions were basically the result of a feeling of insecurity on the part of people who sensed that talking cinema was perhaps less the introduction of new complexities than a radical break with cinema as it had existed until then. A confused lucidity that was quickly stifled because of the urgency of the polemic. The arrival on the scene of a new generation with little knowledge of silent techniques and which was as a result considered incompetent *a priori* led, then, to the novelty of the new art being played down instead of being confronted head-on. Speech was considered as just an extra element (or rather two elements since a distinction was made between speech and sound effects) that could be added on to the accepted procedures of silent cinema. Talking cinema was thus merely silent cinema with speech grafted on and talking films were made by a process of addition of these attributes.

What was Pagnol doing at this time? He was filming the guilty party. Instead of considering speech as the intruder (i.e. as a rival) he installed it, queen-like, at the centre of the image. This reminds me of Sacha Guitry's reply to an assistant who suggested filming a shot of a chandelier: 'There's no dialogue in a chandelier.'

Like Guitry, Pagnol instinctively refuses to film the chandelier because it doesn't talk. What I mean is that this shot of the chandelier would have been appropriate if it had had to replace (signify) speech, i.e. appropriate to that act of compromise promoted at the time by silent film-makers who were attracted by talking cinema, to that audio-visual art, the offspring of an outmoded discourse of images whose muffled echo continued for a while to reverberate through books on theory. As we can see, it isn't ultimately its muteness that defines silent cinema so much as a certain way of manipulating simple elements, and in the new art it isn't so much speech that counts as a certain global apprehension of a synthetic unity. That is why many talking pictures perpetuate the aesthetic of the silents whereas many silent films (notably those of Feuillade, Stroheim and Murnau) can be seen as more or less conscious ancestors of the talkies.[4]

Pagnol, then, films speech. But not just any old speech. In this respect there is nothing more misleading than the term 'filmed theatre'. Bazin was in no doubt about that: 'Theatre can absolutely not be differentiated from cinema on the basis of a pre-eminence of verbal expression over visual action . . . speech in theatre is abstract, like everything on the stage it is itself a convention, the result of actions put into words; speech in cinema on the other hand is a concrete fact, it exists, perhaps not in the beginning, but at least by and for itself; it is action that prolongs it and in a way debases it.'[5] Enough said.

However, if we look more closely, the term 'filmed theatre' does at least have one advantage: it helps us to define a whole category of modern film-makers, from Renoir to Guitry, and from Rossellini to Rouch or to young Eustache. 'Filmed theatre' is in fact a proclamation of the separate identity of a content (theatre) and a container (film). Remember Boudu bounding along the banks of the Marne or Poupon revelling in the sound of the word 'sophism' (*Jofroi*): you have the impression that they exist quite independently from the way the camera has caught them.

And it is the autonomy of what is shown (something Rohmer was arguing for in these columns last month[6]) that generates in the spectator that exquisite sensation of arbitrariness linked to some mysterious necessity called grace.

Silent cinema was essentially functional (like the sentence I have just written): there was no such thing as the well-turned phrase or the polished phrase or the unconventional phrase (which explains why there is no baroque silent art), only the appropriate phrase made any sense. Pagnol and his peers on the other hand based their practice on what was to become the precept of Rossellini, seeing the object of *mise en scène* as being purely and simply *to record the dramatic situation*. Hence the means used were of secondary importance: a scene would only ever be *more or less well* recorded like some news event filmed simultaneously by ten cameramen. The best way to film (and no longer the only way) was thus the simplest one, the one that would be the least obtrusive, and if Pagnol can, in this respect, be considered superior to Korda[7] it is simply because, not being a professional director, he forgot cinema and filmed instinctively. What then is filming except carrying out with a greater or lesser degree of felicity a task of recording that is *indispensable* (without it there would be no spectacle or at least no transmission of spectacle) but *arbitrary* (since the spectacle has an autonomous existence or at least one that is independent of the way it is shown)? This technical work can of course be accompanied by some fine 'effects' of *mise en scène* – like that magnificent wide shot, worthy of Murnau, in *Manon* that gives Hugolin's confession an undeniable tragic grandeur. But can it be denied that this grandeur was already there in the confession itself and that even if it had been massacred by the ineptitude of an amateur cameraman it would still have retained some of its power? Or, to take a more spectacular example, how could a technical analysis of Godard's sketch in *Paris vu par . . .* teach us anything at all about Godard's art (he is the author of the film) since the work of recording (choice of camera angles, framing, etc.) wasn't done by him?

What we are dealing with here is the paradox of a cinema without cinema, at the opposite extreme both from the whole of silent cinema and from a tradition of sound cinema that culminates in the work of Bresson (all Bresson's statements contradict what has been said above).[8]

We could, therefore, divide film *auteurs* into two categories, using what we remember about their films as the basic criterion: we recall a *character* in Pagnol but a *shot* in Bresson. To put it another way, Pagnol would not be a lesser film-maker if he had had nothing at all to do with the technical direction of his films, whereas it is impossible to imagine a single Bresson film that could have been directed by anyone else. That is why criticism so often misses the mark: as a technical analysis, it can almost exhaust the possibilities of exploration of a Bresson film but can't begin to cope with a film by Renoir, Guitry, Rossellini, Pagnol or young Eustache; if it is centred on drama and the intrinsic analysis of performance, it overlooks Bresson and Resnais. And if we could consider Pagnol's *cinematic* genius as going beyond cinema (or stopping short of it if you prefer), it might perhaps be useful to return to what Roger Leenhardt said recently on television: 'I personally thought that it was the scriptwriter who was the most important . . . and that we were going to have a generation for whom the author of a film would be an author in the same way as a playwright is in the theatre. And that there would be specialization with the result, when strong personalities were involved, that the director would be there to apply his technical skills to the author's work, like Jouvet producing a Giraudoux play. I was completely wrong. At least as far as France was concerned. Since what has in fact happened is that all the young writers who were really made to be film authors in the sense I have indicated have increasingly been drawn not just towards directing actors but towards the precise visual organization of their films. Astruc, one of the finest literary minds of our generation, is, for example, much less interested in aesthetics than in the gymnastics of a crane shot . . . Be that as it may, I was wrong and I want to make that clear.'[9]

It will also be clear that an analysis of Pagnol's films ought to begin exactly where this article leaves off: by a scrutiny of the text of his dialogue (for example his penchant for argument or for recipes that are such a recurring feature in his films) and the way it is rooted in a *fiction* (there is a need for a systematic study of Pagnol's dramatic situations), in a *landscape* (we would discover two types of landscape: Marseilles and its hinterland), and above all in *characters* (an inventory would prove what tremendous actors Raimu, Poupon, Fernandel and Scotto were). Landscapes and characters that have become inseparable not from cinema but from the fiction that it conveys.

I would be very surprised if, almost thirty years later, this analysis didn't show that Roger Leenhardt was right.[10]

Translated by Norman King

Notes

1 *'Maudit'*, literally 'cursed' but as used here, and very often in writing about cultural works and artists, with a meaning more closely approximating to 'unjustifiably neglected' or 'misunderstood'.

2 The Biarritz Festival referred to was 'Le Festival du Film Maudit', organized by 'Objectif 49', a ciné-club which grouped together critics and film-makers like Jean Cocteau, Robert Bresson, Roger Leenhardt, René Clément, Alexandre Astruc, Pierre Kast, André Bazin, Raymond Queneau and others who, in Jacques Doniol-Valcroze's phrase (in 'L'Histoire des *Cahiers'*, *Cahiers* 100, October 1959, p. 64), 'dreamed of a *cinéma d'auteurs* . . .'. Jean Cocteau's 'Préface au cinéma maudit', from the 1949 festival, is reprinted in *Cahiers* 161–2, January 1965. Two festivals were held. 1949 included Bresson's *Les Dames du Bois de Boulogne*, Grémillon's *Lumière d'été*, Ford's *The Long Voyage Home*, Vigo's restored *L'Atalante*, plus new films like Tati's *Jour de fête* and Welles's *The Lady from Shanghai*. The second, and last, festival, in 1950, featured the French premieres of Antonioni's *Cronaca di un amore* and Ray's *They Live By Night*. For further background, see Richard Roud, *A Passion for Films* (London, Secker & Warburg; New York, Viking Press, 1983), pp. 80–2.

3 'Le Cas Pagnol', by André Bazin, in Bazin, *Qu'est-ce que le cinéma? II: Le Cinéma et les autres arts*, Paris, Editions du Cerf, 1959.

4 Labarthe's point here resumes very precisely Bazin's theses about realism and the evolution of film language: see note 2 to Labarthe's 'Marienbad Year Zero', in this volume, Ch. 3.

5 Bazin, 'Le Cas Pagnol' p. 121.

6 'L'Ancien et le nouveau: entretien avec Eric Rohmer', *Cahiers* 172, November 1965, translated as 'The Old and the New: a discussion with Eric Rohmer', in this volume, Ch. 7.

7 The first films made by Pagnol's company from his plays were directed by others: *Marius* (1930) by Alexander Korda, *Fanny* (1932) by Marc Allégret, *Topaze* (1932) by Louis Gasnier. After that Pagnol directed his own films.

8 'Bresson affirms, for example, that there is only one place from which a scene can be shot. Sight and vision are, he says, fused into one.' (Author's note.)

9 In 'Roger Leenhardt, ou le dernier humaniste' in the television series (with which Labarthe was long associated) 'Cinéastes de notre temps' (1964).

10 Some of the kind of analysis Labarthe asks for here is provided by Michel Delahaye in 'Le Saga Pagnol', *Cahiers* 213, June 1969.

('Lelouch, ou la bonne conscience retrouvée', *Cahiers du Cinéma* 180, July 1966)

No, Lelouch is not our *bête noire*. You can't reproach a film-maker for not being a genius. Lelouch may lack talent or genius but you have to admire his sincerity and naivety, the courage or stubbornness that made him go on madly working away amid universal scorn or indifference until it turned into praise. The wind is coming from another direction now, and present glory is no less excessive than past contempt. While Lelouch's first five films were sometimes less awful than their reputation, the sixth far from lives up to the one it has acquired. *Un Homme et une femme* has a few nice ideas frantically chasing their tails in search of an *auteur*, but nothing much to distinguish it from the decidedly botched jobs that preceded it. Nothing that is except perhaps that this time the naivety and sincerity have become calculation and swank – sure harbingers of awards and success. Good for Lelouch. Why shouldn't we have one more happy film-maker in France? His film is fashionable, and that's what needs to be explained. *Un Homme et une femme* cannot be considered separately from the triumphant reception it has had from critics and audiences: doggerel passes for poetry, and there are as many (and no doubt the same) lessons to be drawn from the film on the tastes and needs of a particular audience as there are on the satisfaction this audience gets from the film. Every film assumes more or less the meaning of its success, and this is truer of this purpose-built film than of others. [. . .]

Even in the course of interviews and despite the obvious goodwill of the interviewers, the dialogue often dries up: 'Mr Lelouch, what were you trying to do, what were you trying to say exactly in *Un Homme et une femme*?' – 'Well, you know, for me even the first step is too much. . . .' What a wonderfully formulated aphorism, the essential conversation stopper. There's not much to be got out of a man who can proclaim with a kind of primitive joy and pride, 'For me, even the first step is too much'. And what's more, it's quite accurate. Not all of us can be Cournot.[1] It's no shame to be stupid; and in fact it would be foolish to believe that stupidity is necessarily accompanied by shrinking modesty. It's only painful when, as in this case, it aspires to be a profession of faith, a complete programme. Is Lelouch, in his desire to convince us of his stupidity at any price, really that stupid?

Cunning is undoubtedly a form of stupidity but certainly its most civilized form. Verneuil, Cloche, Joannon,[2] all our primitives that is, are careful not to call themselves stupid. It isn't that they are trying to put up a front, they genuinely believe it's the rest of the world that's stupid. Lelouch's case is more complicated. The degree zero he lays claim to is full of subtleties, if not subterfuges.

Rejecting the role of intelligence involves constructing a whole theory of the cinema. Thrusting stupidity to the forefront involves posing as a dumb animal of the cinema. And that's what Lelouch wants to be taken for: a human camera, an instinctive image-maker, an eye without a brain, a swollen sensibility; his intellectual simplicity is meant to offer the surest guarantee of full communion with the world and humankind; and this lack of distance – in both viewpoint and aesthetic or moral principles – clears a space for raw emotion, for a crude, unmediated beauty which can only be driven out into the open by the undefined and ungovernable surges of an abundant intuition. As you see, the idea isn't bad. In a period when the cinema – as we know, the art of pleasing the crowd, public entertainment, spectacle that aims at gut reaction – is unlucky enough to be fed off by a good many more or less intellectual bores like Godard, Resnais and Bresson, it's good that a film-maker should race to the defence of the intellectually underprivileged, the dealers and distributors who form the viewers' élite, assuring them in advance with a great deal of fanfare that here is a film which won't make exhausting demands on them, won't over-tax their brains, that all they need to understand cinema is a heart and eyes (something that élite – wrongly – was beginning to believe less and less). Lelouch's whole art and thought in a nutshell is this: on the one hand a desire to restore idleness and facility to favour, to make people believe that beauty requires no effort, that the pure mind will be amply rewarded, and other such demagogic catch-phrases; on the other hand, to ensure that cinema is seen as a matter of god-given talent, that it has to be made by dumb animals for dumb animals, that instinct dispenses with any need for quality, substitutes for rigour and morality, and that one does not need to think to exist – nor to succeed. The village idiot would find the argument subtle. It culminates in a kind of terrorism: 'If you don't like Un Homme et une femme, it's because you're against simplicity, nature, life. Some noxious kind of intellectualism must be eating at you. You have to recover your innocence to be receptive to beauty.' But I would say that to propose this debilitated cinema first of all means despising the spectator. The desire to be basic means denying the intelligence of the spectator. Setting your sights low means aiming at a lower target. In one sense.

Because in another sense it would be advisable to question the soundness of the base on which these Lelouchian assertions are founded. What are we to do about those instances where a momentum carries the film towards a hypothetical and rejected second level?

1 The sudden reference to a quote from Giacometti: 'If I had to choose between rescuing a Rembrandt or a cat from a fire, I'd choose the cat, even if I let it go afterwards.' What accident drops this cultural reference into the middle of a film which on principle excludes any Godard-type collage? It would have been better to do as Godard would and work fully through such a disruption. Instead it is here dragged clumsily into the situation and the dialogue of the two characters, who act as if they just happened to recall it, and it inclines one to think that Lelouch brings it in as some kind of self-justification: given a choice between filming a Monet seascape and a dog roaming round Deauville, Lelouch opts for life – the dog. Unfortunately, for all that he doesn't stint himself when it comes to filming waves, and more waves, the coast, the beach, piling up the pictorial references.

2 The exchange of remarks between Trintignant and Aimée on the acting profession, achieved by tricks of sound and laborious improvisation, which has her saying (with slight embarrassment moreover): 'No, I shouldn't like to be an actress', etc.

3 A bit of dialogue about the cinema, what it ought to be, why one goes to films, etc.

4 How could cinematic references – instances of degree two – be avoided in a film where the chosen heroes are a continuity girl and a stuntman, where he is killed during a stunt and she is frequently shown at work? Either Lelouch doesn't know what he wants or his affectation of simplicity is just protective camouflage. The life that Lelouch prefers to art is simply a pretext for art. Both life and art lose their point when they're put through this game of Box and Cox which won't come clean. Lelouch's great weakness is thinking he is something he is not: a primitive of the cinema, plunged deep in the heart of life itself; and not accepting what he is: an unreflecting aesthete who will always prefer a beautiful image to an accurate gesture, a zoom to a look, colour embellishment to truth, in short, the camera to cinema, fakery to life.

To give just three quick examples of fakery:

1 The music, used as a vector of images and emotions: a refrain, a song, an obsessive and insistent tune over images of the sunset, the doggie or the couple waltzing, is a way of winning over the audience, doling out emotion. It verges on emptiness, it's sleight of hand, flashiness and fakery because the film-maker is incapable of playing out the full potential of sentimentalism (not everyone can be a Demy, a Reichenbach or a Guy Gilles).

2 Filters are all very nice, but when they don't relate to anything in particular, as in this case, they are a substitute for *mise en scène*. You slap on a filter to mask the vacuity of the shot, to give prolix meaning to something that has none. The filter is a sign heterogeneous with all the

other signs of the shot or sequence, but one which obliges them all to be read globally and combines them arbitrarily to give an illusion of cohesion and logic; which allocates to them a necessity they would not have naturally and which is therefore false.

3 Dialogue part-improvised by the actors. Here the fakery lies in the half-measure. Trintignant and Anouk Aimée are fine, intelligent actors; in other words, when Lelouch gives them their head and leaves the fate of the dialogue to them, something is bound to happen, the inventiveness is there. But here the actors hesitate and stammer a bit. This is noticeable and the intention is to give the impression of spontaneity, naturalness, life. But these are actors who cannot but do it their way. This isn't *cinéma vérité* or psychodrama. The most involuntary hesitations still bear the mark of acting, of composition and premeditation, which makes them a pretence. What is achieved is not truth unsecured by improvisation, but the signs of improvisation alone, the empty mannerisms of truth (redundancies, repetitions, etc.): clichés of what is natural standing for naturalness itself. Note that in these three cases the fakery is related to a kind of naivety which believes itself to be astute, or a craftiness which thinks it is aiming at extreme simplicity. The fakery here is the product of clumsiness and impotence together.

The impotence of the film-maker is compensated by the aestheticism of the camera (one of the keys of the film's success), evident in the excessive and improper use Lelouch makes of the ellipse. All the scenes which are, or ought to be, the dramatic hinges of the film are evaded. When Trintignant and Aimée tell each other about their lives, Lelouch resorts to the trick of replacing this essential confrontation with the image of what they are both supposed to be telling each other about themselves. As a result what we have is no longer the character talking about himself or herself with all that that implies in terms of emotions, reservations, embarrassment or confidence; in short, with all that it requires in terms of work by the film-maker on the narration and *mise en scène*. Instead we have Lelouch showing the spectator what took place. In other words, the sequences of recall, instead of producing a closeness between the main characters or between them and the spectator, completely obliterate their presence and their dramas. These passages become something like parentheses within the dramatic sequence which is nevertheless what produces them. So much so that when something happens in these marginal episodes which must affect the dramatic development of the scene – the death of Anouk Aimée's husband, for instance – Lelouch is forced to go back to Trintignant's face and make him express his reaction – astonishment, pain. But these feelings are then quite theoretical and abstract, mere conventions, an actor's mimicry and no more, because the actor who should be witness to the recital is absent from the scene for its entire duration. What one sees on the screen is neither the accident seen by Anouk Aimée (since she is filmed in it), nor the accident seen by Trintignant through Anouk Aimée (since there is no commentary to make the memory personal), but the event seen through the eyes of a third person, alien to the characters, who imposes a view of things which cannot be that of the main characters and in which they have no part except artificially and externally, through the play of conventions. The voyeur is Lelouch, who prefers his own images to his characters, or rather for whom the characters are only images, malleable at will, fakeable, editable without any concern for truth or even simple narrative effectiveness. The film thus self-destructs even as it seems to progress. Ultimately the whole thing is an ellipse, images replacing other images in order to express images. The reason for this visual logorrhea and the frenetic use of ellipse is the *auteur*'s impotence when it comes to filming the essential thing, which is the action and the drama, and his obsession with deflecting attention to the superfluous, the parasitic and the subordinate: in other words, what is pretty to look at, the photography, beautiful images, everything that represents a flight from cinema. It is said that Lelouch belongs to the generation of the image. But the image in question is the voyeur of images, the devourer of images.

In fact, it is as if the 'pleasure of filming' alone guaranteed successful expression. Lelouch's way of taking the film forward involves an expansion of sequences, an accumulation of shots, a multiplication of images whose chief *raison d'être* is the pleasure they've given him in the filming and in the renewal of that pleasure in the viewing.

The stubborn piling on of gratuitous images in the end invades the dramatic framework like a noxious weed. The incoherence and disorder are here not the effects of art. They are the clinical symptom of a pathological incapacity to choose, eliminate, decide – to direct, in fact. Renoir, Hawks, Rossellini, Bresson, Skolimowski, Straub, Sternberg, all say that directing means suppressing, putting aside, taking away: aiming at the essential. In this respect, the proliferating images of Lelouch's cinema are a disease of cinema, its cancer.

This is doubtless why he enjoys the favour of fashion. Of course prettiness, like gratuitousness, has always been fashionable. Showiness by definition has its customers. But I see the underlying reason for the fashionable success of *Un Homme et une femme* as the fact that it gives the Champs-Elysées crowd a clear conscience. The cinema of ideas and questions, the modern cinema, is never going to do well there. Godard's films make people uncomfortable, as they are intended to. People go to see them, but however much pleasure they get from them it is never an unalloyed pleasure.

Godard's style is in no way the sum of its formal parts. It is its very purpose, which is not just to challenge the language of cinema, but to challenge the world through that language and the language of that world through cinema. The form irritates some people because it runs contrary to their usual experience of cinema and especially to their comfortable view of the world. Lelouch offers them husk without the grain, the envelope without the letter, the image without the world. The consolation is in the no-holds-barred 'audacity', the fragmentation, the improvisation,

104

the frenzy – and the film remains comprehensible and accessible to everyone. Because there is nothing to understand – help yourself to what you want. Lelouch has given the Champs-Elysées a risk-proof way of retrieving the formal mannerisms of the modern cinema, the tinsel of a modernity whose soul has been removed.

Translated by Diana Matias

Notes

1 Cournot: the reference is to Michel Cournot, whose defence of Lelouch in the weekly paper *Le Nouvel Observateur* is referred to in a short paragraph omitted in this translation.
2 Verneuil, Cloche, Joannon: Henri Verneuil, Maurice Cloche, Léo Joannon, three veteran French film-makers referred to here as representative of the 'cinéma de papa' against which the *nouvelle vague* was reacting.

10 | Francois Truffaut: 'Evolution of the New Wave': Truffaut in interview with Jean-Louis Comolli, Jean Narboni (extracts)

('Entretien avec François Truffaut', *Cahiers du Cinéma* 190, May 1967)

Our last interview was more than three years ago[1] and a lot has happened in French cinema since then, so we'd like to ask you what you think of the evolution of the 'New Wave'.

The other night I saw on television a vague argument between Claude Mauriac and Melville. And the only time they were in agreement was when they said, 'Of course, the New Wave was very disappointing'. Then they went on to something else, as though they had stated a fact. That shocked me. If you recall the New Wave as it was originally: to make a first film with a reasonably personal theme before you were thirty-five – well, there was an extraordinary richness there, every promise was fulfilled, and the New Wave started similar movements going in every country of the world, which was something quite unexpected.

The New Wave was born in 1959, and by the end of 1960 it was already an object of contempt. For a year it had some prestige in public opinion. The turning point, the switch from praise to denigration, was marked by the film made by La Patellière and Michel Audiard, *Rue des Prairies*, which was promoted as an 'Anti-New-Wave' film: 'Jean Gabin squares up to the New Wave'. That's where the demagogy started. I mean, the journalists who had launched the movement decided to give people the clichés they wanted to read and nothing else. Before *Rue des Prairies*, when Jean-Luc, Resnais, Malle, me or others were being interviewed we used to say: 'The New Wave doesn't exist, it means nothing'. But afterwards you had to change, and it was from that moment that I declared myself as belonging to this movement. Today, in '67, you have to be proud to have been, and to be, part of the New Wave, like being Jewish during the Occupation.

The New Wave is constantly being attacked, but always in a cowardly way because those who make the attacks don't bother either to define it or to cite names and titles. No need for impulsive list-making, but all the same we can note the emergence during the last three years of Alain Jessua, Claude Berri, José Giovanni, René Allio, Luc Moullet and several others. These aren't occasional film-makers, they're people who'll go on working, who inevitably belong to the New Wave, to the French cinema, and whose films will go to festivals and be shown abroad. . . .

People who say 'The New Wave has failed' without defining what they mean by that, I suppose they're thinking of 'intellectual' films which were not successful at the box-office, and with this in mind they refuse to 'label' films which pleased them or were successful – an arbitrary division since the New Wave is just as much *L'Homme de Rio* as *L'Immortelle*, *Le Vieil homme et l'enfant* as *La Musica*, *Les Coeurs verts* as *Un Homme et une femme*, *La Vie de Château* as *Brigitte et Brigitte*. That's why it's idiotic to generalize all the time, and as someone said, that in itself is a generalization! The New Wave did not have an aesthetic programme, it was simply an attempt to rediscover a certain independence which was lost somewhere around 1924, when films became too expensive, a little before the talkies. For us, in 1960, to make a film was to imitate D. W. Griffith shooting his films in the Californian sun before even the birth of Hollywood. At that time directors were all very young – it's astonishing to realize that Hitchcock, Chaplin, King Vidor, Walsh, Ford, Capra all made their first film before they were twenty-five. It was a young man's profession being a film-maker, and so it should be. So we must have the young men coming on, like Guy Gilles or Lelouch or even younger people, camera in hand, perched on the side of a helicopter, prepared to swell up like a balloon from mosquito bites in the Amazon, etc.

That's a very broad and generous definition of the New Wave . . . It takes in a lot of people: Lelouch, Rappeneau . . .

I don't see how you can define them except by age. Lelouch shoots with a hand-held camera and without a carefully planned script: if he isn't part of the New Wave, then it doesn't exist.[2]

[. . .]

In an interview once you talked of the way you've been criticized for your moderation, your 'classicism', as opposed to some of the aesthetic developments which have been made in cinema during recent years. What's your view of that?

I count on remaining a stranger to these aesthetic developments, since I simply can't do anything which I don't feel deeply. [. . .] I think Rohmer's definition is a good one, when he distinguishes films in which cinema favours the characters from those in which cinema is at the service of the story.[3] However, I don't fit myself in here because I steer a middle course. *Fahrenheit* is somewhere in between these two categories. For the audience it's the story which counts whereas I was more interested in the cinema side of it. But in general I'm more with those who use cinema to tell a story, as in *Les 400 coups* or *La Peau douce*.

From this point of view the best story-teller at the moment is actually Eric Rohmer. In *La Collectionneuse* cinema serves a narrative which is at once extraordinarily subtle and absolutely simple. The film moves with a quiet assurance such as you don't often find in the French cinema. You'd have to go back to *Un Condamné à mort s'est échappé*, where you can sense this mastery, this control being exercised not just over each shot but over the whole film as well.

There are films which are beautiful or moving or sympathetic in their hesitations, their tentativeness, their way of looking for cinema while gliding round it (*La Loi du survivant*, for example), but what impresses me in *La Collectionneuse* is the certainty you can feel in every set-up, every shot change, the 'this is how it is and it couldn't be otherwise' side of it.

La Collectionneuse is also visually beautiful – the neutral, discreet beauty of the Hitchcock Vistavision films. Instead of the usual way films have of alternating day scenes with night scenes, Rohmer succeeds in making us aware of every hour of the day: he has domesticated the sun, the light, shadows, and he's done it without 'effects' which are extraneous to the story being told.

You could see that Bresson, in *Le Procès de Jeanne d'Arc*, was aiming at something which would be all-absorbing – an invisible style, absolute neutrality, an integral and anonymous narrative – but after *Au hasard, Balthazar* and *Mouchette* I no longer think that. Whereas *La Collectionneuse*, which is the most logical film in the world, seems to me, by dint of its precision and its simplicity, to reach that anonymity of execution which sets me dreaming.

[. . .]

Again, my favourite film-makers are all scriptwriter-directors, because after all what is *mise en scène* exactly? It's the *putting together of the decisions made* during the preparation, shooting and completion of a film. I think that all the options open to a director – of script, of what to leave out, of locations, actors, collaborators, camera angles, lenses, shot composition, sound, music – prompt him to make *decisions*, and what we call *mise en scène* is clearly the common destination of all the thousands of *decisions* taken during those six, nine, twelve or sixteen months of work. That's why 'partial' directors, those who are only concerned with the one aspect of filming, even if they're talented, interest me less than Bergman, Buñuel, Hitchcock, Welles, who *are* their films completely.

[. . .]

I'm sometimes unhappy about details in my films, and they can be numerous, but for some time what's given me confidence is the awareness that I've rarely been wrong as far as my intentions were concerned, the preliminary idea, the point of departure. [. . .] The only thing that worries me, as I've told you, is the idea of being 'out', but frankly I have no desire to be 'in'. If it happens, yes, but wanting it to happen is something I couldn't put up with. I just couldn't arrange things like that, just making films which are 'modern'. I approve of that in Godard because it's instinctive to him. In a dozen films Godard has never made any allusion to the past, even in his dialogue. Think about that: not a single Godard character has talked about their parents or their childhood – extraordinary. What's more, a study of what is not in Godard's films would be just as intriguing as a study of what he does put in them. He's an intensely modern person, and the fact that he's Swiss is important. One day someone ought to look at the Swiss aspect of Godard's films – the Switzerland which is the liking for lay-out, watches, modern gadgets, secret bank accounts and all that.

But nearly all the films which imitate Godard are indefensible because they miss the essential thing. They'll imitate his free and easy manner but forget – and for good reason – his despair. They'll imitate the word-play but not the malice.

My distrust of fashion extends to the language people are using nowadays. For instance, I can't bring myself to use a phrase which keeps creeping into *Cahiers*: 'On the level of. . . .' [. . .]

Cinema, for me, is an art of prose. Definitively. The thing is to make films that look good without having an air about them or having an air of nothing to them. I feel very strongly about that, and it's why I can't rise to the Antonioni bait – too immodest. Poetry irritates me, and when people send me letters with poems in them I throw them straight into the wastepaper basket. I like poetic prose – Cocteau, Audiberti, Genêt and Queneau – but only prose. I like cinema because it's prosaic, it's an indirect, unemphasized art, it conceals as much as it reveals. The film-makers I like all have at least this one thing in common – a shared modesty: Buñuel, who refuses to do more than one take; Welles, who shortens his 'beautiful' shots until they're virtually invisible; Bergman and Godard, who play down the importance of what they do by working at top speed; Rohmer, who works like a documentary director; Hitchcock, who's so involved emotionally with his films that he pretends he's only thinking about the money; Renoir, who affects to leave it all to chance – all of them instinctively reject the poetic approach. Just to finish what I'm saying about being 'modern', I don't know if I'm being reactionary, but I don't go along with the critical line which consists of saying: 'After such and such a film it will no longer be possible to watch neatly packaged stories, etc.' Although I like films as new as *Deux ou trois choses . . .*, *Man is not a Bird*, *Barrier* and so on, I think that if *The Magnificent Ambersons*, *Le Carrosse d'or* or *Red River* were here now, in '67, they would be the best films of the year. So I've decided to continue making the same kind of films, which involve either telling a story or pretending to tell a story – there's no difference. Deep-down I'm not 'modern', and if I pretended to be so it would be artificial. In any case I wouldn't be happy with it, and that's reason enough for not doing it.

Translated by David Wilson

Notes

1 *Cahiers* 138, December 1962, translated as (extracts) 'Interview with François Truffaut' in Graham, *The New Wave*.

2 Contrast Truffaut's views here with Jean-Louis Comolli's polemic against Lelouch, 'Lelouch, ou la bonne conscience retrouvée', *Cahiers* 180, July 1966, translated as 'Polemic: Lelouch, or the Clear Conscience', Ch. 9 in this volume.

3 See Eric Rohmer, 'L'Ancien et le nouveau: entretien avec Eric Rohmer', *Cahiers* 172, November 1965, translated as 'The Old and the New', Ch. 7 in this volume.

Part Two

American Cinema: Celebration

Introduction: The Apotheosis of *mise en scène*

As I point out in my general introduction to this volume, '*Cahiers du Cinéma* in the 1960s', the early 1960s saw a considerable increase in the amount of attention being paid to *Cahiers* outside France. One obvious reason was that the *nouvelle vague* had become the vanguard of European art cinema, with the international success of films by Alain Resnais, François Truffaut, Jean-Luc Godard, Claude Chabrol, Louis Malle, Jacques Demy and others (and in many ways regenerating interest in more established French film-makers like Jean Renoir, Robert Bresson, Jacques Becker, Jean-Pierre Melville). This new status of French cinema forced a process of recognition of the critical positions which formed the background of Godard, Truffaut, Chabrol and the other film-makers from *Cahiers*. As this focussing of attention on *Cahiers* went on, *Cahiers* itself was going through a period of supposed 'extremism' associated with newer critical figures. With André Bazin gone, and with Truffaut, Godard and others less active critically now that they were making movies, the work of critics such as Luc Moullet,[1] Jean Douchet, Fereydoun Hoveyda began to appear more frequently and to set a different tone in *Cahiers*.

In some ways, the main critical battles which *Cahiers* had fought in the 1950s had been won, especially of course those around authorship and the *politique des auteurs* and around *mise en scène*:[2] as Hoveyda says in 'Sunspots', 'Few people nowadays contest the fundamental importance of *mise en scène*'. These 'victories' provide the context for the supposed 'extremism' of the 1959–61 period, in which the *politique des auteurs* was rendered into a polemical tool for the validation of popular cinema and the concept of *mise en scène* began to take on new weight and, ultimately, new meanings. This was the period of intense critical debate in Britain and the USA.[3] In Britain Penelope Houston, the editor of *Sight and Sound*, began a defence of traditional liberal values in criticism, arguing that 'cinema is about the human situation, not about "spatial relationships"' and that criticism should examine films primarily in terms of their 'ideas'.[4]

113

In the same issue of *Sight and Sound* Richard Roud expressly confronted *Cahiers* criticism in 'The French Line',[5] attacking its extremism and trying to come to terms with the concept of *mise en scène*, but unable finally to move beyond a failure to comprehend the relationship between form and content which *Cahiers* posited through the idea. Claiming that *Cahiers* insisted upon the supremacy of form over content,[6] Roud reached the distressingly inadequate conclusion that 'the one thing they [*Cahiers* critics] have in common . . . and that we would gain most by adopting, is the firm belief that form is at least *as* important as content'.[7] Hoveyda had been relatively clear about the form, content and meaning relationship in 'Sunspots': 'It is not a question of setting the search for meanings against the study of form'. And Rivette was later to be very clear: 'We have often been accused of defending in *Cahiers mise en scène* in a pure state . . . What we tried to say, on the contrary, is that a film is a whole'.[8] This was the fundamental concept which was to inform both the work of Andrew Sarris in the USA and the work of *Movie* in Britain. Sarris argued in *The American Cinema* that the art of the cinema was 'not so much *what* as *how*. The *what* is some aspect of reality rendered mechanically by the camera. The *how* is what the French critics designate somewhat mystically as *mise en scène*. Auteur criticism is a reaction against sociological criticism which enthroned the *what* against the *how*. However, it would be equally fallacious to enthrone the *how* against the *what*. The whole point of a meaningful style is that it unifies the *what* and *how* into a personal statement'.[9] Chapter 6 of V. F. Perkins's *Film as Film* is titled '"How" Is "What"' and concludes: 'Synthesis here, where there is no distinction between how and what, content and form, is what interests us if we are interested in film as film. It is that unity to which we respond when film as fiction makes us sensitive to film as film'.[10]

Addressing himself to the *Sight and Sound* response to *Cahiers* and the new criticism in general, Sarris pointed out that 'No one seems to question the transcendent merits of the key European films which reflect new intellectual conceptions. What is mainly at issue is the American cinema. . . . At times, one suspects that the argument boils down to *Party Girl*'.[11] What was the 'extremism' that Hoveyda was accused of in his article on *Party Girl* and in the more 'theoretical' essay on *mise en scène*, 'Sunspots'? Calculatedly outrageous references to *Party Girl* offering 'a glimpse of the kingdom of heaven' aside, Hoveyda's approach boils down to what now seem relatively straightforward ideas about subject matter or theme, about authorship and about *mise en scène*. It was, of course, outrageous to defenders of a concept of cinema as being about 'ideas' to have the subject matter of *Party Girl*, as embodied in its script, dismissed as idiotic but, at the same time, irrelevant to its success. But this was only shocking if one did not imagine that in cinema, as Hoveyda puts it in 'Sunspots', '*mise en scène* can breathe real content into a seemingly trivial subject'. Also writing about Ray, a little later, V. F. Perkins was to make much the same kind

114

of point: 'The treatment may or may not have been successful: there is no such thing as an unsuccessful subject'.[12]

Some of Roud's objections in 'The French Line' attach to what he calls Hoveyda's *'critique des beautés'*: 'To Hoveyda, as to many French critics, *x* number of beautiful shots equals a great film'[13] (a view of Hoveyda which John Caughie seems to share when he writes of 'an almost hedonistic pleasure in visual delights'[14]). There is perhaps some truth in these complaints, though it seems to me that Hoveyda is working towards some synthesis of his points into an overall reading of *Party Girl*, towards, as Sarris puts it, 'a theory of the moral relationships which recur in all of Ray's films'.[15] Nevertheless, the process Hoveyda seems engaged in appears to be qualitatively different from, for example, Perkins' conception of 'significant form'.[16]

In a central passage of 'Sunspots' Hoveyda links the concept of the *auteur* inextricably with the concept of *mise en scène*: 'The originality of an *auteur* lies not in the subject matter he chooses, but in the technique he employs, in the *mise en scène*, through which everything is expressed on the screen . . . a film-maker's thought appears through his *mise en scène*. . . . *Mise en scène* is nothing other than the technique which each *auteur* invents to express himself and establish the specificity of his work'.

A year and a half later, in his 'Self-Criticism',[17] Hoveyda was to point out that 'the *politique des auteurs* has had its day: it was merely a staging post on the road to a new criticism' (although, as we shall see, the concept of the *auteur* retains an important, if now more ambiguous, place in his argument). In the sense that the *politique des auteurs* implied simply an 'analysis of themes', this critique is already present in 'Sunspots'. Is the implication that the new emphasis on *mise en scène* somehow undermines the pre-eminent status of the *auteur*? In effect, no, since the conception of the *auteur* which remains – the author as the untrammelled individual, as source of originality – is still, essentially, a romantic one: 'each artist invents his own technique through which he expresses himself'. Hoveyda goes to extreme lengths to dismiss the effects on film-making not just of sunspots but also of production constraints, generic conventions, all social and geographical factors, precisely the factors which, three years earlier, Bazin had argued were crucial to a consideration of American cinema[18] and which, ten years later in *Cahiers*, will assume crucial significance for analysis.[19]

However, as I point out in my general introduction to this volume, John Caughie is surely right to argue in his book *Theories of Authorship* that the new emphasis which begins to become clear here on cinematic specificity – *mise en scène* as defining the nature of cinema – marks the beginning of an important break.[20] First, a wedge is inserted between the *auteur* as a living individual and the *auteur* as a critical construct – what Peter Wollen was later to describe as the difference between 'Fuller or Hawks or Hitchcock, the directors' and '"Fuller" or "Hawks" or "Hitchcock", the structures named after them'.[21] As Hoveyda puts it in 'Sunspots', 'Lang . . .

evolves, changes, ages: his *permanence* exists only at the level of his *mise en scène'*. Second, as Caughie puts it:

> In many respects, the attention to *mise en scène*, even to the extent of a certain historically necessary formalism, is probably the most important positive contribution of *auteurism* to the development of a precise and detailed film criticism, engaging with the specific mechanisms of visual discourse, freeing it from literary models, and from the liberal commitments which were prepared to validate films on the basis of their themes alone.[22]

Third, Hoveyda's observation that '*mise en scène* is not required to represent the real but, through its technical procedures, to signify it' begins to question Bazin's ideas about the ontology of the photographic image and the realist nature of cinema it implied,[23] by pointing, however confusedly as yet, to important distinctions between representation and signification. 'In *auteurist* criticism *mise en scène* begins to be conceived as an effectivity, producing meanings and relating spectators to meanings, rather than as transparency, allowing them to be seen.'[24]

As we have seen, Hoveyda's work at this time was taken to represent an extreme position, a kind of apotheosis of *mise en scène*. But the positions represented by Michel Mourlet[25] and the 'MacMahonist tendency' (so called after the Paris cinema which specialized in showing a certain kind of popular cinema, very often American and, even when not, often associated with the adventure or melodrama genres[26]) were put at a distance even by someone like Hoveyda, as he makes clear. Mourlet's first article in *Cahiers* and the main statement of his general position, 'Sur un art ignoré', in 1959,[27] came with an editorial introduction pointing out that although the journal had a less rigorous and less common position than was often imagined, nevertheless Mourlet's article was at some remove from that position. It was a distance given visible form by the printing of the entire article in italics, an honour also accorded to his later 'In Defence of Violence'. But, said *Cahiers*, since *Cahiers* itself was so often considered extreme, it also liked to print material *it* considered extreme.

In fact, the MacMahonist 'extremism' had some close affinities with more generally accepted *Cahiers* positions (and this was, of course, why it was in *Cahiers* in the first place). Hoveyda, as we have seen, is fully in agreement with the MacMahonists on the pre-eminence of *mise en scène*. And, just as fundamentally, Mourlet and others, like Jacques Serguine, found their theses about the nature of cinema very firmly in Bazin's thinking about realism and the cinema as expounded in 'The Evolution of Film Language'.[28] With them, as with Bazin, there is the rejection of the 'deformation' of the real, particularly by any form of expressionism, and the embracing of ideas of cinema as the 'art of the true' and of basic assumptions about the progress of cinema, through the coming of sound and colour, towards greater 'realism'. The idea foregrounded in Mourlet's 'The Beauty of Knowledge' of Losey not inventing but rather *discovering*,

116

and of being style-less, has distinctly Bazinian overtones, as has Douchet's observation that Losey 'restores the camera to its original function as scientific instrument'.

However, while these familiar perceptions significantly inform Mourlet's two articles here (as well as Douchet's review of *Blind Date*), they are equally clearly being inflected in somewhat special ways. It is worth quoting again (as I did in Volume 1), Mourlet's account of the film experience as elaborated in 'Sur un art ignoré':

> The curtains open. The house goes dark. A rectangle of light presently vibrates before our eyes. Soon it is invaded by gestures and sounds. Here we are absorbed by that unreal space and time. More or less absorbed. The mysterious energy which sustains with varying felicities the swirl of shadow and light and their foam of sounds is called *mise en scène*. It is on *mise en scène* that our attention is set, organizing a universe, covering the screen – *mise en scène*, and nothing else. Like the shimmer of the notes of a piano piece. Like the flow of words of a poem. Like the harmonies and discords of the colours of a painting. From a subject, from a story, from 'themes', and even from the final draft of the script, there spurts forth a world of which the least one can ask is that it does not render vain the effort which gave it birth. The placing of the actors and the objects, their displacements within the frame, should express everything, as one sees in the supreme perfection of the two latest Fritz Lang films, *The Tiger of Eschnapur* and *The Indian Tomb*.[29]

A passage such as this gives some idea of what, in 'Sunspots', Hoveyda refers to as Mourlet's 'monstrous abstractions' and his 'theory of fascination'. Where, for Hoveyda, *mise en scène* embodies meaning, for Mourlet *mise en scène* is at the service of a mystical notion of man, the privileged object of the camera – a point central to 'In Defence of Violence' – being the actor in his physical presence – 'man become god in the *mise en scène*, a hymn to the glory of the body'. In this perspective the film-maker becomes judged by the ability of his *mise en scène* to fascinate us: 'the absorption of the consciousness by the spectacle is called fascination'.[30] The height of achievement of this cinema is then 'to deprive the spectator of all conscious distance, to throw him into a hypnotic state sustained by an incantation of gestures, looks, tiny movements of the face and body, vocal inflections, in the bosom of a universe of sparkling objects . . . in which one loses oneself in order to find oneself again, released, lucid and appeased'.[31] It was not just these ideas which were regarded with varying degrees of outrage and astonishment, but also the way in which these ideas were used to validate a conception of cinema which not only ennobled Lang, Preminger, Fuller and Walsh over Hitchcock, Welles, Eisenstein and Rossellini, but also claimed as among the supreme achievements of cinema movies such as Don Weis's *Adventures of Haji Baba* and Cecil B. de Mille's *Samson and Delilah* and the work of 'B' movie director Edward Ludwig and Italian 'peplum' specialist Vittorio Cottafavi.

'In Defence of Violence' is generally taken to represent Mourlet at his most extreme, most mystical, most fascistic: the passages about Charlton Heston as 'axiom' have become legendary – 'obviously one can go no further in the erection of a system based on one's own tastes', as Richard Roud commented.[32] A concern with violence was by no means new to *Cahiers*: the responsible treatment of violence was an important component of its admiration of American cinema, particularly film-makers like Nicholas Ray and Anthony Mann.[33] But Mourlet's deliberate choice of violent imagery and his obsession with violence, virility, heroism, conquest (and their implied misogyny) move the concern to a disturbing level. At the same time it is worth recognizing that some of the 'excess' associated with Hoveyda's 'Nicholas Ray's Reply: *Party Girl*' and with Mourlet's writing in relation to the concept of *mise en scène* may be valued in helping to raise questions rarely raised in critical writing at this time or since, questions relating to visual pleasure. As Caughie puts it, 'the attention to *mise en scène* gives criticism a way of accounting for the text as pleasurable, pointing to its fascination as well as its meaning'.[34]

1960–1 was a curious period for *Cahiers*, a period even more than usually full of contradictions: the work in this section celebrating the qualities of (primarily) American cinema needs to be seen alongside contemporaneous writing such as Luc Moullet on Godard and André S. Labarthe on *Les Bonnes femmes* in Part I[35] and the growing interest in new kinds of cinema and in Brecht which becomes clear in Part IV.[36] The crypto-fascistic tendencies of the MacMahonists come together with the potential for radicalism of Brecht in the figure of Joseph Losey,[37] who emerges as the consummate film-maker in both of Mourlet's articles (and in the work of the MacMahonists in general[38]) and in Douchet's article on *Blind Date*. Douchet himself points up some of the contradictions very neatly. On the one hand, he begins by almost self-consciously restating, in very similar language, Mourlet's remarks about Losey as scientific researcher for knowledge, as observer rather than interpreter of the world, then proceeds, as if consciously recalling Hoveyda's complaint about Mourlet's lack of 'specific examples', to show what Mourlet's thesis might look like in practical critical detail. On the other hand, Douchet places Losey in the context of Brecht's comments about emotion and thought – apparently very far removed from Mourlet's ideas about fascination and loss of consciousness – claiming Losey for a rational Left, particularly in his lack of sentimentalism.

Despite the similarity of some ideas, Douchet was not specially close, ultimately, to Mourlet and the MacMahonists – there are very clear differences, for example, in their choice of language. And Douchet's work on Hitchcock[39] is in many ways much more in the mainstream of *Cahiers* writing. He draws very directly on, for example, Claude Chabrol's and Eric Rohmer's mid-1950s work on Hitchcock: Chabrol had already spoken of the courtyard of *Rear Window* as a projection of the James Stewart character and discussed the three sections of the window blind,[40] and Rohmer and Chabrol in their book on Hitchcock had taken *Rear Window* as a metaphor for 'the very essence of cinema . . . *seeing, spectacle*'.[41] At the same time, Douchet's emphasis on catharsis and the therapeutic places him much closer to Robin Wood's 1960s work on Hitchcock,[42] even if Douchet's thesis lacks the familiar, almost obsessive, *moral* emphasis so characteristic of Wood's criticism of this period. However, Douchet's discussion of voyeurism and desire, and more generally of the importance of the audience relationship, begins to point forward to a later, and rather different, essentially psychoanalytically-based, Hitchcock criticism.[43]

Notes

1 Luc Moullet is represented in this volume by Ch. 1, 'Jean-Luc Godard' and Ch. 17, 'Questions about American Cinema', a discussion between the older *Cahiers* critics from the 1950s, but see also, for example, his 1959 article, 'Samuel Fuller: In Marlowe's Footsteps', Ch. 20 in Volume 1.

2 See my Introduction to Volume 1 and my 'Introduction: *Cahiers du Cinéma* in the 1960s', in this volume.

3 See 'Introduction: *Cahiers du Cinéma* in the 1960s' and its note 2, in this volume.

4 Penelope Houston, 'The Critical Question', *Sight and Sound*, vol. 29, no. 4, Autumn 1960, p. 163.

5 Richard Roud, 'The French Line', *Sight and Sound*, vol. 29, no. 4, Autumn 1960. Cf. Ernest Callenbach, 'Editor's Notebook: "Turn On! Turn On!"', *Film Quarterly*, vol. 16, no. 3, Spring 1962.

6 Roud, *op. cit.*, p. 167.

7 Ibid., p. 171. Roud persisted in his idea that there was perhaps something aberrant about the importance attached by the French critics and film-makers to *mise en scène*. Much later, talking to Truffaut about Henri Langlois and the Cinémathèque Française, Roud comments: 'Langlois always said that the fact that he showed films without subtitles was what taught you all *mise en scène* because, not understanding what was being said, you really had to concentrate on how the films were put together' (Richard Roud, *A Passion for Films: Henri Langlois and the Cinémathèque Française*, London, Secker & Warburg; New York, Viking Press, 1983, p. 98). This may sound like a neat idea, but of course these critics also talked about *mise en scène* in relation to French cinema, as well as seeing plenty of subtitled or dubbed films outside the Cinémathèque.

8 Jacques Rivette, in 'La Critique: Débat', *Cahiers* 126, December 1961, p. 16, quoted at greater length in my 'Introduction: *Cahiers du Cinéma* in the 1960s' in this volume.

9 Andrew Sarris, *The American Cinema: Directors and Directions 1929–1968*, New York, E. P. Dutton, 1968, p. 36.

10 V. F. Perkins, *Film as Film*, Harmondsworth, Penguin Books, 1972, p. 133.

11 Andrew Sarris, 'The Director's Game', *Film Culture*, no. 22–3, Summer 1961, p. 79.

12 V. F. Perkins, 'The Cinema of Nicholas Ray', *Movie* 9, May 1963, p. 5, reprinted in Cameron, *Movie Reader*.

13 Roud, 'The French Line', p. 170.

14 Caughie, *Theories of Authorship*, p. 13.

15 Sarris, 'The Director's Game', p. 79.

16 See, for example, Perkins' discussion of Ray's *Johnny Guitar* in *Film as Film*, pp. 77–9.

17 Ch. 25 in this volume.

18 See André Bazin, 'Sur la politique des auteurs', *Cahiers* 70, April 1957, translated as 'On the *politique des auteurs*', Ch. 31 in Volume 1, also in Graham, *The New Wave*.

19 Exemplary in this context is the collective text 'John Ford's *Young Mr Lincoln*', *Cahiers* 223, August 1970, translated in *Screen*, vol. 13, no. 3, Autumn 1972, reprinted in Nichols, *Movies and Methods*, in *Screen Reader 1*, and in Gerald Mast and Marshall Cohen, *Film Theory and Criticism: Introductory Readings*, New York, Oxford University Press, 2nd ed., 1979.

20 Caughie, *Theories of Authorship*, Part One: 'Auteurism: Introduction'.

21 Peter Wollen, *Signs and Meaning in the Cinema*, London, Secker & Warburg; Bloomington, Indiana University Press, 2nd ed., 1972, p. 168.

22 Caughie, *Theories of Authorship*, p. 13.

23 See André Bazin, 'The Ontology of the Photographic Image' in Bazin, *What is Cinema? Vol. 1*.

24 Caughie, *Theories of Authorship*, p. 13.

25 Michel Mourlet, critic and novelist, was an active contributor to *Cahiers* 1959–60, his main articles being: 'Sur un art ignoré', *Cahiers* 98, August 1959; 'Trajectoire de Fritz Lang', *Cahiers* 99, September 1959, translated as 'Fritz Lang's Trajectory' in Stephen Jenkins, *Fritz Lang: The Image and the Look*, London, British Film Institute, 1981; 'Le Mythe d'Aristarque', *Cahiers* 103, January 1960; 'Apologie de la violence', *Cahiers* 107, May 1960, translated in this volume, Ch. 12; and 'Beauté de la connaissance', *Cahiers* 111, September 1960, translated in this volume, Ch. 14. From 1961 to 1963 Mourlet was one of the editors of *Présence du Cinéma*, a journal begun in 1959 and publishing twenty-five issues up to 1967, when it folded. When it began, *Présence du Cinéma* published critics associated with *Cahiers* such as Pierre Kast, Louis Marcorelles, Luc Moullet, Jacques Doniol-Valcroze, Michel Delahaye as well as critics associated with *Positif* like Roger Tailleur and Robert Benayoun. From late 1961, when Mourlet became associated with it editorially, its complexion changed somewhat, publishing in 1961–3 special issues on Vittorio Cottafavi (no. 9), Preminger (no. 11), Don Weis (no. 12), Raoul Walsh (no. 13), Riccardo Freda (no. 17), Joseph L. Mankiewicz (no. 18), Samuel Fuller (no. 19). Later issues on Dwan, Tourneur and De Mille confirmed its status as speaking for the MacMahonist tendency. Mourlet's first novel, *D'exil et de mort*, Paris, La Table Ronde, 1961, was published at this time.

26 For a statement of the MacMahonist position see Jacques Serguine, 'Education du spectateur, ou L'Ecole du MacMahon', *Cahiers* 111, September 1960.

27 'Sur un art ignoré', *Cahiers* 98, August 1959.

28 For Bazin's writings in this area, see Ch. 3, note 2, in this volume.

29 Michel Mourlet, 'Sur un art ignoré', p. 27.

30 Ibid., p. 31.

31 Ibid., p. 30.

32 Roud, 'The French Line', p. 171.

33 See, for example, Jacques Rivette, 'Notes sur une révolution', *Cahiers* 54, Christmas 1955, translated as 'Notes on a Revolution', Ch. 8 in Volume 1, and André Bazin, 'Beauté d'un western', *Cahiers* 55, January 1956, translated as 'Beauty of a Western', Ch. 23 in Volume 1.

34 Caughie, *Theories of Authorship*, p. 13.

35 Chs 1 and 2 respectively in this volume.

36 See especially Chs 23 and 24 in this volume. In Ch. 23 Bernard Dort specifically denounces Hoveyda's and especially Mourlet's 'view of the world and of art which is magical' and a view of cinema as a 'privileged art'.

37 See my comments on Losey and Brecht in my 'Introduction: *Cahiers du Cinéma* in the 1960s', in this volume.

38 Jacques Serguine ends his 'Education du spectateur' (see note 26 above) thus: 'One day, on the screen, for the first time, I saw a man sobbing. . . . The film was *The Prowler*. I cannot talk about it, because words would betray it, as they would betray *The Big Night*. What I know is that it did not become schematic, like Lang, did not disperse, like Preminger, did not let itself become corrupted, like Fuller. What it showed – and its frankness and honesty were as upsetting as a punch from a fist – was a being greater than the heroes and more beautiful than the gods: this was a man. Cinema is the art of the true: Joseph Losey is its first artist' (p. 44).

39 Douchet had contributed several important articles on Hitchcock: 'La Troisième clé d'Hitchcock I', *Cahiers* 99, September 1959, and 'La Troisième clé d'Hitchcock II', *Cahiers* 102, December 1959. Douchet's later book (*Alfred Hitchcock*, Paris, Editions de l'Herne, 1967) concentrates on *Vertigo*, *The Birds*, *Psycho*, *North by Northwest*.

40 Claude Chabrol, 'Les Choses sérieuses', *Cahiers* 46, April 1955, translated as 'Serious Things', Ch. 18 in Volume 1.

41 Eric Rohmer and Claude Chabrol, *Hitchcock*, Paris, Editions Universitaires, 1957, translated as *Hitchcock, The First Forty-Four Films*, New York, Frederick Ungar, 1979, p. 124.

42 Robin Wood, *Hitchcock's Films*, London, Zwemmer; New York, A. S. Barnes, first published in 1965, but Wood had already published articles on Hitchcock and, indeed, the same issue of *Cahiers* with Douchet's 'Hitch and his Audience', *Cahiers* 113, November 1960, carried an analysis of *Psycho* by Wood, 'Psychoanalyse de *Psycho*'.

43 See, especially, Laura Mulvey, 'Visual Pleasure and Narrative Cinema', *Screen*, vol. 16, no. 3, Autumn 1975, an article rarely cited these days without the epithet 'seminal', reprinted in Karyn Kay and Gerald Peary, *Women and the Cinema*, New York, E. P. Dutton, 1977 and (abridged) in Tony Bennett, Susan Boyd-Bowman, Colin Mercer, Janet Woollacott, *Popular Television and Film*, London, British Film Institute/Open University, 1981. See also Raymond Bellour, 'Hitchcock, the Enunciator', *Camera Obscura*, no. 2, Fall 1977 (an approach to *Marnie*) and 'Psychosis, Neurosis, Perversion', *Camera Obscura*, nos. 3–4, 1979 (an analysis of *Psycho*). Sandy Flitterman, 'Woman, Desire and the Look: Feminism and the Enunciative Apparatus in Cinema', *Ciné-Tracts*, vol. 2, no. 1, Fall 1978, draws on Mulvey and Bellour's first article. Bellour's second article is a point of departure for Barbara Klinger, '*Psycho*: the Institutionalization of Female Sexuality', *Wide Angle*, vol. 15, no. 1, 1982, while Annette Kuhn comments upon it extensively in her *Women's Pictures*, London, Routledge & Kegan Paul, 1982.

11 | Fereydoun Hoveyda: 'Nicholas Ray's Reply: *Party Girl*

('La Réponse de Nicholas Ray', *Cahiers du Cinéma* 107, May 1960)

> But do you not realize that displeasures and the most mortal of sorrows are hidden beneath the crimson?[1]
>
> Bossuet

Since November 1958, we have been waiting impatiently for a follow-up to the rather disjointed interview which the author of *Rebel Without a Cause* gave to *Cahiers*.[2] Nicholas Ray has at last given it to us, in the most perfect form imaginable – that of a brilliant film.

It is, however – and I readily concede the point to those who are critical of the film – a commissioned piece with an imposed screenplay. Since one knows about the problems that various directors have encountered at MGM and about the way producers like Joe Pasternak operate, it is easy enough to guess that Nicholas Ray wasn't able to introduce anything much in the way of changes to the script or to alter anything at all once shooting was over. If one were to transpose it into literary terms, the story, adapted by George Wells (who so clearly lacks the 'Herbert' of genius) from a short story by Leo Katcher, would seem ridiculous and silly. I accept that too. But do we go to the cinema in order to translate into words the images we see? I shall carefully avoid, therefore, giving any summary of the story of *Party Girl* except in the kind of terms used in publications like *Semaine de Paris* or *L'Officiel des spectacles*,[3] that is in cryptic phrases like 'Rivalry between gangsters in 1930s Chicago' or – if you want precise details – 'Through his sincere love for a young dance-girl, a crooked lawyer is brought back to the path of duty'. We should note in passing our author's constant predilection for the melodramatic situations beloved of scriptwriters of 'bohemian' films: meeting a hot-blooded gypsy girl brings a wayward Romany back to the straight and narrow; the love of an immigrant Swedish girl returns an anti-social cowboy to society; a young girl gives a rebel a cause, etc.[4] Reduced to this level, the subject of *Party Girl* is much the same as in all Nicholas Ray's films. So much for the story. Coming after *Underworld, Scarface* and a long line of gangster films, *Party Girl* could, on a superficial viewing, give rise to numerous pointless comparisons which would prove only one thing: that the person who makes these comparisons frequents the Cinémathèque. One could add that since Robert Taylor was the star of *Johnny Eager*, Nicholas Ray has plagiarized Mervyn LeRoy. In spite of that, or perhaps because of it, Ray's new film proves the mastery of its author and reveals the very essence of an art which is still unrecognized, as our friend Mourlet would say,[5] though even he does not much appreciate the CinemaScope and the Metrocolor.

Party Girl has an idiotic story. So what? If the substratum of cinematic work was made up simply of plot convolutions unravelling on the screen, then we could just annex the Seventh Art to literature, be content with illustrating novels and short stories (which is precisely what happens in a great many films we do not admire), and hand over *Cahiers* to literary critics. I am not attempting to reopen here an old debate which is both pointless and of no interest. But with the regularity of a pendulum, some critics keep harping back to how necessary it is not to neglect the importance of the screenplay, the acting, the production system. Why not, while they are about it, take into account the influence of the planets?[6]

Of course, cinema is at one and the same time a technique, an industry and an art; and like all art, it borrows from other arts. But I am not aware that the diversity of production systems and types of subject-matter has stopped masterpieces reaching us from every latitude. This digression doesn't really take me away from my point. Precisely because *Party Girl* comes just at the right moment to remind us that what constitutes the essence of cinema is nothing other than *mise en scène*. It is *mise en scène* which gives expression to everything on the screen, transforming, as if by magic, a screenplay written by someone else and imposed on the director into something which is truly an author's film.

What is immediately striking in *Party Girl* (dubbed in France with the idiotic title *Traquenard*) is the graceful ease with which it unfolds, the perfect unity of its aesthetic, and the uncluttered immediacy of what it has to say. Ray's need of instant and direct expression, his *discontinuous* technique and rejection of conventions, are once again in evidence. As in our author's previous films, there are frequent lapses of continuity. The scenes relating to the lawyer Farrell's recovery are simply slapdash, no doubt filmed by an assistant. As Vicki Gaye, the dance-girl, arrives at the Swedish hospital, a grotesquely bandaged man comes out through the main entrance leaning on the arm of a nurse, having so obviously waited for the cameraman's signal; later, there is an insert blown up from 16mm and shot in Venice by the notorious Fitzpatrick. Worse still, the back projections seen through the windows of sharp-lined period limousines show the aerodynamic shapes of modern cars. It was out of the question, of course, to reconstruct old Chicago, so Ray takes the precaution of announcing in a flamboyant caption: 'Chicago in the early thirties'. What do we see? A lowish-angle shot of skyscrapers painted on a backdrop with, on the left of the screen, a flashing neon sign suggesting the entrance to a nightclub. The camera tilts down and pans left towards the neon sign. Then there is a long tracking shot closing in on the scene as if to stress even more that from now on the action of the film will take place inside the studio sets and, within them, inside the characters. The few exterior sequences are also filmed in the studio, either in confined spaces or in front of mediocre back projections. Yet the Chicago of the 1930s remains as present as in *Scarface*. It is Ray's *mise en scène* that recreates this invisible presence, through an astonishing use of colour and decor, by an exaggeration of atmosphere (as in the opening sequence at the gangster Rico Angelo's party), by the excesses of the set decoration (Rico's apartment is crammed with showy furniture and oppressively draped with heavy fabrics), by the intrusion of garish costumes, etc. These overbearing interiors, overflowing with gold and crimson, refer us back to a past epoch. I don't want to lapse into a facile chauvinism, but I owe it to myself[7] to point out the heaps of Persian carpets, the miniatures which make up the design of the upholstery on the gangster's armchair and, opposite it, the photographs of dance-girls in their richly gilded frames.

We already know how important decors are for Ray. Didn't he have the living-room in *Rebel without a Cause* modelled exactly on his own living-room because James Dean behaved in it exactly in the way he imagined he would in the film? The last scene between Rico and Farrell takes place in the Southside Citizens Club, in which multi-coloured streamers hang down from the ceiling and confetti litters the floor. This end-of-party atmosphere, and the coat that Rico – like Napoleon on the evening after Waterloo – has slung over his shoulders, are brilliantly suggestive of impending defeat. Another example: the scene on the bridge: Farrell recalls his childhood for Vicki, while in the background the interlocking girders stand out, made to look slightly bluish by Lee Le Blanc's special effects; the whole of this scene is bathed in an atmosphere of unreality reminiscent of the best science fiction films. I will add a word on colour: there seems to be a constant desire to separate the world of the gangsters (in which really garish colours are consistently used), as for example in *Hot Blood*, from the world of the lovers (in which the hues are softened), as in the sequence in the empty mansion in *Rebel without a Cause*. Jean Douchet has pointed out that the real moments of tension occur in those scenes in which the couple are brought together, and that the moments of relief are in fact those when we witness the physical violence of the gangsters.

There is more: an absolutely new element comes into play here, one which proves that in Ray's mind it was not simply a matter of two actions opposed to one another, or of a system like connected chemical flasks, in which the salvation of one of the protagonists would necessarily bring about the destruction of the other.

There are, in *Party Girl*, real gags. One could of course feel the author's sense of humour coming through in *The Lusty Men*, *Run for Cover* or even

124

Wind Across the Everglades. But you couldn't really say there were gags. Here it's quite different. When, for example, Canetto goes into Vicki's dressing room (while Farrell is in prison), he leans on one of the bulbs which decorate the mirror and burns himself. I could quote many other scenes: Rico's breakfast, the way he 'gets even' with Jean Harlow, Canetto's cigarette when he's in court, etc.. A young Persian director, Feri Farzaneh, even saw a deliberately burlesque element in the portrayal of the gangsters. I would not say that he is entirely wrong. I am thinking, for example, of Cookie La Motte's arrival, reminiscent of Marlon Brando in *Guys and Dolls*; of Rico in the back seat of his car, assuming an Arkadin pose;[8] of the final scene between Rico and the couple which dissolves into a kind of burlesque ballet, improvised in front of the bay windows. It isn't a question of comedy but of finding an effective way of stressing the absurdity of the gangsters' world.

There are torrents of inventiveness. Every sequence is a cascade of ideas (in the *mise en scène*, of course!) which advance the action or suddenly imprint on a shot a particular emotive quality. In the dressing room a girl (played by Ray's wife) casually steals some make-up remover; the money given to the dance-girls in powder compacts piled up on the little table in the bedroom; the shadow of the policeman who by turning his head indicates the arrival of Farrell, out of frame; the fur coat which Vicki trails along and finally lets drop; the man sketching during the courtroom scene; the drops of water from the bouquet of roses that cling to Vicki's face; the flashlight picking out the gangsters as they run down Cookie La Motte's boys; the little flame in the grate reflected in the corner of the mirror as Vicki and Farrell kiss, etc. Out of this hotchpotch I will pick two random examples which demonstrate clearly that Ray has little faith in editing devices in themselves, and that he doesn't consider dissolves adequate for suggesting the passage of time. On the evening of Vicki's birthday, Farrell is summoned by the gangsters. When he gets back, much later, Vicki, who has been waiting for him, comes out of the bedroom into the dark living-room, still wearing all her clothes but *barefoot*. Another example: Vicki meets Farrell (a prisoner) in a hotel room and tries to convince him. Dissolve. We then see them still talking together, but one can just make out the impressions their heads have left on the pillow. These are tiny details, it is true, but as a certain kind of publicity material would put it, they are details which change everything.

The obsession with abstraction which Rivette has already drawn attention to in *The Lusty Men*[9] is exhibited here in all its glory. The shortest route between two points being a straight line, Nicholas Ray doesn't hesitate: he moves, as quickly as he can, straight to the essentials, admirably served here by the 'horizontal line' which is what fascinates him in CinemaScope. A few shots before the titles get the plot off the mark as sharply as the starter's gun at the beginning of a race. A few brief images, intercut with concise dialogue, reveal the characters in all their depth. Within five or six minutes we already know all we need to know about the three principal characters: Vicki, Farrell and Rico. We understand right from the start that Vicki's attitude is a way of protecting herself after her harrowing experiences as an adolescent; that the gang leader, Rico Angelo, is attached to Farrell, his lawyer, in a way which is somehow ambivalent. A single shot, a back view of Farrell talking to the city dignitaries, is sufficient to evoke the corruption that was rife in 1930s Chicago.

'The camera,' said Nicholas Ray in his interview, 'is the microscope which allows you to discover the "melody of the look".'[10] For him, as for Fritz Lang, the look has an essential role to play.

Vicki Gaye, standing beside Canetto who is playing dice, looks to her right and, with her, we discover Farrell's back. When a moment later she asks him to take her home, she hears him say something like, 'Are you going to leave Canetto after taking his money?', as if he had eyes in the back of his head; and Vicki comments: 'You don't miss much'. Thus the first encounter between the two protagonists has already taken place through the look. Similarly, when Farrell goes to ask for a star billing for Vicki, the camera pauses on Rico, sitting eating his breakfast, and in his look we read not just a kind of dismay, revealing the ambivalent nature of his attachment to the lawyer, but also, as Simon Mizrahi,[11] Ray's most ardent admirer, has pointed out to me, Rico's certainty that he has found in the dance-girl an effective way of putting pressure on Farrell. I could quote a multitude of examples: Vicki's touching expression at the end of the sequence in Farrell's apartment, when she lets her fur coat fall to the ground; the lawyer's moment of hesitation before he draws a cover over the sleeping dance-girl; Farrell sensing Vicki's look during the courtroom scene, etc.

Close shots, cut into sequences to underline the 'melody of the look', lead me to other observations: there are very few close-ups or distance shots in *Party Girl*. Like *Run for Cover* and most of Ray's other films, it is made up almost entirely of framings which cut off the characters at knee level. There is also a systematic use of dissolves and an almost complete absence of montage. What I mean is that editing isn't an essential part of the film. As in Rossellini's *Viaggio in Italia* and *India*, editing is not an element of language but simply of the exposition of facts.

But if sets, colour, inventiveness and framing constitute important elements of *mise en scène*, the raw materials remain the actors. We've known since *They Live By Night* how good Ray is at capturing the expression of a face, at betraying a feeling by a gesture. Thus Cyd Charisse's dance comes across as a continuation of her taunting of Farrell. A masterful direction of actors: remember the transfiguration of Curt Jürgens in *Bitter Victory* or of Robert Taylor here. As Rohmer noted in a discussion of *Bigger than Life*,[12] Nicholas Ray excels 'by a slight rallentando, a sudden speeding up or an imperceptible pause, in conferring on the simplest gesture the mark of eternity'. After listening to Farrell's confession, Vicki gets up and walks round the sofa; when she is opposite the lawyer, she stops and lets her coat fall to the floor. How can one describe in words what *mise en scène* can convey in a few seconds? No unnecessary words, just expressions, significant gestures, concise dialogue. Not surprisingly, therefore, dubbing destroys the internal harmony of the pattern of relationships so skilfully sketched in by Ray. Camera movements scan the development of the plot without either underlining or predicting it, without the spectator feeling in the slightest way disturbed.

A highly developed pursuit of the aesthetic combined with a contempt for obsessive technique. Ray is no René Clément. It is not continuity or unjustified big close-ups that interest him, but quite simply his actors' expressions. And what do these actors express? A 'homely ideal'? With due respect to our friend Marcorelles, I think he is mistaken when he sees in *Party Girl* merely 'a prodigal talent wasted on rubbish'.[13] Abstraction does not mean simplification. And if I say that the subject of a film matters very little to me, it is because I am convinced that *mise en scène* can transfigure it. And if I add that the whole of cinema is ultimately *mise en scène*, it is precisely because that is how everything is expressed on the screen. And if people insist on thinking that *Party Girl* is rubbish, then I proclaim, 'Long live this rubbish which so dazzles my eyes, fascinates my heart and gives me a glimpse of the kingdom of heaven.' What indeed could be more beautiful than two people struggling against themselves and breaking down the barriers they had ingeniously constructed to shut themselves off from the world (or to dominate it, which comes to the same thing)? For in the last analysis Nicholas Ray's authority is such that he can shape an anecdote which is no better or worse than any other so that it conforms to his own view of the world, his own conception of human relationships. The characters of *Party Girl* are near relatives of those in *Run for Cover*, *They Live by Night* or *Rebel without a Cause*, 'strangers here on earth',[14] people who are wounded in the depths of their being, who have enclosed themselves in a total solitude as if to protect themselves more effectively from a hostile world.

Right from the beginning, Farrell throws down a challenge to this woman to whom he is attracted and of whom he is suspicious. When she comes to his office to thank him, he almost chases her out: 'Selling your pride for $400, that's cheap.' Wounding a cat's pride is a serious matter, and the challenge becomes a bond once the other party picks up the glove. After the trial Vicki counter-attacks: 'You sell your pride higher than I do'; and 'You want pity? You have mine'. From then on they are locked in a combat which leads to love. Vicki and Farrell try to earn a reciprocal esteem. Wounded self-respect is what these two people have been suffering from ever since childhood, and what they are trying to compensate for. 'I feel as if I've been robbed,' observes Farrell as he describes the incident which caused his limp, just as the young protagonist of *Run for Cover* (who is wounded in the leg) thinks the world owes him everything. There is always in Ray's heroes a feeling of inferiority compensated for by a frenetic search for superiority and the domination of others. James

Mason gave us an amazing example of this in one of the finest clinical studies ever presented on the screen: *Bigger than Life*. The violence which is so often a feature of Ray's work revealed in that film the true extent of its significance, with *mise en scène* highlighting Mason's outbursts of aggression (as in the sequence of the father teaching the son). The violence of James Dean and the adolescents of *Rebel without a Cause*, of John Derek in *Run for Cover*, or of Jesse James,[15] expresses quite simply a strong feeling of inferiority and guilt, a lack which these characters experience as a kind of punishment for which the whole world seems ultimately responsible.

In *Party Girl*, though, love will help the heroes to survive the ordeal and to glimpse a life-raft. Vicki becomes, as it were, a woman again, but for that to be possible her ambition has first to be satisfied (thanks to Farrell, she gets star billing in Rico's club). Farrell tries to sever his connection with the gang, but to do that he must rid himself of the feeling of inferiority that made him pick up Rico as the quickest way to success. His limp becomes, from then on, a symbol of this infantile fixation; and his cure is, so to speak, the hinge of a diptych, the first panel of which illustrates an internal struggle and the second an external combat (against the gang and in defence of the woman he loves).

As for the third person involved in this drama, the gangster Rico Angelo, he tends to see in Farrell what he himself is lacking: the intellectual superiority that he does not have and a certain physical attractiveness that has a strong appeal for him. Does this show a homosexual tendency? Perhaps. We should in any case notice the affective nature of the attachment Rico feels for his lawyer. Even in the closing shots of the film, Rico asks nothing more than to allow himself to be convinced that Farrell has not betrayed him. For his part, Farrell remains under the spell of the admiration he felt as a child for the 'boss' of a gang of kids and the hatred he now feels as a result of being saved by this man and of owing him his success.

What the crimson and gold that all these characters dress up in conceals, then, is the secret depths of their suffering. This psychological complexity emerges from the film and not from a twisted imagination. To appreciate this, it is enough to look back at some of the key scenes scattered through the film: the dance-girls in the dressing-room, the lawyer's office, the gangster's breakfast, Nick's speakeasy, the bridge, the Southside Citizens Club, the confrontation of the two women, Rico's welcome-home gift, the train compartment on the Springfield Express, the encounters in the prison and in a hotel room, the final discussion with Rico. Some points may appear obscure – for example, the precise significance of the watch. Clearly, when it appears in the Canetto trial sequence and in the final discussion between Farrell and Rico, it evokes the image of the father which psychoanalysts are so fond of (Bergman used the same symbol in *Wild Strawberries*). But there is something else here too: the memory of Rico rescuing Farrell from the clutches of the kids who were trying to snatch the pocket-watch his father had just given him. The watch, and the walking stick, have become protective attributes, fetishes which by arousing sympathy permit their owner to triumph over a hostile world. The first time Farrell offers the pocket-watch to Canetto after the trial scene, it is in imitation of Vicki's gesture when she gave the money back. Farrell is here abandoning an object he is ashamed of. But when in the final shot of the film he gives his own wristwatch to Stewart, the attorney, it is because the watch-attribute has become unnecessary. He is aware that he has won the fight against himself: no need now for subterfuge!

These few reflections underline the relationship between *Party Girl* and the rest of Nicholas Ray's work. Truffaut, writing about *Johnny Guitar*, has observed: 'All his films tell the same story, the story of a violent man who wants to stop being violent, and his relationship with a woman who has more moral strength than himself, since the hero is invariably weak, a child-man.'[16] I would go a little further than that: all Nicholas Ray's heroes have, in their character, a masochistic side which is more or less apparent. Their violence is merely the counterpart of this masochism. If the inability to be happy reaches a peak in the case of people like Major Brand, Captain Leith,[17] Jesse James or the teacher in *Bigger than Life*, self-destruction is no less present in the other characters. Farrell and Rico are no exception to this fixed pattern. They punish themselves in their own way. But in this respect there are important differences between *Party Girl* and Ray's other films. Previously, each hero's victory left a bitter taste. Leaving aside Curt Jürgens and Sterling Hayden, let's just think about the three James's: Cagney, Dean and Mason.[18] The success of one is often counterbalanced by the death of another (here, as in *Rebel without a Cause* and *Run for Cover*). The films almost always end with an air of pessimism which, at the last moment, undercuts the resolution of the moral crisis. Ray shows himself to be as masochistic as his heroes, and seems to get caught up in a vicious circle. There is nothing like that here: the forty-year-old lawyer and his girlfriend emerge from their struggle completely victorious. One could of course set against this victory the denunciation and death of Rico. But in this new kind of triangle, in which one of the masculine sides has set his sights not on the woman but on the other man, things are not so simple: there is at one moment a real declaration of war between the protagonists. Thus, in *Party Girl*, Nicholas Ray continues and develops his theme.

Is it necessary to add that *Party Girl* is really a tragedy, a Cornelian tragedy as Eric Rohmer would say?[19] Or that Ray mixes genres with a disconcerting ease; that one is aware, as in some of his other films, of a need for lyrical expression, of a return to strong emotions, to melodrama, to a symbolic-objective exteriorization of feelings which is sometimes very basic? But I should perhaps insist above all on one aspect, on the 'cinema and nothing but cinema' that Godard likes to see in Ray's films.[20] The beauty of *Party Girl* does in fact exist only through cinema, a particularly modern cinema which brushes aside all conventions as if they were just the icy perfection sought for by those who have no heart. A cinema which is not afraid of exaggerating, of sacrificing everything to expression and to the effectiveness of a reflex or a look.

I said at the beginning of this article that Nicholas Ray's new film is in its way a continuation of the interview which *Cahiers* published in 1958. *Party Girl* does indeed reply, in colours on celluloid, to the *big* question: the ultimate meaning of an already extensive body of work. Should we be looking for this meaning in Ray's thematic? I have already talked about the subjects he uses. Solitude, violence, moral crises, love, struggles against oneself, self-analysis, the common features of the characters and their preoccupations in the different films – in a word, the constant factors of this universe – have nothing original about them, and belong to an arsenal shared by all the film-makers whom we admire. So where can we locate the deep meaning of his work? *Party Girl* shows us in the clearest way possible: we must look for it purely and simply in the *mise en scène* – not in the apparent answer that Ray gives for the mystery of the world and its inhabitants, but in the way in which he questions this world and imitates life. It is not by examining immediate significance that we can come into contact with the best films, but by looking at the personal style of each author. It should be clear that I think *Party Girl* is Ray's most interesting film to date.

Translated by Norman King

Notes

1 The word used is *pourpre*, purple or crimson: the reference is to the ecclesiastical colour, but crimson is preferred here as it relates more accurately to Ray's colour scheme.

2 'Entretien avec Nicholas Ray', by Charles Bitsch, *Cahiers* 89, November 1958, extracts translated as 'Interview with Nicholas Ray' in Volume 1, Ch. 15.

3 Rival commercial weekly magazines listing plays and films, etc., with potted plot summaries.

4 References to Ray's *Hot Blood*, *Run for Cover* and *Rebel without a Cause* respectively.

5 The reference is to Michel Mourlet, 'Sur un art ignoré', *Cahiers* 98, August 1959.

6 The title of Hoveyda's article 'Les Taches du soleil', *Cahiers* 110, August 1960, translated as 'Sunspots', Ch. 13 in this volume, refers precisely to this point.

7 Hoveyda is referring to his Persian nationality.

8 The reference is to Orson Welles's 1955 film, *Mr Arkadin*, known in Britain also as *Confidential Report*.

9 The reference is to Jacques Rivette, 'De l'invention', *Cahiers* 27, October 1953, translated as 'On Imagination' in Volume 1, Ch. 10.

10 'Interview with Nicholas Ray', p. 123.

11 Simon Mizrahi was later programming assistant to Henri Langlois at the Cinémathèque Française.

12 Eric Rohmer, 'Ou bien . . . ou bien', *Cahiers* 69, March 1957.

13 Louis Marcorelles, 'Lettre de Londres', *Cahiers* 94, April 1959, p. 40.

14 Nicholas Ray, quoted in unidentified interview; cf. 'I have only one working

title: *I'm a Stranger Here Myself*, quoted in Colin McArthur, *Underworld USA*, London, Secker & Warburg/BFI; New York, Viking, 1972, p. 124. The line 'I'm a stranger here myself' is from *Johnny Guitar*: see V. F. Perkins, 'The Cinema of Nicholas Ray', *Movie* 9, May 1963, p. 5 (reprinted in Cameron, *Movie Reader* and Nichols, *Movies and Methods*).

15 The reference is to Ray's *The True Story of Jesse James*, 1956 (UK title: *The James Brothers*).

16 François Truffaut, 'L'Admirable certitude', *Cahiers* 46, April 1955, translated as 'A Wonderful Certainty' in Volume 1, Ch. 11, p. 107.

17 Characters in *Bitter Victory*, Brand played by Curt Jürgens, Leith by Richard Burton.

18 James Cagney plays Matt Dow in *Run for Cover*, James Dean plays Jim Stark in *Rebel without a Cause*, James Mason plays Ed Avery in *Bigger than Life*.

19 Cf. Eric Rohmer, 'Ajax ou le Cid?', *Cahiers* 59, May 1956, Rohmer's review of *Rebel without a Cause*, translated as 'Ajax or the Cid?' in Volume 1, Ch. 12.

20 Godard's review of *Hot Blood*, *Cahiers* 68, February 1957, was titled 'Rien que le cinéma', translated as 'Nothing but Cinema' in *Godard on Godard*, reprinted in Volume 1, Ch. 13.

12 | Michel Mourlet: 'In Defence of Violence'

('Apologie de la violence', *Cahiers du Cinéma* 107, May 1960)

Violence is a major theme in aesthetics. Past or present, latent or active, it is of its nature at the heart of every creative act, even at the very moment it is being denied. To deny that violence exists in a peaceable work is to acknowledge its presence at the deepest level, in the twisted limbs of the work's gestation, and in the exercise of will which with fierce determination moulds the material into shape. Violence is decompression: arising out of a tension between the individual and the world, it explodes as the tension reaches its pitch, like an abscess bursting. It has to be gone through before there can be any repose. This is what makes it possible for me to say that every work of art contains violence, or at least postulates it, if art is a way of appeasing violence through its awareness of the terms of the conflict, and the power to resolve it which this knowledge confers.

Sometimes, cinema is talked about in these pages. Cinema is the art most attuned to violence, given that violence springs from man's actions, that moment when a pent-up force overflows and breaches the dam, an angry torrent smashing into anything that stands in its way. This moment, which the other art forms can only suggest or simulate, the camera catches naturally, taking up the torch which literature hands on. Stendhal is superior to Losey up to the point where in what he is describing the intention, the mental undercurrent, can pass to its incarnation in the material and objective world. It is precisely at this point that Losey becomes immeasurably superior to Stendhal.

Elevating the actor, *mise en scène* finds in violence a constant source of beauty. The hero breaks the spell, introducing into the malign order of the world his personal disorder, in his search for a harmony which is both more real and more elevated. What we are defining here is a particular kind of hero, and his name is Charlton Heston or Fernando Lamas, Robert Wagner or Jack Palance. A hero both cruel and noble, elegant and manly, a hero who reconciles strength with beauty (or, in Palance's case, a splendidly animal ugliness) and who represents the perfection of a lordly race, a hero made to conquer, made to portend or to experience the joys of the world. As an exercise in violence, conquest, pride, *mise en scène* in its purest form comes near to what is sometimes called 'fascism', in so far as this word, through a doubtless interesting confusion, has overtones of the Nietzschean concept of a genuine morality as opposed to the conscience of idealists, hypocrites and slaves. To reject this search for a natural order, this zest for effective action, the radiance of victory, is to condemn oneself to understanding nothing of an art that represents the pursuit of happiness through the drama of the body. It takes the innocence of certain theological minds to find a political meaning in an entity which they see as replacing the devil, everywhere to be found with his pot of black paint.

Charlton Heston is an axiom. He constitutes a tragedy in himself, his presence in any film being enough to instil beauty. The pent-up violence expressed by the sombre phosphoresence of his eyes, his eagle's profile, the imperious arch of his eyebrows, the hard, bitter curve of his lips, the stupendous strength of his torso – this is what he has been given, and what not even the worst of directors can debase. It is in this sense that one can say that Charlton Heston, by his very existence and regardless of the film he is in, provides a more accurate definition of the cinema than films like *Hiroshima mon amour* or *Citizen Kane*, films whose aesthetic either ignores or repudiates Charlton Heston. Through him, *mise en scène* can confront the most intense of conflicts and settle them with the contempt of a god imprisoned, quivering with muted rage. In this sense, Heston is more a Langian than a Walshian hero.

For cinema offers us several kinds of violence. At the lowest level, that of Kazan, a frenziedly drunken puppet show whose consummate expression is the contemptible Karl Malden. This is the dominion of the fake, the adulterated, the artificial, the ludicrous nervous twitch. The puerility of intention vies with the ugliness of its expression, and one has no real sense of an actor among all this gratuitous excess, the experiences of a neurotic aesthete glued on to a puppet on a string who makes a noise when you press his belly-button.

The violence in Welles is more honest, even appears to be purely auto-biographical; but it is cut back, niggardly, blocked, with no reverberations beyond the noisy commotion it likes making. It's like a child kicking the furniture when he bumps into it: a state of mind exemplified by the scene in which Citizen Kane applies himself to wrecking furniture. Blinded by his own personality, Welles can only make cardboard cut-outs to parade before us as he howls into the loudspeakers.

Let us pass over the violence of Buñuel, whose every expression, every passionate impulse has been at the service of ideas which since adolescence we have been unable to shake off. (How many of us discovered cinema because of him, or because of Welles, when we were sixteen or eighteen? But our ingratitude to ourselves, as well, knows no limit.)

A notch higher, Nicholas Ray offers an image of violence which is fuller, more sensual, more real, but alas unbridled:[1] not the immense pressure of a mass of water turning into a torrent when it is released, but a permanent flood, a swamp, James Mason forever on the edge of tears. A critic wrote some years ago that in a Ray film 'violence burns freely, a kind of aura surrounding the hero's actions; it is a violence that declaims rather than a violence that kills.' What this critic did not appreciate was that in what he intended as praise he had hit on the method of a *mise en scène* whose fuse is blown by constant overloading. Any genuine intensity becomes impossible; passion is unravelled into endless bits and pieces.

It is with Raoul Walsh that we encounter for the first time the true beauty of violence, an illumination of the passage of the hero, a manifestation of his power and his nobility, a moment of challenge. This clean, straight violence does not mark a defeat; it charts a road to victory. It is the violence of war or of the lone conqueror, and what it expresses is the courage to live, an awareness of the struggle between man and the elements, man against man, and an unleashing of the will to win. Walsh's *oeuvre* is an illustration of Zarathustra's aphorism: 'Man is made for war, woman is made for the warrior's repose, and the rest is madness.' All true films of conflict and adventure aspire to this view, but only those of Walsh rise to the level of epic or tragedy.

The suffocating world of Fritz Lang is particularly favourable to generating and sustaining violence, but in a very different sense. Constrained, held back, explicit and latent in every act and every look, and in no way diluted by weakness as in Ray, it is in fact like a tiger about to spring. If Walsh's violence is out in the open, Lang's is subterranean, more enduring in its tragedy. Only terror releases it; the earth crumbles around it and the hero is swallowed up.

But the film-maker who strikes deepest into violence and demonstrates it better than anyone is clearly Losey, of whom Aldrich is a mere uncomprehending disciple, a bombastic caricature. Losey, rather than the maker of *The Big Knife*, merits comparison with some of those astonishing reflexes one sees in actors in the work of Ida Lupino or Mizoguchi. Violence in Losey is just beneath the skin, catching that moment when the pulse frantically quickens as with every magnified heartbeat a man flexes himself to face what is in his way. And as it does so, it discovers a calm, a detumescence. This is a violence that opens a door on to peace and announces an unaccustomed surfeit of happiness.

Translated by David Wilson

Note

1 Mourlet's choice of Nicholas Ray here refers back explicitly to the enormously important place Ray occupied for *Cahiers* in the 1950s (and continued to hold at this time, as evidenced by the previous chapter); see particularly Jacques Rivette, 'Notes sur une révolution', *Cahiers* 54, Christmas 1955, translated as 'Notes on a Revolution' in Volume 1, Ch. 8, and the Dossier on Nicholas Ray in Volume 1, Chs. 10–15.

13 | Fereydoun Hoveyda: 'Sunspots'

('Les Taches du soleil', *Cahiers du Cinéma*
110, August 1960)

'The style is the man.'
Buffon

In the days before 'pre-digested' food existed, the aristocratic families of ancient Egypt often employed nurses whose sole job was to chew food before spitting it into the babies' mouths. The superfluous paraphrases of screenplays or themes offered by a good number of film critics incline me to include them in a category not far removed from the Egyptian masticators. But an adult produces enough enzymes to do his own digesting. And that brings us to the heart of the subject, namely the usefulness of criticism.

It is good form for critics themselves to look disdainfully from time to time upon their own profession, to decree its object ineffable or, even better, purely and simply to deny its existence. Thus, our friend Michel Mourlet starts out by postulating the 'non-being' of criticism, so as later to give free rein to his colourful (and sometimes esoteric) lyricism, in order to explain its object in the space of three well-filled pages of *Cahiers*. This kind of contradiction, from which our brilliant sophists extricate themselves with admirable elegance, would merit our attention if Roland Barthes[1] had not already explained its deep-rooted causes, which clearly do not include modesty.

Criticism exists, and its influence is growing daily. In vain are its practitioners decried as eunuchs of the cinema, contemptible scribblers and any number of similar insulting terms: they still persist. Indeed, they make films contradicting the theories which they continue to promulgate in their columns. Should one stop writing about other people's films, when one makes films oneself?

Yes, replies the profession. And why is that? Is judgment incompatible with creation? I will not go into my colleagues' reasons. But the mere fact that a category of human beings bands together into a corporation and

135

presumes to elevate the curious exercise in which it engages into an occupation, leads me quite naturally to wonder: 'But who can do criticism?' The members of the profession often emphasize the difficulty of their work, the knowledge it requires, etc.. But we must not be misled by this smokescreen. *Everyone* can and *must* criticize. It is up to the audience, the ultimate addressee of films, to give its opinion. Which indeed it does. As the audience comes out of the cinema, it confidently exclaims: 'I liked it' or 'I didn't like it'. These lapidary, trenchant formulae sum up the ultimate object of all criticism.

Producers are mistaken in poring over the statistics of cinemagoing. Those figures do not inform us as to the value judgments of the audiences. How can we know if the viewers enjoyed *A bout de souffle* or *Black Orpheus*? One would only have to ask the Institut Français de l'Opinion Publique to do a survey. Sociologists, psychoanalysts and filmologists of all sorts would explain to us the drives which lead the consumers to their peremptory judgments. The author of the work, for his part, would explain his personal reasons, and Georges Sadoul[2] would provide the film-maker's bio-filmography and assess the material conditions of production. Finally, Michel Mourlet would inform us of the 'aesthetic enjoyment' and 'degree of fascination' obtained by viewing the work. We would thus have a complete picture which would satisfy even Luc Moullet, who is elsewhere so hard on cinema authors.[3]

While waiting for an ideal apparatus such as I have described to be set up, should criticism as it now exists be condemned? As regards its daily and weekly versions, my reply would be 'yes'. It seems to me to be both unnecessary and harmful. Not so much because of its content as because of its role in time, the fact that it is published at the very moment when films are released. Consciously or not, it aims to act on the potential audience in such a way as to determine its choice and restrict its freedom. Pages of news leave you free to form your own opinion on what they relate. Not so with the columns reserved for film reviews. These seek to persuade the viewer to rush to the cinema or, alternatively, to stop him from doing so. It is not presumptuous to ask by what right the critic of the daily or weekly paper sets himself up as judge and pronounces sentence. I understand, for example, that many readers of *Le Figaro*[4] obey M. Chauvet's diktats. Without impugning the sincerity of that eminent critic, I pity his readership, who end up denying themselves a viewing of an excellent film like *Time Without Pity*. If the Office Catholique du Cinéma finds it necessary to award films a rating, or other social groups invoke reasons of public order and morality, that is their problem: they are not acting as critics, but as censors. There's a difference!

The situation is worse in the weekly magazines, where there is not enough space to review all the films released. Since, as we say, those absent are always in the wrong, silence here amounts to condemnation. How many viewers were thus lost for the fascinating *Agi Murad il Diavolo*

Bianco (*White Warrior*), which, not to be pretentious about it, did not lack real qualities?

A further problem is that the critics don't see all the films. A glance at our 'Conseil des Dix'[5] is sufficient to show that, for the most part, they rush to see the films that 'have to be talked about'. There is a real snobbery of 'seriousness' running through the cinema world. How many critics saw *Beatrice Cenci* or *Spartacus the Gladiator*?

Finally, one only has to skim through the critics' writings to collect phrases such as these: 'a vigorous *mise en scène*', 'a style unadorned with flourishes and fancy tricks', '(an actor's) heady charm', 'So-and-so will never be a great director because he lacks visual imagination', 'remorseless *mise en scène*', 'excellent music', 'a robust film', 'alert directing', 'authentic acting', 'flabby *mise en scène*', 'austere sincerity', etc. Perhaps, after all, in the critic-reader relationship, these adjectives acquire a particular meaning. But in any case that is not the question. What strikes me as thoroughly objectionable is the anticipatory character of film criticism in the dailies and weeklies. It stops viewers from going to see artistically valid films for reasons of politics, morality, or merely the mood of the moment.

So is criticism for burning? Not necessarily. It has a definite value when it enables the audience to understand its motives, when it brings out movements and talents, when it makes good regrettable omissions or flagrant injustices. But how could it achieve such objectives? In my view, by shifting in time, by taking place not at the beginning but towards the end of a film's run. It is not a matter of predetermining the viewer's choice, but of engaging in a dialogue with him about the work he has seen. If this sort of *a posteriori* reviewing were pointless, why would our daily and weekly papers devote so much space to TV reviews? Let's leave to the publicists and the press agents the job of puffing their products or knocking the competition.

You see what I am leading up to: the only valid criticism at the present time is the criticism conducted in the 'monthlies' (and first and foremost, of course, in *Cahiers*).[6] As regards the dailies and weeklies, if they nonetheless want to keep up with the latest news, they should, it would seem, restrict themselves to 'informative criticism', as brilliantly defined by René Guyonnet,[7] whose ideas transport us, so to speak, from the realm of time to that of space. In fact the central question is neither the 'who' nor the 'when' of criticism, but the 'how'. What criteria serve as a basis for judgments? Guyonnet mentions some of them: political significance, moral interpretation, statement of a personal taste, sophistic method, grammatical correctness, human significance, sociological description, historical criticism. He concludes:

> The best approach is rather to ask what is the film's *raison d'être*, to look for its central meaning, the one which touches people and will make some people say 'I like it', and others, 'I don't like it'. Now, it is certain that this central meaning will often be missed, if one applies only a single grid.

But, when you think about it, doesn't the object which Guyonnet assigns to criticism make it a bit unnecessary? Why go to so much trouble to find out why X likes *Les Bonnes femmes* and Y hates it! Aren't we going round in circles, since the fact that X, Y and their friend the critic do or do not like *Les Bonnes femmes* doesn't tell us much about the aesthetic value of the film. Even if one is subjectivist or extremely relativist, one has to admit that this aesthetic value exists (I am speaking in general, and not about Chabrol's film), if not in itself, then at least in relation to society. I personally prefer *Les Aventures d'Arsène Lupin* to *A la Recherche du temps perdu*, but I know that aesthetically Proust is superior to Leblanc. I can see the central meaning of *On the Beach* or *Moderato Cantabile*, but that is no help at all because that meaning has no influence on the ugliness of those works.

A work of art isn't a chemical substance that can be subjected to various tests. I can see the difficulty of appreciating the aesthetic value of a film, especially after one or two viewings. But I do not see what other object criticism can have. We all make mistakes: that is nothing to be ashamed of, since we have no infallible rules of thumb. If the work of art eludes our grasp, to interrogate it all we can do is to put on the magnifying glasses of a single viewpoint and hope that this close-up view will enable us to find the answer. There is nothing mysterious about this. My remark stems from a fundamental truth which could be stated as follows: only a violent, but controlled, *parti pris* leads to a clear awareness of the world, and of art. (I am of course not talking about a political *parti pris*!)

Personally, I like extreme opinions. Since each one of us can only defend his own truth, it is vain to hope to keep, as our masters suggested, in the path of the golden mean. 'Neither-nor' criticism (as Barthes has called it) leads straight to sclerosis. It will be objected that a film is a mosaic of different elements the combining of which leads to the work of art, so that only a meticulous analysis of all these ingredients can give an account of it.

André S. Labarthe has judiciously emphasized the limitations of this reputedly infallible method, which it seems curious, to say the least, to apply to the cinema.[8] A film is not a juxtaposition of molecular elements that do not modify each other. It is not a well-designed machine,[9] but an organized form with dialectical not logical relationships. What is the point of balancing good scenes against bad, form against content? At most, analysis decomposes the work, but does not give an account of it. Must the advocates of analysis be reminded that a whole is always different from the sum of its parts?

Just as every statement reveals in its author a conception of the world, so every piece of criticism, even the most insignificant, presupposes a theory of cinema. Since other people's beliefs are not my concern, I shall merely reveal my own 'metaphysics'. The blinkers that I have chosen are the *technical* viewpoint, *mise en scène*. But when we say here that the specificity of the cinematographic work lies in its technique and not in its content, in its *mise en scène* and not in the screenplay and the dialogue, we raise a storm of protest. Contrary to a widespread belief, there is no more eclectic team than that of *Cahiers*. But, despite all that distinguishes me from Jean Douchet, I cannot fail to see that through him René Cortade is attacking all those who reduce cinema to technique. Cortade has painted an interesting portrait which unfortunately resembles no one we know.[10] It is easy to credit us with opinions we have never put forward.

When I state that everything is expressed on the screen through *mise en scène*, I in no way contest the existence and importance of the subject matter. I simply want to point out that the distinguishing feature of a great author is precisely his ability to metamorphose the stupidest plot through his technique.[11] It is obvious that if we tried to summarize on paper the plot of *Time Without Pity*, we would end up with a very weak melodrama. But do we go to the cinema to translate images into words? The screenplay, a literary work which has to be read, cannot be criticized through the film, a cinematic work which has to be seen. The story in no way constitutes the basis of the film. As Alexandre Astruc has observed, it is extraordinary, after half a century of existence, to see that the great works which begin to stand out are not necessarily the most important dates in the history of the cinema. Up to now, a snobbery about the subject matter has often weighed on film-makers. Even Lang forced himself to undertake unnecessary chores, such as *Metropolis*. Chabrol has made the point well: there are no big subjects, and no small subjects.[12]

We are often accused of defending 'minor' films and of glorifying works which do not 'mean' anything. It is true that we sometimes point out the importance of thrillers or even 'B or C features'.[13] But what have people got against thrillers and adventure films? It's a strange attitude that sees profundity only in eternal triangles and bourgeois drama. To calm the wrath of Marcabru and Cortade, let me quote Jean Cocteau: 'These books (thrillers) have the great fault that once you start one, you can't put it down. The "thinking minorities" reader, if I may use that expression, retains the strange snobbery of the boredom he takes for seriousness and in which he publicly disowns what he secretly enjoys.' But there is something else: such is the power of the cinema that, under the wand of a great director, the most insignificant 'thriller' turns into a work of art. If Domarchi, for example, quotes Hegel and Kant in discussing Minnelli,[14] he does so neither out of pedantry nor a love of paradox, but simply because cinema is at least as important as theatre, literature or painting! *Mise en scène* can breathe real content into a seemingly trivial subject. Hawks's *Rio Bravo*, for example. And most often it is precisely the mediocre directors who resort to big themes, to try to mask their inadequacy. Unfortunately for them, they only highlight the lack of *mise en scène* in their work, like Kramer in *On the Beach* or Cayatte in *Les Amants de Vérone*.

As a further element of appreciation, we are sometimes offered 'milieu'. But, my dear Marcabru, aren't Kurosawa and Mizoguchi both inspired by the same Japanese civilization?[15] What is it that makes the latter so much greater than the former, if not his brilliant *mise en scène*? The milieu produces the director: that is precisely why I don't believe in it. Marcabru goes even further: 'There is no single, universal cinema, but cinemas governed by geography and time'.[16] Not only have we never argued for the existence of a monolithic cinema, but we do not lump together Lang, Rossellini, Losey, Preminger, Ermler and Mizoguchi on the grounds that they use the same language. But, in our view, they differ more in the individual style of their *mise en scène* than through their racial or geographical origins. When Renoir goes to India, he does not make an Indian film, but a Renoir film. Likewise Lang in America, Losey in England and Rossellini in Germany.

It is true that the *writing* (*écriture*) does not modify the style, if by writing is meant 'grammar'. But *mise en scène* is not writing. *Moonfleet* remains above all a film by Lang, whatever the influence of the English tempera-ment on the screenplay. Lang, for his part, evolves, changes, ages: his *permanence* exists only at the level of his *mise en scène*.[17]

At other times our opponents point to the 'mission' of the cinema which is supposed to grasp man in his true state. The objectivity of the camera, the documentary school, the camera-eye. . . . Haven't we been bored enough, first with *verismo* and realism, then with neo-realism? As if it were a question of recording the images of the world, in the way that cartographers' aeroplanes photograph the relief of the ground! Can't people understand that the mere presence of the camera changes the décor? Cinema which was content to describe things, to give a miserable record of their lines and surfaces, would most infallibly distance itself from reality.

This tendency leads, moreover, to a sort of abject 'voyeurism'. It is also absurd and aberrant. Even supposing that a Rouch or a Rogosin (since those are the two examples constantly cited) were able to lurk with a camera and a tape-recorder in a hovel near Abidjan or Sophiatown,[18] to film the daily life of a black household, his film would not inform us about anything: we would lack the context, in other words the shared memories, the shared perceptions, the situation of the couple, the inner preoccu-pations of each of the protagonists – in short, the world as each of them sees it or knows it is seen by the other. *Mise en scène* is not required to represent the real but, through its technical procedures, to signify it.

Since cinema offers moving pictures, some give first place to photography. Photography is indeed one of the essential elements of the film. But we see the same prestigious names of cameramen appearing in the most varied credits. They put their talent at the service of the director. It is up to the director to know how to use it.

Other critics, noting that a film is a collective work, would like also to take account of the conditions of production and distribution. These elements, coming after the screenplay, the photography, the climate and the milieu, remind me of the theories of the economist Stanley Jevons, who explained the cyclical crises of the economy by the build-up of sunspots, at approximately ten-yearly intervals. Contemporary science demonstrates the links between these solar phenomena and disturbances in our climate. Indeed, we now know that sunspots affect the human metabolism. The director, being essentially human, like other people, is therefore subject to the variations due to sunspots. Why not take account of that, while we are about it, in criticizing their films?

So now I too am launched into general ideas. Is it my fault, when sociologists, filmologists and critics so often talk to us of the Cinema with a capital C? The Cinema is an art. The Cinema is an industry. The Cinema is entertainment. But what exactly is the Cinema? A certain number of very individual films, shown in a certain number of no less individual theatres. Could we please talk about specific films and not go in for Aristotelian logic, with talk of Russian cinema, British cinema, German cinema, etc.? It is only ever a matter of works we have seen. Let's make use of the brilliant lessons which the great Alfred Korzybski[19] gave in his *General Semantics*, and instead of declaring, 'Lang is the greatest living director', let's try saying, '*The Tiger of Bengal* and *The Indian Tomb* are works which achieve perfection'. Long live non-Aristotelian logic!

If my opinions are sometimes close to those of Mourlet and his friends, that doesn't mean I consider myself one of the 'MacMahon school'.[20] Their *res cinematographica* is a monster of abstraction which horrifies me. Mourlet handles general ideas elegantly. How could I argue against him, until he offers examples that would enable me to follow him in the realm of the concrete, the only conceivable battleground? If one applied his theory of 'fascination' to the films he admires, one would want to know by what miracle he is persuaded to prefer *The Adventures of Haji Baba* to *Notte Bianchi* and *Il Boia di Lilla* (*Milady and the Musketeers*) to *Viaggio in Italia*. He seems to me to confuse method with system. He starts by postulating the principle of the pre-eminence of *mise en scène* (on which I entirely agree with him) in order to put forward as an absolute criterion the technique of the directors he likes: Lang, Losey, Preminger and Walsh, in the first rank, and Cottafavi and Don Weis in the second rank. Criticizing the 'metaphysics' of the main contributors to *Cahiers*, he ends up lumbered with his own metaphysics, which is neither better nor worse. Thus he writes about Losey: 'He is the only cosmic director. He represents the fulfilment of the cinematic project inasmuch as he restores the world to its original brutality.' Why can't he see that each artist invents the personal technique through which he expresses himself? The beauty of *Time Without Pity* does not detract from that of *Viaggio in Italia*. Preferring one to the other depends on purely personal tastes.

In any case, *Cahiers* did not wait for the 'MacMahon school' before discovering the essential importance of *mise en scène*. For a long time, with Rohmer, Rivette and Godard (to mention but three), *Cahiers* had been developing a critical tendency which brought in a healthier and purer element of appreciation. The '*politique des auteurs*' was only a necessary stage on that steep path. In approaching criticism, several of us started with what was easiest: the analysis of themes. The consistency of the ideas we found in the films of Lang, Rossellini, Renoir, Welles, etc. struck us so much that we sometimes forgot what was essential. But soon we recognized the self-evident: all our favourite *auteurs* were, ultimately, talking about the same things. The 'constants' of their particular universes belonged to everyone: solitude, violence, the absurdity of existence, sin, redemption, love, etc. Each epoch has its themes, which serve as a back-cloth against which individuals, whether artists or not, act out their lives. At a time when the method introduced by Marthe Robert[21] is revolution-izing literary criticism, are we to remain attached to futile paraphrases when we discuss the cinema? The originality of an *auteur* lies not in the subject matter he chooses but in the technique he employs, in the *mise en scène*, through which everything is expressed on the screen. If you interrogate Ray by analysing the elements of his screenplay and enumer-ating his apparent themes, you are likely to hate *Party Girl*. For the superfi-cial viewer, *The Tiger of Eschnapur* looks like a film of no interest.

As Sartre said, 'One is not a writer because one has chosen to say certain things, but because one has chosen to say them in a certain way'. Why should it be different in our art? Just as 'a painter's thoughts must not be considered separately from his means' (Matisse), so a film-maker's thought appears through his *mise en scène*. What counts in a film is the striving towards order, harmony, composition; the placing of the actors and objects, the movements within the frame, the capture of a movement or a look; in short, the intellectual operation which has set to work an initial emotion and a general idea. *Mise en scène* is nothing other than the tech-nique which each *auteur* invents in order to express himself and establish the specificity of his work. How can one give a general definition of it, when it comes from deep inside each artist and varies with him? The critic's task becomes immense: to detect behind the images the *auteur's* 'manner' and, with the aid of that knowledge, to reveal the meaning of the work. If, as Astruc writes, *mise en scène* is interrogation and dialogue,[22] then criticism is even more so: questioning the work, but substituting a 'how?' for the traditional 'why?'. The work of art is not reducible to an idea, because it is the production of a being, of that something which cannot be thought: its idea is in its very technique.

Few people nowadays deny the fundamental importance of *mise en scène*. But because our art lacks its Littré,[23] words do not always have the same meanings and our vocabulary remains vague. Many critics confuse *mise en scène* with writing (*écriture*). The error comes from literature, where the word 'writing' means two quite different things. When we talk about *mise en scène*, we are indeed thinking of the *precision* of the writing, but a *structural*, not a rhetorical precision: it is not a question of 'fine writing'. That is why phrases like 'correct *mise en scène*' or 'unadorned style' mean nothing at all.[24]

Let me conclude by returning to a recent article by Pierre Marcabru,[25] since he himself indicates the cause of the misunderstanding when he

142

writes: '*Mise en scène*, i.e. camera movements, editing, framing, is the only thing that counts, beyond everything else'.

Marcabru need not worry. Just as Domarchi and Douchet do not aspire to the title of 'Doctors of law' which he awards them, so the *Cahiers* team has no intention of insisting on 'style' and shunning 'intelligence'.[26] If, for years, they have been more interested in *mise en scène*, it is the better to question films and listen to the *auteur*'s answers. Through technique, what we are looking for is the meaning of the work. It is not a question of setting the search for meanings against the study of form. The originality of the films we like often lies precisely in a correspondence between thought and form. And, to paraphrase Marthe Robert, I will say that our aim is to bring out the meaning of films through the technique whereby they achieve their specific character. Our view is similar to that of Guyonnet when he writes: 'While it is true that what counts is *mise en scène*, that this is the creative element, it is equally the case that *mise en scène* is not a pure form, that it does not create in a vacuum, but that, on the contrary, it conveys meaning'.[27]

It goes without saying that such a critical method leads to the greatest severity. But *Cahiers* has never been particularly indulgent towards a certain type of cinema. I am sometimes surprised to hear friends complaining that we praise films made by colleagues who have gone behind the camera. What are we supposed to do? Attack their films even when they are good? Ignore them? I can see that some eulogies may appear unfortunate. They are their authors' sole responsibility. The whole *Cahiers* team does not reduce cinema to *mise en scène*, and I personally do not claim that other critical methods are not respectable and fruitful. Ultimately, the essential thing is that each critic should remain faithful to his own view of things, while recognizing its necessarily limited character.

Translated by Jill Forbes

Notes

1 Roland Barthes, *Mythologies*, Paris, Editions du Seuil, 1955, translated as *Mythologies*, London, Jonathan Cape, 1972.

2 Georges Sadoul, 1904–67, French film critic and historian, occasional contributor to *Cahiers* but long-time film critic for *Les Lettres Françaises*; important figure in development of French cine-club movement; best known for his six volume *Histoire générale de cinéma* and for dictionaries of films and film-makers, originally published in 1965, translated as *Dictionary of Film-Makers* and *Dictionary of Films*, Berkeley, University of California Press, 1972.

3 Apparent reference to Luc Moullet's article, 'L'Ecrivain de cinéma en quête de son paradoxe', *Cahiers* 103, January 1960. Moullet was a major *Cahiers* contributor at this time: see, for example, 'Sam Fuller – sur les brisées de Marlowe', *Cahiers* 93, March 1959, translated as 'Sam Fuller: In Marlowe's Footsteps' in Volume 1, Ch. 20, 'Jean-Luc Godard', *Cahiers* 106, April 1960, Ch. 1 in this volume, and his contributions to the editorial discussion of American cinema from *Cahiers* 150–1, December 1963–January 1964, 'Questions

about American Cinema: A Discussion', Ch. 17 in this volume. Later in the 1960s *Cahiers* much valued his work as a film-maker: see, for example, references in the October 1967 interview with Godard, Ch. 31 in this volume.

4 *Le Figaro* is a Paris daily newspaper; Louis Chauvet was its film critic at this time.

5 'Le Conseil des Dix', literally 'The Council of the Ten', was a regular 'Critics' Choice' feature of *Cahiers*, in which each month three or four *Cahiers* critics joined with six or seven critics from other publications to evaluate the month's new releases with gradings from a blob ('don't bother'), to one star ('to be seen at a pinch'), two stars ('to be seen'), three stars ('must be seen'), and four stars ('masterpiece'). This practice continued until 1968, when it was discontinued on political grounds: see Ch. 36 in this volume.

6 'Here, as elsewhere, the author is expressing his purely personal opinion.' (Original editors' note.)

7 *Esprit*, June 1960. (Author's note.)

8 In his preface to Jacques Siclier's *Ingmar Bergman*, Paris, Editions Universitaires, 1960: 'By situating at infinity the completion of its project, the moment when it finally has a view of the work in its totality, analysis exposes the absurdity of its undertaking: to achieve in a human lifespan (in the best theoretical case) that which only an infinitely extended life could grasp'. Only one analysis finds favour in his eyes, one which is at the same time 'the demonstration of a method of analysis', and which Siclier practises in his study of Bergman. (Author's note.)

9 I mean films that can be regarded as works of art. It goes without saying that the majority of the products that we consume, *faute de mieux*, in fact belong (when they are bearable) in the category 'well-designed machines'. (Author's note.)

10 'But the school in question becomes frankly comical when, after having eliminated all the works which had a human content . . . it immediately endeavours to pour content into those which have none', *Arts*, 8 June 1960. (Author's note.) *Arts* was a weekly arts newspaper, for which Truffaut and Godard, for example, had worked in the 1950s.

11 Cortade writes: 'For them, of course, the screenplay does not exist, or should exist as little as possible. Their ideal film would be one whose *mise en scène*, organized as a series of separate, perfect shots, would bear its own meaning within itself, independently of the story. And as it is impossible to dispense totally with a plot, they would choose the thinnest plot available: a fatuous biblical story, like *Solomon and the Queen of Sheba*, an exotic adventure, like *The Tiger of Bengal*, an American frivolity or a commonplace detective story, like Minnelli's comedies or Nicholas Ray's *Party Girl*. The technique would be all the more striking since it would, as it were, be running neutral', *Arts*, 8 June 1960. (Author's note.)

12 Claude Chabrol, 'Les Petits Sujets', *Cahiers* 100, October 1959, translated as 'Big Subjects, Little Subjects' in *Movie* 1, June 1962, and as 'Little Themes' in Graham, *The New Wave*.

13 *Arts*, 8 June 1960. (Author's note.)

14 See, for example, Jean Domarchi, 'Le Fer dans la plaie', *Cahiers* 63, October 1956, translated as 'Knife in the Wound' in Volume 1, Ch. 30.

15 Hoveyda seems to have in mind the Kurosawa-Mizoguchi debate which took place between André Bazin, Luc Moullet and Jacques Rivette in *Cahiers* 68,

February 1957, 69, March 1957, and 81, March 1958, translated as 'Exchanges about Kurosawa and Mizoguchi' in Volume 1, Ch. 32.

16 'The object viewed, whatever it may be, imposes the laws of this climate on vision, on perception', Pierre Marcabru, *Combat*, 2 April 1960. (Author's note.)

17 'Lang is then completely conditioned by the British climate, and he only has his writing through which to manifest himself. I admit that the writing is very beautiful. But it is only an instrument serving a Stevensonian sensibility and intelligence', ibid. (Author's note.)

18 Hoveyda has in mind Jean Rouch's *Moi, un Noir* (1958) and Lionel Rogosin's *Come Back Africa* (1959).

19 Alfred Korzybski, 1879–1950, Polish-American scientist and writer, pioneer in psychological-philosophical semantics and best known for his 1941 study, *Science and Sanity: An Introduction to Non-Aristotelian Systems and General Semantics*.

20 'MacMahon school': see general introduction to this section.

21 Marthe Robert, *Kafka*, Paris, N.R.F., 1960. (Author's note.)

22 *La Table Ronde*, May 1960; cf. Astruc, 'Qu'est-ce que la mise en scène?', *Cahiers* 100, October 1959, translated as 'What is *mise en scène*?' in Volume 1, Ch. 33.

23 'Littré', i.e. the *Dictionnaire de la langue française* (1863–73), the first scientific attempt to establish etymology and usage in the French language, undertaken by lexicographer Emile Littré, 1801–81.

24 In *Combat*, 2 February 1960, Marcabru denounces 'the absurdity of an immobile criticism, clinging to structures, to writing in its purely grammatical aspects, as soon as an exotic cinema is envisaged', and adds: 'By exotic cinema, I mean anything which escapes from a traditional cinematic style, the Hollywood style in all its splendour, a style which is, incidentally, perfectly compatible with revolutionary writing (cf. *A bout de souffle*)'.

Mise en scène, unlike writing, cannot be correct or incorrect, since it is the 'manner' in which the artist has chosen to express himself. Though we can enumerate many of the elements which contribute to it, *mise en scène* remains difficult to pin down. It is precisely the role of criticism to help the public understand an author's procedure. (Author's note.)

25 *Combat*, 28 May 1960. (Author's note.)

26 'It's no longer intelligence that touches them, but manner, a certain way of doing things. It doesn't matter if the film is silly, the subject grotesque, so long as the writing corresponds to a certain canon that they have established once and for all', ibid. (Author's note.)

27 *Esprit*, June 1960. (Author's note.)

14 | Michel Mourlet: 'The Beauty of Knowledge: Joseph Losey'

('Beauté de la connaissance', *Cahiers du Cinéma* 111, September 1960)

> He worships this body of man and woman which is the measure of anything.
> Paul Valéry ('Introduction to the Method of Leonardo da Vinci').

A is A. Reality offers no ambiguity, rising into the consciousness in the full light of the evidence. It is these constant flashes of light which open the way to knowledge, not those systems which substitute a dance of the mind for the way the world moves on. Nietzsche and Valéry reveal the character of an intellect which entrusts itself to the order in which things happen, their logic being not that of those intellects which bend this ordering of things to their will, but simply the connection between all its parts. Reason is not a searchlight that man turns on an irrational spectacle; it is contained within that spectacle; it has to arrive of its own accord. This is precisely what Hegel, who had some insights, said.

Most directors project on to the world their system, the blurred image of their vision, the distorting lens of their intellect. A worthless piece of work is in the first place a false work, a distorting mirror. We move through these films as in a bad dream, constantly bumping into things we don't recognize. Our only salvation is to escape from this suffocating circle of artifice, and return to the real world which surrounds the cinema, the world which is beating on its door but can't get in.

Losey is the director whose mirror presents a surface so limpid that you forget it is there, that reality itself, in his films, unfolds before us. An unprepared eye, sensitive only to Welles-type provocations, might confuse this naked truth with the lack of ideas in the generality of films. A short time ago, a writer quoted a phrase taken from a presentation I had done on Losey in his weekly magazine so that he could have some lively fun with the word 'cosmic' which I had used to describe the director. He could not, however, have accused me of using it about anyone or at any time. I know of only one director who can constantly make one feel the presence of the world, the pressure of the atmosphere at the centre of a scene, by means of sounds, lights, the identification of the decor with the drama and the drama with the decor. The core of the drama is like the burning heart of a sun whose rays extend and pulsate infinitely into space. Two shots in *Time Without Pity* remind one of this: the first shows London, the bridge over the Thames and Parliament; the clock strikes; without any transition we are with people in a house; the striking of the clock comes to an end, slightly muted by the barrier of the walls. A brief, insignificant detail, but it is enough to register the scene within the totality of the real world.

For an artist to have a 'universe' is an admission of inadequacy, of limitation and, more importantly, of artifice. Stendhal, Racine, Bach, Leonardo da Vinci do not have a universe. They are clearly more interested in certain aspects of the world than in others, which is to their credit, but they know how not to cast these privileged forms in the mould of a caricatural sensibility. One can talk of Kafka's universe. One cannot talk of Losey's universe. What throws Losey's detractors is that it is impossible to refer to that fundamental defect of the creative act by which meaning can be blunted or softened. In this perspective, Hitchcock has a style and Losey does not. The notion of style masks, in this case, a distortion of the truth: Hitchcock, Welles, Eisenstein certainly *invent* forms, but isn't the acknowledgment of this the strongest criticism one can make? The artist does not invent, he discovers; otherwise we detach ourselves from his fantasy creations. The history of art is to a large extent the history of sicknesses of the mind. Very few artists have followed the straight path of the pure vision. By pure vision[1] I mean that absolute clarity of consciousness which is the base on which the true forms of the world are constructed, and which is also called intellect, since, as we have just seen, intellect and beauty are not distinct.

There is an absolute knowledge, a revelation of being, such that to think the opposite is psychologically impossible, a mere intellectual conceit. Holding on to these facts, rejecting a fragile architecture which lacks foundation or support, and rejecting seductive but gratuitous theories, this is what determines a thought – and therefore an art – which is deeply rooted in life. Losey reflects this awareness with the utmost fidelity and ruthlessness. It is a question not of a universe, but of *the* universe; not of a world that may or may not be, but of the real world.

This does not mean that Losey is stuck in the rut of realism, and offers us banality and ugliness as guarantees of truth. His subject is what is most rare, most noble, most passionate in man. But this subject is simplicity itself, and that is why he astonishes. Our habits of thinking break down when we are confronted with precision. We tend to think that people tell us lies; we even think we are being lied to when we're being told the truth. A critic called an (incidentally erroneous) article on *Time Without Pity* 'The Magnificence of the False',[2] and people have talked about expressionism in connection with this film, which opens a door to misunderstanding. Expressionism is not concerned merely to set itself in oppo-

147

sition to impressionism by interposing an organizing will; it involves putting a stress on what *ought* to be important. Now, in Losey's *mise en scène* what appears as essential is so of its own accord, without any external validation, simply because of the rightness of the gesture which characterizes it.

If this art could be defined by a single word, it would be honesty. Whether this honesty is applied to moments of extreme tenderness or extreme violence, it will always be disconcerting, will always seem perverse or naive to those who have lost their innocence, to those who have never run their finger over a rock to trace its grain. It could be described as something born out of an extraordinary conjoining of childhood innocence and lucidity. The world is seen fresh and raw – but understanding is adult and it does not break under the strain. On the contrary, it overcomes it, recovers itself, rises above the apparent chaos, and in total clarity is free to follow its chosen course.

In the same vein, people have talked about the performances being theatrical, which is to confuse theatricality with dramaturgy. A theatrical performance, in the accepted sense, is a performance which is heightened so as to represent feelings whose expression exceeds their actual intensity. A dramatic performance *can* be a performance which expresses extreme emotions in their integrity. I say *can* because more often than not the dramatic falls back on the theatrical when an emotion fails to register of its own accord. But in Losey's case, what we have really is drama, not theatre. If his experience in the theatre has served him well, it is much more in the use of scenic space than in the direction of actors. The space is actually the same, though the footlights and the other conventions of the theatre have disappeared on the screen.

Out of this comes a freedom of gesture which is found nowhere else. We witness the birth of these gestures, which is utterly spontaneous, the sometimes extraordinary way they move in space, and the always sublime way they reach the heart. In the same moment we feel astonishment, and the living and breathing sensation of truth. Never before have we been so close to human beings, their flesh, their nerves, their pulse beat. Losey's genius finds a perfect objectivity: a very studied art achieves the spontaneity of emotion as it happens. Losey is the only prophet: he foresees what does not yet exist in any degree, what is on the point of arising out of nothingness. And he can do this because of his intuitive sense of the actor's being, the possession of what is, bringing with it the power over what might be. This possession (and since *Time Without Pity* was shown recently in Paris we can take it as an example) we find in its totality in the performance of Leo McKern, in whom the madness of domination and pride, contained in every fibre of his powerful body, explodes in fantastic fury, the manifestation of an infinite lacerating passion.

For this light which suffuses both people and objects is there to guide an extraordinary monster, half-blind in a murky universe, to point out to him the sharp edges which have hurt him and which from now on he will know how to avoid. From this monster of the night the light creates a man. The demon of knowledge, the temptation of lucidity – are they any more than a desire to control the universe and impose on it the laws of man? Losey's *mise en scène*, like Valéry's writing, is at every turn an act of knowledge, the vision of a clear eye and the victory of an unprejudiced mind. Their greatness is to have recognized that there is no salvation outside of understanding. Hence their shared attitude towards metaphysics and all arbitrary constructions of the mind. Their domain is what they can feel, touch, control. One can imagine the bafflement of this kind of mind in the face of the extravagant thinking which seems to be all around us.

If beauty and lucidity go together, there can no longer be what we often think of as the 'aesthetic' and the 'moral', two distinct activities given a chapter of their own in the textbooks studied at the Sorbonne; there is only a single movement, for which beauty, morality, understanding are simply different names. The clearest vision chooses the noblest form, and the hand shapes it faithfully. We know no other definition of art. This movement can be seen in Losey's films in its freest, purest and most subtle form. It is this, and this alone, which sets a scene in motion and brings it to a conclusion. A compulsion in continual tension, a choice which is at once proud in the presence of men and respectful of nature, draws this convergence of means towards a central point, the same point for everyone but one which few minds glimpse and hardly anyone reaches. The time for trying to discover the secret of the world is gone. In rage and tragedy, as in ecstatic happiness, the only question is to learn how to live.

Translated by David Wilson

Notes

1 Cf. the title and argument of André S. Labarthe's review of Chabrol's *Les Bonnes femmes*, 'Le Plus pur regard', *Cahiers* 108, June 1960, translated as 'The Purest Vision: *Les Bonnes femmes*' in this volume, Ch. 2.

2 'La Splendeur du faux', Luc Moullet's review of Losey's *Time Without Pity*, *Cahiers* 109, July 1960.

15 | Jean Douchet: 'Hitch and his Audience'

('Hitch et son public', *Cahiers du Cinéma* 113, November 1960)

This article is forbidden to those who have not yet seen *Psycho*. Which is not to say that others are obliged to read it. But it is impossible to examine the film without unveiling its secret. And knowing it will deprive the reader, the future spectator, of a major part of his pleasure. I know this from experience. In his last interview here, Hitchcock narrated his film from beginning to end to Jean Domarchi and me, and mimed it in an extraordinary manner. For more than an hour we saw *Psycho* being born, sequence by sequence and sometimes shot by shot. I say *born* advisedly, because this happened in October 1959 and Hitchcock started shooting in November. And now, in Paramount's small private screening room, we felt that we were seeing the film for the second time. We were deprived of some of the terror felt by the others who were there.

Now this terror is Hitchcock's first, if not entire, objective. Even in the least of his interviews he loves to reveal to us the point at which, for him, creation is based on an exact science of audience reactions. This is not a financial concern (he was actually convinced that *Psycho* would be a failure), nor is it for publicity reasons (though he makes admirable use of publicity, we know, since *North by Northwest*, what he thinks of it), but because he attributes a mission to 'suspense' films. This mission is catharsis. The audience must 'untrammel' itself on the psychoanalytical level, make confession on the logical level, purify itself on the spiritual level. So Hitchcock needs the active participation of the audience.

The proof? *Rear Window*. It is here that Hitchcock exposes his conception of cinema (which is cinema within cinema), reveals his secrets, unveils his intentions. In the film James Stewart, reporter photographer, is first and foremost a spectator. This is one of the reasons for our seeing him confined to his chair. Through him Hitchcock's intention is to define the nature of the spectator, and specifically the nature of the Hitchcockian spectator. The latter is a 'voyeur'. He wants to enjoy the spectacle. What he sees on the screen (and so what Stewart watches in the apartment on the other

150

side of the courtyard) is the projection of his own self. This alone, *a priori*, can hold his interest. In one way or another it is himself that he sees. A spectacle which, after all, would soon become tedious if a precise aspect, a mystery, had not entirely captured his attention. Thereafter his intelligence fixes itself on an idea which grows into an obsession. Reasoning and deduction give way to *subjectivity*, to feelings of desire and fear. The more he desires or fears, the more his expectation will be fulfilled – and way beyond what he is hoping for. So strong is Stewart's wish for a crime to have been committed that the crime materializes and happens for him. In a Hitchcock film it is the spectator who creates the suspense; the suspense only meets the request for it. (Remember Doris Day, also a spectator, at the Royal Albert Hall in *The Man Who Knew Too Much*.) In other words, Hitchcock first excites the worst feelings of his audience and then, through his spectacle, authorizes them to be satisfied. The sense of horror which the audience experiences gives rise to other feelings, pure and noble feelings, which alone allow the first feelings to be cancelled out. Here cinema is not just therapeutic, it is a genuinely magic art.

Which brings us back to the *auteur*'s purpose. Hitchcock's intention is to unmask reality and show it to us in *triple* form. Triple like those three window blinds which are raised one after the other in the very first shot of *Rear Window*. The first reality is obviously that of the *everyday world*, immediately recognizable to the spectator. Which is why Hitchcock takes so much care with it. Since it serves as the fixed base of his structure, the director goes to considerable lengths to portray it with great attention to the truth. In his eyes falsehood is inadmissible. Still less the arbitrary. (We are far removed from Clouzot's *Les Diaboliques*.) Never, absolutely never, does Hitchcock cheat the audience. He sometimes – and wilfully – diverts their attention (as he diverts Stewart, at the moment the crime unfolds, in *Rear Window*), but he always leaves them enough to work on. The spectator can, if he wants, reconstruct in his mind the events which have been unfolded before him. This is especially the case with *Psycho* where everything, down to the last detail, is clearly revealed. Nothing, then, is less justified than the charges of lack of verisimilitude which certain people have levelled at Hitchcock.

The second reality, the second blind, opens on the *world of desire*. For this is just the way that the apartment appears from the other side of the courtyard. Everything that happens in the everyday world – in Stewart's apartment – is inscribed there, projected as on a screen. Stewart's own apartment is duplicated there many times, peopled by forms which are themselves animated by the forces which gave birth to them. These forms-forces personify the secret thoughts, mental attitudes and above all the desires of our hero. And in this world they have a real existence and an active power. Like a huge mirror turned on the everyday, the world of desire produces a reverse image of its situations as well as its thoughts; the world of the couple of Kelly and the (paralysed) Stewart, as well as the couple comprised of Raymond Burr and his bedridden wife; Stewart's latent desire to be rid of Kelly, which is effectively carried out by Raymond Burr. These forms-forces of desire constitute the fundamental component of every Hitchcock film. A psychoanalyst will see it as a representation of the feeling of guilt. Never, however, before *Psycho*, has our director provided so much evidence of it. Here the form is really nothing other than a form endowed with a terrifying force.

Finally, the third reality, the *intellectual world*. This is the main plank of the Hitchcockian oeuvre, the plumb line which connects the two parallel universes and allows them to communicate in this way. This is what the director relies on in all his films. So it is through the intermediary of this world that Stewart, confined in his everyday universe (which is why we never leave his living room throughout the film), can penetrate the world of desire. Inasmuch as he is a spectator, then, what does our hero see? What he believes to be the everyday world, and which is only his own reflection. But the world of desire soon reveals its true nature. A horrible act is committed there, which the hero has not seen but which he imagines. From then on his attention is roused, his intellect is placed at the service of his interest. If Stewart conducts his investigation by a logical process of induction and deduction, working from the slightest clues, his objective is scarcely a noble one. On the contrary. He seeks less to reveal the light than to penetrate the shadows, those shadows in which the killer wraps himself – though a cigarette betrays his presence. In short, he examines the objective facts only so that he may better gratify his own subjectivity, and to satisfy even more an unhealthy curiosity. (Seen in this light, the publicity dreamed up by Hitch for *Psycho* becomes a major constituent of the film: the audience must *want* to be afraid.) From then on he cuts off his right arm – lucid understanding. He finds himself as unarmed as a primitive, subject to the great ancestral fears. His reason wanders wilfully into the irrational, surrenders – defenceless (like Janet Leigh under the shower) – to the all-powerful occult.

Faced with the menacing of the murderer, who has come from the world of desire, a sudden invader of his everyday world, Stewart sees his flashbulbs as an altogether ridiculous ally. The wholly material light is not enough to protect him. 'We're all in our private traps,' someone says in *Psycho*: the Hitchcockian spectator more than anyone else. Because Stewart, at the summit of his curiosity, wants the intellectual distance represented by the courtyard to be physically bridged by Kelly, he unleashes what occultists and magicians fear the most: the counter-shock. If the reader now really needs persuading that *Rear Window* is the Hitchcockian concept of cinema, let him recapitulate the above as follows. Stewart is like a projector; the apartment opposite, the screen; the distance which separates them, the intellectual world, would then be occupied by the beam of light. Remembering also that Stewart is from the beginning the spectator, the reader may conclude that the hero 'makes himself his own cinema'. But isn't that precisely the definition of 'voyeur', the essence of morose gratification?

Well? Well, we must push on with the investigation of this intellectual world. First, the more this world is concentrated on an object of desire or fear, the more intense it becomes, and the more the force of that intensity animates the form it has created. At the same time the form is made explicit and the force is augmented. As in *Psycho*. Let us assume that Stewart comes down from the screen of *Rear Window* in order to sit himself in the theatre, that he becomes each one of us – a spectator. His 'voyeur's' appetite finds sustenance from the very beginning of *Psycho*. The camera indiscreetly enters a room where the blinds are drawn in the middle of the afternoon. And in this room is a couple on a bed, wrapped in an embrace which indicates a great physical attraction. At this point he feels frustrated. He wants 'to see more'. If John Gavin's torso just satisfies at least half the audience, the fact that Janet Leigh is not naked is taken badly by the other half. This aroused desire should logically find its conclusion at the end of Janet's journey. She will be naked, totally, offering herself totally. The sexual act performed on her will also be extreme. So the wish is gratified beyond all hopes.

But let's go back to the beginning of the film. The spectator's feeling towards Janet is at once one of desire and one of contempt. A woman who takes a room in a shady-looking hotel, in the middle of the afternoon and in her own provincial town, does not deserve respect. So he has no problem assigning to her his own worst instincts. Among others, his unconscious desire, and what in his own life he can't bring himself to do – theft. Back now in her office, Janet herself is present at an important transaction. The spectator, who is beginning to be bored by these banal scenes of professional life, wants something to happen. To be precise – and why not? – that Janet Leigh will take the money for herself. The transaction being irregular, there would be no proof and the owner of the money is a really nasty type. Happily, her boss asks her to take the money to the bank. Now the sum involved is $40,000. Moreover, this happens on a Friday: the theft would not be apparent until the following Monday. Janet takes the money. And here she is, on the road.

A motorcycle cop stops her: a simple identity check. We are gripped by a feeling of anxiety. This feeling is soon increased: the cop follows her. What does he want? Have they already discovered the theft? By now we are very anxious for her to get away with it. We are with her all the way. But this altruistic feeling hides our own crime, which Janet Leigh has to commit on our behalf. Apparently sympathetic, it disguises an improper desire. A desire which will be gratified: the cop takes off.

(Why does he let her go? There are essentially three explanations. First, psychological: this woman seems very confused; moreover, she is pretty. It's normal for a cop – a man, after all – to hope that she will ask him for help. Well, she doesn't ask for help. Second, the logical explanation: as a traffic cop he is concerned about Janet Leigh's tiredness. He is professionally obliged to follow her, for fear that she will cause an accident. As it happens, she doesn't cause one. Finally, another explanation – the occult.

The very appearance of the motorcycle cop, reminiscent of the motorcycle cops in Cocteau's *Orphée*, belongs to the domain of fantasy. He is at one and the same time conscience and the Angel of Order, dispatched for a last attempt at salvation. But he cannot save someone who does not want to be saved. If the reader-spectator is familiar with the notions of magic, he knows that the audience's wave of hostility prevents the Angel from accomplishing his mission. Hence, in Hitchcock's films, the extreme importance of the *call*, frequently symbolized by the telephone. Thus in *Rear Window*, Stewart, in sending Kelly to the killer's place, both provokes him and calls him. Inversely, the killer calls him on the telephone before he arrives. In *Psycho*, the fact that the sheriff, in the second part of the film, telephones Bates, throws a singular light on what he represents in the occult order of things. We can only converse equal to equal, man to man, angel to angel, or God to Satan (*North by Northwest*). On the other hand, humans can call on superior powers, whether they are malevolent or benevolent: Teresa Wright in *Shadow of a Doubt*, Farley Granger in *Strangers on a Train*.)

Salvation being rejected by us, and so also by Janet Leigh, she is now prey to every kind of delirium, delivered up to the powers of the night, can't bear the glare of the headlights. Her fatigue makes us want her to stop. Hence our relief when she does stop at the motel. But the strange, mysterious look of the place and its proprietor gives us qualms. We sense danger, the more so because Janet Leigh is alone in these sinister surroundings, alone in her room, with the window wide open, as she looks for somewhere to hide her money (our money). And all she can do is leave it lying there on the night table. From now on we have everything to fear. To fear that the money will disappear while she is eating. And because we have everything to fear, her conversation with Perkins seems too long to us. We want to see this fear verified. Our desire to *see* is about to become even stronger: Perkins, like us, is a voyeur and watches his guest as she undresses. Is he going to rape her or rob her?

Neither one nor the other, but worse. Because our desire and our fear still have nothing real to fasten on to, are still blurred in our minds, the form which they assume is itself imprecise. A sort of shadow, a kind of ectoplasm. But, exasperated by our waiting, they are at the height of their intensity. And the force that we have imparted to this form will be of awesome power. So the form-force commits its outrage.

(It should not be thought that I am extrapolating. On the one hand, I am only describing what we see, what every spectator could have felt. On the other hand, I would point out that *Psycho* was filmed in forty-one days. That scene which lasts a mere forty-five seconds on the screen took six days to complete. Hitchcock has told us about the immense difficulties he and his cameraman Russell faced in rendering this imprecise form. He wanted no tricks; he wanted the effect to come directly from the lighting. In short, he had an extremely precise idea for arriving at this imprecise form. Let us give him the credit, which he claims vigorously elsewhere, of knowing what he is doing and of shooting only what is strictly necessary.)

An outrage, then, at once crazed and fascinating. An outrage which, by filial piety, Perkins attempts to efface. And while he is about this, we are entirely with him. We are involved in his sordid household chores; we accept that Janet Leigh, wrapped in a translucent shower curtain, really becomes what she was for us – a form. We are simply in a hurry for this business to be over. We are also afraid that a passerby, lost on this little travelled road, will discover the crime. That fear is increased when Perkins, having a quick look round the room to see if he has not forgotten anything belonging to Janet, does not see *our* money.

(Which proves that Janet found the best hiding place. 'To appreciate *Psycho* you need a great sense of humour,' says Hitchcock. Especially Hitchcockian humour which is, as we know, a way of inverting our desires; that is, of realizing them in a manner which contradicts our expectations. And is not inversion, moreover, our director's preferred system?)

But Perkins retraces his steps, sees the packet and takes it. We hope that he will discover the money and keep it – in short, that the murder will have a material justification. But as he throws it into the boot of the car, with the body and the victim's other things, we feel relieved somehow. Perkins heaves the whole thing into the slimy, stagnant water of a swamp. The car sinks halfway. Let it disappear, we think. At last it sinks completely, definitively. We heave a sigh of relief. The darkness – or our subconscious – has, we believe, swallowed up for ever our complicity in the theft.

But for this we have become accomplices in a crime. We have climbed a rung on the ladder of guilt. I don't think it would be useful to continue describing the film in detail. What we need to grasp above all is the way Hitchcock's imagination works: how Hitch uses the spectator for the internal progression of his film, how he plays on his fears and desires. The spectator has only to analyse his reactions to the arrival of the private detective. He knows why the form-force, looming for the second time, will be precise, though still mysterious. After this ordeal he has only one wish: to flee. To flee this motel and its inhabitants. But the mechanism which he himself has set in motion can no longer be stopped. From now on he is paralysed, glued to his seat as he approaches the limits of fear. The more so when he discovers that the presumed murderer has been dead for ten years. Now comes the total rout of his logical mind, the collapse of his intellectual world. From here on, for the spectator, everything becomes an object of terror. The simplest thing he sees, however banal, is enough to scare him. Each new scene is an instrument of terror. There is only one possible instinct left to him: prayer and blind faith. He hopes with all his heart that Vera Miles, Janet Leigh's sister who has come looking for her, will be saved. These noble and wholly disinterested sentiments, along with a fear which has reached its highest point, necessarily cause the form-force to reveal at last its true face to the light. It is vanquished.

Hence the necessity, after this testing voyage to the end of the night, to the end of the world of desire, to return to our everyday world. This task can only fall to the intellectual world, but one deprived of all passion, detached from subjectivity, disencumbered by morbid curiosity. In short, scientific reasoning. This explains the psychiatrist's speech. Released now, the spectator can contemplate the object of his terror, that form-force which seems, like a bird of the night, impaled and pinned to the wall. And it excites a great pity in him – a pity which it tries to refuse while seeming to provoke. ('Let them see what kind of person I am. I'm not even going to swat that fly. I hope they are watching. They'll see. They'll see, and they'll say, "Why, she wouldn't even harm a fly".') Our pity may be the last chance of salvation for that form-force which seems forever damned, the chance to emerge from the shadows, like the car pulled by a huge chain from the black waters of the swamp.

In this way, following the example of *Psycho*, and by being situated uniquely in the audience's viewpoint, it becomes easier to understand the multiple relations in Hitchcock's work between the three realities. If the spectator belongs to the world of the everyday, it is quite clear that the screen conceals the world of desire. Is it not the property of the screen to be peopled uniquely by forms animated by forces? These forms, though intangible, are possessed of a reality. If, then, the spectator finds on the screen an exact reflection of his everyday universe, it communicates with him immediately. If he feels that appearances have not been faked to 'get' him, he can't 'disconnect'. He is caught up in a phenomenon of fatal allurement. The more so since, on the screen, Hitch intends to enact what the spectator wouldn't dare to do in his everyday life. The spectator is involved more and more intensely with the forms which are charged with assuming his impulses and his secret dreams. He no longer looks objectively at everyday appearances, but receives them subjectively. There is, however, no intrinsic difference in these appearances; it is the spectator who transforms them, changes their illumination. Here the screen finally becomes for him the only reality. His supreme goal is to penetrate it.

The ideal vehicle for linking these two worlds and allowing them to communicate (spectator with screen, the everyday world with the world of desire) is obviously the intellectual world. For Hitchcock, it is clearly a matter of assigning to it the role of transmission. And the term *vehicle* is really the only one which can take account of all those trains, planes, cars, skis, boats, bicycles, wheelchairs etc. which haunt his universe. We experience them not only as a sign of the passing from one world to the other, but above all as a sensation. As a sensation of allurement, of a slide which nothing can stop. They even give the impression of fatality. The reader will immediately recall the multiple variants which Hitch likes to introduce on a theme which is so close to him. But perhaps never has he so well and so completely 'dreamed' as in *Psycho*. Janet Leigh's long and remarkable car journey allows the material and intellectual passage from one world to another: from objectivity to pure subjectivity. Generally, in Hitchcock, the human body is the first of the vehicles (hence the condemnation of dance, which gives the body its fatal seductive slide – the Stork club in *The Wrong Man*, the *thé dansant* in *Vertigo*, or the waltzes of the merry widows in *Shadow of a Doubt*). And, by extension, a vehicle which encloses a being becomes that being's new body. This is why Janet Leigh, in changing her car, is expressing a profound   desire to change her body, her personality. She wants to save a love, pure in itself, from the sordid material circumstances which surround it. But far from wanting to fight to give that love a noble status, she is only looking for purely external expedients. Far from trying to transform herself, she believes that her wish will be granted by changing her material shell.

So if I believe that occultism is at the base of Hitchcock's work, this is not because I am fascinated by the esoteric, nor even that I think it is fundamental to the *auteur*. It is simply the method of understanding which gives the artist's imagination its greatest opportunity to dream. Moreover, since this doctrine does not contradict the other systems of understanding, it allows an extremely varied vision of the world, one which is adapted to the creator's true temperament. It is certainly true that, in commenting on Hitchcock, we can be satisfied with psychoanalysis. Nevertheless, I don't think this is enough to explain the invention of the forms and their internal dynamics.

Hitchcock's work always depicts some form of duel between Light and Shadow – between, in other words, Unity and Duality. The very first shot of *Psycho*, after Saul Bass's abstract titles, reveals an immense stretch of landscape round a very ordinary-looking town, shot in an extremely harsh light. Here, it seems, all must be immutable – a sense of eternity. Titles specify the place, time and date. In opposition to this light, the second shot establishes an absolute blackness in which we are engulfed along with the camera until a room is revealed, then a bed and lovers embracing. In two shots Hitchcock states his proposition: *Psycho* will speak to us of the eternal and the finite, of being and nothingness, of life and death – but seen in their naked truth. Nothing must please in *Psycho*, which is the inverse of *Vertigo*. This latter film was constructed on seduction, hence on disguise, the dressing up of appearances, the appeal of the images – on its attraction, in other words. Here, all is founded on harshness (and no such detail is spared us), on faces without make-up, on the shock of the montage (a *cut* montage, cutting like a knife). This journey towards death must only frighten, and frighten by its *hardness*.

Translated by David Wilson

16 | Jean Douchet: 'A Laboratory Art: *Blind Date*'

('Un art de laboratoire', *Cahiers du Cinéma* 117, March 1961)

Losey is above all a researcher, his *mise en scène* a method. His declared objective: knowledge. His only apparatus: intelligence, or rather lucidity. His approach is modelled on that of the scientist. The same basic attitude to the phenomena under observation, the same procedures: discover lived experience in its totality, record it like an object, make this object the field of investigation, in short, place lived experience in laboratory conditions. Losey restores the camera to its original function as scientific instrument. That is the mark of his originality.

Does this mean that other film-makers are not fired by the same ambition? The *a priori* concept of reality, the ideal and filtered reality of a Fritz Lang, who creates an abstract universe in which passions pared down to the essentials confront each other, of a Mizoguchi, haunted by the perpetual oscillation of an external and a personal world, of a Raoul Walsh, who glorifies adventure, shows that these film-makers don't have the same concerns as Losey, even though their *mise en scène* is similar and very often superior to his. But what of Nicholas Ray and Rossellini? They too consider lived experience as a whole to be respected *a priori*. Knowledge, for them, thus consists of the sudden intuitive penetration of a reality that has first been laid out for examination. The process is the same for both: going from the outside to the inside, through affectivity.

This means that, in spite of a common point of departure, their procedures are radically opposed to Losey's, since *he* always goes from the inside to the outside. To an instinctive knowledge that is purely artistic in the traditional sense of the word Losey prefers a logical knowledge, one in which intuition and deduction are subordinated to intelligence. This kind of attitude raises the problem of modern cinematic aesthetics which goes far beyond the scope of this article: 'It was one of Brecht's principles, and the only one I am in entire agreement with,' Losey told us, 'that the moment emotion interrupts the audience's train of thought, the director has failed.'[1]

158

If one term can characterize Losey's *mise en scène*, I think it must be that of bursting open to view. It isn't quite true to say that he goes from the inside to the outside. He sticks to appearances, scrutinizing objective relationships and refusing to interpret them. Any other attitude would be unscientific and thus, in his view, unartistic. Because the outside is for him the reflection of internal phenomena, the projection of an interiorized conflict. The gesture refers to what motivates it and to nothing else. Effects reveal only their causes and what generated those causes: the person stripped naked. Losey is the first film-maker who has taken as his only material for investigation – without any reference to morality, metaphysics or religion – the truth of human beings. (The aesthetic argument that Jan, the young Dutch painter, expounds in *Blind Date* [US title: *Chance Meeting*] is, on this point, very clear.)

But if the skin is to burst, if the person is at last to be revealed to the light of day, reality has to be placed in laboratory conditions, that is, shut in and subjected to a high enough pressure to produce the split. That presupposes a dramatic situation pushed to the brink of theatricality. There has to be an acute crisis, a feverish temperature, an emergency operation. Hence that style that is so particular to Losey, a style that is raw, tense, strained, incisive. A style that shocks. For, like *Time Without Pity* and *The Criminal*, *Blind Date* is indeed about an upheaval. An earthquake shatters every illusion of stability. It's the observable manifestation of the tremendous pressures that have built up beneath the earth's crust.

If that is accepted, everything in *Blind Date* becomes clear, gestures and setting, plot and narrative structures. The story begins thus: Jan is hurrying along to his mistress's apartment. It's the first time she has allowed him to go there. The door is open. He goes in. No one there. He makes use of the opportunity to discover what kind of decor his lover has, as if it will help him get to know her better. He laughs at her untidiness, is surprised by the garishness of the bathroom, reassured by a small Van Dyck and, stretching out on the settee, mystified to find an envelope stuffed full of banknotes. He waits. The police arrive. His mistress has been murdered while he has been looking round the apartment. He becomes the prime suspect.

Let's pause for a moment on this opening sequence and Jan's discovery of Jacqueline's apartment and thus of Jacqueline herself. The camera just observes scrupulously the sequence of events, the manifestation of phenomena and their objective relations. First of all Jan's own personality. Excited by this adventure, his true self reveals itself in his attitudes as well as in his reactions, and is apparent in each of his gestures. And because they are the reflection of that true self, his gestures are as rare as they are precious (and sometimes, I admit, verging on preciosity). Like the way our young lover stops suddenly on one leg in the doorway of the bedroom, a position that is emphasized still more by a change of angle. Everything in Jan betrays an unsullied innocence, the unbroken heart of a child eager to be enchanted by love.

Too eager, in fact, for an impartial observer like us, and we can't help thinking there is a hiatus between Jan's nature and the kind of woman he loves, as she is betrayed by her apartment. It visibly belongs to a high-class tart. Some of Jan's reactions make it clear that he is aware of this, but then a tastefully chosen object reassures him. He is in fact willing to let himself be taken in. He is blinded by his love and his trust. He is on the verge of submission, his innocence is threatened. That is the heart of Losey's subject-matter. Jan has to weigh up what he has, take an exact account of its value, sum himself up, in short, study himself, i.e. attain lucidity through a critical self-examination in terms of his relationships with the outside world.

The murder creates the conditions necessary for an experiment of this kind. It constructs an enclosed world in which maximal pressures are brought to bear on him. They bear down with increasing intensity on people shut up in these conditions and lead to a kind of tearing apart that is rendered visually by the *mise en scène* and which is, it seems to me, the basic dynamic of *Blind Date*. This tearing apart comes into being with the hiatus between Jan and the setting. It is developed as soon as the police arrive, when Inspector Morgan also looks round the apartment. This time it is a cold, clinical inspection that leaves no possible doubt about the fickleness of Jacqueline's character or about Morgan's down-to-earth brashness and tactlessness (his gestures, his Welsh accent, his reaction to the mirror in front of the bed, etc.).

The confrontation of two divergent visions of the same interiors and thus of the same woman brings about an even more violent tearing apart, the flashback. This is opposed visually, through its harsh, white, Nordic lighting and bare sets, to the grey photography and the cluttered apart-ment in the first part. The flashback, generated simply by the logic of the situation, is as much a sensual evocation of a love affair as an exact analysis of the relationship between the two lovers and a judgment of their love. As an investigation made necessary by the internal logic of the situation, it brings out the obvious incompatibility between the Jacqueline Jan loves and the owner of the apartment as she is pieced together by the police on the basis of evidence and objects.

That is what Morgan can't help noticing – he has a good nose even if it is blocked. Losey likes to overlay the struggle for lucidity with this kind of physical handicap (Redgrave's drunkenness in *Time Without Pity*, Morgan's cold in *Blind Date*), a handicap that is matched by the blind infatuation of the partner. You have to fight against the fog in your own mind. For Morgan too is involved in this affair, even as much as Jan is. He finds himself caught up in the same quest for truth and thus for his own truth. Hence the pressures he has to submit to. Social pressures that impose a split between his careerism and the more imperative issue of his own self-respect. A simple question of dignity. The problem for Morgan and for Jan is the same: resisting corruption, preserving their integrity. Once they have realized this, after the short struggle that Jan's wounding question provokes in Morgan's office, the resolution isn't far off. The woman – Jacqueline/Lady Fenton – is rediscovered; under the double pressure exerted by Morgan and Jan, her duplicity is blindingly clear. The lie curses the truth. The self has conquered appearances. Innocence goes free.

We would, then, be misjudging Losey, we would indeed be completely misinterpreting his work if we refused to link his aesthetic to a rationalism of the Left. Even, as Domarchi has suggested, of the extreme Left, since Losey categorically refuses any appeal to the sentimentalism the so-called artistic Left is so attached to. His art is a laboratory art. You place a complete lump of lived experience in a jar. You create the most favourable conditions for the experiment. Then you meticulously analyse all the objective relationships that form themselves and you discover that struggle is the vital source of all reality. The struggle of individuals (Jan and Jacqueline, Jan and Morgan), the class struggle, etc. But since the knowledge of the observer is always determined by that of the person observed, the struggle allows this knowledge to develop. In this climate of dramatic conflict, justified violence breaks down ossified structures, pushing the self out on to the surface.

Seizing hold of the inner vibrations of the self: this demand that Jan makes of Jacqueline while she is drawing (whereas she, reflecting her class, seeks only to conceal it) is what Losey demands of his art. An art that despises ornamentation, that uses lucidity to destroy the myth, that grates and shocks. An art that hurts because it allows no compromise. But an art that thirsts after truth. That is why it still repels so many people.

Translated by Norman King

Note

1 'Entretien avec Joseph Losey', by Michel Fabre and Pierre Rissient, *Cahiers* 111, September 1960, p. 5.

Part Three

American Cinema: Revaluation

Introduction: Re-thinking American Cinema

By the early to mid-1960s the critical 'young Turks' of *Cahiers* in the 1950s – Jean-Luc Godard, François Truffaut, Jacques Rivette, Eric Rohmer, Claude Chabrol – had almost become a sort of critical 'old guard'. In addition, all were now more active in production – Godard, Truffaut and Chabrol particularly – and had become less frequent contributors to *Cahiers*.[1] But the occasion of a special issue on American cinema in December 1963/January 1964, eight years after a similar special issue, brought back together most of the older figures for a sort of reassessment of American cinema in the 1960s.[2] The overall tone of disenchantment and nostalgia is markedly different from the vigorously celebratory tone of the earlier issue.[3] It is not so much that the participants thought they had been wrong – though there are some concessions to having misunderstood some aspects of the way the American cinema worked – as a clear recognition that American cinema itself had been changing rapidly, that the 'studio system' was over and that this had changed the nature of its output.[4] At one level we can see a more developed understanding than in the 1950s of both the conditions of production and the role of convention in the 'classical' American cinema and of their likely effects – good and bad – on film-makers. As well as this, one senses the beginnings of an appreciation of US domination of world cinema. Some of these new perceptions were informed, no doubt, by the experience which the former critics now had of making films themselves. At another level what had been seen as one of the strengths of American cinema (and Italian cinema), as opposed to French cinema, in the 1950s – its supposed direct relationship to American society[5] – was thought to have been lost in the process of 'super-production' and the need for obvious general appeal, which provoke Luc Moullet's references to 'alienation'.[6]

It is difficult to resist the thought that the participants in the discussion should have paid more heed to André Bazin's 1957 intervention on the *politique des auteurs*. What Bazin had wanted to insist on, after all, was that the *politique* as then practised failed to take sufficient account of the fact that 'the cinema is an art which is both popular and industrial',[7] and that works were not the product of untrammelled artistic genius but were subject to the determination of social, technical and industrial factors and drew on established conventions. Similarly, in the same essay and elsewhere,[8] Bazin had argued for a clearer recognition of both the economic and the artistic importance of generic traditions.

Whereas 'Questions about American Cinema' focusses on American *cinema*, the discussion in '20 Years On', two years later, takes *critical positions* about American cinema as its focus. Changes in the American cinema itself are a very important part of the background here, but a vital new perspective is provided by the development and recognition of 'new cinema'.[9] Henceforth, attitudes to Hollywood and attitudes to new cinema cannot be separated: the new cinema inaugurated by Godard, by Resnais, by Straub and Bertolucci and 'cinema nôvo' from Brazil and Quebec cinema, thrusts towards new forms in a way which is *critical* in relation to the established forms associated with Hollywood. In Volume 1, I argued that despite the fundamental importance of American cinema for *Cahiers* it was recognized that American cinema could not be exemplary in the sense that the critics and aspiring film-makers could ever hope to make, themselves, a cinema remotely like it. In that sense Italian cinema provided a much more important example.[10] Jean-André Fieschi makes much the same point in this discussion, that 'for us young Europeans who want to make films . . . American cinema *concerns us less* . . . than current Italian, Polish, French or Brazilian films'.

Very different, but related, is the emphasis of Claude Ollier's final contribution to the discussion, which begins to move towards a new vocabulary associated with semiotics – talk of signs and meanings, metaphor and metonymy – which will stress the role of convention, of codes, and whose task will be the analysis and understanding of cinema as a system rather than analysis and understanding directed towards the evaluation of particular films and film-makers. For the moment, however, this new emphasis is there in little more than embryo form and much of the discussion goes over ground relatively familiar from various past arguments about authorship, though with some welcome clarity. The polemical need in the 1950s to establish American cinema as worthy of critical attention is recognized, as is the importance of having achieved this, but the main target of the critique of the *politique des auteurs* is not the mid-1950s but rather the 1959–62 period of 'excess'[11] when, as Fieschi puts it, American cinema became 'sanctified' and *systematically* valued and the *politique* became dogma. In effect, Rivette had already offered this critique in 1961,[12] but Jean-Louis Comolli usefully follows through the implications of the different uses of the *auteur* concept and the 'slippages' between their meanings. In particular Comolli points to problems around the definition of the *auteur* by his themes and the slippage between the identification of the thematic of an *auteur* and the *valuing* of the work of

166

that *auteur*. Inevitably, given the focus of the critique, the discussion also needs to take account of the concept of *mise en scène*.[13] Here, I think, is a more difficult area for the discussion and consequently less clarity, but Comolli, particularly, argues against the use of the concept of *mise en scène* evaluatively rather than as a descriptive term. Michel Mardore usefully points to the past tendency of *Cahiers* to place value on *a certain kind* of *mise en scène*, usually one associated with 'classical' restraint and discretion.[14] It is in this context that the valuing by the contributors to the discussion of a film like *Lilith*, directed by someone not recognized as an *auteur* and in a somewhat 'old-fashioned' way – in any case in a rather self-conscious visual style – focussed very sharply some of the major issues at stake.[15]

In the course of the discussion explicit reference is made back to Bazin's 1957 arguments against the *politique des auteurs* – even more essential background to this discussion than to the earlier 'Questions about American Cinema'. Many of the positions put forward in the 1965 discussion as necessary revision and re-thinking of the *politique* bear a close resemblance to Bazin's earlier critique. Had not Bazin also argued both that the 'theory' behind the *politique* had yet to be produced and that slippages took place between the valuing of *auteurs* and the valuing of films or, as Bazin had put it, 'the negation of the film to the benefit of praise of its *auteur*'?[16] Surprisingly enough, some of Bazin's important points are still not being taken up: his pleas for serious consideration of the role of convention and tradition in the American cinema, for instance, is barely acknowledged (though Ollier's concluding comments take this concern in a different direction). Comolli reaches what was more or less Bazin's conclusion, that American cinema was not, fundamentally, an *auteur* cinema, that *auteurs* in the American cinema were to be found *despite* the system, as exceptions to it. In this formulation, as with Bazin, there is a very clear retention of the *auteur* principle as indispensable, in relation to American cinema as to other cinema.

It is also somewhat surprising, given the juxtaposition of 'new cinema' with 'Hollywood', that the discussion manifests so little awareness of the politics and economics of American cinema and their effects on other cinemas. Comolli's 'Notes on the New Spectator', six months later, moves more consciously towards this awareness, although the emphasis is still formal. Comolli relates the traditional cinema product – 'Hollywood' or, in its broadest sense, 'consumer' cinema – to darkness. In the first place this darkness is the physical darkness of the movie theatre, but by extension it becomes the lack of knowledge and awareness produced in the passive spectator about him or herself and about the world. This represents a considerable shift of position for *Cahiers* (in which Comolli was by then the dominant editorial influence) in relation to American cinema, taken as a whole, from the positions of the 1950s. It is a position which recognizes the ideological functions (and economic base) of 'Hollywood' – although in some ways the position can be seen, as yet, as a return to relatively traditional attitudes to commercial cinema, and Hollywood in

167

particular, as escapist fare for passive spectators. Comolli focuses on the activity of the spectator in relation to the film as his criterion for what constitutes the 'modern' cinema. As yet that modern cinema turns out to be largely the cinema of the *auteurs*, since the *auteur* film 'by definition does not conform to the vague norms fixed by the tradition of dark cinemas'. The *auteur* film is necessarily, therefore, in a kind of oppositional tension with Hollywood conventions, thereby engaging the spectator in a more active apprehension of reality, just as new cinema does. There is in fact a notable tension in Comolli's article: its main points of reference are the Hollywood *auteurs* and yet, just as in the 'Twenty Years Later' discussion the previous year, it is the 'new cinema . . . that must matter most to us'. Comolli's argument here, including the tensions within it, usefully sketches out some of the ideas which were to form the basis of his much more clearly politicized 1969 editorial with Jean Narboni, 'Cinema/Ideology/Criticism'.[17]

Despite the various discussions about the *politique des auteurs*, the idea of the *auteur* survives, as much in American cinema as in new cinema, which will be debated largely in terms of individual film-makers. But it was recognized at least that American cinema posed problems for the *auteur* principle, and that those *auteurs* who survived the reappraisal of Hollywood needed to be 're-read', to be understood in a different light. As I argued in my 'Introduction: *Cahiers du Cinéma* in the 1960s', the late work of *auteurs* like John Ford and Alfred Hitchcock became the focus for critical enquiry into the very idea of authorship and into the nature of cinema, while continuing to be understood and valued in *auteurist* terms. The work of Howard Hawks, like that of Hitchcock, was re-thought partially in terms of being about the cinema. An emphasis on 'deconstruction' – a guarantee of 'modernity' (and, of course, one of the reasons why the work of someone like Jerry Lewis was so valued at this time[18]) – governs Jean Narboni's account of *Red Line 7000*. Like Hitchcock's *Torn Curtain*,[19] Hawks's film becomes a demonstration of the art of minute shifts and variations, playing against the rules in order to reveal the mechanics of narrative construction: '*Red Line* is a masterly presentation of various ways of twisting convention – an epitome of and treatise on deconstruction'. In the 1950s Hawks had generally been seen as a model of classicism and exemplary of the virtues of American cinema – simplicity, lack of pretension, uncomplicated adventure heroes.[20] In the 1960s, in order to continue to claim genius and authentic *auteur* status for Hawks, his classicism must be denied, in a certain measure, and he must be claimed instead for modernism. While Narboni argues for Hawks's work as deconstructive, Comolli argues for an ironical Hawks who conceives his heroes, below their superficial heroism, as ridiculous, futile puppets, in the adventure films as much as in the comedies.[21] As Comolli puts it in a review of *El Dorado*, 'in *El Dorado* ridicule kills more definitively than a Winchester rifle'.[22]

There is a very strong sense in the mid-1960s *Cahiers* writing on *auteurs*, especially within American cinema, that it is strung out uneasily between older critical formulations which are no longer quite satisfactory, but which cannot be denied either, and newer critical formulations, more theoretical and more political, taking shape but – like the pods in *Invasion of the Body Snatchers* – not yet fully formed. At one level we can see this as a – decisive – shift away from the definition and evaluation of the individual *auteur* towards a primary interest – very much implied in the impulse to deconstruct and to discover deconstruction at work – in the nature of cinema itself. At another, closely related, level we can begin to see in the articles of this period a change in the critical vocabulary in use, the frequent recourse to ideas about, for example, structure, repetition, variation. This change testifies to the growing influence on *Cahiers* – not just on *Cahiers*, of course, but on French social and cultural thinking more generally – of the structural anthropology elaborated by Claude Lévi-Strauss and the consequent structuralist re-reading of Marx and Freud.[23] As John Caughie puts it, these new emphases, co-existing with older assumptions, 'indicate a pull between the recognition of the *auteur* as system of consistencies and the film as site of repressions and contradictions'.[24]

These new emphases are perhaps clearest in Claude Ollier's essay 'A King in New York: *King Kong*', possibly because *King Kong* is not essentially an *auteur* film and therefore questions of authorial 'intentions' do not seem to impose themselves significantly (and possibly also because Ollier, strongly associated with the *nouveau roman*, had less stake in past *auteur* positions: this seems also to characterize his contributions to the earlier 'Twenty Years On' discussion about the *politique des auteurs*). The object of the analysis here is to make the film text say what it itself does not say, or cannot say, or can say only by omission. With its concern with the nature of narrative construction, its drawing on ideas about myth, its strong psychoanalytic dimension, its use of Marxist terminology and concern with the ideological functions of the film, this is a 're-reading' which looks forward to the methodologies of later *Cahiers* re-readings much more emphatically than it looks back to critical practices of the past.[25] At the same time we should note the extent to which it draws significantly, in terms of dream configurations and the erotic and in the psychoanalytic sphere generally, on much earlier Surrealist views of the film,[26] as well as the extent to which, in its efforts to relate the film to its social and economic context, it was only doing what Bazin had long ago argued as necessary.[27]

Analyses, re-evaluations and re-readings like those of Comolli, Narboni and Ollier represented here form an essential complement to the more militantly polemical positions about new cinema beginning to be developed alongside them and chronicled in Part Four of this volume.

Notes

1 Rohmer and Rivette remained editorially important until 1965, Rohmer acting as chief editor after Bazin's death in late 1958 until 1963, when Rivette took

over the main editorial role until 1965. See my 'Introduction: *Cahiers du Cinéma* in the 1960s', in this volume.

2 Apart from Bazin, the principal absence was Rohmer, who had recently been ousted from his editorial role: see my 'Introduction: *Cahiers du Cinéma* in the 1960s', in this volume.

3 Three articles from this issue are translated in Volume 1: Eric Rohmer, 'Rediscovering America', Ch. 7; Jacques Rivette, 'Notes on a Revolution', Ch. 8; Claude Chabrol, 'Evolution of the Thriller', Ch. 21.

4 See, for example, my discussion of changes in the American cinema in my 'Introduction: *Cahiers du Cinéma* in the 1960s'. This new perception of American cinema on the part of *Cahiers* is also very clear in the roughly contemporaneous editorial discussion around Resnais's *Muriel*, Ch. 5 in this volume, and in the later discussion of American cinema and the *politique des auteurs*, Ch. 20.

5 See, for example, the 1957 editorial discussion translated as 'Six Characters in Search of *auteurs*: a Discussion about the French Cinema', Ch. 2 in Volume 1.

6 Cf. my discussion of these tendencies in my 'Introduction: *Cahiers du Cinéma* in the 1960s'.

7 André Bazin, 'De la *politique des auteurs*', *Cahiers* 70, April 1957, translated as 'On the *politique des auteurs*', Ch. 31 in Volume 1, p. 251.

8 See, for example, Bazin in 'Six Characters in Search of *auteurs*', p. 33.

9 See Part IV of this volume, and my 'Introduction: *Cahiers du Cinéma* in the 1960s'.

10 See my Introduction to Part III: Italian Cinema, in Volume 1. Cf. Rivette's comments at the end of his 'Letter on Rossellini', Ch. 26 in Volume 1.

11 See Part II of this volume, especially the articles by Michel Mourlet and my 'Introduction: The Apotheosis of *mise en scène*'.

12 Jacques Rivette in 'La Critique: Débat', *Cahiers* 126, December 1961, p. 18, quoted in my 'Introduction: *Cahiers du Cinéma* in the 1960s'.

13 See, for example, Fereydoun Hoveyda's 'Sunspots', Ch. 13 in this volume, in which Hoveyda discusses authorship in terms of *mise en scène*.

14 Essentially, this is the aesthetic elaborated by V. F. Perkins in *Film as Film* (Harmondsworth, Penguin Books, 1972). Perkins values a cinema in which the hand of the director does not impose itself in an obvious way, but this aesthetic is flexible enough to accommodate the often highly expressive *mise en scène* of, for example, Hitchcock or Sirk.

15 See Ch. 20, note 9, for further reading on *Lilith* and Robert Rossen.

16 Bazin, 'On the *politique des auteurs*', p. 258.

17 Jean-Louis Comolli and Jean Narboni, 'Cinéma/Idéologie/Critique I', *Cahiers* 216, October 1969, translated as 'Cinema/Ideology/Criticism' in *Screen*, vol. 12, no. 1, Spring 1971, reprinted in *Screen Reader 1* and Nichols, *Movies and Methods*.

18 See Ch. 20, note 11, for other *Cahiers* material on Jerry Lewis.

19 See my 'Introduction: *Cahiers du Cinéma* in the 1960s' for discussion of *Cahiers* responses to Hitchcock's *Torn Curtain*.

20 See, for example, Eric Rohmer's 'Rediscovering America', Ch. 7 in Volume 1. As Comolli points out, Jacques Rivette's seminal 1953 essay on Hawks, translated as 'The Genius of Howard Hawks', Ch. 16 in Volume 1, was rather more ambiguous in its definition of the 'classicism' of Hawks.

21 Since Rivette's 1953 essay, most critical studies of Hawks have seen the comedies as essentially the inverse of the adventure films. Comolli follows this line here, as do Robin Wood, *Howard Hawks*, London, Secker & Warburg; New

York, Doubleday, 1968; revised edition, London, British Film Institute, 1981; and Peter Wollen, *Signs and Meaning in the Cinema*, London, Secker & Warburg; Bloomington, Indiana University Press, 1969, second edition 1972.

22 Jean-Louis Comolli, 'L'envers de l'Eden', *Cahiers* 192, July–August 1967, p. 22. Interestingly, Robin Wood, in his roughly contemporaneous British study of Hawks, *op. cit.*, comes up with some of the same perceptions, positing, like Comolli, *Scarface* as the key Hawks work, but producing, fully in line with Wood's overall concern with moral universes, a Hawks vitally concerned morally with flawed heroes and the nature of heroism, rather than an ironic Hawks.

23 See my brief discussion of these developments in my 'Introduction: *Cahiers du Cinéma* in the 1960s', in this volume. John Caughie discusses these developments at greater length in his Introduction to Part Two: 'Auteur-structuralism' in *Theories of Authorship*, pp. 123–30.

24 Caughie, *Theories of Authorship*, p. 14.

25 For later, collectively written 're-readings', see, for example, the work on *La Vie est à nous*, *Cahiers* 218, March 1970; on *Young Mr Lincoln*, *Cahiers* 223, August 1970, translated in *Screen*, vol. 13, no. 3, Autumn 1972, reprinted in *Screen Reader 1*, Nichols, *Movies and Methods* and Gerald Mast and Marshall Cohen, *Film Theory and Criticism*, New York, Oxford University Press, 2nd, revised ed., 1979; on *Morocco*, *Cahiers* 225, November–December 1970, translated in Peter Baxter, *Sternberg*, London, British Film Institute, 1980. Cf. Pascal Kané, 'Re-lecture du cinéma hollywoodien: *Sylvia Scarlett*', *Cahiers* 238–9, May–June 1972.

26 See, for example, Jean Ferry, 'Concerning *King Kong*', originally published, under the name of Jean Levy, in *Minotaure*, no. 3, 1934, republished in *Midi-Minuit Fantastique*, no. 3, October–November 1962, translated in Paul Hammond, *The Shadow and its Shadow: Surrealist Writings on the Cinema*, London, British Film Institute, 1978.

27 See particularly Bazin, 'On the *politique des auteurs*'.

17 | Claude Chabrol, Jacques Doniol-Valcroze, Jean-Luc Godard, Pierre Kast, Luc Moullet, Jacques Rivette, François Truffaut: 'Questions about American Cinema: A Discussion' (extract)

('Questions sur le cinéma américain: sept hommes à débattre',[1] *Cahiers du Cinéma*, 150–1, December 1963–January 1964)

[. . .]

Jacques Rivette: Another thing has disappeared,[2] I think, also seven or eight years ago, and that's original screenplays. Eight years ago, inasmuch as there were genres like the Western or the crime film, and particularly inasmuch as scriptwriters were paid an annual salary by the companies, some of these scriptwriters wrote personal stories, within the confines of the existing genres, knowing that if they stayed within the limits of these genres and respected their appearances, they could find in them a way of expressing themselves. Between 1940 and 1950 there were many interesting films made from stories written directly for the cinema.

[. . .]

I think it divided 50 per cent adaptations, more or less faithful, and 50 per cent original stories, written directly for the screen by people who had been hired in the first instance to adapt a Niven Busch or a Chandler. These people, after they'd proved their know-how by writing adaptations which were increasingly unfaithful, ended up by getting their producers to let them write a story of their own invention, as long as it stayed on line. That's something that has practically ceased to exist, I think – the American film made from a script written directly for the cinema.

Luc Moullet: There's a very good reason for this change, which is that the book publishing *industry* has only taken off in the United States during these last few years. Today it makes more money than the cinema: America has started to read.

Rivette: Which explains why more and more films are being made from best-sellers.

Claude Chabrol: There are programmes on television of the 'Reading for Everyone' kind (the same phenomenon is happening in France), in which somebody comes on to sell his concoction and if the viewers find

172

him sympathetic, next day they go and buy his book, which otherwise they don't read . . .

Moullet: They read the last page, where the book is summed up.

Rivette: But if a lot of people have bought the last page, that makes them want to go and see the film.

Pierre Kast: Turning best-sellers into films has become an absolute rule . . .

Chabrol: It always has been a rule to some extent. But nowadays I think nine out of ten American films are adapted from best-sellers – either from books . . .

Jean-Luc Godard: Or from events . . .

Kast: Yes, like *The Longest Day*.

Godard: Even the life of Christ is adapted from best-sellers and not straight from the Bible: they pay someone four million for the rights to make the life of Christ!

Jacques Doniol-Valcroze: But if structured genres have disappeared as such, are the reasons for that really economic ones? The anti-trust law[3] threatened the industry and its traditions; but in '55 this first crisis was resolved. . . .

Chabrol: I've an explanation, but I'm not sure if it's the right one. When these guys got the message that people were no longer going to the cinema, they did the wrong thing. They said to themselves, we've got to have a complete change, we've got to make what we haven't been making and stop making what we have been making. And they went off on new tracks which were actually the wrong ones, since people weren't going to the cinema simply because they had television; now they're starting to go again. So I think the genres are going to come back, and the next instalment, in four years time, will be about the rebirth of the crime film and the Western, quite simply because the producers will have to get back to their old formulas, as it was before '55 . . . So if you start saying that in '58 the American cinema was in full flight, you'll just get laughed at. In '58 it was desperate!

Doniol-Valcroze: But if, in '55, there was already a big shortfall as far as production was concerned, distribution was doing well. And if genres no longer exist, you can't just say 'television' because the initial crisis had already been nipped in the bud by '55–56.

François Truffaut: Television has swallowed up the 'tried and tested' genres and films have become more individualized. These are films made by producers, and producers who are setting up a deal prefer to go in with a big book which was being talked about last year than to film an anonymous script. It's become more personal, in the European manner. A film's existence depends on its producer; and that's surely one of the consequences of the anti-trust law.

Chabrol: Whereas when people were under contract, there was a system of production which was self-generating. If you had a hundred people under contract, you made them do the kind of films you were paying

173

them for. If you'd hired thirty people to make crime films, you made crime films.

Doniol-Valcroze: But by '55 MGM had already fired forty of its fifty scriptwriters.

Rivette: And they've since fired the other ten!

Truffaut: At the moment MGM is like Cocinor-Marceau [the French distribution company]. The big companies have become distribution networks which are willing to take on different products, whereas before, when you went to see a film you knew from the first reel more or less how it would end.

Rivette: Just from the quality of the photography, or the sets or the style of the direction (for example, there was more cutting in Universal films than in MGM films) you knew what company it was.

Chabrol: Universal editors would have eight shot-reverse shot cuts compared to four in an MGM film.

Truffaut: You could even go so far as to say that MGM films told stories which often spread over a good many years, while the films of the other companies dealt in moments of crisis. In the end, you liked American cinema because the films were similar; you like it less now that all the films are different.

Doniol-Valcroze: American cinema, then, has become Europeanized . . .

Godard: Just as European cinema has itself changed . . .

Rivette: Let's just say that they've moved towards each other: American cinema has taken eight steps in this direction to European cinema's four.

Godard: As a matter of fact, there's been a great falling off in the general quality. The reason we used to like the American cinema was that of every hundred American films 80 per cent, say, were good. Nowadays of every hundred American films 80 per cent are bad.

Truffaut: I agree. It was the know-how one appreciated. Now it's intellect, and intellect is of no interest in American cinema.

Godard: As with Anthony Mann, who was a great director when he was paid by the week and under contract. Now he makes *The Fall of the Roman Empire*.

Rivette: The main point is the fact that the big companies, who were production companies, have become distribution companies who make deals with independent producers.

Chabrol: When they haven't become oil wells . . .

Rivette: This is what accounts for the rise during the last eight years of United Artists, the first company to follow this policy. Eight years ago United Artists was a second-rank company compared with MGM: now they are just as important.

Chabrol: All the same I think there are still some people under contract. Minnelli, for instance, is still under contract at MGM.

Rivette: Yes, but that's the exception. These people are the survivors of the old system. Which raises a question: who are the people *making*

174

films now, since every film made now is made in isolation? You realize that it's everybody: veteran producers from the big companies, who are nowadays entirely in charge of their films, actors, directors, even scriptwriters who have had a success and have managed to get control of their own productions. For these people, who make each of their films as an independent project, what's the financial criterion they base themselves on? They have to get finance from a big company or from a bank (which comes to more or less the same thing). So what can they do? Only one thing: set the thing up, get their film rolling on the basis of a *title*.

Chabrol: What counts for them is to have a title, certainly, but also actors. This is why actors are so powerful at the moment: we're back in the era of the stars.

Rivette: So we have a cinema which no longer has any time structures. I mean that when there was such and such an actor or such and such a director under contract, a way of doing things, a system would last ten years – a particular producer's idea could last ten years. . . . The films being made now are entirely of the present moment, but 'spatial': that's to say, a system which is valid for a single film, but a film aimed at the whole world.

Chabrol: The history of *The Train* is oddly characteristic. What happened was that there was Arthur Penn who had the idea for the film, and his producer who is tied up with the William Morris agency. They go to see Lancaster. But the moment he's on board, he's running the ship.

Rivette: Why, though?

Chabrol: Because he's a star.

Rivette: Because what you have is a cinema of playing for stakes: so everyone tries to raise the ante by betting on Lancaster. Which is why Lancaster has so much power and importance. He himself is left behind by this kind of general manoeuvring going on around him, by the size of what's involved in this throw of the dice. That simply leaves him behind.

Chabrol: Still, it was he who gave Penn the boot.

Truffaut: It's almost part of the system.

Rivette: I think that in a case like this everyone is *pushing* Lancaster to give Penn the boot because everyone is concerned that the stakes should be as high as possible.

Chabrol: What makes Frankenheimer more important than Penn?

Truffaut: It's not a change of director, it's a change of *film*.

Godard: It's quite simply because Penn didn't tilt the camera when he was shooting the engine in *The Train*. He didn't use any tilt shots, that's all it was. Which meant it wasn't 'epic', it wasn't a super-production. There was no sense of alarm, the train's arrival wasn't startling. It's the Selznick method of twenty years ago.

Kast: What's characteristic, and a kind of counter-proof, is the way Zanuck made Wicki's film *The Visit*. His original notion was to shoot the film on location in Yugoslavia, with a small budget. But he said to himself: 'Wicki is the greatest director in Europe, I'm going to make him the greatest director in the world'. And the result was: 'We can't make the film for less than three million dollars.'

Godard: Previously, he wouldn't have needed to make a calculation like that, because all over the world he had a circuit of cinemas which would show the film automatically. There's no such thing now: so the product has to be transformed, adapted to other needs. There used to be an automatic world market, but today there are conditions attached.

Doniol-Valcroze: The companies no longer control the cinemas they had up to 1947, before the anti-trust law.

Chabrol: They control them all the same.

Godard: Since 1950 Paris has had a great many cinemas under American control. In fact, the American cinema has never been more powerful. From the point of view of domination, not a single film gets off the ground today without sooner or later being bought by America or without the Americans being involved in one way or another.

Rivette: It's starting to become increasingly a kind of world cinema, or at the very least a cinema of NATO and SEATO.

Doniol-Valcroze: Half the world market.

Godard: I'm a film-maker, and I make films by myself. But whether you're Stanley Kramer or MGM, you make more or less the same kind of films. And if I make a film with Kramer, I won't come out of it better than with MGM – worse, on the whole.

Previously, the producer was an individual. The money and the producer were one and the same thing, not an abstract, diffuse presence, but a man you had in front of you and whom you fought against. Whereas today what's most difficult is that, since the producer is every-body, you don't know who to talk to, you've got to fight a general state of mind. When you want to place a script today, there's no precise person you can talk to, and that goes on for months. Before, you used to go and talk to Goldwyn. Today, ten people are producing a film: it's the intellectual middlemen who make the film in the end.

Truffaut: We should perhaps admit that we were wrong several years ago when we welcomed the emancipation of the American cinema, because in reality it was the beginning of the end – starting with Stanley Kramer and the disappearance of traditional methods of making films. We used to say that we liked the American cinema but its film-makers were slaves; what would it be like if they were free men? Well, the moment they become free they make lousy films. The moment Dassin is free, he goes to Greece and makes *Celui qui doit mourir*.[4] In short, we liked assembly-line cinema, pure manufactured cinema, where the director was an operative for the four weeks of shooting, where the film was edited by someone else, even if it was the work of a big director. This is what Ophuls said in *Cahiers* 54,[5] but we didn't reckon how vital it was, for the American cinema, to work in these conditions. Because very few people deserve to be free in the cinema: freedom implies being in control of too many different elements, and it's rare for people to have the talent for all the stages, all the different moments in the making of a film.

On the other hand, there was a great modesty in the American cinema, which came out of the hard face of business. Mr Goldwyn didn't give a damn for prestige – he had several prestige films a year – but he was particularly proud of the power of his production company. The moment films become individualized (in their working and production methods), producers identify themselves with a film, they're more concerned with the rewards, the Oscars. This turns it into a cinema with all the faults we criticize European cinema for, and none of the advantages.

Godard: Six years ago, I had for the first time the opportunity to make a film. At that time, I was only thinking in terms of American cinema, in terms of the films that I knew. It was the model to imitate. Nowadays it's the thing not to do.

Moullet: But the Americans thought the opposite. And instead of creating a new American cinema on the same basis but with a different character from the one that existed ten years ago, they made a copy of European cinema, except that they only kept its most superficial aspects. Previously, the American cinema was a national cinema, with extremely solid foundations, whereas today it's really alienated.

Godard: What was good about American cinema was that it was spontaneous, at whatever level; now it's become calculated. The American character is not that well suited to calculation.

Chabrol: People were prisoners and tried to escape. They've become a lot more cautious and timid than they were before. It's a crazy thing. I'm sure today Dassin couldn't even imagine doing *Thieves' Highway*.

Truffaut: It's not a film that a free man wants to make. You have to be on the payroll to make this film – it was good payroll cinema.

Kast: Better good payroll cinema than bad director's cinema.

Godard: The first time you make a film, you say, 'If only I had a free hand . . .'; and the fifth or sixth time, you realize that certain constraints are a good thing, and that the problem of being free in the cinema is part and parcel of the cinema.

Truffaut: Every time you met an American director in Paris, you were always struck by his modesty: he thought of himself as being just a cog in the wheel.

Rivette: A true modesty – or a false one.

Truffaut: No! A true modesty.

Rivette: Hawks and Ford were not cogs.

Truffaut: I'm talking about Nicholas Ray.

Chabrol: But Ray suffered from it.

Rivette: That said, I think we must take the American cinema as it is in 1963, and not be universally pessimistic. For example, this genre cinema has its good side. But it also has its awful side. When you have another look at some American films from 1940 to 1950 (leaving out the films of the great directors like Ford, Hawks or Hitchcock, which are special cases), you're sometimes very happily surprised. And sometimes appallingly let down. Generally speaking, it's the ambitious films you feel appallingly let down by, and the frankly commercial films you're very happily surprised by.

Truffaut: That's absolutely right. *Desperate Journey*,[6] which was shown again on television, is tremendous.

Rivette: Whereas Ophuls's *Caught* is very irritating. Ophuls was given a script to shoot which obviously didn't interest him for a moment. Being given something to do means it's less well done.

Kast: What one might say is that many directors, who could give of their best within that kind of set-up, find themselves being abruptly transplanted into a set-up they're not made for, one whose risks they're not ready to take, because freedom entails risk . . .

Rivette: In fact, we liked Ray's films a lot, but we also liked the films of Stuart Heisler. Obviously you didn't put them in the same category. But it's clear that for some years different personalities, like Ray and Heisler, were obliged to comply with a kind of pre-existing set-up. But it's difficult to know precisely what was involved in this set-up. Today you see directors who were supported by this set-up suddenly caving in. Mervyn LeRoy created a misleading impression when he was at MGM, because he was given good actors, good scripts. Without this supporting framework, he's no longer anything – nothing. On the other hand, some directors, such as Preminger, have managed to profit from this freedom. Preminger's recent films are more interesting than his earlier films, even if you can argue about them. Others, though, like Ray, were lost in this freedom.

Truffaut: The equivalent for Ray of Preminger's freedom was when he made *Rebel Without a Cause*.

Godard: Ray worries about himself too much. He asks himself too many questions, and in the end he's his own worst enemy. He needs someone who can sense when his ideas are good and when they're bad.

Kast: Something else survives from the old system. Jane Fonda told us[7] that what she was most struck by in *The Chapman Report* was the extent to which Cukor wasn't free to do his own editing.

Godard: It must be said that Cukor could have done so had he wanted to. But as it happened, he didn't want to have to fight to get into the editing room, he didn't want to have to fight to make an arrangement; if he wanted to, he could pay for an editing suite at his own place. And then, that's not to say that this would be better or worse. What struck me when I was talking to Nicholas Ray was that every time I said I very much liked one of his films, he said, 'Yes, there are one or two shots that I quite like; there's a fine tracking shot there; good camerawork in that one. . . .' Things like that. American directors don't suffer, whereas with European directors, whether they're good or bad, if they have a word cut from an hour and a half's dialogue, they're as miserable as sin . . . Even Ray, who's more sensitive, who's one of those rare people with an *auteur*'s mind, doesn't get at all agitated by this kind of thing. He's sad, but that's different.

Doniol-Valcroze: When we said that the American cinema has become Europeanized, it's more on the level of structures than the way its directors behave.

Godard: At the same time, it's based on something else. Preminger offered me a film in the United States and I said to him: 'I'd like to do a Dashiell Hammett novel. . . .' He didn't go along with this because he wanted me to do something on New York.

Rivette: *A bout de souffle* on Main Street.

Godard: What I wanted to do was a little Western.

Rivette: Obviously Preminger can't understand that.

Godard: In the United States no one understands it.

Truffaut: I think the decline of American cinema began when they wanted to make films on the actual locations. The stars were very keen on this because they admired Italian neo-realist films, and also it allowed producers to use their blocked funds in various countries. In the old days the American cinema used to build forests in the studio – as in *Sergeant York*. The moment they went off to film Argentina *in* Argentina, it went downhill.

Rivette: When they go to Argentina, they choose what looks like what they used to do in the studio.

Moullet: My feeling is that the major factor, in the cinema as elsewhere, is the disintegration of the pyramid. The whole strength of American cinema was in its pyramid structure: there were forty films which weren't bad and five masterpieces. These days, there are almost as many great films as there are middling ones. It's the death knell for any activity.

Chabrol: To get a hundred good films in any country you have to make five hundred.

Truffaut: America was the only country where the unambitious film had quality. That remains a unique phenomenon.

Translated by David Wilson

Notes

1 The original subtitle for the article, 'Sept hommes à débattre' (literally, 'Seven Men Discussing') is an allusion to the French title of Budd Boetticher's Western, *Seven Men From Now, Sept hommes à débattre*. André Bazin's review of the film, which had acquired the status of a minor legend, in *Cahiers* 74, August–September 1957, is translated as 'An Exemplary Western' in Volume 1, Ch. 23.

2 This discussion had begun with some rather desultory comments on the relative

disappearance of genre cinema, and had been prefaced by a reminder that the earlier special issue on American cinema, *Cahiers* 54, Christmas 1955, had contained articles on the evolution of various genres – André Bazin on the Western (translated as 'Evolution of the Western' in Bazin, *What is Cinema? Vol. 2*, reprinted in Nichols, *Movies and Methods*), Jean Domarchi on the musical, and Claude Chabrol on the thriller (translated as 'Evolution of the Thriller' in Volume 1, Ch. 21). The initial comments about the disappearance of genre cinema stemmed from the observation that no one had proposed articles on genre for the 1963 special issue.

3 Anti-trust laws were used against the major Hollywood companies throughout the 1940s, but the process by which, essentially, exhibition became divorced from production and distribution is usually taken to begin with the Supreme Court verdict in the Paramount case, May 1948, and the consent decrees which followed. The history of these changes is detailed in two anthologies on the American film industry: Tino Balio, *The American Film Industry*, Madison, University of Wisconsin Press, 1976, revised ed. 1983, and Gorham Kindem, *The American Movie Industry: The Business of Motion Pictures*, Carbondale and Edwardsville, Southern Illinois University Press, 1982. See also, for example, Lea Jacobs, 'The Paramount Case and the Role of the Distributor', *Journal of the University Film and Video Association*, vol. 35, no. 1, Winter 1983.

4 Cf. the thesis on Jules Dassin elaborated in Colin McArthur, *Underworld USA*, London, Secker & Warburg; New York, Viking, 1972), where Dassin is seen as having the self-conception of a Romantic artist, 'believing his prime responsibility to be to his own act of creation rather than to the necessity of communicating to his audience or to the rules of pre-existing artistic forms. He would regard himself as producing his best art when least trammelled. . . . But where his Hollywood films suggest a craftsman who might have become an artist, most of his European films suggest a talent lost in the process of trying to create Art'. (pp. 93, 101).

5 Max Ophuls, 'Hollywood, petite île', *Cahiers* 54, Christmas 1955 (special issue on American cinema).

6 *Desperate Journey*, a 1942 Warner Bros. picture directed by Raoul Walsh, with Errol Flynn, Ronald Reagan, Nancy Coleman.

7 'Jane Fonda par Jane Fonda', an interview in *Cahiers* 150–1, December 1963–January 1964, the same special issue on American cinema in which this discussion appeared.

Jean-Louis Comolli: 'The Ironical Howard Hawks'

('H.H., ou l'ironique', *Cahiers du Cinéma* 160, November 1964)

Who is H.H.? The more there is of him, the less, if we aren't careful, we know about him. Each time he makes a new film his old ones are talked about again, but only to be lost sight of even more than they were.

His latest film, *Man's Favorite Sport?*, refers back to *Bringing Up Baby* in its details, to *I Was a Male War Bride* in it substance and to *Monkey Business* in everything else; but these correlations don't help at all, quite the contrary: instead of helping to explain, for example, what might be central in these very diverse films, they simply cross-multiply images of this elusive centrality that are sometimes the right way up and sometimes upside down; and you need real cunning to find that centrality or to make sense of it – if women are men, that doesn't quite mean that men are women; both sexes flirt with the transsexual but both stop short of crossing over to the other side – even a cat couldn't tell which kitten was which; and besides, in *Bringing Up Baby*, love – or the fury which passes for it – tends to deprive the man of the attributes of his profession, whereas in *Man's Favorite Sport?* the same love – or the blindness which passes for it – confers on him and encumbers him with those same attributes; the more our *auteur* advances in a straight line, the more we seem to be going round in circles! We haven't yet reached the stage where an adequate schema of Hawksian situations and their inter-relationships can be drawn up; what can already be guaranteed is that if you add them all up one by one, they cancel each other out.

And even if, from one film to the next, H.H.'s trajectory seems to be a straight line in its obstinacy, this is only the straightness of a sophist. Instead of concluding, the film's conclusion leaves the film in a state of suspense, which doesn't mean that it isn't finished or that the possibility of more effective endings is excluded, but neither are these other endings allowed for any more than a given film allows for the equally inconclusive endings of the other films.

There isn't one of his films that doesn't end abruptly with an about-turn, that doesn't turn away from itself and from what it was advocating in a final reversal, stopping short of a conclusion or continuing well beyond it. Take for example the end of *Red River*, which seems to run counter to the whole film – but which doesn't, of course – all the more so since the film spends its time avoiding itself, thwarting itself and since it begins, amazingly, with the end of some other film, with the resolution of a *real* Western, one that *Red River* merely comments on and criticizes. But there are also the endings of *Sergeant York*, *To Have and Have Not*, *The Big Sleep*, *Monkey Business*, *Bringing Up Baby*, which are just ellipses, like the ending of *Man's Favorite Sport?*, or reversals (like that of *Male War Bride*). These are the fundamental principles of comedy but they recur with an astonishing frequency in the 'dramas' (very strange dramas). *This* is the film-maker who, not unreasonably, has long been quoted as an example of classic cinema in its purest state and whose genius has, not unreasonably, been considered as self-evident.[1] That's fine as far as I am concerned. But, looking at his films, we have in the end to ask ourselves what kind of classicism we are talking about here and whether we don't have to consider the evidence as something quite different from simplicity or immediacy even if it is founded on these two qualities; whether Howard Hawks and his films, which usually do quite well at the box-office, don't simply make us call into question a whole referential system, all our neat little ready-made ideas about the 'classic', about the wisdom of the great Americans – and thus about seminal heroes, about the whole construct of myths that have had so much to do with our love of American cinema, myths of free and responsible men,[2] of women who weren't *femmes fatales* but aware that they were there at the right time, myths of purity and simplicity which, if we took the trouble to investigate them, would all turn out to be based on the much more consistent myth of the grandfather who fascinates children.

Why should we hesitate any longer to confront a simple fact which is as real as it is worrying: from his first steps through to his latest offspring Hawks has never been either a classic in the classic sense of the term or the master of 'simplicity' and even less of the obvious (something that has been inferred from a misunderstanding of Rivette's idea[3]). His only 'evidence' is that of the lynx: he sees without being seen.

The only constant in his films is that he always talks about Man. That, I suppose, is enough for all the strengths and virtues which adolescents attribute to manhood to be conferred on this Man just on the credence of the capital letter. It is in any case enough to have stopped people going to look more closely at the kind of man Hawks talks about and how he talks about him. It is evidently not a man who is free and fulfilled, a model person, that he takes as his subject and model. However heroic his heroes are, they are always a little bit ridiculous and viewed with a trace – an affectionate trace – of condescension by the director. Take Wayne in *Red River*, *Hatari!* and *Rio Bravo*: yes, you are confronting the toughest of heroes and the truest. At least you, we spectators, see him like that. The Hawksian viewpoint is quite other. It seems quite likely that Hawks doesn't give a damn about heroes, about *his* heroes. For the film-maker, perfection isn't a good subject. Men who have fulfilled themselves in their own particular field are of no interest and there's no story in the simple-minded – or else, if that's what you really want, you have to ask Rossellini or Olmi but not Hawks. That is why you can't take literally his so-called (he's the one who says it) passion for 'specialists'. It is a strange kind of passion that sets out to catch these 'specialists' in the crudest of life's traps, that plays on their speciality to ridicule them, making them human in the process. This tough, grave and uncompromising sheriff is a loser, Hawks's camera says in an aside. But keep that to yourselves because heroes must always be right. No, Wayne, the fearless hunter, the ambitious cowboy, the incorruptible sheriff lives a life that is just a series of failures and renunciations. He isn't simply 'unhappy' (that's why he needs to be attractive to women), he has always missed out on what matters most because he is a 'specialist' or more exactly because Hawks doesn't film true heroes any more than he films ideal men.

H.H. operates in fact on two levels. He isn't naive, he isn't wet behind the ears. He knows what works in cinema – the exemplary – and he knows that it is to an extent in the nature of cinema to invest in dreams and to set itself up as an example.

His films are, then, exemplary, full of characters who at first glance (he rarely allows you a second one) can seem exemplary, perfect, wonderful. In this way he wins over the crowds a little, warming the hearts of adolescent dreamers. He is, in this respect, a demagogue; but that isn't his fault: cinema is even more demagogic and you can't make films without cinema. Fortunately for us (and for cinema), Hawks is too sincere – or too lucid – to believe for a moment in his prototypes. He is concerned about what the audience likes but at the same time he reserves the right to back the intelligence of that same audience to the hilt: he shows us something of the heroes right-side-up but always contrives at one moment or another to reveal the wrong side in an extremely unflattering situation, one in which they cannot in fact show their worth, only their inability to live out their lives, to go beyond their preconceptions.

This is a good lesson in logic, a good lesson in cinema. Take it or leave it, this is what constitutes Hawks's genius, he leaves the door wide open. Perhaps, too, his presence is swept away by the draught: he is the supreme example of the man and the artist that you can't pin down.

His films are like that too. We still don't know what he or they are, we just know a few things *about* them. *He* remains one of the great directors – even his size makes you look at him a bit at a time; *they* are perhaps the most complete and most accomplished body of work that exists, and this, again, complicates everything. There seems not to be a single topic or theme that hasn't been touched upon and subtly demystified or perversely mythified while still giving the impression that it is only ever Man and his ideals that are at stake. But we have already seen that Hawks only concentrates on this Man because he is a man of straw. The attitude, the notorious manner of this Hawksian man, is also straw-like, except when it's wooden: he is always the best man around except when he really needs to be.

It has become a cliché that the ethic of his heroes and their stories is facing up to things. But it's rather that they efface themselves as quickly as they can to avoid completely losing face. I am thinking here of the most frequently quoted examples, the Bogart of *To Have and Have Not* and *The Big Sleep*: but how can you avoid noticing that he takes action only when he has to, and that far from sometimes leading to a pay-off this action is only a last resort, a way of escaping with some of his dignity still intact. Bogart isn't the hard man with a soft heart or the tight-lipped fighter, he is a kind of casual amateur who shows off as much as he can and bows and scrapes politely to women after stringing them along just long enough to have a bit of fun. Marlowe is a pathetic character, as demonstrated by the killings he is unable to prevent. Like everyone else he hasn't much of a clue what is going on in *The Big Sleep*. It is only after he has crawled through dozens of mouse-holes, lots of dirty business and some whopping great lies – all Hawks's characters lie, about themselves, about what they are going to do, and not just for the sake of it but for fear of being caught out – that he reaches a degree of awareness and morality. Nothing to get excited about!

Hawks's characters tell copious lies but he *has no compunctions about telling them either.*

To take just one example – *Hatari!*: he has said over and over again that Wayne and the other actors didn't have stand-ins, whereas it is clear from beginning to end that they did and that the whole film is faked. I hasten to add that it is all the more beautiful as a result. But *Hatari!* of all films! A film that has itself become a myth. It's Adventure, Africa, Adoration. . . . We'd do better to move on down the alphabet, it's a film about ridicule, senility, worthlessness.

You only have to notice that in every single case, including Hatari!, *the thrilling career that pits the hero against the universe (all that should be in inverted commas) is merely child's play.*

It may indeed not be easy but it's kid's stuff all the same: driving cars, hunting wild animals, playing at cowboys and Indians or cops and robbers, playing with model aeroplanes, playing war games, playing at detectives, come on, none of that's for real, it's just fooling about. Childhood or second childhood. Hawks doesn't show us these trivialities just for the fun of it, believe you me. No, it's not through impotence or anything of that order that his films only present us with futile puppets. It is perhaps – but this clue is so carefully concealed that it really is invisible – it is perhaps, as we are sooner or later obliged to admit, just to show us that they are indeed mere trivialities and likeable puppets that disintegrate as soon as they come up against life, that it's all lies, lies that evaporate as soon as there is the slightest drama, the slightest glimpse of reality: love, death. The key to Hawks's work (and it isn't for nothing that

H.H. ranks this film above all the others) is *Scarface* with its pitiful hero. All the rest are just various kinds of surrogates for this tragic infant. What Hawks says about *Scarface* only makes sense if you also take into account the characters in *Only Angels Have Wings* or *The Big Sky* or all the other films.

It's been thought until now that there is a hiatus between Hawks's comedies and the serious films. Not so. There are the same marionettes with the same demons pulling the same fragile strings, there are the same sour masquerades, the same blithely admitted gratuitousness, the same ephemeral swagger that disintegrates as soon as the slightest difficulty, the barest necessity of life is encountered.

What can we conclude except that Hawks is exactly the opposite of the worthy figure with deep humanitarian concerns he is so often made out to be in devotional literature: he is, in essence, the most discreet humorist of the century. And since humour has nothing to gain from discretion, it has passed unnoticed. It is no coincidence that his heroes are stupid, ignorant and clumsy, that they lack sensitivity and tact, that they are misfits and losers; it is a well-deserved hell since all these numerous shortcomings are passed off as exemplary virtues. It is intelligence taking its revenge. An intelligence that is all the more subtle in that it devotes all its energies to an almost obsessive desire to throw you off the scent, to sell the dummy, to pass off carefully planned strategies as improvisations, lies as expressions of sincerity, men as women and utter crassness as intellectual power. An intelligence that is all the more evident in that it presents the criticisms it wants to make as if they were apologies and thus manages to keep itself entirely in the background so that you won't notice it is there. From the heights that separate him from his heroes and his films, Hawks must be enjoying himself immensely.

Because it is hidden, his message can only carry all the more insidiously. In the service of the lie, cinema speaks the truth; it lies in the service of truth and can thus serve it better.

An intelligence that is dissimulated, an *auteur* whose only self-revelations in his films are lies (those in which he shows himself most clearly are *Scarface, Twentieth Century, Man's Favorite Sport?*), a perpetual play of reversals, of phoney rhymes, of false values presented as though they were true, an irony that is all the more vicious because it is concealed; and at the same time a corpus of films in which the point is never undermined, the objective, on whatever level it is located, always attained; a cinema whose practice is consonant with its nature – the effacement of the *auteur* in his work, in his films. That is what would make Hawks appear to be a trumped-up classic if he hadn't always been a true modernist.

Translated by Norman King

Notes

1 Jacques Rivette, 'Génie de Howard Hawks', *Cahiers* 23, May 1953, translated as 'The Genius of Howard Hawks' in *Movie* 5, December 1962 (abridged); modified

translation (complete) in Joseph McBride, *Focus on Howard Hawks*, Englewood Cliffs, N.J., Prentice-Hall, 1972, reprinted in Leo Braudy and Morris Dickstein, *Great Film Directors*, New York, Oxford University Press, 1978, and in Volume 1 of this series, Ch. 16. Rivette's article begins: 'The evidence on the screen is the proof of Hawks's genius . . .'.

2 Comolli has in mind, for example, Eric Rohmer's view of Hawks: see Eric Rohmer, 'Redécouvrir l'Amérique', *Cahiers* 54, Christmas 1955, translated as 'Rediscovering America' in Volume 1, Ch. 7.

3 See note 1, above.

19 | Claude Ollier: 'A King in New York: *King Kong*'

('Un roi à New York', *Cahiers du Cinéma* 166–7, May–June 1965)

In 1925, the captive brontosaurus brought back from *The Lost World* and exhibited as a fairground attraction in London broke loose from its chains, wrought considerable destruction around Piccadilly Circus and headed for London Bridge, where it slipped, sprawled headlong, and brought the bridge tumbling down under its weight. Six years later, Willis O'Brien, creator of the models and techniques used in these special effects, was asked by Merian C. Cooper (co-director with Ernest Beaumont Schoedsack of *Grass*, *Chang*, *The Four Feathers*, *Rango*, and later producer of some of John Ford's best films) to prepare a series of designs illustrating a project for a film about a giant gorilla. Aided by Mario Larrinaga and Byron L. Crabbe, O'Brien duly produced twelve tableaux likely to have clarified Cooper's ideas.

> The very first sketch showed King Kong on top of the Empire State Building, clutching the girl in his hand and being machine-gunned by the planes. The second showed Kong in the jungle, shaking the tree-trunk in order to throw off the sailors. Then in the third, Kong was beating his breast and defying the sun, with the girl this time at his feet. There were twelve sketches in all. During shooting, eleven of them were meticulously reproduced in live action sequences.[1]

So the adventure of filming *King Kong* in fact started with its closing sequence. It would be interesting to know in what order the screenwriters who ultimately worked out the details of the action – James Creelman and Ruth Rose (Mrs Schoedsack who, contrary to some reports, was never a stripper) – actually elaborated the episodes. It would not really be surprising if they did in fact work backwards: the most fertile fictions are sometimes born this way, since the very fact of proceeding backwards forces the author, on pain of death, to find an absolutely irrefutable chain of causality (usually finding it fairly quickly, since the 'impossible' links eliminate themselves, as it were); whereas if he proceeds in the supposedly more normal forward direction, the possibilities spread out before him like a fan, much too diffuse to ensure a necessarily healthy growth, and the ineluctability of the plot suffers. The retrospective method, on the other hand, stands a good chance of imposing a self-evident truth, indisputable even though it may conflict with everyday logic and likelihood. The hard facts follow abruptly on each other's heels, driven by some obscure subterranean impulse, and one no more feels the need to query them than the scriptwriter, borne back into the fiction's darker reaches, was at liberty to suppress the gifts of divination forced upon him.

It may be that Creelman and Ruth Rose did in fact proceed in the manner most spectators (and readers) imagine to be the way of sensible screenwriters: going clockwise rather than back-tracking an ineffable course of time. The fact remains that the motifs governing the film are all comprised in O'Brien's initial conception, a veritable blueprint synthesizing the fiction: Beauty, a prized jewel wrested from her doomed social milieu, bearing witness to the mortal combat engaged by mechanized civilization and the gorilla-god of primitive nature (she seems distinctly less terrified than at the 'beginning', and not only, it would seem, because fear exhausts itself through its own expression); the furious Beast, who pathetically defends her rather than himself against the flying machines, since he is shot in the back by the daring US air force Spads while momentarily relaxing his vigilance to check on the safety of his protégée; the theme of the omnipotence of public entertainment, of the commercial interests it involves and consumes to the point of exhaustion or catastrophic (but possibly welcome) disaster; as a corollary to this, the extravagant role played by publicity in the star system, with the prehistoric beast promoted to the status of star revealing itself to be a god of love, and therefore of destruction; finally, and most notably, the elaboration – rendered in concrete form by the presence of the monster on top of a skyscraper – of a parallel between the primitive island and the modern metropolis; one might add, for the record, yet another demonstration of the unshakeable faith of those 'explorers' Cooper and Schoedsack in the cinema's capacity – and calling – to make itself a vehicle for any delirium whatsoever.

Product or not of a backwards logic exploding from that grandiose image, the script for King Kong, which combines three celebrated tales – The Sorcerer's Apprentice, Beauty and the Beast and The Lost World – is uncommonly rich in its implications. It is rather disconcerting to see how, in describing this masterpiece of symmetry, even the most laudatory critics of thirty years ago used the term 'infantile' which can still be heard from the mouths of many a favourable spectator today. (In that autumn of 1933, of course, when the Place Clichy was dominated by an enormous pasteboard Kong covering the façade of the Gaumont-Palace, French audiences were deprived of the film's opening reel, happily now restored for their admiration in the current reissue.) At first glance the narrative is doubtless not the most remarkable aspect of this remarkable movie. The power of *King Kong* of course derives primarily from a visual splendour unequalled in the genre, from the brilliance of its oneiric imagery, and from a capacity for erotic suggestion astonishing enough to have caused generations of schoolgirls to fall for the great ape, protective perhaps, but terrifying to say the least.

The workings of this plot nevertheless deserve further examination. What, to begin with, is it about? It's about a compleat *auteur* (backer, producer, scriptwriter, cameraman, director) preparing to set out once more for virgin territories to film another of the never-before-seen spectacles which have made his name. The originality of this 'setting in the abyss' derives from the fact that it is surrounded with the same atmosphere of secrecy as the story of the actual voyage: to the unforeseen – relatively foreseen – of the film to be shot is added an unforeseen element through the parsimonious details offered concerning the second story. There is of course an obvious motive for this precaution: if the crew knew what awaited them at the end of the voyage, they would probably never sign on. But more particularly, this process of gradual, grudging revelation adds to the overall feeling of an 'adventure movie'. And in so doing it also offers an opportunity to clarify certain facts or to hint with delightful anticipation at things to come. If, for example, that daredevil of celluloid Carl Denham has involved a girl in one of his productions for the first time, it is because the critics – and therefore the public – have earnestly demanded that he freshen his formula by adding sex to the exoticism. The project in hand is to a large extent, therefore, a response to collective demand. Moreover, the circumstances in which Denham himself comes ashore to pick his female star off the streets are not left to chance: what attracts his attention is a piercing cry, provoked by an act of aggression as the fruit-vendor brutally grabs his victim. Around this voice, potentially a shriek of anguish, the mystery of our dual suspense is polarized; a mystery which Denham does not dissipate until they are lying off the island. Naturally he has a scenario in mind, or rather an outline singularly modern in conception since he envisages, within a set framework and with certain given data – an unexplored land, a primitive people, a young American woman, a legendary creature neither man nor beast and in essence seemingly divine – very sizeable unstable areas in which complete improvisation will reign. The theme chosen is that of Madame Leprince de Beaumont's celebrated tale; in detail, scenes will depend on what happens during shooting. Like some Rouch of prehistory hatching a monstrous psychodrama, Denham puts the time spent at sea to good use by fashioning his Beauty: a costume specially designed for the role, exercises in mime, voice tests in the higher registers, a conditioning to fear. As for the Beast, he will direct it as best he can, backed up by gas grenades. Note the classic mythic nature of the island: the Norwegian sailor who passed on the map had never seen it himself; it was a native, survivor of a shipwreck, who told him about it. The ritual elements of the late nineteenth-century adventure yarn, along with its earnest tone, the sense of leisureliness, the naive and slightly fusty tone, are also scrupulously preserved: a storm to be outrun, a course deviating from normal shipping routes, an uneasy captain, a restive crew, clammy heat, torpor, fogs and reefs. But the island does indeed exist, and so does Kong, whose name echoes in the ears of the sailors like some vague memory rooted in the mists of time.

The first day's shooting exceeds all expectations the heir to the Scandinavian 'discoverer' may have cherished. Very soon overtaken by events more cinematic than he could ever have dared hope (the natives seize his leading lady and take over the *mise en scène*), deprived of the initiative but wresting it back through strong-arm tactics, Denham substitutes the spectacle itself for an exotic film spectacular, subjugating the monster and shipping it aboard with the intention of exhibiting it in New York along with the heroes who captured it – one of the rare instances in which the spectacle itself is likely to be more impressive than a record of it on film. Like Denham, we have had our fill as far as adventure is concerned. But there is another way of telling the story with equal fidelity: an inveterate speculator, spurred by the unprecedented economic depression that is shaking his country to its foundations, realizes that he must stage an absolutely extraordinary show to stave off the crisis. Leaving the country – where the authorities, faced with a grave, unforeseen peril, have responded with neither a coherent plan nor any effort towards a fundamental revision of the system, leaving the hapless populace trembling before the spectre of poverty – he sails to an unknown, almost entirely virgin island whose primitive inhabitants are similarly exposed to a terrible menace, permanent in this case, indeed virtually eternal, but who have come to terms with it in a form of exchange that seems to have worked hitherto to everybody's satisfaction. Intoxicated by the scent of profit, totally failing to recognize the native wisdom which he treats with the contempt befitting an honest white racist, he manages within a record time – like the foolish merchant of the fairytale who sets too little store by Beauty – not only to bring terrible deaths upon several of his companions, but to destroy the delicate balance set up by the local witch-doctors. Roused and despoiled through his foolish intervention, the monstrous creature shatters the age-old ramparts and lays waste to the village.

Even this is not enough for Denham. Still driven by his contemptible purpose, he mobilizes the resources of technology in order to ship the gigantic, vengeful creature to his own country, thereby unthinkingly placing the life and property of many of his compatriots at risk. Only the very latest weaponry enables him to lay the bogey. So, through the fault of one of its own citizens desperately seeking a constructive solution, the menace hovering over the New World, hitherto on a human scale, is now reinforced and redoubled by a much more terrible threat from nature, superhuman, enigmatic, in defiance of reason, a retaliation by savage forces which inevitably looms as a sanction: it is contact with a tainted, unjust society, degrading to the individual, that drives Nature in all its 'horror' and long-forgotten bestiality to intervene and try to rescue the only being worth saving from the chaos that threatens her and which it destroys. The element of provocation is vitally important here: it was the white man who broke the pact by taking back the proffered sacrifice. To ignore the laws of Nature – or to animate and violate them – is to unleash a cataclysm.

Setting aside the social and moral implications of a second half in which the themes and their figurations combine and interweave so as to 'reconstitute' the ultimate vision of the gorilla – dominating the city over which it brandishes the threat of sovereign retribution – in all its original simplicity, let us consider two spatial locations equated by a 'puerile' script of remarkable complexity. The topography of the island, for a start: Skull Island seems very similar to all those imaginary islands in the shape of hemispheres, skulls or inverted teacups – like the Back Cup of *Facing the Flag*, admirably animated by Karel Zeman in *The Fabulous World of Jules Verne*, who draws his inspiration from the steel engravings by Roux for the Hetzel collected edition of Verne. Here, a narrow peninsula extends to the foot of a huge mountain, exactly like the tip of Manhattan beneath the skyscrapers. An ingenious native tribe survives as best it can in the lowlands close by the dreaded barrier, just as the civilized population swarms round buildings where the powers-that-be sport with and mysteriously control its destiny. But in both cases the bulwark ensuring security and prosperity eventually gives way; even the razing of the main gateway in the barrier has its symbolic echo in the unthinkable 'contemporary' catastrophe of the Wall Street Crash which blew the financial floodgates wide open. In each case the equilibrium is destroyed, the only difference being that for the people of New York the two dangers are cumulative, while it is a white man who sounds the alarm going to summon help from black natives he has just accused of cowardice and for whose deaths he is responsible. Once stirred up and let loose, King Kong rather unfairly attacks black or white without distinction. The whites admittedly rid the island of his presence, but did not Kong also rid it of giant beasts on occasion? All that is left for the natives to do is to bury their dead and rebuild the gateway before the real monsters, the truly vile and bestial ones with whom no pact is possible, can breach it in their turn.

A parallel is thus drawn between two jungles. Thanks to virtuoso special effects reaching a peak of skill and sumptuousness here, the jungle of Skull Island – created out of models, transparencies, articulated armatures and stop motion photography – transfers its oneiric power of suggestion to that other more modern island, made up largely of very real views of New York. This way in which the fantastic spreads by contamination from one world to the other of course constitutes the film's prime source of power. But there is another, relating to the laws governing each of these worlds, which deserves some attention. Students of market values would certainly find matters worthy of analysis here.

191

Against her will, the heroine Ann Darrow puts each of them to the test: as a token for barter (initially almost worthless, relatively valuable as soon as Denham hires her), she finds herself promoted to current coinage by the natives of Skull Island. Then another promotion: in King Kong's hand she becomes the object of a love cult. Rescued by Denham, her stock goes down a couple of points but her exchange rate soars vertiginously. By reclaiming her and placing her out of reach of his money-grubbing peers, Kong saves her from a degrading 'fetishization': the wrath of god is explained as much by the theft practised on him as by the disrespectful attitude of the theatre audience to the couple starring in the drama. Ann's turbulent fate is thus closely linked to the conditions of life prevailing in her social group: in triumph as in terror it is exemplary, and this is what the shrill modulations of her scream express throughout. 'Your only hope is to scream,' Denham tells her on the boat. From the very outset this scream predestines her to rape, and the misadventures of Ann in *King Kong* prefigure those of another similarly predestined American heroine, the Melanie Daniels of *The Birds*. The link between individual and collective destinies, through progressive amplification and eventual generalization, is continually established in both films: Melanie conjures the birds to attack, as Ann does with the gorilla; in her wake, first the limited group, then society in general and the entire country become prey to destruction. The famous 'overlong' opening to *The Birds* corresponds exactly to the first part of *King Kong*, where nothing uncanny happens, nothing but progressive tremors of apprehension in the 'chosen one' rapidly communicating themselves to ever-widening social circles. In *King Kong*, the retracing of the heroine's past which served as the object of investigation and analysis in *The Birds*, is elided and condensed into Ann's scream, into that exceptional faculty she possesses for expressing terror which brings her to Denham's attention, just as Mitch is drawn to Melanie on the strength of her 'innocent' little machinations. This said, New York is saved from destruction, Denham pronounces his funeral oration over the body of the vanquished beast, and he has the final word, whereas Hitchcock's screen remained occupied by thousands of winged creatures, menacing, observing a truce between two attacks. But the prosperous America of 1963 could afford to indulge an ending fraught with uncertainty and danger; the America of 1931, the year in which *King Kong* was conceived, could not dispense with the happy ending. (Not until the year of *The Birds*, 1963, could one see New York obliterated by the US President's own hand:[2] the *ne plus ultra* of a screenwriter's daring in a time of fatted calves.)

But to return to Ann's nightmare. With the lights of New York echoing the torches of Skull Island, all the scenes in which blonde Fay Wray (delightful Mitzi of *The Wedding March*, Eve Trowbridge in *The Most Dangerous Game*) changes masters – one eye licentious, the other apprehensive – take place at night: Denham carrying her off, her seizure by the natives, Kong first taking possession of her from the sacrificial altar, then again as a prelude to his irresistible climb up the skyscraper. The one exception is when Driscoll reclaims her during the fight between Kong and the pterodactyl (or pteranodon?), concluding a non-stop series of clashes which constitute the acute phase of the experience. Interposed at this point are two vertical plunges, perhaps one of the best devices the cinema has seized on to express the phenomenon of temporary relief as nightmare fades: the climb down the providential creeper, then the vertiginous plunge into the water incredibly far below. Terror dissolves, crystallizes, dissolves again in admirably interwoven sequence, resolved in Ann's sinuous flight, her hair flying free and her body relaxed for the first time since the start of this terrible series of convulsions and battles to the death. (The fall from the clifftop is worth comparing to certain perspectives of flight featured in Norman Z. McLeod's *Alice in Wonderland*, made in the same year.)

Another sequence communicates one of the most hallucinatory sensations of incredulity ever seen on the screen. This is the one in which a helpless and terrified Ann, having fallen from the treetop where Kong had placed her for safety, looks on as her protector and the tyrannosaurus fight to the death. Here a slight difference in shading between the foregound shots involving Ann and the middle distance where the monsters are battling away contradicts the impression of proximity sufficiently to cast doubts as to the distance that really separates the two locations. The brutes are indeed close by since they batter several times against the now uprooted tree-trunk, yet their confrontation (in medium long shot) is taking place at a problematic, 'unthinkable' distance. Ann's terror derives equally from the immediate vicinity of the spectacle (and the intense danger that implies) and from a suspicion one senses growing in her as to the reality of what is happening. (If, moreover, there were any 'everyday' logic to the affair, it would surely be quickly snuffed out by the staggeringly terrible punishment the combatants inflict on each other.) But at this point the 'splitting' of the action is obvious. To a large extent Ann is attending her own nightmare. A similar though less evident sense of dislocation hovers almost constantly over the fight scenes: for instance in the overly speeded-up motion of the brontosaurus which emerges from the swamps and pursues the sailors through the jungle. Here several effects of different origin combine as they come into play: the more or less visible ruptures in depth shots achieved by multiple printing, the rupturing transition from long shot to medium shot of Kong (or indeed that extraordinary dolly in to his enraged features), and above all the jerky movements caused in filming frame by frame. One can see how even the defects, certain imperfections or slight lapses in perception of movement, far from destroying or lessening the credibility of what we see, in fact contribute to the sense of overwhelming oneirism, so true is it that the world of dreams is one of spatial effects, optical dislocations, sequential breaks and general discontinuity. Together, the 'dubious' space created by O'Brien's in-depth montages and the need to film in fragmented motion compose a visual universe which perfectly realizes the 'collage' effect basic to any nightmare vision: stippled space and stippled time, gaps, fringes, overlaps and incompatibilities in action, zones of imponderable duration, void, into which apprehensions of unreality tumble headlong. In the same way, the occasional errors in proportional scale noticeable here and there between Kong and his surroundings also add to the radical compartment-alizations characteristic of dreams, where the relative sizes of people and objects are constantly evolving. (It is a pity that a scene in which the sailors hurled into the precipice were devoured by giant spiders – and which was shot – was not retained in the final cut, apparently at the film-makers' own wish.)

From a purely visual point of view, O'Brien's creations – both on paper and on film – have a strange, sumptuous, pullulating beauty: this jungle, comprising vegetation that is geographically unlikely and animals more legendary than scientifically prehistoric, stems directly from engravings inspired by several centuries of adventure stories. In the scene involving the underground lake, for example, one finds the same chiaroscuro as in many an illustration for Jules Verne or Paul d'Ivoi (a very similar lake, for instance, where the hero, hunted and taking refuge in a grotto, had to tackle a giant octopus single-handed and in total silence since his enemies were prowling nearby). In certain compositions involving rocky escarp-ments, the affinity with Gustave Doré is obvious. We know, too, that the painting of Skull Island reproduces Arnold Böcklin's celebrated 'Isle of the Dead': a few years earlier, Fritz Lang had similarly used elements from three Böcklin paintings for two sequences in his *Die Nibelungen*. As for the animation of the King of the Jungle, secrecy continues to shroud the various techniques used simultaneously or by turns. The character is so indubitably driven by a vital spark of life – one might almost say of humanity – that it is difficult to disabuse spectators, impressed by his magnificent demeanour and movement, of the notion – totally unfounded – that the role of Kong was played by a human being. Finally, in so far as cruelty is concerned, horror in its whole gamut of dark, basic sensations (suffocation, oppression, vertigo, pulverization, burial, ingestion, sinking, strangulation, dismemberment), the film offers many terrible, matchless displays: witness the image of an enormous paw with hooked claws care-fully crushing an unfortunate black into the spongy mire.

King Kong, a masterpiece of the fantastic and certainly one of the finest and most disturbing examples ever made, recalls a period in cinema when every true audacity was permitted and often inscribed on the screen. There can be no doubt that it owes its resounding success to the competence and cohesion of an exceptional team of film-makers. The heart of the matter probably lies less there, however, than in the source of inspiration on which that team chose to draw. Through literature, painting and engraving, O'Brien and his collaborators revived a rich tradition of illus-trated myths and legends, and this is certainly the direction to follow in preference to the sort of breathless leap into some pseudo-atomic science fiction instanced most recently at its lowest ebb by the drearily ugly *Goldfinger*. One regret, perhaps: that the scriptwriters did not faithfully follow the story Denham had intended to film to its conclusion. Another possible happy ending would have lifted crucial doubts as to the Beast's other guise, a mystery that remains shrouded. How would Kong have looked if, in those last moments, Ann had loved him?

Translated by Tom Milne

Notes

1 Interview with Merian C. Cooper, *Midi-Minuit Fantastique* no. 6, June 1963, p. 40.
2 In Stanley Kubrick's *Dr Strangelove, or How I Learned to Stop Worrying and Love the Bomb*.

20 | Jean-Louis Comolli, Jean-André Fieschi, Gérard Guégan, Michel Mardore, Claude Ollier, André Téchiné: 'Twenty Years On:[1] A Discussion about American Cinema and the *politique des auteurs*'

('Vingt ans après: le cinéma américain et la politique des auteurs', *Cahiers du Cinéma* 172, November 1965)

In the history and the landscape of 'cinephilia' the most burning issues and dangerous passages have been, and still are, the politique des auteurs[2] and American cinema. From their first issues to the present, Cahiers have pursued a parallel defence and illustration of both which has turned them into the basic options, the necessary preliminaries to any move towards full recognition of the cinema as a major art.

The time has now come to look at the balance sheet. At the end of the day, the two-pronged battle to win acceptance for the politique des auteurs and American cinema comes up with two contradictory results. On the one hand, the signs are all for proclaiming a victory. Apart from a few crabby critics whose ideas (or lack of them) were never open to change, all who stand for an act of faith in the cinema – critics, magazines, film societies, fans – are now aware of the reality of the concept of auteur and the soundness of the politique, just as they are of the historical and aesthetic importance of American cinema. On this front, the battle has been won more decisively than anybody could ever have predicted. Now it needs to be pursued on other fronts, and it is up to the new cinema to carry on the struggle.

But on the other hand, even as they won the field, the politique des auteurs and the cause of American cinema soon exceeded the limits of their initial definitions, as is inevitably the way of attractive causes.

In the name of one cause or the other, misuse, excess, misguided ideas, flights of fancy have multiplied at every opportunity. The more meaningless they became, the more they assumed mythical status; the more they traded in particularities, the greater their claim to absolute values. In sum, options and speculations became dogma and system.

It is these excesses which concern us here. We challenge the elevation of the politique des auteurs *into dogma and the systematic valorization of the American cinema. It seems to us that to cling to rules which admit no exception, systems which object in advance to any contradiction, is to restrict both the richness of the*

196

cinema and our ability to understand it – something constantly confirmed by recent films, whether American or European, and indeed by the evolution of cinema as a whole.

We do not intend, therefore, to burn former idols. On the contrary, we mean to keep close company with the cinema on its voyage of self-discovery. The age of auteurs *is both finished and yet not finished. The age of American cinema is perhaps still to come. For the moment what matters is seeing that the beauty of the cinema knows neither rules nor boundaries, that it gives the lie to the laws that supposedly contain it, and that it can be seen in the early films as often as in the most recent; in fact, that it is faithless and capricious and that it matters less to rediscover it than to be surprised by it each time. We are not the teachers or the judges of a cinema which has been fully achieved, we are witnesses to a cinema in the making.*

The debate that follows has as its sole aim to ask, or ask once again, those questions that to us seem serious. We have turned circles long enough not to get giddy when the round is over and it is time to start again.

Basically, the cinema has always had to be discovered. And surely it is up to our readers to say so too?

Jean-André Fieschi: What we need is clarification of the misunderstanding or misunderstandings which for some years now have led cinephiles as a whole astray on the American cinema and the concepts of *auteur* and *mise en scène* as *Cahiers* itself presented them – in often confused and sometimes over-theoretical terms. First there is what might be called the ill-conceived sanctification of the whole of American cinema, which the great majority of cinephiles regard as not just fundamental and especially privileged, but even *magical*. On this particular point, I'd say there has been a fairly radical change (and obviously I'm not talking here about Chaplin, Welles or Hitchcock, but about Walsh, Hathaway or Stuart Heisler, and all those craftsmen, great or small, to whom we owe the quality of commercial cinema, entertainment and genre film). We have been forced to concede that once you divest the American cinema of its magical function, which it largely owes to the charm of the exotic, then for us young Europeans who want to make films, it is not exemplary in the way that has been claimed rather irresponsibly. American cinema, with certain notable exceptions (Sternberg, Welles, Hitchcock, Lang, and all our '*auteurs*'), *concerns us less*, except simply as film enthusiasts and consumers, than current Italian, Polish, French, or Brazilian films. And we have to concede that the qualification '*auteur*', to the extent that it implies a value judgment (I'll come back to that), is not applicable to a hundred film-makers or more, but to a much more limited number who need defining as precisely as possible.

Jean-Louis Comolli: The concept of the '*auteur*' as argued by *Cahiers* was at first, I think, fairly close to that of the writer or painter: a man who controls his work in accordance with his own wishes and is himself totally immersed in it. The issue for the critics and future film-makers

197

of *Cahiers* was to assert that in cinema as a 'collective art' artists were able to present their own 'world view' and to express their personal, even private, preoccupations. In short, that the individual and creator was not effaced in the collective work of creation, rather the reverse . . .

Michel Mardore: Bear in mind that intelligent people in the United States, like Richard Brooks, see the *producer* as the *auteur* of the film; in other words, it's he who gets together the ideas, chooses the cast and the technicians, and takes responsibility for the product. What we've been thinking of as the *auteur* is a specialist film worker.

Fieschi: When you read an interview with Minnelli – a nice man, but he doesn't have much to say – and then an interview with John Houseman who produced Minnelli's films, it's obvious that the *auteur* is not Minnelli but Houseman. The same goes for a number of musicals; the contribution of Arthur Freed, who chose the scripts, choreographers, actors, designers and directors, is more important than that of the director in question.

Even in the case where a film-maker becomes his own producer, he still has a boss; it's a bit like self-censorship in certain fascist countries. Nothing obliges films made by this method to be more liberal or courageous than those produced by Zanuck. There are, to put it mildly, some very odd things about our beloved American cinema. Take Vidor, for instance, dissociating himself from the sublime ending of *The Fountainhead*. This is one of those films, and it doesn't only apply to the American cinema, where the individuality of a man and a creator are asserted with the greatest strength and the fewest concessions. So it seems Vidor himself, even though it meant being against his own masterpiece, was infected by the producer mentality.

Comolli: The *politique des auteurs* was at one and the same time an ambitious assertion – allowing cinema all the prestige of a complete and separate art – and a very modest one – the cinematic *auteur* was quite simply the equivalent of the writer, painter, or musician, confronting his work as they confronted theirs. At the same time, this definition was married to a premise which derived less from a critical appreciation than from a value judgment. From the point at which the quality of *auteur* was recognized in a certain film-maker his films accorded each other a mutual value so that each succeeding film by that '*auteur*', when it wasn't absolutely excellent, had to be 'interesting' at least.

In other words, recognition was given to a certain *fidelity* of the *auteur* to himself, to certain constants in interpretation, theme, expression, etc. Which not only characterized the film-maker and every one of his films, but signalled their essential interest.

This led to a kind of slippage. A confusion arose between the concept of *auteur* and the concept of theme: you only had to identify certain constants, a particular obsession in a film-maker, for him to be labelled an '*auteur*' – which is fair enough – and for him to be considered great – which is in most cases not justified.

And on the other hand, if for some reason you liked a film-maker who had previously not been recognized as an *auteur*, you fought tooth and nail – and what's more, successfully – to uncover some kind of 'thematic' in his *oeuvre*, thereby automatically authenticating the *auteur* and demonstrating the presumed quality of his work. To put it in a nutshell, every great *auteur* had a thematic, every film-maker you decided to call a great *auteur* had a thematic and the slightest trace of a thematic meant that the *oeuvre* fell within the *politique des auteurs*.

The phenomenon we are dealing with here is the stretching of the *politique des auteurs* to the point where the *auteur* and his subject matter endow each other with a mutual value. Obviously, even the worst film-makers have their obsessions and they deal with them. Badly, naturally. And they're of no great interest.

Fieschi: The question of the thematic is on the whole one big joke – at least in the terms proposed. Ford's could make a breviary for reactionaries. As for Walsh's, it boils down to two or three basic principles in adventure stories; it obviously doesn't ever guarantee the success of a particular film. *Distant Drums* is a fairly close reworking of *Objective Burma* which in no way explains why the latter is a great film and the first is not.

Comolli: In the same way you can say that Fuller's thematic isn't the most interesting thing in the world. If you're looking for *ideas* in film-makers, better look elsewhere. I'm not sure they are best expressed in film.[3]

Fieschi: Take another example: the plot of *My Fair Lady* is undoubtedly more Cukorian than that of *The Chapman Report*, which is one of this *auteur*'s masterpieces, while *My Fair Lady* is to say the least debatable, despite all that can be said for it by a commentator as dangerous as Téchiné.

André Téchiné: *The Chapman Report* may be superior to *My Fair Lady* but that takes nothing away from the latter, whatever you may think. By comparison with the Broadway musical, Cukor goes for an astonishing 'vacuum'. In the film there is a clear rejection of spectacle, or to be more precise, the spectacular. Cukor's case is special and the same goes for any American film-maker taken independently; there are only exceptions and it's their areas of overlap that make it possible to turn them into dogma, rob them of their complexity and emasculate them. So the way opens up to those who only know how to follow and not to original creators.

Comolli: All this again brings up the question of what an *auteur* is in the cinema. Does the quality of *auteur* rest in fidelity to themes and in the uniformity of their treatment? Or shouldn't we reduce their number and make that *quantity* correspond rigorously to the essential *quality* of the works. Historically, those we have called *auteurs* were in the first place great film-makers: Hawks, Rossellini, Hitchcock, Lang, Mizoguchi, Buñuel, Renoir . . . To extend the *auteur* quality is to devalue it.

This means that if the *politique des auteurs* could appear to have a real base in the case of a few great film-makers, it was because of the preliminary *choice* of those particular film-makers; in other words a gamble was taken on them. A certain *taste* precedes the *politique des auteurs* and is its basis. When the *politique des auteurs* is applied indiscriminately and then found wanting, it's a question of bad taste. It's not the interest of a particular thematic which decides the value of a work, the two are reciprocal. We need to avoid confusing continuity of theme with aesthetic consistency.

Gérard Guégan: Bostonians hated the American West and those who planned its conquest, with the result that history worked itself out without them. The reception given to cinema from the other side of the Atlantic after the Liberation is not without analogy – the same scorn, the same fervour. And as always, faith did the rest. That faith gave criticism the term 'Hitchcocko-Hawksian'. The era (*L'Ecran Français*[4] had sunk into pathetic anti-Americanism) invited violence. A new kind of orthodoxy seemed to be taking shape – the *politique des auteurs*. You must admit that when you read the *Cahiers* of the time now, it's impossible not to be aware that there are no criteria for the choices made. Their absence undoubtedly favoured the systematization of the *politique* which, with time, risked becoming just a grid to be applied to any product. In an article which inevitably became the focus around which the critique of criticism organized itself, Bazin himself deplored the thinness of the theory: 'But,' he wrote, 'that is not the main point, at least to the extent that the *politique des auteurs* is practised by people of taste who know how to watch their step.'[5] Who isn't tempted to see the key to all our problems in the second part of that statement? The fact is that in the period of Truffaut and Rohmer you could count the errors of judgment on the fingers of one hand. Various elements had to be resolved and given an organic coherence, and they managed to do this.

In their absence, since life had to go on without them, a code was set up which, necessity being the mother of invention, was more than once modified in the face of films by Ulmer or Walsh, to name only two. From distortion to distortion, the postulate evolved into a law that was utterly unacceptable. It was evoked wherever the occasion served. Brooks, Welles, Wilder and Donen were thrown out of the club. Immediately, a clan formed to take them in; even better, minor tribes pitched camp at the approaches to the Musée du Cinéma to demand respectable status for Daves and Corman. The *politique des auteurs* had become an elegant way of proclaiming that the moon was made of green cheese.

Mardore: If we are going to get our point of departure straight, we ought to start by standing Truffaut on his head. It's now more than ten years since Truffaut demanded a commitment from his readers with the aim of getting the *politique des auteurs* through.[6] Basically, he told them: 'You like four or five films by Kazan, three or four by Clément. Better to choose once and for all between Kazan and Clément than to quibble over the quality of *every* film'. By that he was implying a superiority of personality, of thematic. In a way it was a kind of gamble, a lottery in which right values were part of the game while wrong values, even when they accidentally succeeded, were thrown out. This tactical point of view has broken down in our day. The film has begun to be more important than the *auteur*, the reverse of what the historians thought. They believed the cinema was impersonal in its infancy and personal in its adulthood.

Guégan: Take the most recent Minnelli film. Lots of people saw us as brutally rejecting what everybody adored, or seemed to adore. And I'm afraid we have to plead guilty.

Aren't we really responsible for a terrorist regime which reduces all thought to the acceptance of normative values, which demands the depersonalizing of every film viewer? Yet to pass over in silence today the insignificance of the latest Minnelli film would mean in the end failing to distinguish the successes from the failures in his work. We ought to decide once and for all: Minnelli's art draws its greatness from its subordination to American conventions: for example, build a world which is in all respects like the real world and then distort it in the filming; suppress the first element and you have *The Sandpiper*.

The failure of a Welles film has a different flavour altogether: he teaches us that an *auteur* can make mistakes but that his mistakes are a thousand times more exciting than the half-successes of someone else, that *The Stranger*, despite its failings, prefigures from within *Touch of Evil*. Just as ignoring the marvellous courage of Autant-Lara's *Le Journal d'une femme en blanc* so as to exalt the phoney daring of *My Fair Lady* leads to a denial of the art of our time, so elevating the past in order to authenticate the future is a fraud. And that's the function often assumed by thematic criticism, because for it the thought exists before the work and gives it a place in some idealist continuity.

Take Walsh, whom some people prefer to Welles. What would happen if we took it into our heads to harangue our readers at length on the homage to be paid to him by the Cinémathèque? A break with the readership . . . I don't think so. At most a bit of friction which would lose all its importance in the long run because all that would be retained of his films is the bit that charms. From *Gentleman Jim* to *A Distant Trumpet*, if we consider just the last twenty years, there are ten films for which we would continue to fight. But to demand that all the other films should be adduced to shore up the hypothesis of a second level is like inviting a violent end – the beauty of Walsh's films is in their effective reducibility to a unique vision, their proclamation of intent throughout the screening. Having said that, did we turn up our noses at *A Distant Trumpet*?

There is an advantage to be drawn from the critical status of these film-makers and that is the break with a closed and corrupted faith, a renewal of scepticism without which nothing lasting will ever be built; without which we would have discarded the latest Mackendrick or the latest Mulligan. It is up to others to concern themselves with developing something that can't be considered here except as one point of view arising out of a general discussion, and to say in what sense Straub, Bertolucci, Groulx, Forman and Skolimowski inaugurate not so much a new cinema as a new *critical platform*.

Mardore: We no longer have the right to overlook happy accidents in the name of some absolute *politique des auteurs* because the time has come to envisage an *open* cinema, that is a non-dogmatic cinema. In such a perspective everyone has their chance. This does not mean throwing over theories and alliances, it means a total approach to cinema. There should no longer be films that are *maudits*,[7] at least not as far as film criticism is concerned.

American cinema was in any case never 'everything'. Bergman and Buñuel had their defenders. *Cahiers* is supposed to have a tendency. But in fact you have to distinguish several things and several periods. In the beginning, before this magazine was founded, the *auteur* of a film was a complete *auteur*. He created the script, the music, directed the actors, controlled the photography, etc.. Chaplin is the prototype. At a pinch, there's Welles or Sternberg. After that the *auteur* was the creator (or rewriter) of the script who, at a secondary level, dominated the *mise en scène*, even though in the mind of the cinephile the *mise en scène* takes first place.

Every interview with American film-makers confirms that – aside from legal questions of role or 'signature' – they in effect controlled the script. It's on that basis that the notion of *choice* has developed. Since the Americans, and certain European film-makers too, saw themselves as the controllers of both the direction and the script it was important to settle the point. The 'personal vision' or world view seemed to be an absolute criterion, on the same principle as pure *mise en scène*. The notion of 'continuity' (of inspiration and theme) prevailed over diversity.

An 'interesting' director deserved to have the least of his products examined. The 'uninteresting' director did not even merit the slightest account of the best of his productions. The *politique des auteurs* was consciously and deliberately arbitrary. It is against that arbitrariness that we are reacting.

Guégan: It may be appropriate at this point to recall an old principle of this editorial board: the one who liked the film best wrote about it. It's a principle which inevitably produced extravagant claims for quality. Time and again in fact, promise fell away into a pedantic enthusiasm which was dubious, to say the least. A vague, irritating terminology got rid of any real or likely objections. However that may be, let's not forget that this enlightened policy only existed by virtue of a chart standard better known under its label of 'Le Conseil des Dix'.[8] The mystery (was there really one?) vanished when you looked at the review of a film alongside the verdict of the wise or unruly Ten. Nothing earned the accolade of unanimity. There was always a black mark and one or two stars governing destiny and depriving it of its element of the unknown. Given a dead heat the two camps banned cults, allowed personal prefer- ence free reign and partisanship when they saw fit. Nevertheless, current experience of film society audiences shows that only praise reaches the readers and the exception makes the rule. All in all, our relations with them recall Pavlov and his dogs – the conditioned reflex.

Fieschi: It's a question of clarification through examples and it's precisely at the level of examples that things get complicated. There are, let's say, about sixty American film-makers who have signed their name to films that are well-made, interesting or enthralling for various reasons, whether for their plot, or because they had Bogart or Cooper, or for some intuitive sense of landscape and other aesthetically pleasing details.

Of course, these aspects are far from negligible. They have a great part to play in the physical pleasure of the spectacle which America has brought to perfection. But not overlooking them does not mean seeing them only at the expense of more fundamental ideas. We all know that cinephile's aberration of only seeing in a film that wonderful moment when Jack Elam crushes a cigarette butt into the left eye of a one-legged Apache chief while whistling the 'Marseillaise', or the retort which Lee Marvin spews out a moment before he is rubbed out by a hail of machine-gun bullets. The *politique des auteurs* rapidly degenerated into a *politique* of the craftsman and then of the jobber. These days it is fairly general practice to search the work of Ray Enright or Joseph Pevney for the curiosities we used to excuse in a Ford or a Boetticher. Soon we'll have the age of Henry Levin or Jean Negulesco.

Excesses of this kind are evidence of the irreversible victory of Amer- ican cinema, and it is precisely because a particular battle has been won that we must once again show ourselves to be demanding. Films and film-makers are no longer unjustly ignored by the cinephile audience, even if they are by distributors. The time has therefore come to discuss things more calmly and to recognize that *The Sandpiper*, *In Harm's Way*, even *Lord Jim*, are bad films. This in no way robs *The Bandwagon*, *Angel Face* and *Elmer Gantry* of their merits. Similarly, to praise some film by Gordon Douglas, Hathaway or Stuart Heisler does not mean that their *oeuvre* as a whole has to be taken into consideration. No doubt we are reaching the impossible stage as far as a theory of cinema in general, and American cinema in particular, is concerned; but for years, if *Cahiers'* position was to be productive, a certain rigid dogmatic control was needed. So were the appropriate classifications to separate the wheat from the chaff.

Today we have to recover some sense of the film *itself*, which does not, however, imply abandoning our basic options concerning people like Hawks, Hitchcock, Ford and Kazan. We have to be alert, able to recognize that *Lilith* (and *The Brave Bulls* makes no difference) is one of the finest American films of recent years.[9]

Mardore: Cinephiles are cut off from the most elementary truths of existence. If there have been excesses on the side of the *politique des auteurs* and the worship of *mise en scène*, perhaps this has something to do with the personality of people who had no contact with reality. The point is not whether Tourneur's *mise en scène* transcends the image of a man kissing a woman, but what Tourneur thinks about love, the texture of the woman's skin, her lips, the man's desire, etc.. All these are things you never come across in the aesthetic critic's analysis. Those small touches in the *mise en scène* which Truffaut defined and the transcendence of the plot by the film-maker's eye are no longer enough to satisfy us. The subject matter stands beyond the artifices which validate it.

Comolli: To get back to the most modest and ordinary sense of the term *auteur* – the author of the film – it's possible to put into practice a *politique* of good and bad *auteurs* as far as European film-makers are concerned since the interesting ones are all, quite apart from the success of their films, of necessity *auteurs* from the outset. But American cinema continues to pose the same problems and their complexity in the end rules out any systematization of the *politique*, or the actual quality of *auteur*. Every case is a special case. You find complete *auteurs*, complete non-*auteurs* and all the degrees between total freedom and total submission, between personal expression and anonymous creation. What are we to conclude from this if not that it is impossible to try to set up a rigorous and dogmatic *politique des auteurs* for the American cinema? *American cinema, basically, is not an auteur cinema*: the reverse of European cinema. *Auteurs* in America are *exceptions*; the rule they confirm is not that of a consistency and invariability in their work, but of their extreme fragility, complexity and formal plasticity. This makes for constant transformations to meet any new situation, and in the last analysis renders them resistant to any global definition and alien to any thematic schema. Every great American film-maker is an exception, contradicting even more exceptions.

As for the norm in American cinema, at the rank and file level it is made up of producer's films which by some miracle (and it is the miracle which fascinates all cinephiles) is from time to time pierced by a fragment of personal expression from the film-maker. The fact that everything is in league against the film-maker expressing himself makes it all the more admirable and exemplary to us, however little it shows up.

But that 'miracle' in itself is not enough to turn any American film-maker into a great film-maker. Nor is it enough to turn current American cinema into a cinema of personal expression, a cinema of *auteurs* in keeping with their *politique*. The American cinema is great because of the film-makers who break free from it. It was enough to see *a few* Capra films to be able to re-evaluate this film-maker, who was previously in disfavour. The same goes for Ford. We should need to see all Walsh's films in order to counter that kind of over-hasty re-evaluation and make us consider only *a politique of the oeuvre confined to its best examples*.

On the other hand, and this is no less important, the American cinema we love and defend is not the *whole* of American cinema. You only have to see a few Lubitsch films to give Preminger his true, more modest place. The battle has still to be fought as far as Lubitsch, DeMille, Capra and even Ford are concerned.

Fieschi: Ultimately, in fact, the true *auteur* is inconceivable in American cinema. Think of Sternberg's and Chaplin's silence, Welles's exile, the withdrawals of Ray or Mankiewicz.

Téchiné: A point of view that's, let's say, more objective and historical, brings out quite clearly the way the American cinema has developed and the vanity of the rather hasty theories it has inspired. Economic upheavals, provoked by the growing exodus of Hollywood studios and linked to the disappearance of the big production companies, have changed more than just the industrial conditions. The gradual movement towards decentralization has resulted in more than just a transformation of market laws. It's now clear that the disruption of the conditions of film-making generated by the financial breakdown is ruling out or restricting particular genres like the musical comedy without, properly speaking, producing genres to replace them.

The continued existence of American cinema is not made up of constants and analogies in which it is possible to distinguish main lines which can be erected into a system. On the contrary, rather than a survival or a clear break, it shows a continuous movement, shifting logically by reference to a precise context.

Films as different in story, theme, and subject matter as *The Chapman Report*, *Lilith* or *Splendor in the Grass*, which show the same concern with splintering the narrative, tell us more about America and its cinema than does the continuing existence of conventional forms verifying or seeming to confirm established theories. It is at this level that the three films I've mentioned can be said to be connected. The innovatory idea one can begin to distinguish in a historical sense starts from this simple fact.

Comolli: In short, if you ask what characterizes an *auteur*, what makes a film-maker an *auteur* in the strong sense of the term, you fall into a new trap: it's his 'style', in other words the *'mise en scène'*, a notion as dangerous, risky, infinitely variable and impossible to pin down as *auteur*.

Mise en scène means two things, one obvious – the directing *process*; the other mysterious – the *result* of that process. So when criticism talks about the *mise en scène* of a film, passes judgment on it and discovers some special beauty in it, it is sustaining a confusion – which may only be one of terminology – between what is seen on the screen, i.e. a result, and what is deemed to have produced the result, i.e. a set of means, a series of acts. But in precise terms these means, these acts have no intrinsic value: they are worth only what the result, the film, is worth. The latter established the value of the former and not vice-versa. In other words, the fate of the *mise en scène* is to be wiped out just at its culminating point. The film, as the result of the *mise en scène*, replaces it in every aspect, substitutes an artistic reality for the operational reality. Only that artistic reality achieves concrete existence as an aesthetic object, thanks to the *mise en scène*. Once the film is made, the *mise en scène* has only an abstract or phantom existence. Or a dogmatic one.

In other words again, the *mise en scène* is not and cannot be the object of aesthetic appreciation. Its end product, the film, may make such a claim. *Mise en scène* is not an object and not a work of art. Nor is it an expression of anything. It is a means of expression – stylistic, rhetorical, technical, etc. You can't judge a means. Conversely, the essence of the cinema doesn't lie in its means. The *mise en scène* is not part of the order of values. In *Cahiers* it has played the role of an artefact; it was brought to the forefront because it was claimed that the criteria for the beauty of a film were to be sought in the *mise en scène*, but this was only an illusory explanation. The beauty of films has to be looked for in the actual reality of films as objects.

Mardore: The question is not to deny *mise en scène* in favour of 'style', which in any case should not be so different from it, but to distinguish the people with a genuine personality from those with 'obsessions'. *Character*, as Welles would say, remains the sole criterion. We don't take enough account of the personality, of everything the *auteur* carries in himself, what he represents in the world, the power he has to express the world. There are no aesthetic criteria, just criteria of the individual. Cinephiles have denied this in the name of some 'pure *mise en scène*' which is the least definable notion imaginable. In fact the least gifted person whose personality 'explodes' in the work will always carry the day over the most skilled technician. We have to learn that there aren't any rules. Intuition and sensibility triumph over all theories.

Fieschi: The notion of 'character' stressed by Mardore is in fact of primary importance for a correct definition of the *auteur*. And I should add that it's better to have a bad character than no character at all. Over a period of time people like Huston and Wilder, who have after all had more failures than Wyler or Preminger, have over them the advantage of a *line* followed with obstinacy if not always with rigour. The fact that that line culminates in films like *The Night of the Iguana* and *Kiss Me Stupid* is sufficient proof of its validity.

Mardore: The arbitrary definition of '*mise en scène*' carried with it an *a priori* refutation of all heresies and variants. Ten years ago a film like *Lilith* would have been violently panned, and precisely in the name of the *politique des auteurs* and *mise en scène*. *Lilith* uses visual effects, camera angles, and cutting devices which would have appeared obsolete and anti-aesthetic. In the mind of the *politique des auteurs* the American cinema limited itself to a denial of any dramatic, 'demiurgic' intervention from the *auteur* in question. That over-simplification condemned *a priori* all mannered, baroque, in the end non-conventional, forms (since simplicity and effacement are variants of convention). In *Lilith* it is impossible to pinpoint the extent of Rossen's intervention. A writer who uses an archaic form, the preciosity of another age, isn't necessarily retarded or simple-minded. He may have chosen the style in order to give himself a certain narrative distance. We don't have the right to lay down the law, to elevate one form at the expense of another. We have to defend the notion of a pluralism of styles against a desiccated classicism, which in any case was never there in the minds of American film-makers. The important thing is to throw off the aesthetic and moral shackles.

Guégan: But people will ask, where is *Cahiers* going? A way forward has been suggested by Jacques Rivette in *Les Lettres Françaises*, on the basis of an Allio film. The inverse of the (so-called) Brechtian criticism of the 60s does not mean rejecting the original notion. We still need to consider its lessons and not sink into a criticism based on what the script says. Our question mark has to be placed over the effect: where does it come from and how does it work?

Viaggio in Italia raises just such a question. You remember, George Sanders and Ingrid Bergman are at a party. Ingrid is happy. She smiles at us. Next shot: Sanders looking at her. Then Ingrid in frame again. The meaning is reversed. The themes held in this series of shots reflect a general idea, but Rossellini's actual style makes it special. This is the way we ought to go. In an analogous sequence, *Pierrot le fou* re-poses the questions. Responding is understanding. This means rejecting years of uncertainty, winning back lost ground and cultivating it. In a remarkable preface to *La Vie de Rancé*, Roland Barthes suggests that Chateaubriand's yellow cat is perhaps all of literature. We have to find it in the cinema we love. Then the time will come when it will be natural to enjoy the company of *The Enforcer*, *I am a Fugitive from a Chain Gang* and *Night and the City*, films without an *auteur* admittedly, but which nevertheless prompted Bazin to write, 'What is so admirable in the American cinema is that it cannot help being spontaneous'.[10]

We are closer than ever to a genuine *politique des auteurs*.

Claude Ollier: While on the subject of *auteurs*, it ought to be stressed that Jerry Lewis,[11] along with Penn, is the only *auteur* to have emerged in the American cinema in the last five years. The reason in my view does not lie in some consideration of a thematic order, or in some other notion of obsessional characterization. It would be much more accurate to say that it's because he has created new forms. I believe that the idea of the *auteur*, i.e. of style, inevitably opens out on to the need for analysis of that kind. There would be several steps to such an analysis, namely:

1 an inventory of the forms concerned along a line of relevant *oeuvres*;
2 a basic analysis of each form (for example, an analysis of gags based on the intermittent use of sound);

3 a comparative study of these forms and earlier burlesque in order to establish the points at which innovation occurs;

4 the classification of these formal innovations according to whether they affect (a) the acting, (b) the narration, (c) the distance the actor establishes between himself and his creation;

5 an examination of meanings, implications made by signs which have previously been indexed and analysed.

Perhaps, at the point we have reached, it is in fact absolutely essential to speak of the cinema in terms of formal innovation. Make no mistake about it, what draws our interest to a particular film is that it strikes a new *note* – what Céline called 'a minor music'. But that 'minor music' can only be the art of using metaphor and metonymy to assemble a new personal discourse out of both new and traditional forms.

The originality of a creative and innovatory *mise en scène*, which is the hallmark of an *auteur*, must be analysed in terms of signs and meanings. If certain films in current production interest us (Brazilian, Polish, Italian, French) it is because we are intrigued by the *forms* they create. Our task is to establish what it is that intrigues us in them and what links can be established between them and earlier forms.

There is no reason why cinema should differ in this respect from music or literature. However more complex it is, the problem remains the same: forms have a future, an irreversible development. The critic's role is to determine the precise extent of that innovation and, as a result, the extent of what has to be shed.

Translated by Diana Matias

Notes

1 'Twenty years on': not from the founding of *Cahiers du Cinéma*, in 1951, but from 1945. That is to say, what is at issue in the discussion is the development of film criticism in France in the 1945–65 period, including the battles over American cinema in *L'Ecran Français* (see Ch. 7, note 12), the critical work of *La Revue du Cinéma* (see my Introduction to Volume 1) and the founding of *Cahiers* (and *Positif*) in the early 1950s, very much in the traditions of these earlier journals.

2 '*La politique des auteurs*': the phrase, often given in English as the '*auteur* theory', is left in French. Clearly, throughout this discussion, there are references to 'theory' but, certainly in its original usage in *Cahiers* in the 1950s, the *politique* was much more a *policy*, a proposition, a principle, a strategy – what Mardore calls, later in the discussion, 'a tactical point of view' – than it was any kind of theory. We have wanted to retain this difference in original meaning. The translation to '*auteur* theory' is usually associated with Andrew Sarris and his articles 'Notes on the Auteur Theory in 1962', *Film Culture*, 27, Winter 1962–3, and 'The American Cinema', *Film Culture*, 28, Spring 1963, later elaborated in his book *The American Cinema: Directors and Directions 1929–1968*, New York, E. P. Dutton, 1968. In fact, Luc Moullet uses the phrase '*auteur* theory' in his 1959 essay on Sam Fuller in *Cahiers* 93, translated as 'Sam Fuller: In Marlowe's Footsteps' in Volume 1, Ch. 20, where he talks (p. 149) of 'Truffaut's celebrated

auteur theory'. André Bazin had long before pointed out the relative *lack* of theory involved in the concept in his article 'De la politique des auteurs', *Cahiers* 70, April 1957, translated as 'On the *politique des auteurs*' in Volume 1, Ch. 31: 'as the criteria of the *politique des auteurs* are very difficult to formulate the whole thing becomes highly hazardous. It is significant that our finest writers on *Cahiers* have been practising it for three or four years now and have yet to produce the main corpus of its theory'. (pp. 256–7.)

3 Cf. Luc Moullet's opening to his essay on Fuller in Volume 1, Ch. 20.

4 *L'Ecran Français*: see Ch. 7, note 12.

5 André Bazin, 'On the *politique des auteurs*', Volume 1, p. 257.

6 François Truffaut, 'Une Certaine Tendance du cinéma français', *Cahiers* 31, January 1954, translated as 'A Certain Tendency of the French Cinema' in *Cahiers du Cinéma in English*, no. 1, 1966, reprinted in Nichols, *Movies and Methods*.

7 '*maudits*': see Ch. 8, note 1.

8 '*Le Conseil des Dix*': see Ch. 13, note 5.

9 See, for example, Jean-André Fieschi, 'Le film unique', *Cahiers* 177, April 1966, on *Lilith*, translated as 'The Unique Film' in *Cahiers du Cinéma in English*, no. 7, January 1967. *Cahiers* 177 contained other material on Rossen, also translated in *Cahiers du Cinéma in English*, no. 7.

10 André Bazin, 'On the *politique des auteurs*', p. 251.

11 Jerry Lewis was an important figure for *Cahiers* in the mid-1960s; cf. Godard's comments in his 1967 interview, Ch. 31 in this volume: 'Lewis is the only one in Hollywood doing something different . . . the only one who's making courageous films . . . He's been able to do it because of his personal genius'. *Cahiers* devoted considerable space to Lewis in issues no. 160, November 1964, and no. 175, February 1966, with an interview and articles on *The Family Jewels* by Serge Daney, Sylvain Godet, Claude-Jean Philippe and André Téchiné, all of which is translated in *Cahiers du Cinéma in English*, no. 4, 1966. *Cahiers* 197, Christmas 1967–January 1968, was a special issue devoted to Jerry Lewis but only the 'Petit lexique des termes lewisiens', compiled by Jacques Aumont, Jean-Louis Comolli, André S. Labarthe, Jean Narboni and Sylvie Pierre, has been translated, as 'A Concise Lexicon of Lewisian Terms', in Claire Johnston and Paul Willemen, eds, *Frank Tashlin*, Edinburgh, Edinburgh Film Festival in association with *Screen*, 1973; this lexicon appears to pick up on the kind of analysis Ollier lays out here.

21 | Jean-Louis Comolli: 'Notes on the New Spectator'

('Notes sur le nouveau spectateur', Cahiers du Cinéma 177, April 1966)

One of the aims of filmography taken as a science is to arrive at a scientific understanding of the qualities which condition the way film is seen – sharpness, depth, subtlety. The only way to achieve this is to subordinate these abstract qualities to the conditions of viewing, which one imagines to be more tangible.

While, for the most part, the material factors are themselves capable of a whole range of variations and adaptations (there is after all nothing more fragile than the technical norm), there is one condition which is constantly met to the point where it seems a necessary and indispensable part of viewing, and moreover up to the point where it is accepted as natural, normal and ontological. That condition is the darkness of the theatre. Granted there are a number of technical reasons to justify and require the watching of films in the dark. Perhaps the screen's light would really lose something in daylight. But although up till now darkness has been the absolute rule, I don't believe that optical considerations alone provide sufficient reason to make darkness the natural milieu of film. All the other kinds of spectacle – theatre, circus, opera and concerts – adapted themselves to varying degrees of part-light (if not to full sunlight as in the case of classical Greek theatre). Only cinema, although born in the relative half-light of cafés, developed and established itself well away from daylight, admitting no light other than the one it gave off itself. Sociologists and psychologists have of course frequently observed that the darkness of film theatres has other functions and effects apart from those favouring a better viewing of the film. While it may be one element of the technical requirements, darkness is also the location of phenomena of a different order of complexity which – through and beyond the film, in and beyond the spectator – involve people and society. In other words, they bring into play in a sense the psychological and social function of cinema.

In this connection it has to be clearly understood that cinema, while an art, is also a language, a system of signs which uses a breadth of metaphor

210

in order to signify. Like literature, which is tied to words, it is a language or languages and so a form of expression, but perhaps this is more true in an absolute sense of film because the image relates in a more absolute way than words do to the world as the conscious mind sees it, because words are the tools of the world of consciousness itself. What is remarkable about cinema is the degree to which art and life are linked and merged in images filled with the world and a beauty filled with meaning. As a result there is some point in considering cinema from the angle of its meanings and functions (obviously, it is only in the 'writing' – we would say *mise en scène* – of the individual film-maker that these are worked out clearly and distinctly); considering it in other words in terms of forms and the formal questions they pose rather than in terms of themes (the themes that the works themselves deal with).

The darkened film theatre is the theatre of myths, provoked by and provoking those content to be led along by the screen. We are familiar with the phenomena of fascination, transference, ecstasy – the 'projections' of spectators in tune with the projection of the film. The so-called commercial or consumer cinema (whatever its aesthetic merits, it has until now been the most obvious part of cinema) merely responds to these needs and nourishes them. And in so doing, it sustains the surrounding darkness, making it more indispensable than ever. There is a long-standing and constantly renewed agreement between the darkened film theatre and the commercial cinema; each represents the other's means of survival. It would be very difficult to decide which has contributed most to maintaining the conventions on which both are founded. True, what is referred to as 'current production' has its constants, stereotypes, narrative conventions, standardized acting and characters, and true too that these conventions are seen by a great many spectators as unalterable laws; but the heavy burden of responsibility for them is borne almost entirely by the darkness of the auditorium. Conditioning to darkness activates to full effect a kind of reflex in the spectator entering a cinema – expectation, desire even, for familiar forms, recognized patterns, the whole homogenized apparatus.

First, and perhaps most important, there is the sense of leaving the world of everyday life and entering a darkness close to that of the confessional or the bedroom; the shores of the dreamworld. The dark in the theatre invites the spectator to see the film only as an ingenious dream mechanism (sadly and usually of the crudest and emptiest kind); in other words, as a denial of living, a bracketing off of the world (even if the alternative is a world just as crude and futile).

Whatever advantages to the spectator accrue from this negative and sublimatory use of the cinema (loss of inhibition, fulfilment of frustrated desires, etc.) it leads inevitably to an equilibrium: a stabilization of needs and offers, demands and responses, in which the same remedies (because proved effective) are brought to the same ills, these then being reproduced in the same way from endless fictitious cures. Effects are made to balance their causes, or made void in what is tantamount to total stagnation. This is the way the film industry functions when it is working at maximum efficiency.

And if the cinema amounted to no more than this industry with its simple rules, if there were no great film-makers and artists to cause trouble, mess up the cards and disturb the whole mutually tranquillizing producer–consumer osmosis game (by rubbing conventions the wrong way, using secondary illusions to frustrate primary ones), the chances are that film would go on reeling in and out inside a closed circuit, forever repeating the same forms. And, since they produce the same effects, the same series would be doled out again and again, like some old ham still trotting out the business that once made him a star.

The prototype for this kind of closed-circuit cinema, where supply and demand seem tailor-made for each other, has for more than thirty years been represented by Hollywood films (both the B features and the more 'ambitious' films, with the exception of Hawks, Hitchcock, Lang, Ford, Fuller, DeMille, Sternberg, Preminger, Ray, etc. – in other words, apart from the *auteurs*, precisely because they sought to opt out of Hollywood, or to subvert it). There has, in other words been a golden age, not of cinema, but the industry; a true golden age, because in that period needs were instantly satisfied, a moment out of time, outside history, a shadow zone in the history of cinema itself, the inert mass in its process of evolution. If you look at things from this point of view it becomes easier to understand that American cinema's 'nostalgic' followers are in the end nostalgic not for the golden age of an art (because every moment in the life of an art is tragic and for that reason inscribed in the history not just of the arts but of mankind as well). They are yearning rather for a kind of paradise lost, a pre-natal state with a kind of foetal relationship between spectator-child and industry-mother. What dedicated supporters of the American cinema love in it has never been the beauties, the bold strokes, or the new forms delivered by the free-ranging talents of Hollywood. On the contrary they have, sadly, been in love with the automatic and problem-free satisfaction of their desires (if such unconscious impulses can be called desires).

Spare me all those lectures on the grandeur of the Hollywood cinema if what you mean is the perpetuation of this condition, these immature relations which have excluded any element of risk and made the chance happening impossible, if in fact it means this way of putting cinema and spectator somewhere outside the world and time – there's nothing great about such a perfect mechanism. I would rather see the power of the American cinema in those film-makers who cannot be reduced to such a level and who, far from being willing to put up with this fluctuation-proof stock market, have attempted to put a spanner in the works (the Lang of *Fury* and *Beyond a Reasonable Doubt*; the Ford of *The Grapes of Wrath*, *The Long Voyage Home*, *She Wore a Yellow Ribbon*). The truth is that however successful their films were, they always treated the spectator (without his always being aware of it) like an adult and not some self-indulgent day-dreamer.

Closed-circuit cinema, deliberately cut off from the development of cinematic forms, has known only one advance (still at the industrial level) in the shape of increasingly higher bids for greater demand and increased consumption through advertising campaigns which exaggerate consumer needs and puff up the offered allurements. (This is true of the super-productions – last-ditch efforts to expand an already over-saturated and over-ecstatic market.) As for aesthetic innovations, bold inventions of style, they are inevitably produced by rebels against the system who are more or less consciously *auteurs* and are not working for the darkness of the film theatres, but against it.

Thus the existence, even the new dimensions, of what has been called *'le malentendu'* (misapprehension) is not at all surprising. Entering the cinema the spectator is at once imprisoned by the dark. It has conditioned him to receive certain impressions and to expect a series of standardized emotions. He has to make a genuine effort to resist and pull back if he is going to appreciate even the most minor film made by an *auteur* (which by definition does not conform to the vague norms fixed by the tradition of dark cinemas). Once in the blackness he has to stay awake if he is to understand something about films which decline to treat him as if he were asleep. (Conditioning and habit play an important role here. The average spectator, if he has been an average frequenter of darkened cinemas, will, strangely enough, have retained from his half-sleeping state only the element of repetition, sameness and conformity. His cinematic 'education' wipes out the extraordinary and retains only the clichés and conventions which in his eyes pass for normal cinema. He sees anything that contradicts them as unnatural, or as failure. It is equally well known that children quickly 'grasp' the most complex and unusual narrative structure and are not disturbed by the wildest ellipses; in other words they show an open-mindedness which is precisely what prolonged experience of the cinema as 'entertainment' closes off for ever.)

This is no doubt why the *auteur* cinema is only just tolerated by the spectator, and even then with bad grace. There is a wide gap between the state of a spectator in a darkened cinema and the state of receptivity or lucid participation demanded by any film not made simply for the consumer. Why? Either the film is a natural extension of the dark, an ante-chamber of dreams, so that the spectator, having left the world behind, denies himself and others, and himself as another. Alone, he follows the sweet, simple thread of a dream which envelops him like a cocoon; the world unfolds its shapes before his eyes with dreamlike ease. There is a hypnotic sympathy at work which any encroachment on antici-pated forms and expected themes would shatter painfully. Or the film, despite and beyond the darkened cinema, aims to be an extension of and comment on the outside world. If that is the case the spectator is lost. On the one hand, he remains subject to the theatre, drawn by it towards the habitual satisfaction of his expectations: which the film does not give. On the other hand, the film confronts him with himself and others; its images continually draw him to the world, sustaining an awareness which the dark of the theatre is trying to deny him.

You could consequently argue that there is a conflict between the responsible cinema (which, from Griffith to Renoir and from Lang to Godard, we would consider to be the modern cinema) and the place in which it operates. The 'misapprehension' referred to earlier comes from the fact that modern cinema (which openly confronts the world as well as art; see Godard's films) always has to pass through the dark (omission of the world, obliteration of art). What modern cinema needs is lighted theatres which, unlike the darkness, neither absorb nor annihilate the clarity which comes from the screen, but on the contrary diffuse it, which bring both the film character and the spectator out of the shadows and set them face to face on an equal footing.

What characterizes the modern cinema is precisely this: the spectator is the hero of the film and the film is his apprenticeship for that thankless central role. How can we understand a cinema which puts us on stage if we are incapable of understanding where we are and who we are? *Cinéma vérité*, the film investigation, eye-witness accounts, film interviews, of which almost all yesterday's great film-makers were the precursors and which have exercised such an influence, whether directly or not, on the film-makers of today, are the best illustration of this need for clarity and for conscious action, as necessary to the new cinema as they are to the new spectator. The major use television makes of *cinéma vérité* is no accident; the small screen is often the only one which opens on to a lighted 'theatre'. Indeed, re-seeing the great works of cinema on television confirms this: if you are not obsessed with dark cinemas and do not try more or less to recreate the conditions of watching in the dark, in other words if you re-view films in a half-light that helps concentration, you see them differently and better than in the cinema. You watch them from a level of confidence and equality. The formulae no longer create an illusion. The aesthetic pleasures are charged with more meaning.

True, this lighted room is also a dream, but no longer the dream of escapist cinema. It is rather the dream of a cinema participating in life, and ultimately in fact our reflection on life. (This is the sense in which we can today 'live the film'.[1])

As Moullet, that precursor, said of his *Brigitte et Brigitte*: 'It's a film you go into to find reality, and come out of to lose distance, to re-enter the fiction of the street.' There is no doubt that in the long run the new cinema (which is the cinema that must matter most to us) will call up this new kind of spectator who will come to judge the world and acknowledge himself in the true light in which both will be shown on the screen. The new spectator will, to quote Sternberg, never tire of calling for 'more light'.[2]

Translated by Diana Matias

Notes

1 'Live the film': the phrase appears to be a reference to Comolli's earlier, fundamentally phenomenological, approach to cinema as elaborated in 'Vivre le film', *Cahiers* 141, March 1963.
2 In fact, of course, Josef von Sternberg was quoting Goethe's last words, *'mehr Licht'*, Sternberg, *Fun in a Chinese Laundry*, New York, Macmillan, 1965; London, Secker & Warburg, 1966, p. 309.

22 | Jean Narboni: 'Against the Clock: *Red Line 7000*'

('Contre la montre', *Cahiers du Cinéma* 180, July 1966)

For Hawks's *oeuvre*, which has survived more or less intact beyond the reach of time for more than forty years, notions of transformation and flux are as strange as any idea of an evolving and enduring existence. It has survived first 'archaeologically', if I'm allowed the term, in that it has been able to accommodate itself unproblematically and cheerfully to all attempts at re-evaluation, questioning, revival and re-examination. Every critic, whether his starting point was traditional criticism or criticism of a more determinedly 'modernist' stamp, has been able to find much to admire in it.

Next it has survived in terms of style. Right from the start, there were no signs of any initial hesitancy or nervousness, the chance element and the dangers of excess were kept to a minimum, and the style achieved a level, a clarity and an authority which it was obstinately to maintain for more than forty years.

Then there is the structure of the films, characterized by Rivette's celebrated phrase as 'the same feeling as the agonizing wait for the fall of a drop of water'.[1] Hawks's films are as far from the gentle ascents of Rossellini as they are from Kazan's halting progressions, as far from Sternberg's spinning out of time as they are from Mizoguchi's amplification of it. Instead we have a tenacious, obstinate, repetitive temporality moved forward by accumulation and tautology rather than straight progression or the sudden take-off. Hence the eddies round a fixed centre in Hawks, the violent way of marking time, the rhythm of the films – their attraction is that of an orchestral suite or a fugal continuum. Figures harmonize to order; parallel lives, dislocated on the formal level, forge links in a chain rather than influence each other. Only two of Hawks's films deal explicitly with the problem of time: his absolute masterpiece, *Monkey Business*, and his failed film, *Land of the Pharaohs*, and then only to denounce the disastrous consequences of too strong a belief or an illusory faith in notions of age and posterity, youth and immortality.

216

Gertrud has often been called a magnificent film because there an 80-year-old man's vision of love is given in terms so utterly youthful, absolute and complete.[2] The real reason is that in asserting the clear primacy of love in our lives it demonstrates at the same time, without in any way cheating, that only an old man could have expressed it in that way. The same is true of death as Cocteau saw it, disillusionment in the last of Lang's films, loneliness and shame in Mizoguchi. In Hawks there is nothing of that: no broadening of the point of view, no deepening of perception, no maturing of style, nor any new gravity of tone. *Red Line* seems like the work of someone ageless (it would not be quite accurate to call it the view of a young man). It's as if for Hawks everything, every element of a film and every film in the wider context of his *oeuvre*, was being presented once and for all in a unique present.

His cinema has to be taken integrally, because in every case it is presented as such. His films have a profound integrity: the cards are always open to view, always displayed and never marked. But the players' hands always remain out of sight and the result is always surprising. Must we today reproach Hawks for giving away (a bit of) the secret of the game in his turn, for showing how it's done and the mechanics of things, the relations between them rather than the things themselves, shorn of course of a measure of their substance (which never encumbered them much); the connections between them, their successive accommodations to each other, their arrangements and interlinkages? Shouldn't we instead be marvelling at the fact that even while we are shown the process and the instrument, the method and the material, the result is each time unexpected, and now more than ever?

What we have here is a cinema that has to be taken in its entirety, a vast nervous system, a magnetic field, a multi-layered network. It conjures up the belief voiced by Edward G. Robinson in *Tiger Shark* that a man can only enter heaven whole (repeated in *The Big Sky*). So it is with Hawks's films, which posterity and our own rather remotely connected generation will have to accept as a totality, a whole *oeuvre*, and not as a series of films. Here the earth has never been enriched or over-nourished (there is no profuseness about Hawks) but the parts are arranged in varying ways, distributed differently, and balanced according to surprising orders and structures which arise when and where one least expects them. This is a unique instance of achieving saturation level with the smallest possible number of elements. 'She's not bad,' says Mike to Lindy in *Red Line* as they watch a dance floor where some twenty girls are gyrating. 'Which one?' Lindy understandably asks. That sums up Hawks: the sure eye that homes in on the detail in the mass, and does so unerringly every time (and thanks to his profound honesty and clarity we too know who and what it's all about). The themes, characters and situations which are repeated, redistributed and developed in every case require our discriminating attention, not the prematurely complacent sighs of boredom that *Red Line* elicited from the critics. It is easy and naive to accuse Hawks of having a tendency towards the conventional, or at least of carrying on as if he were unaware of it. He has always been able to adapt to the laws of genre, far from the poetic transmutations of a Ray and equally far from the sombre lessons of Lang, in order to bend them and corrupt them surreptitiously, playing against the rules the better to change the nature of the game, imperceptibly, without bombast but with tenacity.

Red Line is a masterly presentation of various ways of twisting convention – an epitome of and treatise on deconstruction.

1 Take the structure of the narrative: at the beginning of the film a few extraordinary but simple shot-reverse-shots bring us into the rich possibilities of the situation alongside a hero 'we'll never leave'. But that's exactly what we do. A moment later he kills himself. The film thus begins like the end of a film so as to culminate in something like the middle of another – the car caught by the camera and fixed in motion while the chorus of women announces other films to come (or gone?).

2 A conventional situation, clearly announced as such, is opened up and then cut off: the first meeting between Gabrielle and Mike, in a night-club, which is brusquely cut short.

3 A convention is taken up, dropped, and then picked up again at the last moment: the scene where Mike and Gabrielle go off for a Coke, provoked by a chance but fateful meeting; only Hawks treacherously muddies our view of Sirius, first by an alternating sequence which totally compromises space, making it contingent, unlocatable and heterogeneous. The sequence is followed, very contra-conventionally, by Miss Queneau's conversation about place-names, but a kiss brings us back to conventions, in the nick of time.

4 Convention self-destructs by overdoing it and declaring itself: the reconciliation between Mike and Gabrielle in the rain where the dialogue outdoes the 'happy end' theme and sets up a clear ironical distance.

5 References to earlier situations are refreshed by a new setting or development, or by their impact with other familiar elements: Julie with her motorbike and glasses (the boyish side of Ann Sheridan in *I Was a Male War Bride*) very quickly turns hyper-feminine (in the swiftest resolution of the boy-meets-girl theme in the whole of Hawks's *oeuvre*). Julie: 'Don't treat me like a boy any more!' Next shot: 'Do you think I'm sexy?' (to the boy in bed with her). Or the amputation theme and the gag about the arm in a plaster cast, this time connected to macabre effect.

One could go on and on recording situations in *Red Line*. A mechanistic cinema, it will be said. But would Roussel or Poe be any the less great for having included 'Comment j'ai écrit certains de mes livres' in *Locus Solus* or 'The philosophy of composition' in 'The Raven'? What is at issue has really much more to do with the highest form of the model-maker's cinema, the work of a handyman in the best sense, the art of minute shifts, minimal and infinite variations. It's a case of everything being there in very little, and not the opposite.

Translated by Diana Matias

Notes

1 Jacques Rivette, 'Génie de Howard Hawks', *Cahiers* 23, May 1953: see Ch. 18, note 1 for translations. The quotation comes from 'The Genius of Howard Hawks' in Volume 1, p. 129.
2 The importance of *Gertrud*, and Dreyer's work in general, can be seen in the reviews of *Gertrud* by Michel Delahaye and André Téchiné in *Cahiers* 164, March 1965, and in the interview by Michel Delahaye, translated in *Cahiers du Cinéma in English*, no. 4, 1966, reprinted in Andrew Sarris, *Interviews with Film Directors*, New York, Bobbs-Merrill, 1967, and the article 'L'archaïsme nordique de Dreyer' by André Téchiné, both in *Cahiers* 170, September 1965.

Part Four

Towards a New Cinema/New Criticism

Introduction: Re-thinking the Function of Cinema and Criticism

As we have seen, in *Cahiers* in the 1960s neither thinking about contemporary French cinema nor re-thinking about American cinema can be considered separately from a more general debate about 'new cinema', a debate absolutely central to the development of the journal in this decade. What was 'new cinema'? Where did it come from? Why was it so important for *Cahiers*? What new form or forms of criticism were appropriate to it or did it make necessary?

The *nouvelle vague* itself was in many ways an important component in the development of a new cinema.[1] Among the factors generating debate about new cinema arising out of the *nouvelle vague* was the impact of new documentary forms emerging in the late 1950s and early 1960s under the name of *cinéma vérité* or (in the later, now more generally accepted term) 'direct cinema'.[2] Although examples of direct cinema from the US were important, in France over the first ten years of the *nouvelle vague* Jean Rouch occupied, with his *cinéma vérité* films, a position of importance rarely acknowledged outside France. As Jacques Rivette comments in his 1968 interview 'Time Overflowing' in this volume: 'Rouch is the force behind all French cinema of the past ten years . . . In a way, Rouch is more important than Godard in the evolution of the French cinema'. In retrospect particularly, the work of Rouch was felt to have changed some of the fundamental assumptions about cinema: 'Rouch . . . upset the boundaries between fiction film and document . . . direct puts back into question the shooting methods of traditional cinema', as Michel Marie puts it.[3] Clearly, if paradoxically, the impulse towards *cinéma vérité* or direct cinema represents both an extension of André Bazin's conception of realism[4] (and, of course, an extension of Cesare Zavattini's neo-realist principles[5]), *and* a decisive break with them.[6] Jean-André Fieschi, retrospectively again, elaborates the point:

223

From *Moi, un Noir* onwards, the camera assumes an entirely new function: no longer simply a recording device, it becomes a *provocateur*, a stimulant, precipitating situations, conflicts, expeditions that would otherwise never have taken place. It is no longer a matter of pretending that the camera isn't there, but of transforming its role by asserting its presence, by stressing the part it plays, by turning a technical obstacle into a pretext for revealing new and astonishing things. A matter of creating, through the very act of filming itself, an entirely new conception of the notion of the filmic event.[7]

Though perhaps less clearly, a good deal of this importance of direct cinema was perceived at the time. Fereydoun Hoveyda's 1961 article, *'Cinéma vérité*, or Fantastic Realism', on Rouch's *Chronique d'un été*, ends with a clear recognition of the importance for a *'new* cinema' of Rouch's work, and Louis Marcorelles's 1963 essay 'The Leacock Experiment' begins with the idea of *cinéma vérité* as an extension of neo-realism and as a crucial contribution to the exploration of realist fiction undertaken by the *nouvelle vague*. In another assessment of Rouch, Michel Delahaye pointed very clearly to the way in which Rouch's shooting and editing strategies could be seen as a source of renewal for fiction cinema. He describes Rouch at work on *Moi, un Noir*:

From a car he had followed and filmed Robinson, interrupting himself from time to time – but no question of interrupting Robinson – to reload his camera.

Nor was there any question of editing, of making the sequences obtained in this way flow together. What to do? Nothing. Let the nature of things make itself known – neither edit nor fit together, but put the sequences end to end: a style was being born.

Truffaut, who knew nothing about all that, was very shortly afterwards faced with an analogous problem, when he found himself faced with an impressive number of shots of Jean-Pierre Léaud replying to questions from an unseen psychologist whom certain circumstances prevented from being actualized in reverse cuts.

There too the solution was to put the shots end to end, so that the Indochina war sequence in *Moi, un Noir* was to become one of the highlights of *Les 400 coups*.

Both Rouch and Truffaut knew how to accept an impossibility and, into the bargain, found themselves coming out with its transformation into a superior possibility.[8]

Such strategies are partly what Marcorelles has in mind in 'The Leacock Experiment' when he talks about direct cinema in relation to the outdated conventions of traditional Hollywood cinema, and very much what Claude Beylie, writing about another *cinéma vérité* film, meant by these new techniques representing a return to 'a kind of *infancy of the art*'.[9] But it is Hoveyda's article which looks forward most clearly from *cinéma vérité* to a 'new cinema' (despite its insistence – typical of the period – on a 'certain way of showing the world' through the *mise en scène* as the work of authorship[10]). Hoveyda's comments on the mixing of the fictional and the documentary modes recall strongly both Jean-Luc Godard's comments in interview[11] and his practice in his films, as do his comments about *Chronique d'un été* being both the film and the 'notebook' for the film (as Hoveyda points out, rightly, this is something 'absolutely new', giving us 'all the conditions of the experiment') and about Rouch's cinema having become 'interventionist', setting up a dialogue with the spectator.

As integrated into the work of Godard in the 1960s and beyond, these formal innovations have often been argued to have their source in Brecht's ideas on theatre.[12] But this perspective – strongly associated with post-1968 *Cahiers* and *Screen* in Britain and their reading of Brecht – is not at all the one adopted by Bernard Dort's 1960 article 'Towards a Brechtian Criticism of Cinema'. For Dort the specific *means* of Brecht's epic theatre[13] has to do with theatre, while its *object* is to

> offer the audience recreated images of social life – that is, images of social life rendered comprehensible, and from which the audience may derive a lesson for their times, by means of a constant movement between identification with the characters which are presented and understanding of the historical situation which has made these characters what they are. . . . The spectacle should be such that it appears neither universal nor as a projection of the viewer's subjective world, that it is clearly dated and placed in time and space, and that it is not a story which is valid for all times and in all places. Its primary function should be to reveal the history of a time and place to us, enabling us to see what is particular in things, people and events, and to see them with new eyes.

Given the later readings of Brecht, it is important to understand the perspective on Brecht offered here because it is precisely in this perspective that Marcorelles, in 'The Leacock Experiment', claims Leacock's direct cinema as 'the perfect counterpart of what Brecht was trying to do in the theatre, allowing for the difference between the two modes of expression'. This very different idea of what 'Brechtian cinema' would look like is elaborated by Marcorelles in his later book:

> . . . in direct cinema, and first of all in Leacock's films, reality is given to us raw with all its instant, provocative qualities. Unlike Brecht's theatre, which rejects the fake realism of the bourgeois theatre and seeks to give us social reality by distancing the audience from the stage and the action, Leacock's cinema, denouncing the fake realism of what is said to be the only possible cinema – that of performance – moving us to take a more intense part in real action, gives us the tool needed to discover on the screen how things *really* happen. Here 'reality' can be seen at first glance, if it has been filmed with the right skill. Then the social fiction that underpins all our actions can be revealed, the drama we act out each day for society. By this new relationship with the lightweight synchronized camera, the person filmed, whether an actor or not, appears to our eyes and ears in a new dimension . . . .[14]

As I argue in my 'Introduction: *Cahiers du Cinéma* in the 1960s', in retrospect the early 1960s look to be a period of real contradictions. On the one hand, the critical positions of *Cahiers* had triumphed, alongside the successes of the *nouvelle vague*; as a result general attitudes to the cinema, and particularly American cinema, had changed, and that triumph had then perhaps pushed *Cahiers* critical positions into dangerous areas;[15] Godard felt that *Cahiers* was going downhill now there were no positions to defend. On the other hand, most obviously in the 1960 special issue of *Cahiers* on Brecht, Bernard Dort and *Cahiers*'s own (always independent and divergent) Louis Marcorelles were preparing a different field of battle, indeed a different war. Just as Marcorelles at the end of his article in that issue directly confronts and attacks the most cherished positions of *Cahiers*,[16] so does Dort – the *politique des auteurs*, the demand for cinematic specificity, the primacy of *mise en scène*, mystical ideas about 'the immediate beauty of the real' – in favour of a view of cinema as a form of mediation of the real world. There is no doubt that in the years following this issue on Brecht the concerns which Dort and Marcorelles put on the agenda became of increasing importance, coinciding as they did with radically changing attitudes to American cinema.[17] Nor is there any doubt that a general self-questioning of critical values and methods began to take place, alongside the deliberate opening up of critical perspectives in disciplines outside of film.[18]

Fereydoun Hoveyda's 1961 'Self-Criticism', noting the general imprecision of critical language, makes manifest the desire to find a more 'scientific' critical language and gives some sense of this 'opening up': his main points of reference are Saussure, Merleau-Ponty and the nature of signification in language,[19] Marx on literature, Lévi-Strauss and anthropology, Lacan and psychoanalysis.[20] This may seem a somewhat startling array of references for an essay dated 1961, when *Cahiers* was generally reckoned to be thoroughly obsessed with American cinema, authorship and *mise en scène*! Naturally, Hoveyda's attempt at self-criticism is equally marked by precisely those concerns of the time, producing some (retrospectively at least) difficult juxtapositions of ideas such as: 'A film is its *auteur*. And the *auteur* is a human being. All that we can do is try to grasp his singularity, the "signifying structure" he has erected'.

As explained in my 'Introduction: *Cahiers du Cinéma* in the 1960s', there were powerful forces in French culture which were moving *Cahiers* into new critical areas, just as cinema itself was moving in new directions. The new critical areas, associated with Jacques Rivette's assumption of editorial leadership,[21] were marked explicitly by the series of interviews with what *Cahiers* called 'certain outstanding witnesses of contemporary culture',[22] the first of which was with Roland Barthes. The relationships between the new areas of concern are very much at the centre of the interview with Barthes, in which the by now familiar problems of applying linguistics to the cinema are addressed relatively clearly: given the analogic nature of the photographic sign, can there be a cinematographic 'language'? Can structural analysis provide a means of breaking film down into signifying units and of discovering codes at work? Is the (existing, at least) cinema essentially narrative in nature and are syntagmatic relationships therefore of primary importance? The interview with Barthes thus usefully lays out the groundwork for a semiotics of the cinema, a semiotics which, in relation to theatre, Barthes saw as arising from Brecht's work,[23] and a semiotics which Barthes's follower Christian Metz was beginning to attempt to elaborate around this time.[24]

The struggle for a new criticism went on alongside, and was intimately bound to, the search for a new cinema. In so far as there was a distinction between 'modern' cinema and 'new' cinema, new cinema was generally understood to engage more directly with social reality – an engagement which Dort and Marcorelles had emphasized in the Brecht special issue. In the 1950s a frequent complaint about French cinema had been that it lacked precisely this quality of engagement with contemporary social reality,[25] a quality which had been admired in Italian cinema (and in a different way in American cinema). This point was clearly restated in relation to the new French cinema in the May 1962 special issue of *Cahiers* on Italian cinema. Work by film-makers such as Vittorio de Seta, Ermanno Olmi, Francesco Rosi, Pier Paolo Pasolini was seen as inheriting the essentials of neo-realism while pushing towards greater interiorization and towards a greater degree of critical analysis, thus differentiating it from the French *nouvelle vague*. Jacques Joly, in 'A New Realism', noted that the new Italian cinema was necessarily Leftist and that, as a result, 'this cinema is in opposition to the French *nouvelle vague*, born in a France exhausted by political contradictions and research into language . . . Above all, the young Italian cinema aims to be engaged, *impegnato*, which is not the sign of an attitude of mind but a vital necessity for an Italian . . . On both sides of the Alps the interrogation of traditional language and story translates into the desire to get at the truth, but in Italy that truth is a partial and momentary one, that of *man in his situation.*'[26]

This is the essential context for Jean-André Fieschi's account of *Bandits at Orgosolo*, rooted as it is in a perception of the differences between the personal, individual interior realism of the French *nouvelle vague* and the greater engagement with social reality of the new Italian cinema. Fieschi's review reflects the critical tensions of the time. It draws on critical positions of the past – the convergence of the qualities of the American and the Italian cinemas, its closeness to Bazin's account of *Bicycle Thieves*[27] (Fieschi: 'the art of showing restored to its original dignity') – while looking forward. American cinema, yes, but with the recognition that American cinema is no longer enough. Bazin, yes, but with the recognition that a clearer social, political edge is necessary. Its central question looks forward: what will modern cinema be?

Noticeably different are the terms – derived from Freud and Marx via Foucault – in which, three years later, the same Fieschi addresses another Italian film, Marco Bellocchio's first feature, *Fists in the Pocket*. Here, the importance of the film is precisely in its *politics*, in its break with 'the fundamental choices of neo-realism', and in particular neo-realism's humanism, in favour of 'contestation'. Bellocchio, Fieschi argues, achieves 'the ambition of every young film-maker – he holds up a mirror in which his generation can see the conditions of its own existence'.

'New' or 'young' cinema was always a broad term, able to include within its general designation films as different from each other as *Fists in the Pocket*, Rouch's films, *Bandits at Orgosolo*, Godard's films, *Switchboard Operator*, Quebec films and 'cinema nôvo' films from Brazil, independent American films. It is precisely this range of work to which Comolli refers in his 1967 article 'A Morality of Economics'.[28] But the article also allows us to see how much more overtly politicized the idea of new cinema – and cinema in general – was becoming in the later 1960s, and the extent to which the positions usually associated with *Cahiers* in the post-1968 period were in fact already well developed long before 1968. The terms in which Comolli writes here are similar to those in his editorial 'Situation of New Cinema'[29] and in his 'Notes on the New Spectator',[30] both from 1966, but are considerably clearer: clearer about the 'revolutionary' nature of the changes in cinema taking place, clearer about the relationships between production, consumption and aesthetic practices, clearer about the political function of cinema and about the political tasks of criticism.

For Comolli, as for *Cahiers* as a whole, Jean-Luc Godard was the crucial figure in the development of these significantly more politicized ideas about cinema, and Godard's work had exemplary status in this respect. It is not at all surprising, therefore, to find these ideas being articulated in the interviews with Godard and with Jacques Rivette translated here[31] (though the one year gap between the interviews, Rivette's coming some months after the events of May 1968, makes a big difference in the relative clarity and confidence of their formulations). Godard, for example, is very clear about the death of American cinema and the rottenness of the whole commercial system, a system worth working in only to change or destroy it from within, as about the need to make a different kind of cinema with a different kind of function.[32] For both Godard and Rivette the political nature of all cinema is tied closely to the nature of the film image and its representational status[33] and to conventions of narrative. Hence, of course, Rivette's interest in theatre as subject matter, as a means of reflecting upon cinema.

It is in this context that, just as Fieschi found *Fists in the Pocket* emblematic of new cinema in 1966, so in 1968 Jacques Aumont finds Dusan Makavejev's *Switchboard Operator* exemplary at this later stage of the development of a new cinema for its 'open narration'. Aumont argues that *Switchboard Operator* is one of those films which offer 'several ways into a reading of one and the same narrative', thus allowing modern cinema to cast off 'the shackles of Representation' – precisely the essential rejection of realism (representation and narrative) which Jean Narboni proposes in his note 'Towards Impertinence'. In this perspective the radical or revolutionary importance of a film like *Switchboard Operator* lies in its formal strategies, its questioning of traditional modes of construction and reading.[34]

In the years following the Barthes and Lévi-Strauss interviews in 1963–4 the search for a 'new cinema' had gone on alongside a marked growth of interest in new theory in the pages of *Cahiers*. As Christian Metz put it in a 1965 essay in *Cahiers*, 'On the Impression of Reality in the Cinema', whereas in the 1920s every critic of cinema had also been a 'theorist', now 'we believe, more or less surely, that the criticism of individual films states all there is to be said about film in general'.[35] Metz, from his theoretical perspective, insisted that each film was 'first of all, a *piece of cinema*'. Of course, in a very different theoretical register, this had been very much André Bazin's way of working and thinking, the essays in *What is Cinema?* being generally inspired by individual films.[36] For *Cahiers* at this time, Metz's perspective implied a shift away from 'films' and 'criticism' of films towards cinema as language and cinema as institution. As a commentator from outside film theory, Allan Megill, describes the general shift, the 'structuralisms' associated with Lévi-Strauss and Barthes (and Lacan and Althusser) 'can be most succinctly characterised as attempts to move the centre of intellectual concern away from the speaking subject and toward the structure of the language being spoken'.[37] Structuralism and semiotics depended on some form of language, and it is not surprising that much of the theoretical work published in *Cahiers* in these years concerned itself, in one way or another, with the fundamental question posed by Barthes in the 1963 interview: was cinema a language, or did its representational, analogical nature prevent it from being considered as a language? This is one of the central concerns of Metz's 'On the Impression of Reality in the Cinema' and (though he takes a very different direction) Pier Paolo Pasolini's 'The Cinema of Poetry'.[38]

This question is central, again, to the curious short article, translated by *Cahiers*, by Martin Heidegger on cinema and the Japanese Noh play, in which Heidegger sees a denial of the representational 'plenitude' associated with cinema.[39] In introducing Heidegger's short article, Patrick Lévy argued that those traditions of representation had also been interrogated by the work of Robert Bresson, an interrogation being continued by Godard and Rouch.[40] Thus, issues about the representational nature of cinema meet up with the polemics for new cinema, and these were central to the Christmas 1966 special issue of *Cahiers* on 'Film and Novel'. Bernard Pingaud, for example, in his attempt to relate the *nouveau roman* to the new cinema, begins with precisely the question of whether cinema is a language.[41] And Christian Metz's developing work on semiotics – focussing on the syntagmatic relations of narrative organisation – tries to provide semiological underpinning to the sense that 'modern' film-makers like Godard and Resnais – 'the two great poles of modern film' – were 'renewing' traditions of representation and narrative.[42] In this argument, new cinema is 'critical' in that it involves levels of deconstruction of traditional film (primarily in narrative rather than representational terms), demanding a different spectating consciousness.

This was also the context for Noël Burch's 1967–8 series of *Cahiers* articles on film aesthetics.[43] As Annette Michelson puts it in her introduction to the English publication of these articles, they intervene in and reflect 'the terms of a debate on *the politics of illusionism*',[44] a debate the two poles of which were represented by André Bazin and Sergei Eisenstein, and a debate continuing in the 1960s, as she saw it (like Patrick Lévy and Metz), in the film practice of Godard and Resnais (and anticipated by figures like Bresson). Historically, she argues, this moment 'inaugurated the possibility of a renewal and redirection of critical energies and an end to cinema's alienation from the modernist tradition'.[45]

On the whole, the more theoretical work published in *Cahiers* in these years was undertaken by writers from outside the journal rather than by its principal and regular editors and contributors. Although this distinction began to disappear in the late 1960s (as the later articles and interviews in this volume testify), we have seen that the emphasis in the writing of Jean-Louis Comolli and Jean Narboni was rather different, more rooted in former critical practices and now becoming more overtly political.

Both Jean-Louis Comolli and Jean Narboni were involved in the interviews with Godard and Rivette and it is striking to see how both filmmakers, though Rivette especially, in collaboration with their interviewers, work towards positions very similar to those outlined by Comolli and Narboni in their 1969 editorial 'Cinema/Ideology/Criticism'.[46] Fundamental to these positions is the rejection of a cinema of spectacle or entertainment, in favour of, as Rivette puts it, 'the idea of an ordeal either imposed on or at least proposed to the viewer, who is no longer the comfortable viewer but someone who participates in common work – long, difficult, responsible work'. Rivette recognizes that a revolutionary cinema, in France at least, can only be

> a cinema which questions all the rest of cinema . . . Films that content themselves with taking the revolution as a subject actually subordinate themselves to bourgeois ideas of content, message, expression. While the only way to make revolutionary cinema in France is to make sure that it escapes all the bourgeois aesthetic clichés: like the idea that there is an *auteur* of the film, expressing himself. The only thing we can do in France at the moment is to try to deny that a film is a personal creation.

In their interviews both Godard and Rivette place Ingmar Bergman and *Persona* at the very centre of such a conception of a modern, political cinema. Anglo-Saxon readers, certainly readers in the 1970s *Screen* tradition, are likely to find this puzzling – just as it was puzzling to find Bergman and *Persona* so prominently endorsed in Comolli and Narboni's editorial. Rivette himself unlocks part of this puzzle in his comment about rejecting 'the idea there is an *auteur* of the film, expressing himself . . .

Bergman's films are something completely different from Bergman's vision of the world, which interests no one'. In Britain and the USA, of course (as in France in the 1950s[47]), Bergman was, precisely, the unquestioned *auteur*, the romantic artist expressing himself *par excellence*, and what interested everyone was, precisely, 'Bergman's vision of the world'. The dominant reception of Bergman's work in Britain, represented at its most intelligent by Robin Wood, emphasized the essentially moral concerns of the 'artist'. Wood's response, at least, was always a complex one, recognizing fully as it did the crisis of traditional forms represented by a film like *Persona*. Contrasting Bergman with Godard, Wood comments: 'Bergman has never . . . shown any inclination to be *avant-garde*, and the "advanced" aspects of *Persona* were determined solely by the content: they are not evidence of a desire for deliberate formal experiment, but purely the expression of Bergman's sense of breakdown and disintegration'.[48] The emphasis here is never in doubt: the function of criticism of Bergman's work is to elaborate the artist's moral world view. Really no one in Britain or the USA produced an analysis of Bergman's work which is much like Comolli's observations on *Hour of the Wolf*,[49] concerned as they are with reflection upon the nature of film representation and narrative and their relationship to the intentions and control of the director/artist. In Britain views like Wood's were so influential and so defined the critical interest of Bergman's work that it became more or less 'illegible' in the terms that Godard, Rivette and Comolli find interesting and propose here.

I began this introduction to the section on new cinema and new criticism by pointing to the importance of *cinéma vérité* or 'direct' cinema for the development of a new cinema in the 1960s. As Michel Marie puts it, 'this technique imposed a redefinition of cinematographic fiction in that it makes evident its own processes of representation and the process at work in all the successive operations of producing a film from the shooting script to mixing. In "direct", fiction no longer pre-exists before the shooting but is truly its *product*'.[50] In the late 1960s *Cahiers* became particularly interested in the ways in which, in films like Rivette's *L'Amour fou*, Bertolucci's *Partner*, Rohmer's *La Collectionneuse*, and in films by directors like Godard, Philippe Garrel, Straub, Jancsó, Cassavetes, there was 'an increasingly apparent recourse – in the "fiction" film – to the modes of direct cinema'.[51] Comolli's interest in his 1969 essay, and here in his and Sylvie Pierre's observations on Cassavetes' *Faces*, is precisely in the way in which direct cinema 'compels the cinema to redefine itself', primarily at the level of representation and narrative, the function of the image (and hence also at the level of ideology), but also, clearly and inextricably, at the technical and economic levels.

The October 1968 issue of *Cahiers* in which the material on *Faces* appeared was devoted to 'Four American Film-Makers': Shirley Clarke, John Cassavetes, Andy Warhol, Robert Kramer. American cinema, yes, but, variously, independent, politically and/or aesthetically radical. American cinema, but part of a new cinema. But if it is appropriate to end this volume with articles like those on *Faces* – very much the critical other face of that traditional American cinema which had been so fundamental to the past of *Cahiers* – it is also appropriate to end with the flurry of editorials from the spring and summer of 1968, and particularly the editorial on changes in the editorial strategies of *Cahiers* itself. Six months after Comolli had asked 'Why? Where? How? When?' criticism needed to struggle,[52] *Cahiers* found itself very much in the arena, fighting, debating, taking action. The 1968 editorials presented here bear eloquent testimony to the militant posture adopted by *Cahiers* as it fought for the politicization of film culture through 'The Langlois Affair'[53] and the Estates General of the French Cinema.[54] Finally, the *Cahiers* editorial for August 1968, announcing editorial changes, recognized that *Cahiers* had been complicit with the 'system' and expressed its determination to be no longer so, by very consciously putting at the centre of its attention what the system had marginalized, and vice versa. *Cahiers* was, in other words, already heavily and openly committed to the political and theoretical project which would preoccupy it in the aftermath of May 1968.

Notes

1 This question is also discussed in my 'Introduction: *Cahiers du Cinéma* in the 1960s', in this volume.

2 Louis Marcorelles, in *Living Cinema: New Directions in Contemporary Film-Making*, London, George Allen & Unwin, 1973 (originally published as *Eléments pour un nouveau cinéma*, Paris, Unesco, 1970), traces the development of a new cinema from the decisive break which he takes 'direct' cinema to represent.

3 Michel Marie, 'Direct', originally published in *Lectures du film*, Paris, 1976, translated in *On Film*, no. 8, Spring 1978, reprinted in Mick Eaton, *Anthropology-Reality-Cinema: The Films of Jean Rouch*, London, British Film Institute, 1979. Marie's points about the effects of direct cinema on traditional cinema are addressed by Jean-Louis Comolli in 'Le détour par le direct', I and II, *Cahiers* 209 and 211, February and April 1969, extracts from which are translated in Williams, *Realism and the Cinema*.

4 For Bazin's writing about deep focus and realism, see Ch. 3, note 2, in this volume. Bazin's writings about Italian neo-realism are collected in Bazin, *What is Cinema? Vol. 2*.

5 For Zavattini's ideas on cinema and realism, see Ch. 3, note 4, in this volume.

6 Cf. Mick Eaton, 'The Production of Cinematic Reality', in Eaton, *op. cit.*

7 Jean-André Fieschi, 'Slippages of Fiction', in Eaton, *op. cit.*, p. 74. See also Ch. 24, note 5.

8 Michel Delahaye, 'Le Règle du Rouch', *Cahiers* 120, June 1961, p. 7. Cf. Fereydoun Hoveyda's discussion of *Les 400 coups* in *Cahiers* 97, July 1959, translated in Volume 1, Ch. 5.

9 Claude Beylie, 'La Nature crie', on Mario Ruspoli's *Regard sur la folie*, *Cahiers* 137, November 1962, p. 56.

10 Cf. Fereydoun Hoveyda's 1960 article 'Sunspots', Ch. 13 in this volume.

11 See, especially, the 1962 interview, translated as 'From Critic to Film-Maker', Ch. 4 in this volume.

12 See, especially, Colin MacCabe, 'Realism and the Cinema: Notes on Some Brechtian Theses', *Screen*, vol. 15, no. 2, Summer 1974, reprinted in Tony Bennett *et al.*, *Popular Television and Film*, London, British Film Institute/Open University, 1981; Colin MacCabe, 'The Politics of Separation', *Screen*, vol. 16, no. 4, Winter 1975–6; Kristin Thompson, 'Sawing Through the Bough: *Tout va bien* as a Brechtian Film', *Wide Angle*, vol. 1, no. 3, 1976; Colin MacCabe, *Godard: Images, Sounds, Politics*, London, Macmillan, 1980. Views more or less counter to these are argued by, for example, Dana Polan, 'Brecht and the Politics of Self-Reflexive Cinema', *Jump Cut*, no. 17, April 1978, and Alan Lovell, 'Epic Theater and Counter-Cinema's Principles', *Jump Cut*, no. 27, 1982.

13 Brecht's major statement on 'epic theatre' is 'The Modern Theatre is the Epic Theatre', in Brecht, *Brecht on Theatre*.

14 Marcorelles, *op. cit.*, p. 123.

15 See Part II of this volume, 'American Cinema: Celebration'.

16 See my 'Introduction: *Cahiers du Cinéma* in the 1960s', in this volume.

17 See Part III of this volume, 'American Cinema: Revaluation'.

18 See my general discussion of this in 'Introduction: *Cahiers du Cinéma* in the 1960s', in this volume.

19 Cf. the end of Hoveyda's '*Cinéma vérité*, or Fantastic Realism', Ch. 24 in this volume, where Hoveyda sees in *Chronique d'un été* 'the seed of an attempt to set up new relationships between sign and meaning . . . in "cinematic language"' and compares this to what Alain Robbe-Grillet and Michel Butor were doing in relation to literary fiction.

20 For Saussure, see Ch. 25, note 2; for Merleau-Ponty, see Ch. 24, note 11; for Lévi-Strauss, see 'Introduction: *Cahiers du Cinéma* in the 1960s', note 75; for Lacan, see Ch. 24, note 9.

21 See my 'Introduction: *Cahiers du Cinéma* in the 1960s', in this volume.

22 Ibid.

23 Ibid.

24 For details of Metz's work, see Ch. 3, note 3.

25 See, for example, the 1957 editorial discussion 'Six Characters in Search of *auteurs*', Ch. 2 in Volume 1.

26 Jacques Joly, 'Un nouveau réalisme', *Cahiers* 131, May 1962, pp. 7–8.

27 Bazin's account of *Bicycle Thieves*, along with his other main writings on neo-realism, is in Bazin, *What is Cinema? Vol. 2*.

28 This range is also clear in Michel Delahaye's later effort to draw up a balance sheet of new cinema, 'D'une jeunesse à l'autre: classement élémentaire de quelques notions et jalons', *Cahiers* 197, Christmas 1967/January 1968.

29 See my 'Introduction: *Cahiers du Cinéma* in the 1960s', and its note 83, in this volume.

30 Ch. 21 in this volume.

31 Both interviews are in extract form: see Ch. 31, note 1 and Ch. 38, note 1 for details.

32 Godard, of course, had talked of constructing a new cinema on the ruins of the old already back in 1962, although in rather different terms, or with rather different meanings: see Ch. 4 of this volume.

33 Cf. Jean-Louis Comolli's 1967 review of Godard's *La Chinoise*: see Ch. 31, note 8.

34 Robin Wood offers an excellent analysis of Makavejev's film in Ian Cameron, *Second Wave*, London, Studio Vista, 1970, concluding in a way not incompatible

with Aumont's points, but with rather less overt emphasis on formal and theoretical implications and radical potential: 'Where Eisenstein uses montage primarily to reinforce, Makavejev uses it to modify, to call into question, to contradict. It becomes in his hands a marvellously complex and subtle medium for the definition of contemporary uncertainties. His films suggest that truth, if it exists at all, is many-sided, and composed of an elaborate complex of contradictions' (p. 33).

35 'A propos de l'impression de réalité au cinéma', *Cahiers* 166–7, May–June 1965, translated as 'On the Impression of Reality in the Cinema' in Christian Metz, *Film Language – A Semiotics of the Cinema*, New York, Oxford University Press, 1974, p. 3.

36 André Bazin, *What is Cinema? Volumes 1 & 2*.

37 Allan Megill, *Prophets of Extremity: Nietzsche, Heidegger, Foucault, Derrida*, Berkeley, Los Angeles and London, University of California Press, 1985, p. 189.

38 Pier Paolo Pasolini, 'Le "cinéma de poésie"', *Cahiers* 171, October 1965, translated as 'Pier Paolo Pasolini at Pesaro: The Cinema of Poetry' in *Cahiers du Cinéma in English* no. 6 (December 1966), reprinted in Nichols, *Movies and Methods*.

39 Martin Heidegger, 'Sur le cinéma, le Japon et le Nô', *Cahiers* 186, January 1967.

40 Ibid., pp. 45–6.

41 Bernard Pingaud, 'Nouveau roman et nouveau cinéma', *Cahiers* 185, December 1966 (special issue on 'Film et roman: problèmes du Récit').

42 Christian Metz, 'Le cinéma moderne et la narrativité', *Cahiers* 185, December 1966, translated as 'The Modern Cinema and Narrativity' in Metz, *Film Language, op. cit.* Metz discusses the sequence of the flight from Paris in Godard's *Pierrot le fou* as not conforming to any of his syntagmatic types. Perhaps taking off from Metz's discussion, David Bordwell analyses the same sequence in Bordwell, *Narration in the Fiction Film*, Madison, The University of Wisconsin Press; London, Methuen, 1985, in his chapter on 'Godard and Narration'. Like Patrick Lévy, above, and Noël Burch and Annette Michelson, below, Bordwell also sees Bresson as involved in interrogative modes of narration, offering *Pickpocket* as his main example of 'Parametric Narration'.

43 For details, see Appendix 2; translated as *Theory of Film Practice*, London, Secker & Warburg, 1973.

44 Ibid., p. xi.

45 Ibid., p. xii.

46 Jean-Louis Comolli and Jean Narboni, 'Cinéma/Idéologie/Critique I', *Cahiers* 216, October 1969, translated as 'Cinema/Ideology/Criticism' in *Screen*, vol. 12, no. 1, Spring 1971, reprinted in *Screen Reader I* and Nichols, *Movies and Methods*.

47 See, for example, Jean-Luc Godard, 'Bergmanorama', *Cahiers* 85, July 1958, translated in *Godard on Godard*.

48 Robin Wood, *Ingmar Bergman*, London, Studio Vista; New York, Praeger, 1969, p. 171.

49 See also Comolli's review of *Persona*, *Cahiers* 188, March 1967, translated as 'The Phantom of Personality' in *Cahiers du Cinéma in English*, no. 11, September 1967. The closest to Comolli's perspective in English is perhaps Susan Sontag's essay on *Persona* in *Sight and Sound*, vol. 36, no. 4, Autumn 1967, reprinted in Susan Sontag, *Styles of Radical Will*, New York, Farrar, Straus & Giroux, 1976, in Stuart M. Kaminsky, *Ingmar Bergman*, New York, Oxford University Press,

1975 and in Leo Braudy and Morris Dickstein, *Great Film Directors*, New York, Oxford University Press, 1978.

50 Michel Marie, 'Direct', in Eaton, *op. cit.*, p. 38.

51 Comolli, 'Le détour par le direct', *op. cit.*, in Williams, *op. cit.*, p. 225.

52 See my 'Introduction: *Cahiers du Cinéma* in the 1960s', and its note 84, in this volume.

53 'The Langlois Affair', in which Henri Langlois was dismissed from his post as director of the Cinémathèque Française, then later reinstated, has often been seen as a sort of curtain-raiser for the events of May 1968, in the sense that it demonstrated that, with sustained action, governmental forces could be taken on and even be defeated. For further reading on 'The Langlois Affair', see Ch. 34, note 1.

54 The Estates General of the French Cinema: for further reading, see Ch. 35, note 1.

23 | Bernard Dort: 'Towards a Brechtian Criticism of Cinema'

('Pour une critique brechtienne du cinéma',
Cahiers du Cinéma 114, December 1960)

Brecht and Brechtianism have become so fashionable that even the most diehard anti-Brecht critics and producers are ripe for conversion. One critic, who scarcely two years ago considered Brecht of no significance whatsoever and devoted all his time to the 'discovery' of Ionesco, now believes that Brecht's achievement 'is on a par with that of the great novelists and great Soviet film directors in the way he has created a new theatre art',[1] while a second, who used to state that Brecht should, 'be produced in a way that suits the individual and national personality of the French', now swears exclusively by the strict Brechtian orthodoxy: 'Until someone proves the opposite – and I do not see how anyone could – the best and indeed the only way to perform Brecht remains to copy the Berliner Ensemble'.[2] Even the neologism 'distanciation',[3] which used to be so frequently derided and so strongly rejected, is now so widely accepted that Louis Malle was recently able to use it when describing Catherine Demongeot's performance in *Zazie dans le métro*.

It can be seen that enthusiasm for Brecht has now reached cinema circles. I do not know if the producers have been affected (even though I suspect that Raoul J. Lévy[4] has . . .), but the critics now refer to Brecht, and sometimes invoke his name, and they have begun airing their Brechtian jargon. *Positif* has been thoroughly infected[5] and *Cahiers du Cinéma* will be shortly, for Louis Marcorelles has been doggedly undermining its defences for a number of years. Eric Rohmer casually referred to Brecht in its pages last October[6] and this was an unmistakable sign that a Brecht epidemic was about to break out at *Cahiers*. Indeed, it may be triggered off by the present issue.[7] As a result, we may even catch the defenders of cinematic specificity boning up on 'A Short Organum for the Theatre'[8] or or the 'Hitchcocko-Hawksiens' professing their faith in the Berliner Ensemble.

However, this phenomenon is more serious than it appears at first sight. It undoubtedly does contain elements of Parisian snobbery and it may be reinforced by the coincidence of Bertolt Brecht's initials with those of

Brigitte Bardot.[9] But it cannot be reduced to such things, and I believe it has a deeper explanation which is related to Brecht's *oeuvre* – I mean his works as a whole: plays, theoretical texts, productions for the Berliner Ensemble – which is of a kind that may not be able to change the cinema, but can change the way we look at films and the way we think of the cinema as an art and a language.

I know that such a remark will appear paradoxical. *A priori* Brecht's *oeuvre* has nothing to do with the cinema. Indeed, it rejects and strongly refuses all relation with the cinema in its open claim to be specifically and exclusively theatrical.

One of the first Brechtian commandments is that the audience should never forget it is at the theatre. Hence the absence of illusion: the sources of light are visible, the sets are schematic with placards and billboards to indicate time and place or to summarize the action. Brecht's theatre has no inferiority complex in relation to the cinema. Brecht is not Piscator: his intention is not to have the stage take on the dimensions of the world. The theatre is enough for him, and his theatre, in either austere[10] or extravagant[11] fashion, is determined to be just theatre.

So the cinema and Brecht's theatre would appear to be incompatible. Whenever a film-maker has got hold of one of his works, the result has been either a failure or a betrayal.[12] Pabst's *Threepenny Opera* is a betrayal, whereas Cavalcanti's *Herr Puntila and His Man Matti*, though filmed with extraordinary insight into both the play and the cinema, is a failure. There are also the film projects which were abandoned as a result of more or less obscure disagreements between Brecht and his producer or director. This is the case with the *Mother Courage* that Staudte was supposed to direct.[13]

A film such as the Berliner Ensemble's *Mother* does nothing to reduce this incompatibility. In this film the cinema is at the service of the theatre in the humblest of ways: to preserve a performance.[14] This is all that the cinema was asked to do. To find the beginnings of a mediation between Brecht and the cinema we have to go right back to *Kuhle Wampe*, the film Slatan Dudow directed in 1932 from a screenplay by Brecht and in close collaboration with him. But the resulting film does nothing to prove Brecht's compatibility or otherwise with the cinema, at least for the modern viewer who does not understand the many historical references to the contemporaneous German political situation and therefore cannot appreciate this avowedly propagandist film. But it is still true that many of the film's best scenes, such as the discussion on the S-Bahn, take us back to the theatre and recall, for example, the debates in Brecht's didactic plays. Here the cinema is standing in for the theatre but it is not replacing it: it does not exist as an autonomous language.[15]

So what was Brecht's personal attitude towards the cinema? In the absence of sufficient documentation it is difficult to be sure, but one thing is certain: Brecht was a regular cinemagoer just as he was a great reader of detective stories and newspapers of all kinds. The America he evoked in many of his plays, long before visiting the country,[16] derived from the crime novels and gangster films of the silent era. But Brecht seems to have confined himself to being a 'consumer' of cinema. Even when he got to Hollywood and worked on a number of screenplays[17] in order to make a living, he still retained this attitude. Indeed, he appears to have maintained it deliberately since he noted in his *Journal*[18] of the period: 'For the first time in ten years I am not writing anything of my own', and, 'all I am doing is writing for money'. This was how he described Hollywood:

> Every day to earn my daily bread
> I go to the nearest market where lies are bought
> Hopefully
> I take up my place among the sellers.[19]

The one exception to Brecht's lack of esteem for the cinema was his admiration for Chaplin's work,[20] which he knew very well. In Hollywood he became friendly with Chaplin and, according to one report, considered him 'one of the only two directors worthy of the name in the world'.[21]

Similarly, Brecht's theories would seem to exclude the cinema. In every production, Brecht's efforts were directed towards creating a *distance* between the different elements of the spectacle and between this spectacle and the spectator. But doesn't this appear to be a direct denial of the cinema which is based on film as continuity, on the viewer's identification with one or another of the characters, and on his involvement in the spectacle? When Brecht wishes to condemn 'the effects of the (dramatic) theatre on the spectators', his description of the audience might well be felt even more relevant to the cinema. 'Looking about us, we see somewhat motionless figures in a peculiar condition: they seem strenuously to be tensing all their muscles, except where these are flabby and exhausted. They scarcely communicate with each other; their relations are those of a lot of sleepers, though of such as dream restlessly . . . True, their eyes are open, but they stare rather than see, just as they listen rather than hear . . . Seeing and hearing are activities, and can be pleasant ones, but these people seem relieved of activity and like men to whom something is being done. This detached state, where they seem to be given over to vague but profound sensations, grows deeper the better the work of the actors, and so we, as we do not approve of this situation, should like them to be as bad as possible.'[22]

A study of the techniques Brecht recommends in order to achieve theatrical effects which disturb this state, the *alienation* or *distanciation* effect which 'allows us to recognize its subject, but at the same time makes it seem unfamiliar',[23] would bring out the great differences between Brecht's requirements and what goes on in the cinema. Such a study cannot be carried out here, but Brecht's expectations of actors may be cited as an example. The actor is asked that 'at no moment must he go so far as to be wholly transformed into the character played',[24] and 'the actor no longer has to persuade the audience that it is the author's character and not himself that is standing on the stage';[25] he must in fact indicate, by the way he acts, that 'he narrates the story of his character by vivid portrayal, always knowing more than it does and treating its "now" and "here" not as a pretence made possible by the rules of the game but as something to be distinguished from yesterday and some other place, so as to make visible the knotting-together of the events'.[26]

Here Brecht's *teaching* contradicts not only the lived experience of all film viewers (which is an experience based on immediacy and identification), but also the very conditions under which film actors work. Does this mean that we must abandon any attempt to think about the cinema in Brechtian terms and simply solve the question by seeing a contrast between Brecht's view of the theatre as active and critical, and a view of the cinema as an activity of pure consumption, something entirely passive? I do not think so, for our analysis is far from complete: so far I have only analysed the Brechtian system with regard to its *methods*, but not its aims and structure.

Before proceeding to the latter, however, it should be pointed out that although Brecht's theatre techniques would appear incompatible with the cinema, there are nevertheless certain parallels between Brecht's epic theatre and the work of the great creators of the cinema such as Chaplin or Eisenstein, and these parallels are particularly striking since Brecht was never tempted by the illusion of using cinema techniques.

Alienation or distanciation is simply a means to an end, and the risk is that if one only takes account of these techniques Brecht's epic theatre turns into frozen rhetorical gestures. Brecht's theatre may be described more in terms of his essential determination to offer the audience, in an art form ('the easiest form of existence', according to Brecht), recreated images of social life – that is, images which are rendered comprehensible and from which the audience may derive a lesson for their times, by means of a constant movement between identification with the characters which are presented and understanding of the historical situation which has made these characters what they are.

The first requirement in the epic theatre, therefore, is that the viewer should be able to *look afresh* at what he is shown. As early as *The Exception and the Rule*, Brecht asked of him:

> What is not strange, find it disquieting!
> What is usual, find it inexplicable!
> What is customary, let it astound you.[27]

The alienation techniques are designed precisely to make such a fresh look possible. The spectacle should be such that it appears neither universal nor as a projection of the viewer's subjective world, that it is clearly dated and placed in time and space, and that it is not a story which is valid for all times and in all places. Its primary function should be to reveal the history of a time and a place to us, enabling us to see what is particular in things, people and events, and to see them with new eyes. That is the principal role of staging (*mise en scène*) in Brecht's plays – an essential role which allows for a comparison with the concept of *mise en scène* in the cinema. There is nothing decorative and nothing magical in it. For Brecht, staging (and adaptation was part of it) consisted above all in provoking the spectator's 'unfamiliar look on things, a look as difficult to achieve as it is productive'.

What they look at is the real, concrete relationship between man and his time and place, with History – a relationship which is realized through an *action*: a twofold action since it is both the action of society on man and of man on his society.

As can be seen, when the Brechtian system is analysed in this way it does not exclude the cinema. Quite the reverse. What art form better than cinema, in fact, can stimulate such a fresh look, can allow the viewer to grasp daily life in its most concrete manifestations and, through this immediate grasp, lead him to a historical understanding? I need go no further for an example than *Monsieur Verdoux* which, without any misuse of terms, may be called an exemplarily Brechtian film.

André Bazin's remarkable analysis of *Monsieur Verdoux*[28] remains valid in this perspective. What does Bazin say? As he stated, Chaplin's film causes a double movement of identification, which is at the same time one of discovery and one of understanding. At first, the viewer cannot help but be on the side of the elegant and charming fifty-year-old, Verdoux. But his identification with Verdoux is undermined by his crimes and it proves impossible to continue to stick by a murderer, especially when the murderer is not presented in a romantic light or as the victim of fate, as Fritz Lang's M is. So we are therefore led to take the side of the society which condemns him. But Verdoux's final transformation into Charlie Chaplin[29] runs counter to the second movement of identification: the death of M. Verdoux/Charlie Chaplin is a judgment on society, on *this* society which condemned him to death and which had previously forced Chaplin to become Verdoux. Thus our reading of the film is completely reversed: this was the society which created Verdoux and this is the society which is now getting rid of him because he reveals too much about it and because he has literally betrayed it. As Bazin writes:

Society knows it is guilty but cannot acknowledge the fact. When Monsieur Verdoux explains to the tribunal that all he has done is to apply, down to the last detail, the fundamental law of social relationships, the received wisdom of modern life that 'business is business', society of course covers its face and cries scandal, and all the louder because the point has gone home. Its attack on Monsieur Verdoux will be all the more savage because it refuses to see in him a parody of society, an application *ad absurdum* of its rules of the game . . . *Monsieur Verdoux* is at once a paradox and a *tour de force*. *The Gold Rush* went straight for its goal. Verdoux takes society in the rear like a boomerang;

240

his triumph is in no way indebted to the ready and dubious help of ethics. The myth is self-sufficient, it convinces by its own inner logic.[30]

In *Monsieur Verdoux*, Chaplin does not condemn society in advance for moral or sentimental reasons; he goes one better than that – he exposes it. The logic of Verdoux's attitude ultimately reveals the historical logic of the society in question, and Verdoux's condemnation by that society, far from exculpating it, turns on and condemns the society itself. Thus *Monsieur Verdoux* is one of the most formidable and subtle films of social criticism ever made, in just the same way that Brecht's plays are plays of social criticism.[31] Yet there is a difference – in *Monsieur Verdoux* there are none of the positive elements which, for Brecht, were associated with the existence of the people, that people which may be wrong, which may be complicit with its oppressors, but which, in the final analysis, must 'be a source of good'.[32]

Rather than attempting a Brechtian analysis of some of the films that have recently opened in Paris and which have been enthusiastically received by the critics, let us try to indicate what such an analysis might be like, to get a sense of the efficacy of a Brecht-inspired approach when applied to a cinema very far removed from the positions which Brecht adopted. There is no doubt that a director such as Antonioni, for example, shares with Brecht the desire to look at the world in new ways, untrammelled by the blinkers of traditional morality and with the concern to rediscover moral values, but only following a close examination of reality, that is, moral values which conform to the real world rather than to some hypothetical, eternal human 'nature'.

This is why Antonioni refuses the traditional kinds of dramatization which the cinema, particularly the French cinema, has inherited from the bourgeois theatre. Everything is important to him: what counts is not that a given character corresponds to a given type or has a given personality, nor even that he says particular things, but rather what links a particular character and the articulation of particular things. What counts is *what links the two things*: the way we live everyday life, the way we exist in the world and in relation to things. Antonioni's films above all show us these relations, unlike, for example, the theatrical (in the bad sense of the word) films of directors such as Duvivier or Autant-Lara which only offer us characters and a setting (and even when the settings are 'natural' they often merely reflect and caricature the characters). In Antonioni's films there are no characters and no sets but people in an environment (whether 'natural' or social does not matter – even the island setting of *L'Avventura* belongs to a particular environment: it's a setting for rich people) who are held together by relationships which change throughout the film as they live through a certain amount of time.

One might even go further. In *Il Grido* and *L'Avventura* I detect one of the most basic themes of Brecht's art: the combination of contingency and destiny. Consider *Mother Courage*, for example: seen from outside, her life has all the appearances of fate – and she is smitten at the end, just like Oedipus. But if we look a little closer we can see that the gods have nothing to do with this, and that she alone is responsible for her own fate. She could, at any moment, have said no to war and changed her life. But although she was totally aware of this possibility she never decided to do so.

Cannot the same be said of Antonioni's heroes? At any point, Aldo [in *Il Grido*] might not perhaps have been able to turn the clock back and try to win over 'his' wife again, but he could at least have chosen to settle down and love the woman he had ended up with. But consciously or not (and this is of secondary importance) he chooses refusal and the slow descent towards the river. He chooses his fate. Like Sandro and Claudia in *L'Avventura*, who are free to welcome or to flee the growing love between them.

But why these choices? Why is freedom converted into destiny in this way? Here, Brecht and Antonioni diverge. It is not simply a psychological chance that Mother Courage cannot manage to tear herself away from war and say no to it; Brecht explains that Mother Courage is also the product of a particular society in which war is inextricably bound up with money. Her theoretical freedom to say no to war is translated into a practical impossibility of taking such a decision. Thus by showing us Mother Courage, Brecht is inviting us to reflect on the society she belongs to (which is also, to some extent, our own): what he called *the social gest* is revealed beyond the links of cause and effect in everyday life. Nothing is insignificant, nothing exists simply in itself; every word, every gesture, every action a character performs refers back to society and tells us both about that society and about that character.

At this level, in Antonioni's work, things become confused. We are made to realize, at the outset, that the affair between Sandro and Claudia is specifically bourgeois, just as Aldo's is specifically working-class. But instead of explaining or making clear the basic relationship between his heroes and their environment, Antonioni diminishes its importance and makes it vague. Thus we perceive Aldo, Sandro and Claudia as representatives of humanity in general, as symbols. We lose track of the specificity of their stories and begin to share in their pathos. They take on all the ills of our age, ills which are inevitable and probably incurable. Fate is insidiously restored to omnipotence, and what Antonioni makes us see afresh is simply a new aspect of something that is as old as can be: man's perpetual misfortune.

If a film such as Chabrol's *Les Bonnes femmes*, which is extremely different from Antonioni's works, were subjected to a similar analysis, similar conclusions would emerge. The thesis, or the *fable*,[33] in Chabrol's film is excellent: it set out to show the alienation of the 'girls' of the title not so much at its source (their working conditions) as in the consequences of it which are specific to each individual (inability to cope with their own freedom),[34] and it enabled social relations to be understood on the basis of strictly individual forms of behaviour. Chabrol rapidly turned his back on the wealth of meanings contained in the story: sometimes he portrays his 'girls' in the typical manner of the worst kind of pre-war episode films; sometimes he gets carried away by the stupidity which animates his heroines (such a movement from the over-particular to the over-general is, after all, common: it is the usual passage from naturalism to symbolism). Instead of rendering their adventures intelligible, he makes them more obscure and more doomed than they were at the outset, to such a degree that they are reduced to simple references to the original sin of all female existence.[35]

A final example is Louis Malle's *Zazie dans le métro*. Malle's aim – to place 'an upright and unruffled little girl, who is always the only one who's right, who is never affected by anything, who is a way of looking at things'[36] in the centre of a contemporary big city – coincides with the desire to describe a social phenomenon at a distance, to show it while making it appear strange in the viewer's eyes. In this respect comedy, which, as Brecht pointed out, 'is less likely than tragedy to fail to take human suffering seriously enough',[37] can often turn out to be an extremely effective weapon. This was precisely the technique Brecht adopted in *The Visions of Simone Machard*, in which a very young child performing an act of heroism without being aware of it (she dreams she is Joan of Arc) is what brings to light the contradictions of the French middle classes who, in June 1940, were ready to play the collaboration game with the Germans, though they had previously been jingoistic patriots.

But instead of telling Zazie's story, Malle weaves his inventions round it. He fills it out with often brilliant variations which have nothing to do with the story. Zazie disappears in the bustle of the city, which Malle films in a crescendo of images full of sound and fury. His film is metaphorical, hyper-naturalistic, but not epic or realist. Unlike *Monsieur Verdoux*, for example, a film in which every meaning is mediated, everything in *Zazie* is immediate and so everything is symbolic. Zazie herself no longer has much to do with it, and if she were eliminated the film would not be much different. Malle has simply given us his own view of 'urban terror'.

Brecht, of course, never laid claim to total objectivity. But all his work is subjectivity trying to be objective: it is the transformation of consciousness into *knowledge of a concrete and useful kind*. As he liked to say: 'The poet does not speak in sacred language. He must speak a true language. The theatre does not serve the poet but society.'[38]

Film criticism, at least as it is practised in *Cahiers*, opposes this fundamental position. Some of its watchwords, for example *la politique des auteurs*, were useful in their time, but may now lead critics into subjective blindness and even into what André Bazin called the 'aesthetic personality cult'.[39] Other slogans go even further: the demand for 'cinematic specificity', 'the absolute primacy of *mise en scène*' (this latter being considered an 'act of knowledge'),[40] the definition of cinema as a means to describe the immediate beauty of the real, etc., derive from a view of the world and of art which is magical, a view which also holds that the cinema is the only art there is – a privileged art. Such criticism is mesmerized by its object (the cinema) and thus tends to isolate cinema to an increasing degree, to divorce it from its possible meanings, to deny it its *mediatory* role, and to reduce it to a statement of its own essence. In so doing, criticism of this kind destroys itself as criticism.

It is therefore high time that a new school of criticism replaced this scholasticism and broke the vicious circle in which such criticism is increasingly enclosed, so as to introduce a new and more real dimension into this game of mirrors which makes films disappear into thin air. What is needed is an attempt to understand the work not at the level of the 'humanistic' intentions of its *auteur* but at the level of its meanings – the work understood as *mediation*.

A Brechtian approach to the cinema could fulfil such a role and, without neglecting the undoubtedly valuable contribution of some of the analyses carried out by our metaphysically-minded critics, could challenge the ends and means of cinema today from a historical point of view. The work would be looked at from the standpoint of how responsibly it handles its methods in relation to its *fable*, and its *mise en scène* in relation to its meanings, as well as the relation between film and audience. Criticism of this kind would give cinema back its status as language and its function as art, and it would enable it to get away from the extremely dangerous fascination with its own myth.

Although I still do not know how film-makers can be 'Brechtian', I am sure that Brechtian criticism of the cinema is both possible and necessary today. A little Brechtianism may seem at rather a remove from the cinema, but a lot of Brechtianism can only bring us right back to the cinema, and with great urgency, because the cinema is less able than any other art to shirk the problem of responsibility for its forms and its meanings.

Translated by Jill Forbes

Notes

1 Pierre-Aimé Touchard, 'Brecht et le brechtisme', *Le Monde*, 29 October 1960. (Author's note.)

2 Morvan Lebesque, 'Bertolt Brecht, le fabuliste', *Carrefour*, 17 August 1960. (Author's note.)

3 The term *Verfremdung* cannot be satisfactorily rendered, and the conventional translations, *distanciation* and *alienation*, do not bring out its full meaning. Here is a quotation from one of Brecht's descriptions of acting which will help to clarify the term:

> The actor must play the incidents as historical ones. Historical incidents are unique, transitory incidents associated with particular periods. The conduct of the persons involved in them is not fixed and 'universally human'; it includes elements that have been or may be overtaken by the course of history, and is subject to criticism from the immediately following

period's point of view. The conduct of those born before us is alienated (*Entfremdet*) from us by an incessant evolution.

It is up to the actor to treat present-day events and modes of behaviour with the same detachment as the historian adopts with regard to those of the past. He must alienate these characters and incidents from us. Characters and incidents from ordinary life, from our immediate surroundings, being familiar, strike us as more or less natural. Alienating them helps to make them seem remarkable to us. Science has carefully developed a technique of getting irritated with the everyday, 'self-evident', universally accepted occurrence, and there is no reason why this infinitely useful attitude should not be taken over by art. It is an attitude which arose in science as a result of the growth in human productive powers. In art the same motive applies.

'Short Description of a New Technique of Acting which Produces an Alienation Effect', in Brecht, *Brecht on Theatre*, p. 140. (Author's note, adapted.)

4 Raoul J. Lévy, 1922–66, producer and scriptwriter, best known for launching Roger Vadim and Brigitte Bardot with *Et Dieu . . . créa la femme*, 1956; continued to produce both Vadim (*Sait-on jamais?*, 1957) and Bardot (*En cas de malheur*, 1958, and *Babette s'en va-t-en guerre*, 1959). His films around the time this article was written include Peter Brook's *Moderato cantabile* and Henri-Georges Clouzot's *La Vérité*, both 1960.

5 Cf. *Positif 35*, 'Encyclopédie permanent du cinématographe: B.B. (infection). The Berliner Ensemble's performances at the Théâtre des Nations attracted a tightly packed crowd of film-makers and film critics who were discovering Brecht or claimed they had always known his work. Rightly or wrongly, accurately or inaccurately, the terms *Brechtian, non-Brechtian, Brechtian criticism, Brechtian film* are in the process of becoming the most widely used terms in the cinema.' (Author's note.)

6 Eric Rohmer, 'Photogénie du sport', *Cahiers* 112, October 1960: 'Hawks does not have to chase after the modern, because he is already a master of modernism. I would lay a bet that his example will long continue to be as stimulating as that of Picasso, Joyce or Brecht, whom we in fact got to know before rather than after him'. (Author's note.)

7 I.e. *Cahiers* 114, December 1960, the special issue on Brecht in which this article appeared.

8 Brecht, 'A Short Organum for the Theatre', in *Brecht on Theatre*.

9 *Cahiers* as is well known, has always made great play with the Karl Marx/Marx Brothers homonym. (Author's note.)

10 In his *Lehrstücke*, or didactic plays. (Author's note.)

11 In works as different as *The Threepenny Opera* and *The Caucasian Chalk Circle*. (Author's note.)

12 Ben Brewster discusses Brecht's relationship with the film industry in 'Brecht and the Film Industry', *Screen*, vol. 16, no. 4, Winter 1975–6, focussing on the film of *The Threepenny Opera* and on *Hangmen Also Die*. Both films are also discussed by Martin Walsh in 'The Complex Seer: Brecht and the Film', *Sight and Sound*, vol. 43, no. 4, Autumn 1974, reprinted in Walsh, *The Brechtian Aspect of Radical Cinema*, London, British Film Institute, 1981.

13 The Berliner Ensemble has recently completed a film of *Mother Courage* which is fairly close to their stage production but which, unlike *Mother*, is designed

for commercial distribution. (Author's note.) This was a DEFA production in East Germany, 1961, directed by Peter Palitzsch and Manfred Werkwerth, after the Berliner Ensemble production directed by Brecht and Erich Engel, with Helene Weigel and Ernst Busch.

14 Cf. Louis Marcorelles, 'D'un art moderne', in this issue of *Cahiers* (i.e. *Cahiers* 114). (Author's note.)

15 *Kuhle Wampe* has been significantly re-positioned and revalued since this time: see, for example, James Pettifer, 'Against the Stream', and Bernard Eisenschitz, 'Who Does the World Belong To? The Place of a Film', both in *Screen*, vol. 15, no. 2, Summer 1974, and Pettifer, 'The Limits of Naturalism', *Screen*, vol. 16, no. 4, Winter 1975–6.

16 Brecht made his first trip to New York in 1935. (Author's note.)

17 Notably *Arch of Triumph* (adapted from E.-M. Remarque) [directed by Lewis Milestone, 1947] and Fritz Lang's *Hangmen Also Die*. The latter seems to have been the screenplay to which he made his greatest contribution, but Brecht did not like the way Lang directed the film and had his name taken off the credits for the screenplay, leaving only 'from an idea by Brecht'. (Author's note.)

18 Quoted from information given by John Willett who was able to consult Brecht's as yet unpublished *Work Diary* in Berlin. (Author's note.)

19 The title of the poem is 'Hollywood', quoted from Bertolt Brecht (John Willett, ed.), *Collected Poems*, London, Eyre Methuen, 1976, p. 382.

20 One of the sources of *Herr Puntila and his Man Matti* is undoubtedly *City Lights*: like Chaplin's millionaire, Puntila has two personalities, a good one when he is drunk, and when he is sober the personality of a property owner and capitalist. (Author's note.) Martin Walsh, *op. cit.*, briefly discusses the influence of Chaplin on Brecht, pp. 16–17, and quotes Brecht in relation to Chaplin and epic theatre, from 'The Question of Criteria for Judging Acting: Notes to *Mann ist Mann*', *Brecht on Theatre*, p. 56.

21 The other, of course, being Brecht himself. (Author's note.)

22 Brecht, 'A Short Organum for the Theatre', in *Brecht on Theatre*, p. 187.

23 *Ibid.*, p. 192.

24 *Ibid.*, p. 193.

25 *Ibid.*, p. 194.

26 *Ibid.*, p. 194.

27 Bertolt Brecht, *The Measures Taken and other Lehrstücke*, London, Methuen, 1977, p. 60.

28 André Bazin, 'Le Mythe de *Monsieur Verdoux*', *La Revue du Cinéma* 9, January 1948, translated as 'The Myth of *Monsieur Verdoux*' in Bazin, *What is Cinema? Vol. 2*.

29 'We see Verdoux next being led away across the prison yard in the dawn, between two executioners. A small man in his short sleeves, his arms tied behind him, he moves forward toward the scaffold with a kind of a hop, skip, and a jump. Then comes the sublimest gag of all, unspoken but unmistakable, the gag that resolves the whole film: Verdoux was Charlie! *They're going to guillotine Charlie!*', Bazin, *What is Cinema? Vol. 2*, p. 109.

30 *Ibid.*, p. 108, p. 113.

31 As well as Bazin's essay, the radical political meaning of the 'parable' of *Monsieur Verdoux* is proposed by Pierre Kast in 'Des confitures pour un

gendarme', *Cahiers* 12, May 1951, translated as 'Flattering the Fuzz' in Volume 1, Ch. 29.

32 About Schweik, Brecht wrote: 'Of course, he is not a positive character, but nothing around him is positive either: only he is a source of the positive. (. . .) Because he is so indestructible he can always be exploited, but this also means that freedom will always come from him in the end'. (Author's note; source not given.)

33 *Fable* is the term Brecht uses, following Aristotle, Goethe and Schiller, to refer to the basic story told by a work. (Author's note.)

34 The shop sequences are the least successful parts of *Les Bonnes femmes* because they are not accurate and because the shop-owner character is caricatured by Pierre Bertin. (Author's note.)

35 Dort is probably concerned here to refute some of the claims for 'objectivity' in relation to *Les Bonnes femmes* made by André S. Labarthe in 'Le plus pur regard', *Cahiers* 108, June 1960, translated as 'The Purest Vision: Les Bonnes Femmes' in this volume, Ch. 2. The association of Chabrol with supposed Brechtian practices persisted: a review of *Ophélia* and *Landru* by Jean-André Fieschi, *Cahiers* 143, May 1963, was entitled 'Si nos brechtiens'.

36 Cf. Yvonne Baby's interview with Louis Malle, *Le Monde*, 27 October 1960. (Author's note.)

37 Bertolt Brecht, 'Remarks on *The Resistible Rise of Arturo Ui*', in Brecht, *Collected Plays, Vol. 6*, New York, Random House, 1976, p. 457.

38 Bertolt Brecht, 'A Note on Directing', in *Théâtre Populaire*, no. 39, Autumn 1960. (Author's note; source not otherwise known.)

39 André Bazin, 'De la politique des auteurs', *Cahiers* 70, April 1957, translated as 'On the *politique des auteurs*' in Volume 1, Ch. 31, p. 257.

40 Michel Mourlet, 'Beauté de la connaissance', *Cahiers* 111, September 1960, translated as 'The Beauty of Knowledge', in this volume, Ch. 14: 'Losey's *mise en scène*, like Valéry's writing, is at every turn an act of knowledge; it is the gaze of an innocent eye and the conquest of an ingenuous mind'. Doubtless Dort also has in mind articles such as Fereydoun Hoveyda's 'Les taches du soleil', *Cahiers* 110, August 1960, translated as 'Sunspots' in this volume, Ch. 13.

24 | Fereydoun Hoveyda: '*Cinéma vérité*, or Fantastic Realism'

('Cinéma vérité ou réalisme fantastique',
Cahiers du Cinéma 125, November 1961)

Jean Rouch's new film [*Chronique d'un été*] reminds one of 'La Pléiade', that collection of de luxe editions which combine a novel and the author's 'notebooks' for the novel, often in the same volume. But cinema, as one might expect, has the edge on literature in this field. A 'Pléiade' reader can, *if he wants*, refer to the 'notebook'. He can refrain from doing so, or he can read one and then the other. But anyone watching Rouch and Morin's work *has* to be aware of the 'notebook' – and in the order in which the authors have decided to present it to him. In this case the 'notebook' and the 'novel', if I may be allowed to use literary analogies in respect of a film, are inextricably entwined in the way the film is constructed, and are seen to be indispensable to one another.

However, this use of analogy smacks too much of its Aristotelian origins to account for the cinematic reality of *Chronique d'un été*. So let us dedicate it to the memory of Alfred Korzybski,[1] and instead confirm that if, as Rouch has said, *La Pyramide humaine* is a film of a film, then *Chronique d'un été* is both a film and the film of this film. Normal logic would require us to speak of each of these two aspects in turn. But we must beware of the traps set for us by the Aristotelian tradition. A film *and* the film of this film, yes; but with their images continuously interwoven so that in the end what we have is something *sui generis*, something absolutely new. The danger of analysis is that it can dismantle this profound unity and lead us into false conclusions. Taken bit by bit, Rouch's film does not escape criticism. But considered as a whole, it can only be supported.

I say 'Rouch's film' advisedly. I don't want to deny the very considerable contribution of Morin, or the very personal contribution of the protagonists. *Chronique d'un été*, more than most films, is a collective work. But it inserts itself immediately and so well into Jean Rouch's itinerary, it is so much part of the development of his style and his ideas, that we are obliged to accept it as being properly *his* film. It is proof, if proof be needed, that regardless of how much collaboration or co-operation there

248

may be, the director remains the only master of his ship. *Marienbad* and *Hiroshima* are films by Resnais, and by Resnais alone. Only those with scant regard for the cinema could couple the name of the author of *Nuit et brouillard* with that of Marguerite Duras or Alain Robbe-Grillet. We should not be deceived by an artist's modesty when he announces, 'We wanted to do this or that'. A certain way of revealing the world matters more than the arguments at issue. This is the law of art which determines that in cinema ideas are forged in the crucible of *mise en scène*.

There's that loose phrase again: a phrase that Rouch detests, claiming for himself the role of a simple instrument, an extension of the camera, compensating for the limitations of the apparatus, a kind of 'living camera', but – precisely that – *living*. Niels Bohr[2] has noted that in physics the observer disturbs the object being observed. The fact is that Rouch, after so many films, has become a real director. A director who can be beguiling even as he is going out of his way to plead an absence of direction. And if these ideas of his could at a pinch be applied to his first films, it has been a different story since *Les Maîtres fous* and *Moi, un Noir*. The 'paternalist' attitude which, unconsciously, he showed towards colonized peoples shaped his style and in the end contradicted his original intentions. It was this that prompted my reservations about his African films. Now that he is turning his attention towards white people, towards his own country, this paternalism has vanished.

In any event, there is not a single shot in his latest film which is not *directed*, even the scene in the deserted Les Halles building when Marcelline talks about her deportation. We are moved not just by what she says, but in particular by the way both the words and the setting are inscribed within the frame of the camera as it moves. A simple idea of *mise en scène*, if you like; but an idea of *mise en scène* all the same. There is no need to invoke the Heisenberg 'uncertainty principle'[3] to know that impartial observation is a myth. And if the alleged objectivity of the camera momentarily succeeds in reviving the myth, it's not long before the fundamental ambiguity of the apparatus operated by a film-maker has been exposed.

'Cinéma vérité', like 'kino eye' before it, is only a decoy, a lark-mirror[4] held in front of the audience to make them believe that they are seeing their own image. What does Morin mean by 'cinéma vérité'? A cinema which 'overcomes the fundamental opposition between fictional cinema and documentary cinema . . . Jean and I are agreed on at least one point: you have to make a film which has a total authenticity, as real as a documentary but with the content of a fictional film – that is, the content of subjective life, how people exist.'[5] What was the result for Morin and Rouch as regards this definition? It was a curious inversion: the 'fictional' element turns into documentary (subjective life looked at from the outside) and the documentary side becomes fictional (overloaded with subjectivity). It could not have been otherwise, since the 'fundamental' opposition between the documentary film and the fiction film only exists in the mind of its authors and not in cinematic reality.

Let's pause for a moment on this paradox. I have said that 'fictional' cinema is no more 'subjective' than documentary, or anyway as subjective.

This is the first panel of the diptych. Cinema can only deal with what is 'human' through the intermediary of things, and can only deal with the exterior through the intermediary of the interior. It can only be objective. Whether its subject is fictional or documentary, the image is there in all its material density and there can be nothing transparent about it. The deserted Les Halles building does not denote Marceline's solitude; it *is* that solitude. When Angelo climbs the steps at Petit-Clamart, this does not denote the drama of the working man. Rouch was well aware of this when he said that 'This climb *becomes* a kind of poetic drama'.

The second panel of the diptych: cinema aims equally to be subjective. The image aims to go beyond itself, as image, to denote the 'interiority' which its objective angle of vision denies it (motivations, intentions, thoughts, etc.). From this point of view, I take *Nuit et brouillard* to be as 'subjective' as *Hiroshima mon amour*. To create a blend of documentary and interiority, Rouch and Morin make use of monologues, discussions, questions: spoken language, that is, not cinematic 'language'. In doing this, they are not offering us anything in the way of *truth*. If we are moved by Marie-Lou's monologue, it's not because of the words she speaks but because of the extraordinary play of her eyes and her features.

Once again *Chronique d'un été* reminds me of what we know of atomic physics. I hope readers will forgive me if I use scientific notions in an attempt to make my argument clearer. To represent the properties of light and electricity, some experiments suggest to us the idea of particles. Other observations are interpreted in terms of wave propagation. These two representations are *complementary*. They are only apparently contradictory: the two types of experiment are mutually exclusive and cannot be done simultaneously. The two panels of my diptych are not so far removed from this complementarity. They are exclusive, but they complete one another. Moreover, taken in the Morin and Rouch sense, *'cinéma vérité'* is only a figment of the imagination, belonging to the pre-Einstein era.

Where is truth, where is authenticity? Or rather, what truth, what authenticity is conveyed by the leading characters of *Chronique d'un été*? What do we know about them, apart from a few 'scraps' thrown to us? What are their hidden motivations? From this point of view, the film is missing a number of items: a context and a history for the characters, their innermost preoccupations and so on: in short, the world each of them sees, in its totality. I have already had occasion to state my view of *'cinéma vérité'*,[6] and there is no need to labour it. Besides, Rouch himself hardly believes in it, and he is very careful not to fall into the rut of neo-realism. He is aware that, just as the word is not the thing, so cinema is not life.

Far from being a realist work, *Chronique d'un été* seems to me rather to be a fantastic film. The fictional form sometimes used by writers to bring author and character together, in exceptional narratives, has point here.

Rouch and Morin question their characters and are questioned by them in turn. At each juncture problems of construction present themselves to the authors, which they work out with the full co-operation of the protagonists. The impossible becomes possible, and a door opens on a world which is far more interesting than the facade that the neo-realists construct for us. *Chronique d'un été* belongs within what Bergier and Pauwels[7] call 'fantastic realism'. And it is not the least merit of the film that it introduces us to unfamiliar perspectives, instead of confirming us in our own.

Having taken note of the indissoluble interdependence which exists between the observer and the system observed, Rouch breaks the mould of cinematic narrative. Isolating the experiment from the rest of the world is not enough to authenticate it; it is also necessary to isolate the observer from his apparatus of observation. But if we take into account the circumstances of the experiment, we can gain some understanding of it. This is what Korzybski has called 'the consciousness of abstraction'. Rouch and Morin possess this consciousness. They are honest enough to enter the arena, to put themselves on stage (and into question). This is something that Rouch has not done before. And something that Rogosin[8] has never done. They set before us all the conditions of the experiment. The observer is observed. They don't hide from us their interventions or their responsibility for the *real* evolution of the characters and themselves. I will come back to the way the film ends, which seems to me to be very fine. For the moment, let's say that with Rouch cinema has become *interventionist*.

What makes *Chronique d'un été* such an exceptionally rich film is that one discovers other films in it – to the nth degree – hidden under the first film. What is revealed is a film about the influence of cinema which provides us with much more information about this subject than all the works of filmology past and future. And what we derive from it is an essay on how to make a film that is worth more than all the lessons pouring out of the film schools.

We find here too a film about sociology which brilliantly demonstrates the non-existence of that science whose experts confront us from behind a screen of published papers. To the extent that they wanted to conduct a sociological inquiry, Rouch and Morin have been unsuccessful. The 'discoveries' they make have long been common knowledge: that working on a production line is boring, for instance. Which brings me to the film's most tiresome aspect, and perhaps also its most debatable.

Chronique d'un été is in certain respects an *alimentary* film, in the literal sense of that word. From the outset its makers have decided, not without a certain childish innocence, that people are more relaxed when they eat together. So we have a whole series of scenes in which the characters are seated round a table. These spontaneous discussions serve, in fact, to create an impression of unwanted unreality. The 'actors' don't even appear to be eating, and an unsuspecting audience might easily assume that Rouch has deliberately put bits of food on the table 'to make it more real'.

Some people have criticized the film on the grounds that it is unrepresentative: the people chosen for it are unusual, not typical enough, too individual and so on. I really can't see the point of this criticism. 'Types' are a figment of the imagination, statistical averages: in real life they don't exist. Rouch is not trying to enter the world of definitions. The characters in *Chronique d'un été*, like the characters in any good film, neither want to nor can represent anyone but themselves. What we see in the film is not the Renault worker, but Angelo; not the office worker, but Marie-Lou. The complaint arises from a misunderstanding. In the many statements they have made, Rouch and Morin often talk in general terms of the problems which concern them: 'How do you sort out your life?', 'How do you live?', etc. One might assume, then, that Rouch wanted to tackle a general problem. But this is to forget that, happily, and unlike literature, cinema ceases to exist if it leaves the domain of the concrete world. It is precisely because the film has no wish to generalize or to prove anything that it emerges as a sympathetic enterprise.

On the contrary, it is precisely by focusing on individual, flesh-and-blood characters, and by skilful direction, that Rouch manages to hold our interest in the film, despite its numerous imperfections. There are not many works which set up a dialogue with the audience in this way. The audience is hooked and can't escape: they are involved and obligated. Moreover, some of them object to having their resistance broken like people under psychoanalysis: like the patient directing his 'aggression' against the analyst, they turn on the film and on Rouch or Morin or both of them, as the case may be. In a sense, this reaction seems to me to be justified. Everything that is true or allegedly true (in the cinema) can be dangerous. Fiction eliminates from its subject-matter what I might call its 'degree of concern'. Just as horror films (momentarily) channel our anxieties by drawing us into their fiction. Only 'true' films can prompt the spectator to ask questions about himself (and fiction can also be true) and change his life. It is not a case of describing human reality (an impossible task: total knowledge of living structures is a contradiction of life itself), but simply of getting the spectator involved. And that's where it hurts.

There is, however, another side to the coin. Just as in a real conversation, there are some scenes in the film where we watch the characters' gestures and expressions and through this 'physical' observation try to fill in the gaps in what they are saying. The 'psychodrama' method can often lead to 'full' discourse in the Lacan sense.[9] More often, however, the psychoanalyst only has 'empty speech' to bite on. In this case, sign language becomes a kind of code which lends itself to interpretation. And as we watch *Chronique d'un été*, we can't help interpreting those irrevocable signs that are the *physical* reactions of the individuals which Rouch's camera shows us. Nevertheless, a great deal of the information we need to verify our inferences is missing, and nowhere in the film do Rouch and Morin think to make up for our ignorance.

This inevitably arouses in us a feeling of frustration. Which brings us to one of the limitations of Rouch and Morin's venture. By insisting on their desire for non-intervention and spontaneity, they forget to give us a more complete table of contents. Many necessary details are missing. Many flat, ineffective scenes telescope segments of undeniable beauty. Moreover, what is the spontaneity we are talking about? That of the protagonists? But they are conditioned – as in a psychodrama or the free association techniques of psychoanalysis – by the given facts of the *game*, by having the project explained to them, by the presence (reduced to a minimum though it is) of the camera, etc. Then are we concerned with Morin's spontaneity, or Rouch's? To judge from the scenes they appear in, Morin is nothing less than spontaneous and Rouch is a match for his partner. And to claim that by not having a script you avoid preconceived ideas is to forget that the centre of 'active' preconceptions is located precisely within the unconscious. I'm not really convinced by Rouch's comments on using the camera as a stimulus. So what game is he playing? Ethnographer? He no longer really is one, the film-making side of him having taken over. Psychoanalyst, then? But he falls a long way short of the specialists, and he scarcely profits from his own experiences. (Much could be said about the survival of 'paternalism' after so many endeavours, about Rouch wanting to follow up his characters outside the film with his sharp sense of 'responsibility', about reintroducing a black into a film in which he has nothing to do, etc. But this falls outside the scope of this article.) What is interesting is not Rouch's experiment, but the *cinematic* result he obtains, which we shall try to render in plain language.

Since I have several times mentioned psychoanalysis, I will add now that just as an opportune 'punctuation mark' lends its own meaning to what is said by a subject under analysis, here also 'editing' carries a significant weight. I am well aware that Rouch in a sense disclaims editing, saying that he prefers just putting shots end-to-end in chronological order.[10] But we should not forget Merleau-Ponty's[11] dictum: 'When we speak, we don't necessarily have a better idea of what we are saying than those who are listening to us.' Rouch suggests that 'It is almost impossible to break up the order of filming; because the people have evolved in such a way that if you want to stay close to them you have to show them in terms of their evolution . . . This evolution is in my view the subject of the film.'[12] This statement, like all utterances, conceals its metaphysics: does Rouch believe in an evolutionary process that is constant and regular? His film belies this completely, since his editing insists on fits and starts, wobbles, twists, turnarounds, leaps forward, moments of crisis. I have spoken of complementarity. Rouch's editing is composed precisely of images that are complementary and irreducible, alternating 'objective' segments (Renault factories, the *Cahiers* editorial office, etc.) with flashes of the 'subjectivity' of the characters. On occasion the editing consists of a simple movement of the camera within a sequence-shot (the conversations at table, for example). So where is the purported chronology? In fact, Rouch is ambivalent: in one sense he conducts his argument on a conscious level, and in another from the depths of his unconscious. On the surface he deals in Aristotelian logic, happily contradicted by the film itself. Moreover, isn't the so-called 'absence' of editing actually part and parcel of editing itself? It's high time we stopped pretending that what happens in a film has anything to do with *reality*: the evolution of Rouch and Morin's characters, hinted at in *Chronique d'un été*, does not happen *in* the film but outside it. Chronology, like time itself, is an invention of the mind, and Resnais was quite right to demolish it in *Marienbad*.

In the final analysis, *Chronique d'un été* provides us with much more information about Rouch and Morin than about the material the camera is supposed to convey. It is not ethnology or sociology which interests them, but the possibilities of cinema. With a few ideas to start from they rush headlong into a film, only to find themselves in the end with quite different ideas. Despite appearances, they do not collaborate; each works for himself, while at the same time trying to make the film a joint enterprise. This explains, as I see it, a certain sense of duality, of disjointedness, in more than one sequence. But, as I've said, with the aid of his camera's 'cunning' Rouch wins through in the end.

The possibilities of cinema? Psychoanalysts have long been aware of them, in their use of the camera and films to expedite treatment. If it were only an experiment, *Chronique d'un été* would interest me much less. So where lies the interest (beauty, I would say) of this otherwise incomplete, imperfect, untidy, frequently misleading but always fascinating film? In the account it gives us of the collaboration between Rouch and Morin. The real subject of the film is not the evolution of Marceline, Angelo or Marie-Lou, but that of Morin and Rouch, whose initial enthusiasm and strength of purpose is broken against the wall of life. The final sequence, where the authors are seen evaluating what they have achieved, acquires an almost sublime nobility. With great honesty they confront their failure, knowing that this failure is about to return each of them to solitude. For all that, this is not an empty failure. It is not fruitless: it has given life to a film of extraordinary richness. If the end of the film coincides with the end of Rouch and Morin as partners, the adventure isn't over yet. Rouch and Morin, one feels from their farewell gesture, will harness themselves to new creative endeavours.

I have already indicated some of the criticisms which the film has not failed to elicit from 'purists'. I shall refer to one of them in concluding. This concerns the 'poor' quality of the photography, the 'errors' of continuity and so on; in short, what learned Aristarchus types pompously term 'writing' [*écriture*]. I have a horror of this word applied to cinema, but that is not the issue. *Chronique d'un été* could undoubtedly have been more *extrinsically* well made, and I have sometimes criticized my friends for their systematic disdain for 'good composition'. But in the end their prejudice has its uses, considering the confusion which now reigns in the world of cinema and perhaps also in the other arts. There is a great tendency to confuse 'good writing' and artistic expression. The recent tirade by Michel

Butor,[13] proclaiming the need in literature to learn to *write badly*, seems to me to apply equally to cinema. Only on these terms can we one day disentangle ourselves from that mesh of 'rules' in which the enemies of cinema like to entwine our art to prevent its being renewed. In any event, I admit to being not in the least disturbed by 'writing' in the films of Rouch or of Godard.

There is much more to be said about this attempt at *new* cinema which *Chronique d'un été* represents. Like several other contemporary works, the film contains the seed of an attempt to set up new relations between sign and meaning,[14] in terms of what it is appropriate to call 'cinematic language'. In their way, a Rouch and a Resnais bring to cinema a convulsion similar to the one a Robbe-Grillet or a Butor have introduced into literary fiction. With them, the old notions of beauty, truth, feeling are exploded, or rather given a different context. But that is another story.

Translated by David Wilson

Notes

1 Alfred Korzybski: see Ch. 13, note 19.
2 Niels Bohr, 1885–1962, Danish physicist; the 'Bohr theory' (1913) explained how radiation was emitted by atomic hydrogen.
3 Werner Karl Heisenberg, 1901–76, German physicist who elaborated the 'uncertainty principle', which posited that it is impossible to measure simultaneously both the position and the momentum of a particle.
4 A 'lark mirror' (*miroir aux alouettes*) is a decoy for larks in the form of a curved piece of wood set with small mirrors, mounted on a spindle and twined by a string.
5 *France-Observateur*, 22 December 1960. (Author's note.) Cf. Jean-André Fieschi: 'What Rouch then films, he is the first to attempt: not just behaviour, or dreams, or subjective themes, but the indissoluble amalgam binding them together. The film-maker's desire is to devote himself to the wish of his characters. To follow them step by step, along the basic lines of Zavattini's neo-realist principle, but with the sights set on what their speech reveals at least as much as on their behaviour. Embodying their disappointments, their daydreams, their desires' ('Jean Rouch' in Richard Roud, *Cinema: A Critical Dictionary*, London, Secker & Warburg, 1980, p. 905; reprinted in Mick Eaton, *Anthropology-Reality-Cinema: The Films of Jean Rouch*, London, British Film Institute, 1979, as 'Slippages of Fiction: Some Notes on the Cinema of Jean Rouch', p. 73).
6 In 'Les Taches du soleil', *Cahiers* 110, August 1960, translated as 'Sunspots' in this volume, Ch. 13.
7 Jacques Bergier and Louis Pauwels, literary critics well known for their study of the fantastic, *Le Matin des magiciens: introduction au livre fantastique*, Paris, Gallimard, 1960.
8 Lionel Rogosin, US documentary film-maker best known for *On the Bowery*, 1956, and *Come Back Africa*, 1959.
9 Jacques Lacan, psychoanalyst and teacher whose attention to the productivity of language, related to 'structuralist' currents of thinking, in a radical re-reading

of Freud, provided a materialist theory of the subject. Lacan's most significant writings and period of greatest influence come well after the date of this article, his work being a vital influence on *Cahiers* at the end of the 1960s and into the 1970s. Writings include: *Ecrits* (originally published Paris, 1966), London, Tavistock, 1977; *The Four Fundamental Concepts of Psychoanalysis* (originally published as *Le Séminaire de Jacques Lacan*, Livre XI, Paris, 1973), London, Hogarth Press, 1977. Lacan's work is discussed in, for example, Rosalind Coward and John Ellis, *Language and Materialism*, London, Routledge & Kegan Paul, 1977, and Caughie, *Theories of Authorship* (see 'Notes on Terms').

10 Cf. discussion about editing in Eric Rohmer and Louis Marcorelles, 'Entretien avec Jean Rouch', *Cahiers* 144, June 1963, pp. 6–8.

11 Maurice Merleau-Ponty, 1908–60, philosopher and author associated with Existentialism whose work attempted to bring together phenomenology and Marxism.

12 *France-Observateur*, 22 December 1960.

13 Michel Butor, novelist and critic associated with the *nouveau roman*; his novels include *L'Emploi du temps*, 1956, *La Modification*, 1957, *Degrés*, 1960.

14 Cf. André S. Labarthe's comments in 'Marienbad année zéro', *Cahiers* 123, September 1961, translated as 'Marienbad Year Zero' in this volume, Ch. 3.

('Autocritique', *Cahiers du Cinéma* 126, December 1961)

Using words to discuss films is not the least of criticism's paradoxes. If we admit that cinema is something new, then we have to recognize that literary language is ill-equipped to cope with it in a way that is either adequate or coherent. Our Indo-European languages, whose origins are lost in the mists of time and whose rules were codified around 350 BC by Aristotle, could indeed not foresee that there would be a seventh art. And so critics, drawing on an existing vocabulary, have invented (and continue to invent) new meanings as and when their individual concerns have made them necessary. Unfortunately, while they were about it, they didn't get themselves together (and still haven't) to produce an agreed lexicon, and have thus added to the general state of confusion, reinforcing a whole series of misunderstandings that make us question how useful their work is. The terms 'writing', 'style', *'mise en scène'*, etc. are served up over and over again with meanings that vary from one critic to another, and yet no one seems to find it necessary to provide a definition. Using undefined terms to talk about cinema is indeed a very convenient way of exercising one's profession: the reader has either to recognize his 'incompetence' or accept and pretend to understand the mystifications that are thrown at him.

The 'technical' description of a film provides the critic with an alternative approach which nevertheless resembles the first in that the reader doesn't necessarily understand the production process and indeed usually knows nothing about it. In both instances he may not want to admit to being an ignoramus. But there is still the danger that he may protest and, responding to pressure from the readership, many dailies and weeklies are increasingly relying on non-specialists for their film pages. I personally can well understand this reaction. Firstly – and I wrote about this at length last year[1] – I believe that everyone can and should engage in film criticism. Secondly, I admit to finding specialist criticism of the kind I have described above monumentally boring. When someone talks about 'pure beauty' in a piece on Mizoguchi, I am sorely tempted to ask him to explain to me what 'impure' beauty might be. When someone else throws in my face an expression like 'the highest degree of perfection', I can't help wondering about the 'model of perfection' and the 'scale of values' that underpin this affirmation. Similarly nothing irritates me more than critics' obsessive need to declare that X or Y 'is' or 'is not' the 'part' he is 'playing' more or less well. Compared to what? And how does the critic know that? Judgments like these really make us think that the critic sees himself as superior to the director and in some way outside the film. Pride and presumption! We can easily detect in these approaches the failings of a mode of analysis that separates out the various elements in order to assess them one after the other as though the whole was just the sum of its parts. Yet another of the traps of Aristotelian logic! How could we not approve of the spectator's revolt against the critics?

And I become even more convinced when I look at other ways that critics have gone awry. Many writers on cinema make, for example, analogies with literature that are extraneous to the film, like an anecdote which is, when it comes down to it, completely irrelevant. And what about those hyper-specialized critics that some journals so jealously protect? You could describe their prose as a mishmash of metaphysics, aesthetics, philosophy and cinematography. This most recent of approaches often results in articles that are both pretentious and unreadable, and at best in texts that are hermetic. Then, of course, there are those who just summarize the screenplay: they indeed do the least harm, but I can't see why one should translate the story of a film into words; it's treating the spectator as if he were blind! Lastly I should mention the critics whose contribution can ultimately be reduced to 'I like it or I don't like it'; I have nothing against them – I have too great a respect for each person's right to express an opinion; I will just say that they seem to be pursuing a logic that proceeds by 'yeses' and 'noes', a logic that isn't borne out by the facts.

Whatever you think, it is hard to avoid comparing film criticism to a conversation in which everyone talks and no one listens. And given its blithe tendency to present definitive views of very different works, to quote philosophers and literary authorities, psychologists and academics, you would think it was in possession of the key to the universe. I can't resist the temptation of quoting a text of Eric Satie: 'The critic's mind is a department store; you can find everything in it: orthopaedics, sciences, bedding, arts, travelling rugs, a large selection of furniture, writing paper, smokers' requisites, gloves, umbrellas, knitwear, hats, sports, walking sticks, spectacles, perfume, etc. The critic knows everything, sees everything, hears everything, eats everything, confuses everything and still manages to think. . . .'.

These remarks apply of course just as much to my own writings, otherwise this article couldn't have been entitled 'Self-criticism'! But self-criticism involves a sincere attempt to formulate new guidelines. I will, then, make use of this opportunity to try to sort out some of the conflicting ideas that are floating around in my head as the year draws to a close.

It is really as though many critics admit to the existence of an 'original text' of which the film is just a translation. Thus, when they draw attention to 'perfection' or to 'shortcomings', they give the impression that they are passing judgment with reference to an absolute that is located somewhere outside the work, to some universal standard. Referring to spoken and written language, Saussure[2] remarked that signs taken individually signify nothing, that each of them expresses less a meaning than a 'gap' in meaning which distinguishes it from all the others, and that it is this 'lateral relationship' between signs that confers meaning on them. The ambiguities of cinematographic language are greater still. We have to cast aside the absurd illusion that the image is more accessible than ordinary language. Nothing could be more misguided! And where cinema is concerned, we could apply, word for word, what Merleau-Ponty[3] has to say: 'Language does not presuppose a table of concordances, it reveals its own secrets . . . it is just a monstrance. Its opaqueness, its obstinate self-reference, its introversion and introspection are precisely what constitute it as a spiritual power: for in its turn it becomes something like a universe, able to contain the world of things by transforming them into their meanings.' Ultimately, it is as though the critics I am referring to have access to an absolute cinematographic language or, at the very least, that what they think they know about cinema is a pinnacle and that if a film-maker wants to be an artist he must make use of the same tools.

There exists, of course, a basic set of procedures that constitute, as it were, the 'empirical' language of cinema, one that directors can draw upon as a shared inheritance. Within the appearance of the empirical language of the screen there is, however, a hidden second-degree language in which signs once more assume the 'vagueness' of the painter's colours, the musician's notes, the novelist's words. Bergier and Pauwels[4] are quite right to stress the reality of what they call 'texts with several meanings'. So-called 'commercial' film-makers limit themselves to a 'correct' use (one that keeps to pre-established rules) of the 'empirical' language: their films are purely and simply indistinguishable from the story that is being told. They are at best translators into images ['metteurs en images']. They select signs for a pre-determined meaning. Although critics are often speaking about all films, I want to repeat that what I am saying here applies only to the other kind of cinema, the one in which 'utterance' is truly 'expressive' as it feels its way round an intention to signify that isn't guided by pre-existing definitions and in which a good measure of the implied is visible at every moment. *That* kind of cinema necessarily strains the 'procedures' of the empirical language, giving them new meanings as it goes along even though everything may still look the same. One of my friends rejected *Léon Morin, prêtre* on the grounds, among others, that the large number of dissolves demonstrated infantilism and was in any case tiring or showed up a lack of sophistication in the narrative. Yes, of course these dissolves 'signify' the passage of time, but also the disarray of an individual consciousness and of an epoch, which isn't at all what they are supposed to mean in the 'empirical' language of cinema. I don't want to launch here into a critical examination of *Léon Morin, prêtre*. I just want to say this: if we are going to be fair to Melville, we owe it to him to look at some of the narrative devices he could have used but rejected, and to sense how they would have affected the 'chain' of images, how far Melville's style was the only one possible for his meaning to be made clear.

Something happens in cinema that is in certain ways reminiscent of the 'probability factor' in physics. In each particular instance several possibilities present themselves and if the film-maker selects the most likely one, he has succeeded. It is up to the critic to examine the probabilities and attempt to show that the director has or has not opted for the best one. There is of course a mixture of subjective and objective factors in this task, often making hasty judgments both difficult and dangerous. However that may be, the critic should force himself to 'shake' the apparatus of cinematographic narrative to see if he can get a new sound out of it or lay bare the 'lateral' and 'oblique' meanings hidden within it. Marx understood that perfectly well with regard to Balzac. Let me take up here another remark of Merleau-Ponty that seems directly applicable to cinema: 'The novel as account of events, as expression of ideas, theses or conclusions, as prosaic and evident significance, and the novel as work on style, as oblique or latent significance, exist in a relationship which is simply homonymous'. A certain way of showing modern society in a large number of American films (for example *Some Came Running*, *Party Girl*, *Anatomy of a Murder*, *Blind Date*, etc.[5]) is more important than their stories or the messages they are apparently putting across.

It is indeed right to condemn formalism. But people forget that, rather than over-rating form, it debases it by separating it off from meaning. This formalism is no different from a cinema of subject-matter that ignores form. One can't be content to judge Stanley Kramer or Autant-Lara on their intentions alone, however laudable these may be. It isn't enough to protest against atomic suicide or war, you still have to produce a work of art that disturbs the spectator and makes him ask questions. Otherwise you would be denying the very existence of art, you would be forgetting the fundamental truth that language is not just a simple tool in the service of an object that is outside it, that language contains within itself its own 'metaphysics'. Language sets fearsome traps even for those who claim to be operating only on the level of art, or who say that they are uncommitted (as if art could be cut off from other social activities, as if the uncommitted was not already a precisely determined commitment). By demonstrating the structural relations between language and the laws of society, Lévi-Strauss's studies[6] have amply proved the vacuity of such attitudes. The infantile and unaesthetic image that many of today's film-makers, young and old, have of the world transpires in *Le Déjeuner sur l'herbe* (and in many 'New Wave' films). It is easier to play on false naivety than on intelligence, to celebrate the past than to look to the future. The *politique des auteurs* has had its day: it was merely a staging-post on the road to a new criticism.

Personally I am inclined to agree with Marcabru[7] when he distinguishes between several different kinds of cinema. Except that instead of four kinds I see an infinite number. But that is another story. What I want to suggest is that there are different levels and that these must not be confused. You cannot speak of Autant-Lara, Cottafavi, Rossellini, Preminger and Losey in the same terms. You can of course like or dislike all of them, but they are on different levels all the same, even when they charm or irritate us. This tendency to confuse things to which *Cahiers* seems to have been contributing recently invites a response. The tendency of the daily and weekly press to resort to non-specialists is not, I think, an unrelated phenomenon.

This leads me to clarify my ideas on the critic's function. In many respects, it resembles that of the psychoanalyst. Does he not, in effect, have to reconstruct through the film the discourse of the *auteur* (subject) in its continuity, bring to light the unconscious that underpins it and explain the particular way it is articulated? The unconscious is indeed, as Lacan[8] would say, marked by a gap; it constitutes as it were the censored sequence. But, as in psychoanalysis, the truth can reveal itself; it is written not in the 'visible' sequence of images, but elsewhere: in what we call the *auteur*'s 'technique', in the choice of actors,[9] in the decors and the way actors and objects relate to these decors, in gestures, in dialogue, etc. A film is a kind of rebus, a crossword puzzle. Or rather it is a language which sparks off a debate, which doesn't end with the screening of the film but engenders a real searching.

Of course, just as the psychoanalyst can let himself be lured into a false interpretation, the critic can get things wrong. When we go into darkened theatres, we take with us the whole weight of our prejudices, our education, our heredity – in short, the whole of our personality. You can't leave your past in the cloakroom, and trying to empty your mind is a vain hope. The ideal observer exists only in fiction! The critic says as much about himself as he does about the film he has seen. He must never forget that this is how a two-way circuit is established. The act of criticism creates an opposition between two sensitivities, each of which possesses its own individual history. It would be too easy to praise a film to the skies just because the worlds of the critic and the film-maker coincide. That would not be praising the film, it would be self-congratulation! Every critic should declare his 'metaphysics' to his reader, making it clear where he stands with regard to the reader.

What is at stake is not guiding the reader as if the critic were adopting a kind of superior position, but explaining what we think we have noticed. And in doing this, we must not forget that the film we are discussing is never the film itself. The map, as Korzybski[10] says, is not the terrain! The critic should make this observation his first principle. As a work that has an objective existence outside of ourselves, the film cannot be the object of an exhaustive study. Whatever we can say about it will never be the film. We extract some details and leave aside many others. We will never be able to exhaust all its meanings. A film is its *auteur*. And the *auteur* is a human being. All that we can do is try to grasp his singularity, the 'signifying structure' he has erected.

In one sense, the critic's problem is a problem of language. We have to translate into the language of everyday life an artistic language which has a different logic. This ought to incite writers on cinema to resort to accepted concepts only with the greatest reticence and the greatest prudence. When we talk about films we are in a situation not unlike that of the 'popular' scientist attempting to explain specific relativity and general relativity to an audience that knows practically nothing about mathematics. The phenomenon of cinema involves so many things on which no serious or definitive work has been done that it is impossible at the present moment to talk about it with any degree of certainty. In trying to grasp its meanings, we are groping in the dark, we are trying out theories. We have to have the courage to admit that this is the case. I can't remember who wrote: 'Literary justice is never in the domain of the temporal, and in the spiritual it is never absolute.' This is even more true of film criticism.

The problems raised by film criticism are, as we see, of the same order as those raised by the seventh art itself. You cannot aspire to solve them once and for all. As soon as some are clarified, others emerge. Film criticism is still in its prehistory! I admit, then, without shame, that I frequently let myself be carried away by my own prejudices. But that does not mean I am abandoning my attempts to construct a non-Aristotelian approach to cinema. Where have I got to? That's another story that I will perhaps write one day.

When the militants of young cinema tell me that their films are addressed only to one sector of the public, I can't help thinking of pornographic literature. It too is addressed to a limited audience and geared to specific tastes! And it very rarely produces works that stand up to scrutiny! Besides, when an author embarks on a book or a film he always has at least an unconscious ambition to move heaven and earth. That is why I am very careful not to dismiss a work on the grounds of 'frivolity'. It happens more often than you would think that great things are balanced on the head of a pin. But they can just as easily (and perhaps more frequently) be stood on more substantial objects. As Valéry[11] said, the world of ideas is a thousand times stronger, more fabulous and more real than the world of the heart and the senses.

Confronted by all the pitfalls that beset film criticism, some of which I have mentioned above, we must ask ourselves about the usefulness and the justification of this strange activity which allows you to claim the right to state publicly what you think about a film. Let me have recourse once more to a quotation. One can apply to film-makers what Merleau-Ponty says about writers: 'We who speak do not necessarily know better what we are saying than those who listen to us.' To the extent that criticism also 'speaks', this remark applies just as much to *it*. What this does is open out a space for the 'criticism of criticism' or – which comes to the same thing – for 'self-criticism'. But it is time I stopped.

Translated by Norman King

Notes

1 Fereydoun Hoveyda, 'Les Taches du soleil', *Cahiers* 110, August 1960, translated as 'Sunspots' in this volume, Ch. 13.

2 Ferdinand de Saussure, 1857–1913, founding figure of concepts of the structural nature of language with his (posthumous) *Course in General Linguistics* (originally published Paris, 1915), London, Fontana/Collins, 1974; Saussure's work is discussed in, for example, Rosalind Coward and John Ellis, *Language and Materialism*, London, Routledge & Kegan Paul, 1977.

3 Maurice Merleau-Ponty: see Ch. 24, note 11.

4 Bergier and Pauwels: see Ch. 24, note 7.

5 See, for example, Fereydoun Hoveyda, 'La Réponse de Nicholas Ray', *Cahiers* 107, May 1960, translated as 'Nicholas Ray's Reply: *Party Girl*' in this volume, Ch. 11, and Jean Douchet, 'Un art de laboratoire', *Cahiers* 117, March 1961, translated as 'A Laboratory Art: *Blind Date*' in this volume, Ch. 16.

6 Claude Lévi-Strauss: see 'Introduction: *Cahiers du Cinéma* in the 1960s', note 75.

7 Pierre Marcabru, film and theatre critic, theatre for the weekly arts paper *Arts*, then film for the paper *Combat*; extensively referred to by Hoveyda in 'Les Taches du soleil', Marcabru also figured in the round-table discussion on criticism in the special issue on criticism, *Cahiers* 126, December 1961, which contained the present article by Hoveyda; Marcabru published a history of world cinema since 1940, *Allons au cinéma*, Paris, Gallimard, 1964.

8 Jacques Lacan: see Ch. 24, note 9.

9 That is why it is pointless to say that the actor is or is not the character. The choice of actor is already in itself a declaration of intent. The actor may well be imposed. But a director can make the best of that situation by playing up other aspects that are in a dialectical relationship with the characters. (Author's note.)

10 Alfred Korzybski: see Ch. 13, note 19.

11 Paul Valéry, 1871–1945, thinker, essayist, critic and poet.

26 | Louis Marcorelles: 'The Leacock Experiment'

('L'Expérience Leacock', *Cahiers du Cinéma* 140, February 1963)

If we exclude that kind of 'degree zero' cinematic writing represented by the *reductio ad absurdum* of *L'Année dernière à Marienbad*,[1] the tendency of modern cinema since 1945 has been increasingly to advance the quest for realism. Set against the naturalism of pre-war cinema was Italian neo-realism, a term general enough to include some very different personalities but precise enough to indicate that what was involved was a return to the real, with natural settings and natural speech, non-professional actors, and a rejection of familiar dramatic forms all serving to renew the stock of conventions available to the director. The attempt by Richard Leacock and his collaborators in Drew Associates[2] to establish a cinema which is even more immediate, more closely connected to reality – what Robert Drew calls 'filmed journalism' and Leacock 'cine-reportage' – pushes back the boundaries of realism in the cinema and should, in the near future, open up to the fiction film an entirely new field of investigation, a territory which our own 'New Wave' has hardly begun to explore.

Richard Leacock has expressed in these pages[3] his enthusiasm for the new camera which Morris Engel, director of *The Little Fugitive*, developed to give him a great deal more freedom in shooting his third film, *Wedding and Babies*: 'I'm involved in a big narrative film shot on regular 35mm stock with direct sound and no post-synching. The dialogue was recorded in a lot of different places, notably in the streets of New York on the occasion of an Italian festival, and without in any way that you could notice interfering with the normal life of this district.' Leacock is not the last to celebrate the little revolution in filming methods which neo-realism brought in (he particularly admired *Due Soldi di Speranza*[4]). 'This meant we could film anywhere at all, without being tied to the cumbersome sound equipment and without being troubled by "noises off" . . . But it was a spontaneity created by the skilful application of what I can only call a dying technique.' These two quotations are a good illustration of how for Leacock the problem of sound is primary:[5] there was here a close

264

relationship between sound and image which in the studio could only be re-created artificially.

At about the same time, Jean Rouch was involved in making *La Pyramide humaine*, and tearing his hair out as he sat jammed in the back seat of a car in Abidjan because he couldn't use synchronized sound to record the very lively conversation going on in the front of the car between Nadine and one of her suitors. Rouch has never had the same objective as Leacock. There is not – as some simple-minded people seem to imagine – a heaven or a hell where Rouch, Ruspoli,[6] Leacock and others dance a jig on the grave of good old family cinema. From the outset Rouch has shared with Leacock a strong sense of the outmodedness of some of the conventions of delivery and performance employed by actors, and how discontinuing these conventions means that new techniques must be used. But granted these shared ideas, the two film-makers adopt a very different approach and are as far apart in their objectives as it is possible for them to be.

For Rouch, cinema is a means of communication – communication between the director and his actors, between the protagonists themselves, between the auditorium and the screen. What matters is to open as many eyes as possible to a reality which is hidden from us by prejudice, habit, the social conventions of the moment. Leacock is no different, but he does have clearly different aims. This passage by him in the Spring 1962 issue of *Film Culture*, for all the apparent simplicity of its argument, expresses a notion of cinema which in my view at least is revolutionary, because all his talent, all his efforts to perfect his technique, are directed wholly towards the fulfilment of his stated purpose, as I shall attempt to show in more detail later:

> Tolstoy envisioned the film-maker as an observer and perhaps as a participant capturing the essence of what takes place around him, selecting, arranging but never controlling the event. Here it would be possible for the significance of what is taking place to transcend the conceptions of the film-maker because essentially he is observing that ultimate mystery, the reality. Many film-makers feel that the aim of the film-maker is to have complete control. Then the conception of what happens is limited to the conception of the film-maker. We don't want to put this limit on actuality. What's happening, the action, has no limitations, neither does the significance of what's happening. The film-maker's problem is more a problem of how to convey it. How to convey the feeling of being there.[7]

One notices in Leacock the absence of any claim to convey anything but the truth. The accent, certainly, is on communication, as with Rouch, but communication in the sense of reproducing in the most accurate way possible a reality already laid bare by the director. He doesn't prime or provoke this reality; he doesn't create situations. It is enough for him to integrate himself into a given world, to live with his character or characters without making himself noticed, in search of that little spark by which a character is revealed. From the very outset, one senses immediately what separates this way of approaching reality from that of Zavattini[8] previously, regardless of any question of direct sound. Zavattini believes that the insignificant, the banal, the uninteresting also has an importance, that what makes for boredom in life should also be boredom on the screen. Leacock (English in origin but long since settled in the United States) has only to open his eyes to capture life in perpetual motion. Americans, as they say, live at a continuous high pitch. All you have to do is choose, out of all these high points, the most revealing.

A parenthesis here, in order to stress the distinctive character of the Anglo-Saxon mind, which is as different from the Latin character as it is from the Slav; which is the natural enemy of theory; which does not, like the French mind, feel the need to refine its intuitions into equations, or, like the Russian mind, wish to convince itself ten times over of the rightness of a decision. Life in America is a serial in itself: the future President of the USA, like the racing driver at Indianapolis, is driven by a desperate pursuit of success. Money, being successful – that is the nerve, the motor. It is a world ruled by brute force, and no one is embarrassed by it or tries to conceal behind vague moral arguments its jungle character. As Godard said, one can't imagine an American doing nothing. The cinema of Richard Leacock is ideally suited to this society in perpetual motion.

It should not be thought, however, that it's a matter of easy thrills or sensationalism at all costs. Conversations with Leacock himself and with his friends and close colleagues have convinced me that the aim is to catch the essence of a person, those moments of abandon when an individual, either because he is too tired or very relaxed, does not bother to protect himself in the presence of other people. For the film-maker it is not at all a case of trying to dig deep into the consciousness, but of trying to lay bare the hidden motivations which drive the American individual to commit himself in one direction or another. Everyone has his reasons, as Jean Renoir liked to say; and it is these reasons which can be revealed by a close observation of individual behaviour. But Leacock will never have the detachment of a sociologist: even more than the reasons, it is the emotions he wants to catch, the very movement of living.

What is this realism worth? Whatever is made of it by those who practise it. The method itself means nothing; what counts is how it is applied. Take *Primary*, where for some time – impartially, as far as their respective appearances on the screen are concerned – we follow Senator Humphrey and the future President Kennedy. Which of them is the more sympathetic, has the more guile, etc.? Having had the chance to meet Kennedy in Washington, and having watched Humphrey in the lions' den of the Senate, I will simply say that the self-confident Kennedy of 1962 is no longer the gauche, uncertain if very capable Kennedy of 1960. Humphrey, on the other hand, has lost none of his radical-socialist plainspokenness. If Kennedy defeated Humphrey in these primary elections, it was because he was more energetic and showed a more developed skill at reaching the electorate. The result of the election, which was unknown to Leacock,

Drew and the Maysles brothers when they were filming *Primary*, is as it were engraved in the images, irrespective of the fact that this result had been known for a long time when the film was shown. Kennedy shakes a thousand hands, Mrs Kennedy brings along her sex-appeal and a couple of Slavic words for an audience of Poles; in the evening, alone in his office, the future President is literally worn out. Humphrey, on the other hand, relies simply on goodwill and common sense, as he talks to the voters like the Frank Capra of *Mr Deeds* and *Mr Smith*.

For Leacock and Drew, synchronized sound is not merely a technical device but a fundamental requirement. *Eddie* [*Eddie Sachs at Indianapolis*] starts with a bank of seats collapsing, exactly as it happened, but the editing does not make it entirely clear to us. Mrs Sachs cries out, in the middle of the race, at the exact moment of the pile-up which will eventually endanger her husband. The continuity in space which so preoccupied Bazin[9] here becomes simultaneity in time, except that we can't say that the authors have really solved the problem. Mrs Sachs's shout is inimitable; it could not have happened in absolute conjunction with the image of the accident on the screen. There is always a gap. Inevitably, in the editing, you notice the tricks and devices of conventional cinema. Here one comes up against an inherent limitation of the genre – a limitation we shall have to accept, in the hope that its irritating effects can be limited by an exercise in integrity.

This feeling that Leacock and his colleagues offer us the reality of individual people as never before, and yet that there is something missing, must be attributed, I think, to the real weaknesses of the system – weaknesses which nevertheless should not obscure its decisive contribution. In the interview which appears later in this issue, Robert Drew makes a point of the fact that he is trying to reduce comment to as little as possible. Unfortunately, in the films which he and his team made later, and which I was able to see in New York, one is struck by the progressive encroachment of this element, whether it is there to make up for inadequacies in the filming or to give a more precise orientation to the action. *Petey and Johnny*, for example, records the activities of Johnny, a Puerto Rican gang leader in Harlem, who is taken up by Pete, a black social worker. Richard Leacock shot much of the material – street scenes, a gang meeting, a vigil round the body of a young victim of the gang wars. From time to time in the film we watch this Pete, a black who grew up in the slums himself, and who spends his life trying to free his friends from the effects of poverty. Pete belongs in the category of reformer; if Johnny fools around, it is because he has yet to find a soul-mate. At the end of the film, as in reality, Johnny goes to the hospital to see his girlfriend, who is about to give him a child and whom he will marry. This unhappy story requires that the film has to be centred on the social worker's point of view. As it happens, the violence of the images works against the reformer's altruism. We sense that things have been manipulated to turn it into a model case. Though I should say that I have seen much worse.

Flaherty's former cameraman is the first to know how derisory are these panaceas which are no such thing; and the first to be sharply critical of some of the films of the Drew Associates team, such as *David*, about a young drug addict who undergoes a detoxication cure at a special clinic on the coast. Here too one notes some very fine shots, but one looks in vain for an underlying structure, an in-depth view. As I write, the Drew Associates experiment may be no more than a memory, if Time Inc., its sleeping partner, has cut off its funding. This will be regrettable; yet there is a visible gap, a dichotomy, between the intensity you can expect in each individual technician's filming and the collective nature of the work. The Leacock-Drew method has as its premise a fierce pursuit of the truth, a desire to flush out – without in any way being sensational – people's hidden impulses. Given the multiple collaborators, there will inevitably be a multiplicity of points of view, which they try to harmonize in the editing. Each shot or part of a sequence or sequence-shot which works gives us a sensation of life, of being present at a real event, such as we rarely get from the cinema. But if in the same sequence we have three such segments, dynamically filmed but filmed by three different cameramen, there will be a slight shift in the editing. If one of the cameramen is mediocre or heavy-handed, a hole will appear which has to be filled. Something was wrong at the outset, regardless of the increasingly marked tendency to plug the holes with comment – that is, to force conclusions.

So why stick with an experiment which has run out of steam? Because Richard Leacock (and he was the first to do so) saw the need for a new direction. He saw that the cinema had to change its ways or die; that cinematic technique was now offering new possibilities and making new demands. From his work with Robert Flaherty he has visibly preserved a loathing for everything that smacks of artifice, convention, Hollywood frills: over-made-up stars, gargantuan sets, celestial lighting, actors doing their number. No real person lives and behaves like an actor in a Hollywood film. And the fact is that after seeing *Primary*, *Eddie*, *Kenya*, and a recent and at times remarkable film on Pandit Nehru [*Nehru*] it becomes more difficult to accept the rules of the game as played by Californian cinema. Max Ophuls's ideal of an American actor – set him in the groove and he glides along without budging an iota – no longer seems as satisfying as it did, say, twenty years ago. In bringing us close to people, watching them breathe almost, and without cutting them off from their natural setting or background, Leacock takes the Italian neo-realist revolution a stage further. The individual, whether actor or not, is part of a totality. The film-maker is under an obligation to convey that totality.

'Cinema is a terribly difficult art,' Richard Leacock is fond of saying. Certainly cinema allows us to look at the world in a way that no other mode of expression has been able to do. But in so doing it makes almost impossible demands on the film-maker, beginning with a refusal to juggle arbitrarily with a reality that exists before we even think of examining it. Unlike music, which can have no concrete existence, or painting, which depicts a world made motionless, or literature, which is from the first a projection *beyond* the present, a return to the past or an anticipation of the future, cinema has as its substance an immediate, experienced reality. Its purpose is therefore to reconstitute the unfolding of this reality in all its dimensions, while trying to avoid confusing cinema and reality. Cinema, the art of movement, has as its primary object the rediscovery of interior movement through exterior movement, while respecting what is natural in life and in individual human beings (the Rousseau side of Flaherty and his followers). Technically, on very successful days, as Leacock himself acknowledges, the film-maker films in continuity, so to speak, an action which he has managed to catch 'live' in the camera. The editing is in the filming, even if one cannot talk of 'caméra-stylo', which always involves a resort to literature and its vernacular. Before he writes, thinks, converses, man lives, from day to day. This is admirably illustrated by a sequence from a film shot in India last year by Leacock and two assistants. Camera in hand, Leacock follows Mr Nehru on an election campaign in a village, stalking him; well positioned microphones catch the sounds of the place and record what Nehru has to say.

In this cinema, all is harmony. The camera has just to be there, moving slightly to the left at one moment, tilting upwards at another, to capture the sense of close communication between the demigod and his followers. In ten minutes we are shown Nehru the old man, Nehru the demagogue, Nehru the Buddha. A vision emerges of a sorry man wholeheartedly dedicated to his own myth. The Nehru we see is certainly an intimate portrait, but it is also a Nehru in action, a Nehru whose character is perfectly caught for us, but without there being a single moment of identification by the film-maker with the ideology of his subject. This kind of cinema is, I think, the perfect counterpart of what Brecht was trying to do in the theatre, allowing for the difference between the two modes of expression. Richard Leacock – wrongly – rejects the fiction film. But I am convinced that before long anyone who wants to make actors perform will more or less have to start, if he wants to keep them in control, with little films that are witness to the Leacock spirit, with actors who can completely and very physically project themselves into their roles.[10]

The object of the Leacock method, when it is successful, is to restore to filmed reality its vitality, its truth, without ever pretending to make a judgment. It precludes the film-maker intervening in the life of the person being observed, the ordering of events, or the forcing of an improper interpretation. Politically, the brief portrait of the Kenyan settler [*Kenya*] – which some people find deplorable, others moving, according to whether you think in black or white terms – is the one which most accurately defines the terms of this 'filmed journalism'. But the Nehru sequence already mentioned suggests higher, veritably Tolstoyan, ambitions: every possible judgment can be made in respect of this old man of immense vitality, revealed as it were in his most secret ambitions. This 'possession' of his subject by the film-maker, this osmosis between reality and film, offers us a new kind of awareness which is incompatible with any other. It clearly belongs in the category of poetry.

Translated by David Wilson

Notes

1 Cf. André S. Labarthe, 'Marienbad année zéro', *Cahiers* 123, September 1961, translated as 'Marienbad Year Zero' in this volume, Ch. 3; the 'degree zero' reference is presumably to Roland Barthes, *Le Degré zéro de l'écriture*, 1953, translated as *Writing Degree Zero*, London, Jonathan Cape, 1970.
2 A full-length study of Drew Associates can be found in Stephen Mamber, *Cinéma Vérité in America: Studies in Uncontrolled Documentary*, Cambridge, Mass., and London, MIT Press, 1974.
3 Richard Leacock, 'La caméra passe-partout', *Cahiers* 94, April 1959.
4 *Two Pennyworth of Hope*, directed by Renato Castellani, 1951.
5 Cf. Michel Marie on the crucial function of sound in 'Direct', originally published in *Lectures du film*, Paris, 1976, translated in *On Film*, no. 8, Spring 1978, reprinted in Mick Eaton, *Anthropology-Reality-Cinema: The Films of Jean Rouch*, London, British Film Institute, 1979.
6 Mario Ruspoli: Italian documentary film-maker working in France; two of his *cinéma vérité* films at this time made a particularly strong impression, *Les Inconnus de la terre*, 1961, and *Regard sur la folie*, 1963.
7 Richard Leacock, quoted in Jonas Mekas, 'Notes on the New American Cinema', *Film Culture*, no. 24, Spring 1962, p. 9. Leacock's 'manifesto', 'For An Uncontrolled Cinema', appeared in *Film Culture*, no. 22–3, Summer 1961, reprinted in P. Adams Sitney, *Film Culture Reader*, New York, Praeger, 1970, published as *Film Culture*, London, Secker & Warburg, 1971.
8 Cesare Zavattini: see Ch. 3, note 4.
9 André Bazin and spatial continuity: see Ch. 3, note 2.
10 In his article in *Cahiers* [Cahiers 94, *op. cit.*] on Morris Engel, Leacock wrote: 'I had the feeling that the camera could follow all the subtleties of the thing that are usually lost in normal conditions of filming'. (Author's note.)

27 Jean-André Fieschi: 'Neo-neo-realism: *Bandits at Orgosolo*'

('Néo-néo-réalisme', *Cahiers du Cinéma* 141, March 1963)

No one could be more pleased than we are that American cinema has on the whole won the war that history said it had to win (and not just by winning over the critics). We don't deny that there is still work to be done in this field, for example a true assessment of the great achievements of Mankiewicz or the often underestimated qualities of film-makers like Allan Dwan, Jacques Tourneur, Douglas Sirk, etc., directors who have been unjustly kept out of the limelight.[1]

Even so, as things stand, a reflection on aesthetics based solely on American cinema runs the risk of falling into a new academicism: liking Preminger or Fuller is all very well, liking only them or the cinema they represent just leads us back into the dead-end many critics are already trapped in. The point is not to replace one tradition based on quality by another, even one that has excellent credentials, but to create the conditions in which cinema can thrive on its contradictions without getting bogged down in a caste-based security which would sap its vitality.

And, just as a few years ago the postulates of new criticism were partly based on the confrontation of convergent qualities (yes indeed) of the young generation of American directors and neo-realism (the links between Ray and Rossellini for example[2]), we now have to establish new connections with the intention of forecasting, on the evidence of recent trends (it is too early to say whether this will be successful or not), what the probable or desirable evolution of modern cinema will be.

What are these trends? If you will permit a totally subjective response, I won't hesitate to affirm that the markers that can guide our reflections are, on the one hand, the work of Jean Rouch, the most open of all current work, and on the other the ultimate achievements of those two great directors who are still in the avant-garde, Renoir and Rossellini (especially in *Le Testament du Dr Cordelier* and in *Viva l'Italia*). And also those two 'young cinemas' that are still from time to time dismissed as terrible twins but that I think of as exemplifications of an essential complementarity: I am referring to the young French cinema and the young Italian cinema.

This complementarity derives from a different attitude on the part of their authors with regard to the notion of realism. It is axiomatic that every good film, whatever its point of departure, encounters along its way both realism and the fantastic[3] (by which I mean the sense of mystery inherent in all things when they are looked at in a particular way), since it is in the very essence of cinema to spark off that synthesis that the other arts could by their very nature only aspire to with no hope of succeeding. And yet it is a fact that while they often showed a sensitivity to the real and even to the mundane that is, all in all, quite new, the young French directors nevertheless constructed in their best films – as if to prove their right to be considered as *auteurs* – what could be called personal mythologies. Godard is the ultimate consecration of a *romantic* and profoundly *individualist* mythology. After his two confessional films, Truffaut has been seduced by an essentially *poetic* mythology (Demy too, though he has particular qualities of his own): the exploitation of the fantasies of the gangster novel in *Tirez sur le pianiste*, the attractions of the magic of the past in *Jules et Jim* and of the *future* in Bradbury.[4] As for Rivette, his meticulousness allows him to create in *Paris nous appartient* a mythology that is *abstract*. In spite of his obsession with the event shown in all its ludicrous pettiness, Rohmer invites us to unravel the meanings of a *moral* parable.[5] And there is Chabrol, who gives us the key to his fascinating world of refracting prisms in *Ophelia* . . .

It is, then, precisely when our *auteurs* seem to be the most realist that they are in fact the furthest away from realism, and you would be wrong to take as a criticism of the *nouvelle vague* what I consider to be its most original aspect. After all, the *interiorized* realism displayed is at least as important as the other kind. (Besides, these are creations which are still too close to their point of origin and the way they will develop will certainly take us by surprise.)

Perhaps because they attach more importance to their screenplays (probably following Zavattini's example), the best of the young Italian directors are on the other hand more able to integrate their personal views into an objective realist framework, whether this realism is historical (Francesco Rosi in *Salvatore Giuliano*), poetic (Valerio Zurlini in *Cronaca familiare*) or documentary: De Seta in his *Banditi a Orgosolo*, which I am at last going to discuss after a digression which must seem very long. If the terms realism and objectivity seem vague, it should be added that the principal characteristic of the young Italians as opposed to the young Frenchmen is didacticism. How does *Banditi a Orgosolo* illustrate this didactic quality and what are its characteristics?

De Seta's first intuition was to recognize that the most particularized of geographical locations (the mountains of central Sardinia) would not detract from the universal and exemplary nature of the film: the beauty of a rock is the beauty of all rocks, just as the need to reach a social awareness is the same as that of any other awareness; and to realize that austerity would increase the force of his message rather than detract from it. Thus the formal elements of the film (a man, a child, sheep and mountains) and the plot (a shepherd is accidentally implicated in a murder, has to go into hiding, and is forced to play out the role imposed on him) are reduced to basics. As a result De Seta can make the generality of his point and the particularity of his illustration exactly coincide.

Certainly the film is linked to a profoundly Italian cinematic tradition whose specificity it would not be useful to examine here. What matters is how it goes beyond that tradition by realizing its full potential. *Banditi a Orgosolo* does in fact succeed in bringing together the preoccupations that to an extent underpin Visconti's *La terra trema* on the one hand and De Sica's *Bicycle Thieves* on the other. But these two films couldn't avoid the traps into which the personalities of their *auteurs* lured them: Visconti allowed himself to be seduced by the theatricality of the real and, magnifying his historical document by recourse to sumptuous composition and framing, he couldn't resist the temptations of a social opera, whereas De Sica remained faithful to his demagogic tendencies (whether they are sincere or not is not at issue) and wallowed in the mawkish, lachrymose paternalism that is characteristic of his films. The desire to show people reaching an awareness of unacceptable social realities and then to transfer this awareness from the characters in the film to the spectator was thus compromised by their formalism, plastic in one instance, moral in the other. If the documentary – the neo-realist idea of the document as spectacle of everyday life offered to the senses and to reflection – can conjure up the real as enchantment and transform the banal into lyrical fact, this lyricism must even so be the result of a hidden metamorphosis that is imperceptible to the eye and yet does not pre-exist the look. The lyrical (if you like, the sense of the immediate beauty of the real) has then to be integrated into an analysis. De Seta's film *is* analytical on the level of its apparent progression (the real is not immediately available in its totality but is gradually revealed piece by piece, a revelation that is emphasized by editing which is both particularly effective and dictated by the logic of the characters themselves – contrary to Flaherty's practice, it is subordinated to and doesn't exert a tyrannical hold over the significance of the action), and synthetic on a second level, that of the spectator called upon to pass his own judgment on a case with all the evidence at his disposal and thus obliged to abandon his passivity in order to bring about the ultimate transformation, conferring on the film a full and complete existence. You have to go back to Donskoi's *Mother* to find such a clear and consistently dialectical expression of a theme so dear to film-makers of the Left.

I readily concede that this is not in itself enough to guarantee the beauty of the work but, before going on, it is worth stressing at this point that at least the primary objective has been realized. But it is the way De Seta effects a shift from an initial didacticism (critical realism) to an aesthetic sublimation of this (poetic realism) that makes him interesting: in short, how his *mise en scène*, as vehicle for the Idea, becomes a form that appeals to the emotions.

The feeling of injustice in *Banditi a Orgosolo* arises from the shepherds being prevented by an almost abstract force from finding, in spite of the hostility of their natural habitat, an inner peace whose radiance would be strong enough to restore it to a Virgilian serenity: when the warm breath of the sheep sends the child off to sleep, the harmony of the shot *proves* how powerful this peace is. The shadow of the Carabinieri on the child's face in the next shot is enough to destroy it: an indiscreet and outrageous intruder, the shadow disturbs a natural order of things in the moment of its fulfilment.

De Seta's talent as film-maker shows itself in the balance he establishes between the art of narration and the sense of looking: the narrative never interrupts the continuity of the gaze, the gaze never obstructs the rigorous development of the action.

The gaze is first and foremost an extreme sensitivity to objects as well as to people, to their physical presence which the barrenness of the setting shows up in all the splendour of its simplicity. The film thus becomes a lucid poem imbued with a restrained benevolence, a poem that gives us an intimate glimpse of men's faces frozen as they lie in wait or pearled with sweat after the chase, of convivial attitudes when it is time for sleep, of the dogs rummaging around in the ferns; a poem that reveals to us the beauty of a tree stump, of the meagre, scattered bushes of the *maquis*, of the mattness of the sky, of the flickering flames, of the coarsely woven velvet of the men's jackets, above all of the obsessive presence of the rocks made blinding by the sunlight and darkened by the coming of night.

This is indeed a cinema of total knowledge in which the love of people merges with the intuitive apprehension of things. It makes you understand the vanity of all recourse to gushing sentimentalism or to rhetoric. Left to itself, the art of showing is restored to its original dignity. It is from being distanced enough to avoid the trap of a mawkish complicity which would detract from the clinical nature of his analysis that De Seta's look derives its force. Yet he doesn't sink into the frigidity of a third-person psychology that tries to objectify what cannot be objectified.

I can then, in conclusion, return to my point of departure and reaffirm that cinema has everything to gain from contact with and development of this return to origins since, just like romanticism and surrealism in litera-ture, neo-realism is not a *school* (for all Zavattini's doctrinal extremism) but a tendency, a force that is still active in cinema; we need it as much today, if only as a stimulus, as at the moment of its official recognition. For all the classicism of their writing, the young generation of Italian film-makers which has learned from it continues to innovate. I hardly need stress that *Banditi a Orgosolo* is truly the work of a cinematic *auteur*, although it uses approaches that are quite different from those of young French directors. That is what I was calling the complementarity of the two cinemas. Will they be able to consolidate the points they have in common? It is perhaps from this synthesis that the next new wave will emerge.

Translated by Norman King

Notes

1 In the mid-1960s some amends were made for the critical neglect of such American directors: interview and other material was published on Mankiewicz (*Cahiers* 178, May 1966, translated in *Cahiers du Cinéma in English*, no. 8, February 1967), Tourneur (*Cahiers* 181, August 1966) and Sirk (*Cahiers* 189, April 1967), among others.

2 See Volume 1, Parts 2 and 3.

3 Cf. Fereydoun Hoveyda, 'Cinéma vérité ou réalisme fantastique', *Cahiers* 125, November 1961, translated as '*Cinéma vérité*, or Fantastic Realism' in this volume, Ch. 24.

4 The reference is to Truffaut's project of filming Ray Bradbury's *Fahrenheit 451*, realized in 1966.

5 The reference is presumably to Rohmer's *Le Signe du Lion*, 1959, but Fieschi's emphasis on the *moral* parable side of Rohmer reminds us that Rohmer had in fact also just begun his *contes moraux* cycle, with *La Boulangère de Monceau*, 1962, and *La Carrière de Suzanne*, 1963.

28 | Roland Barthes: 'Towards a
Semiotics of Cinema': Barthes in
interview with Michel Delahaye,
Jacques Rivette

('Entretien avec Roland Barthes', *Cahiers du
Cinéma* 147, September 1963)

*Where does the cinema fit into your life? Is your view that of a spectator, a critical
spectator?*

Perhaps one should begin by talking about one's cinemagoing habits, the
place of the cinema in one's life. I do not myself go to the cinema very
often, once a week at most. As for my choice of film, well, this is never
basically completely free; I would no doubt prefer to go to the cinema
alone since, for me, watching a film is an entirely projective activity; but
as a consequence of your social existence, you usually go to the cinema
with someone else or in a group, and once that's the case, the choice of
film ceases automatically to be straightforward. If my choice were purely
spontaneous, it would have to be totally improvised, unaffected by cultural
or crypto-cultural imperatives of whatever kind, guided by the obscurest
forces of my inner self. What poses a problem for the cinemagoer is that
there is a kind of more or less diffuse moral obligation to see certain
films, there are imperatives, necessarily cultural in origin, which are quite
powerful when you belong to a cultural milieu (if only because you have
to go against them to be free). As with all other forms of snobbery, this
isn't always a bad thing. You are always, as it were, carrying on a dialogue
with these laws of cinematographic taste, which are no doubt so strong
because cinematographic culture is so new. The cinema is no longer a
primitive phenomenon; classicism, traditionalism and the cinema of the
avant-garde can now be distinguished, and the very evolution of this art
brings you back to the problem of evaluation. So that, when I choose,
there is a conflict between films that *have* to be seen and the idea of total
unpredictability, total availability which the cinema still represents for me
or, to be more precise, films which, left to my own devices, I would like
to see, but which are not the ones singled out by this diffuse culture in
process of formation.

*What would you say about the present level of this culture, diffuse indeed, where
the cinema is concerned?*

Diffusion, in this case, is the result of confusion, by which I mean that a kind of crossing over of values can take place in the cinema: intellectuals start defending popular films, and the commercial cinema is soon able to absorb avant-garde productions. This process of *acculturation* is peculiar to our mass culture, but goes on at a different pace in different genres: in the cinema, it seems very intense; in literature, the barriers are much more formidable – I don't think it's possible to follow contemporary literature, literature in the making, without a certain knowledge, I'd say even a technical knowledge, since contemporary literature is all about technique. The cultural situation of the present-day cinema is basically contradictory: the cinema brings techniques into play, hence the need for a certain knowledge, and a feeling of frustration if you do not possess it, but, unlike literature, it is something other than its technique: can you imagine a *littérature vérité* on the lines of *cinéma vérité*? With language, it would be impossible; truth is impossible with language.

And yet you find constant references to the idea of a 'cinematographic language', as if the existence and definition of this language were universally acknowledged, whether the word 'language' is taken in a purely rhetorical sense (for instance, the stylistic conventions attributed to the low-angle shot or to the tracking shot), or whether it is taken in a very general sense to indicate the relationship between a signifier and a signified.

In my own case, it is probably because I have not succeeded in bringing the cinema into the sphere of language that my approach to it is purely projective and not analytical.

Isn't it, if not impossible, at least difficult for the cinema to enter this sphere of language?

One can try to situate the difficulty. It would seem to us, so far at any rate, that the model of all languages is *parole*, articulated language. Now, this articulated language is a code, it is based on a system of signs, signs which are non-analogical (and which therefore can be, and are, discontinuous). The cinema, on the contrary, presents itself at first sight as an analogical (and moreover, continuous) expression of reality; and it is not at all clear how you go about introducing into an analogical and continuous expression an analysis of a linguistic type. For example, how can the meaning of a film, of a fragment of film, be cut up (semantically), how can it be varied? A critic wanting to treat the cinema as a language, putting aside the metaphorical inflation of the term, would therefore need to begin by working out whether in the filmic continuum there are elements which are not analogical, or whose analogical character has been deformed, transposed or codified; elements which are structured in such a way that they can be treated as fragments of language. These are practical research problems which have not yet been explored and which could be: you would need to begin by running experimental tests of some kind, and after that you could see whether it's possible to establish a semantics, or even a partial semantics, of film (a partial semantics is surely what it would be). It would be a case of applying structuralist methods and isolating filmic elements, of seeing how they are understood, which signifieds they correspond to in this or that instance and, by varying them, of seeing at what point a variation in the signifier entails a variation in the signified. Linguistic units, in the proper sense, would then have been isolated, and from these you could construct the 'classes', systems and declensions.[1]

Doesn't this overlap with certain experiments carried out at the end of the silent era, on a more empirical level, by the Soviets – experiments which were not very conclusive, except when the linguistic elements were taken up by someone like Eisenstein in the context of a poetics? But when this research remained on a purely rhetorical level, as with Pudovkin, it was called into question almost immediately; it is as if the link between film and semiology only has to be suggested to be called into question.

In any case, even if you managed to establish a kind of partial semantics on precise points (that is to say for precise signifieds), you would still have a lot of difficulty explaining why the whole film is not constructed as a sequence of discontinuous elements; you would then come up against the second problem, the fact that signs are discontinuous – or that expression is not.

But even if we managed to discover these linguistic units, where would that get us anyway, since they are not intended to be perceived as such? The signified does not implant itself in the same way, on the same level, in the spectator as in the reader.

Our view of semantic phenomena is no doubt still very narrow, and what we find basically hardest to understand are what could be called the large-scale units of meaning. There is the same difficulty in linguistics, since stylistics has not advanced very far (you have a *psychological* stylistics, but structural stylistics does not yet exist). Cinematographic expression probably also belongs to this order of large-scale units of meaning, corresponding to global, diffuse, latent signifieds which are not in the same category as the isolated and discontinuous signifieds of articulated language. This opposition between a micro- and a macro-semantics might perhaps be another way of considering the cinema as a language, allowing us to pass from the level of *denotation* (where, as we have seen, the primary, literal units are fairly difficult to pin down) to that of *connotation*, that is to say the level of the global, diffuse and, as it were, secondary signifieds. A possible starting point might then be Jakobson,[2] and the rhetorical (rather than strictly linguistic) models for which he claimed a very wide sphere of application, corresponding to that of articulated language, and which he applied, in passing, to the cinema; I am referring to metaphor and metonymy. Metaphor is the prototype of all signs which can substitute for one another on grounds of similarity; metonymy is the prototype of all signs whose meaning overlaps because they are contiguous or, if you like, mutually contagious. For example, a calendar shedding its leaves one by one is a metaphor; and it would be tempting to say that in the cinema, any editing effect, that is to say, any meaningful contiguity, is a metonymy and, since editing is what the cinema is about, that the cinema is a metonymic art (for the moment, anyway).

But isn't editing also impossible to isolate as an element? You can edit anything, from a six-frame shot of a gun to a huge five-minute camera movement showing three hundred people and perhaps two dozen intersecting actions; these two shots can be edited one after the other, but that doesn't put them on the same level . . .

What would be interesting, I think, would be to see whether a cinematographic procedure can be converted, systematically, into a signifying unit; whether the structural procedures correspond to units of filmic reading. Every critic's dream is to be able to define an art by its technique.

But the procedures are all ambiguous; for example, according to classical rhetoric, the high-angle shot signifies domination; but you can find hundreds of examples where it doesn't have this meaning at all.

Ambiguity of that kind is normal and that isn't really the problem. Signifiers are all ambiguous; the number of signifieds always exceeds the number of signifiers; if that were not the case, there would be no literature, or art, or history, or any of the things which can bring about change. The power of a signifier derives not from its lack of ambiguity, but from the fact that it is perceived as a signifier – I would say that things matter less in isolation, whatever their meaning may be, than in their relation to other things. The link between signifier and signified is much less important than the way in which the signifiers relate to each other; the high-angle shot may well have meant what you say, but we know that this rhetorical approach is out of date – the analogical relationship between 'high-angle' shot and 'domination' strikes us as naïve, especially now that a psychology of 'denial' has taught us that a valid relation can exist between a content and a form which common sense would say is its very opposite. If the high-angle shot triggers off a meaning, it is this triggering-off of meaning that matters, and not the meaning itself.

Isn't that the point – after a first 'analogical' phase, isn't the cinema already moving out of a second anti-analogical phase via a more supple, less codified use of 'figures of style'?

It strikes me that if the problems of symbolism (since analogy raises the issue of symbolism in the cinema) are becoming less sharply defined and less pressing, this is due above all to the fact that of the two main linguistic paths indicated by Jakobson, metaphor and metonymy, the cinema seems, for the moment, to have chosen the metonymic or, if you prefer, syntagmatic path, the syntagm being an extended, ordered, realized fragment of signs or, in other words, a segment of narrative. It is very striking that, in contrast to the kind of literature where 'nothing happens' (the prototype of which would be Flaubert's *L'Education sentimentale*), the cinema, even when it is not geared to popular demand, is a discourse from which storytelling, anecdote, plot (and therefore *suspense*) are never absent; even incredible adventures – anecdotes taken to the point of caricature – are not incompatible with good cinema. In the cinema, 'something is always happening' and, of course, this is closely linked to the metonymic/syntagmatic path I was referring to a moment ago. A 'good story' is in fact, structurally speaking, a successful series of syntagmatic 'dispatchings': given such and such a situation (such and such a sign), how can it be followed? There are a certain number of possibilities, but not an endless number (the fact that there are limits to what is possible is the basis of structural analysis), and this is why the director's choice of the next 'sign' is significant. Meaning is indeed freedom, but a freedom kept in check by the restricted number of possibilities; each and every sign (each and every moment of the narrative, of the film) can only be followed by certain other signs, certain other moments. This operation which consists in taking a sign (in the discourse, in the syntagm) and adding on another sign (according to a finite and sometimes very restricted range of possibilities) is called *catalysis*: in speech, for example, the sign 'dog' can only be catalysed by a small number of other signs (barks, sleeps, eats, bites, runs, etc., but not sews, flies, sweeps, etc.); the filmic narrative/syntagm is also subject to rules of catalysis, which the film director no doubt practises empirically, but which the critic or analyst should try to recover, since of course each dispatching, each catalysis, makes its contribution to the final meaning of the work.

The director's way of looking at it, we would guess, would be to have a more or less precise idea of the meaning beforehand – which he will realize afterwards has been more or less modified. While he is working on the film, he is hardly ever concerned with the final meaning; he constructs a series of small-scale filmic units – but how does he know which way to go? The guiding principles would be interesting to establish.

He can only be guided, more or less consciously, by his basic ideology, by his approach to life – the syntagm is as responsible for meaning as the sign itself, which is why the cinema can become a metonymic, as opposed to a symbolic, art without losing any of its responsibilities – on the contrary. I remember Brecht suggesting to us on the journal *Théâtre populaire*[3] that we should organize an exchange of views (by correspondence) between himself and young French playwrights; the idea would have been to 'play' the putting together of an imaginary play, that is to say a series of situations, as one would a game of chess; the first person would have put forward a situation, the second would have chosen the following one, and of course (that was the whole point of the 'game'), each move would have been discussed as a function of the final meaning, or in other words, for Brecht, ideological responsibility. But there are no French playwrights. In any case, you can see that Brecht, as an acute theoretician – and practitioner – of *meaning*, was very much aware of the syntagmatic problem. All this would seem to prove that exchanges between linguistics and cinema are possible, provided you choose a linguistics of the syntagm rather than a linguistics of the sign.

The idea of the cinema as a language may never perhaps be fully workable; but we have to pursue it all the same, if we are not to fall into the trap of simply enjoying the cinema as a meaningless object – as an object of pleasure and fascination which cannot be explained. The fact is that the cinema always has a meaning; so that an element of language always comes into play . . .

Yes, of course, the work always has a meaning; but the point is that the science of meaning, which is currently all the rage (fashionably productive, as it were), teaches us paradoxically that meaning is, so to speak, not contained within the signified. The relation between signifier and signified (that is to say, the sign) appears initially as the very basis of all 'semiological' reflection; but later on, we take a much broader view of meaning, and the signified becomes far less central (everything we have said about the syntagm goes in this direction). We owe this broadening of our perspective to structural linguistics, needless to say, but also to someone like Lévi-Strauss,[4] who showed that meaning (or to be more exact, the signifier) was the highest category of the intelligible. And the (human) *intelligible* is basically what interests us. How does the cinema make manifest or converge with the categories, functions, structures of what is intelligible as elaborated by our history, our society? A 'semiology' of the cinema might offer some answers to this question.

It is surely impossible to produce anything that is unintelligible.

Absolutely. Everything is meaningful, even nonsense (which has at least the secondary meaning of being nonsense). Man is so fatally bound to meaning that freedom in art might seem to consist, especially nowadays, not so much in *creating* meaning as in *suspending* it; in constructing meanings without, however, making them rounded and complete.

Perhaps we could take an example; in Brecht's productions, there are linguistic elements which do not initially lend themselves to codification.

As regards this problem of meaning, the case of Brecht is fairly complicated. On the one hand, as I was saying, he was very aware of the techniques of meaning (and in this he was highly original, given that Marxism in general has tended to ignore the responsibilities of form); he knew how even the most humble signifiers, like the colour of a costume or the positioning of a projector, take their full share of responsibility; and you know how fascinated he was by oriental theatre, where meaning is highly codified – or rather, *coded* – and consequently not very analogical; also, we saw with what care and attention to detail he worked on, and wanted people to work on, the semantic responsibility of 'syntagms' (epic art, which he favoured, is moreover highly syntagmatic); and of course, all these reflections on technique were geared to a political meaning. *Geared to*, but not perhaps *determined by*; and it is here that we begin to see ambiguity in Brecht from the other side. I wonder if the *committed* meaning of Brecht's work isn't finally, in its way, a *suspended* meaning. You remember that his dramatic theory involves a kind of functional division between the stage and the auditorium: it is for the work to ask questions (in the author's own terms, obviously – this is a responsible art), and for the audience to find the answers (what Brecht called the *outcome*); the meaning (in the positive sense of the term) leaves the stage to go down into the auditorium. In short, there is indeed a meaning in Brecht's theatre, and this meaning is very powerful, but it always takes the form of a question. Which perhaps explains why this theatre, while being critical, polemical and committed, stops short of being militant.

Can this approach be extended to the cinema?

It always seems very difficult and rather pointless to transport a technique (and meaning comes under this heading) from one art to another, not because the genres have to be kept separate, but because structure depends on the materials used. The theatrical image is not made from the same materials as the cinematographic image, it does not offer itself up in the same way to segmentation, duration, or perception. The theatre strikes me as a much more 'rudimentary', much 'cruder', art than the cinema (theatre criticism, similarly, strikes me as more rudimentary than film criticism); and it is therefore closer to practical tasks of a polemical, subversive and oppositional kind. (I am not talking about the theatre of consensus, conformism and consumer satisfaction.)

A few years ago, you raised the possibility of determining the political meaning of a film by examining not only its argument, but also the process whereby it is constituted – the left-wing film relying, broadly speaking, on lucidity and the right-wing film on an appeal to magic . . .

What I now wonder is whether certain art forms aren't necessarily, by their very nature, their very techniques, more or less reactionary. I think this is true of literature; I do not think that a literature of the left is possible. A problematical literature, yes, that is to say a literature of suspended meaning – an art which provokes answers, but does not give them. I would say that literature at its best is just that. As for the cinema, I have the impression that it is very close to literature in this respect and that, by virtue of its materials and structure, it is much better equipped than the theatre to assume that very particular responsibility of form which I have called the technique of suspended meaning. I believe that the cinema finds it difficult to deliver clear meanings and that, in the present phase, it ought not to do so. The best films (for me) are those which are best at suspending meaning. Suspending meaning is a very difficult operation which requires a great deal in the way of technique, as well as total intellectual commitment, as you have to get rid of any parasitical mean-ings, which is extremely difficult.

Have you seen any films which seemed to be achieving this?

Yes, *The Exterminating Angel*. I don't think that Buñuel's warning at the beginning of the film (I, Buñuel, assure you that this film has no meaning), I really don't think that this is Buñuel striking up a pose, I think it actually defines the film. And when you look at it in this way, the film is a joy to watch – you can see how meaning is continually suspended without, of course, ever being nonsense. The film is not in the least absurd; it is full of meaning; full of what Lacan[5] calls *signifiance*. But it does not have *a* meaning, or even a series of little meanings. And by that very fact, it is a profoundly unsettling film, one which calls into question far more than mere dogmatism or narrowly held beliefs. In the normal way, if consumers of film lived in a less alienated society, this film ought, as the common expression puts it, to 'make people think'. You could also, if you had the time, show how each of the meanings which are constantly gelling, whether you want them to or not, get drawn into an extremely fast, extremely intelligent 'dispatching' towards the next meaning, which is itself never definitive.

And this continual 'dispatching' is the movement of the film.

There is also, in this film, an initial success which explains the overall success: because the story, the idea, the argument, are so clear-cut, an illusion of necessity is created. The rest seems to follow on automatically. Up until now, I wasn't all that keen on Buñuel; but in this film, one has to admire the way in which Buñuel has managed, on top of everything, to include his full range of metaphor (his films have always been very metaphorical), his complete arsenal and personal reserve of symbols; the clarity of the film's syntagmatic development and the fact that each 'dispatching' is perfectly executed mean that everything gets taken in.

And besides, Buñuel has always been so totally open about his metaphors, so scrupulous about maintaining the distinction between what comes before and what comes afterwards – this was already a way of isolating metaphor, of putting it in quotes, hence going beyond it or undermining it.

Unfortunately, for most of his fans, Buñuel is defined above all by his metaphors, by the 'wealth' of his symbolism. But if the modern cinema has a direction, it's in *The Exterminating Angel* that the pointers are to be found . . .

Talking of 'modern' cinema, have you seen L'Immortelle?

Yes. . . . My response to the film is complicated by my (abstract) relations with Robbe-Grillet. I'm not happy about it, because I never wanted him to make films. . . . Well, there you have your metaphors. . . . In fact, Robbe-Grillet doesn't destroy meaning, he scrambles it. Robbe-Grillet thinks that by scrambling a meaning he's destroying it. It takes more than that to destroy a meaning.

And he gives more and more emphasis to a meaning which is more and more banal.

Because he 'varies' the meaning, he does not suspend it. Variation imposes an increasingly definite meaning, of an obsessional kind: a small number of signifiers subject to variation (in the musical sense of the term) refer to the same signified (which is the definition of metaphor). In *The Exterminating Angel*, on the contrary (to go back again to Buñuel), quite apart from the way in which repetition is derided (at the beginning, in the exactly repeated scenes), the scenes (the syntagmatic fragments) do not constitute an immobile (obsessional, metaphorical) series, they each participate in the progressive transformation of a society from freedom to constraint, they construct an irreversible time span.

And what's more, Buñuel observed the rules of chronology. Ignoring chronology is all too easy; it's a false assurance of modernity.

We are coming back to what I was saying at the beginning: one likes the film so much because there is a story; a story with a beginning and an end and an element of suspense. All too often nowadays, modernity amounts to a way of cheating with the story or with psychology. The most immediate criterion of modernity, for a work, is not to be 'psychological', in the traditional sense of the term. But at the same time, no one really knows how to get rid of this business of psychology, this business of emotional ties between human beings, this relational vertigo which, paradoxically, is no longer handled by works of art but by the social sciences and medicine. Psychology has been reduced to psychoanalysis which, however intelligent or wide-ranging their approach, is practised by doctors; the 'soul' has become a pathological fact in itself. Modern works have ceased to have anything to say about interpersonal, inter-human relationships. The great movements of ideological emancipation – or let us say, without any possible ambiguity, Marxism – did not pay much heed to the private individual, and that was no doubt as it had to be. But we know very well that the private individual is still in a mess, there is something still not quite right: for as long as people go on having rows, there will be no shortage of questions to ask.

The one big subject of modern art is really the possibility of happiness. And at the moment, in the cinema, it is as if people are saying that you can't be happy in the present, so you have to look to the future in some way or other. Perhaps in the years ahead, we shall see a new idea of happiness being advanced.

Yes, I think you're right. None of the major ideologies, or visions of the future, is concerned with this at the moment. We have a whole literature devoted to utopian visions of outer space, but no one has created the kind of micro-utopia which would involve the dreaming up of new psychological or relational worlds. But if the structuralist law of the rotation of needs and of forms operates in this sphere, it shouldn't be long before art takes a more existential turn. Which is to say that the sweeping anti-psychological statements of the last ten years (statements to which I have myself contributed, of course) should be reversed and cease to be fashionable. However ambiguous Antonioni's art may be, it is perhaps for this reason that he touches a chord and strikes us as important.

In other words, and to sum up our expectations: what we would now like to see would be syntagmatic films, films that tell a story, films of 'psychological' interest.

Translated by Annwyl Williams

Notes

1 The reader can refer, with interest, to two recent articles by Roland Barthes: 'L'Imagination du signe', *Arguments* no. 27–8, and 'L'Activité structuraliste', *Les Lettres nouvelles* no. 32. (Author's note.) Both essays, translated as 'The Imagination of the Sign' and 'The Structuralist Activity' respectively, appear in Roland Barthes, *Critical Essays*, Evanston, Illinois, Northwestern University Press, 1972.

The work of Christian Metz, a follower of Barthes, aims, precisely, at trying to discover 'linguistic units' in film: see Ch. 3, note 3.

2 Roman Jakobson, best known theoretician of the 'Prague school' of linguistics; see, for example, Jakobson, *Selected Writings*, The Hague, Mouton, 1970.

3 *Théâtre populaire*, theatre journal edited by Barthes and Bernard Dort; it had been very important in the presentation and popularization of Brecht in France during the late 1950s.

4 Claude Lévi-Strauss: see Introduction to Part 3: 'Re-thinking American Cinema.'

5 Jacques Lacan: see Ch. 24, note 9.

('Le haut-mal', *Cahiers du Cinéma* 179, June 1966)

The kind of controlled fury, the methodical and calculated anger that marks out right from the beginning a radically new space – in which we can nevertheless all recognize and identify the demons of our own adolescence in spite of the deliberately exceptional nature of the mode of affabulation – bring powerfully into play the elements of a protest whose violence and impact lead us back to *L'âge d'or* and *Zéro de conduite*: like Buñuel and Vigo, Bellocchio uses the forms of a dramatic poem to express the virulent arguments he deploys in his search for vengeance while at the same time preserving all that is excessive and outrageous in his message by a constant recourse to irony. Even so, it would be far too restrictive to limit consideration of *I Pugni in Tasca* to its value as a denunciation or to its poetic qualities. We witness the precise construction of a world and at the same time a clinical enumeration of its symptoms of decomposition, diseases of the body and of the mind. The declaration of bankruptcy and decadence, which is not just that of a particular family but of a whole class, is made without the slightest recourse to romantic symbolism, without a trace of nostalgia for the past or smugness about the failure and misfortune of others. If, from the apparently very specific discourse he chooses to pursue, Bellocchio deduces a general significance which is structured and spread through the whole film, he does this by relying exclusively on the analysis of behaviour. Thus, avoiding the trap of individualism, the impassioned nature of his demands becomes clear through an unusually powerful drive towards critical lucidity. And if he has chosen to abandon his characters to the grip of the 'falling sickness' that the ancients thought was of divine origin, it is no doubt because only epilepsy, the most spectacular and most 'theatrical' of all mental illnesses, could allow him to indicate a less evident but more fatal disease, one where spasms and convulsions are only visible traces or metaphorical symptoms. Or rather, the characteristic alternation of crises and periods of remission help to make Sandro the privileged witness of a decadence he sometimes suffers

286

from and sometimes contributes to; he is marked out as one of the elect by the conflicting symbols which drag him into the abyss, the impossible meeting point of an extreme lucidity and an extreme abnormality. And the dialectic of the torturer and the victim has never been more immediately apparent than in this man possessed who bears within himself the stigmata of a universal but unspeakable secret: the secret of a childhood which must be destroyed by fire for the adult to be able to exist and which, since he can't burn, he allows to consume him until he reaches the final ecstasy as death strikes him down.

But what makes this young man's film exceptionally great is less the masterful, almost playful way he shuffles the whole pack of myths handed down by Greek tragedy to the whole of Western drama which still thrives on them today, than the insolent authority with which he makes his characters break the most inadmissible taboos; a fascination with morbid behaviour cannot possibly be an adequate justification for the vertigo experienced by the part-shocked, part-complicit spectator witnessing the matricide and fratricide committed by Sandro. It is a feeling that can be compared only to certain pages of Georges Bataille (*L'Abbé C* and especially *Histoire de l'oeil*).[1] It had seemed to us that cinema, by its very nature (and in spite of some of Buñuel's transgressions), was constrained to set aside that feeling, to ignore it or at the very least to transpose it with a greater or lesser degree of prudence and success. But Bellocchio has no compunction about making it the central feature of his film. Let us make no mistake about this: it is an act of aggression whose effect cannot be mitigated by reducing it to a morbid exhibitionism or a monstrous self-gratification. What is at stake is quite the opposite: cinema has acquired here a form of protest that was previously unthinkable. The film doesn't spare the bourgeois conception of the family or the accursed obscurantism of a narrow-minded Christianity, but if that was all it would remain at the level of the anecdotal or the picturesque. Don't insult us by referring to Mauriac or Hervé Bazin[2] here! No, what Bellocchio calls into question is of a more general and radical nature, it is the duplicity and the hypocrisy of a degenerate humanism which, in spite of de Sade, Freud and Marx, still presides over the actions of individuals and the destinies of nations. (Michel Foucault[3] says in a recent interview: 'Humanism has been a way of resolving, in terms of ethics, values and reconciliations, problems which could not be resolved at all. Do you remember what Marx said? Humanity only asks questions that it can answer. I think we can add: humanism pretends to answer questions it cannot ask! . . . Our immediate task is to liberate ourselves definitively from humanism and in that sense our task is a political one.')

It is of course in that same sense that Bellocchio's film can be called political: just consider, in this respect, how decisively *I Pugni in Tasca* breaks with the fundamental choices of neo-realism. . . . It is now the whole person and not just man in society that is at the centre of the debate and the focus of the discourse. That is why you could not seriously claim that the exceptional terms of reference Bellocchio uses to define the environment he sets out to analyse (epilepsy, matricide, incest) could have been quite other. As Edgar Allan Poe says – the quotation is approximate: 'The normal person is subject to all the forms of madness, the madman only to one.' And it isn't the least of the film's qualities that the microcosm it describes presents us with a disturbing anthology of different modes of behaviour in which even the most self-assured 'normality' cannot avoid recognizing some of its basic elements: narcissism, sadism, lack of awareness are presented in a state of hypertrophy so that they can be identified more easily.

The proliferation of interconnected themes and patterns in *I Pugni in Tasca* is so rich that any attempt to describe them runs the extreme risk of becoming merely a fastidious catalogue of significances. It would probably be more profitable to make a systematic study of the forms used to bring about a convergence of themes and images. We would need to demonstrate that Bellocchio relies less on powerful moments and spectacular scenes to generate insecurities than on the more ordinary, everyday scenes in which Sandro's solitude is set alongside that of a sad child (and an inkwell spilled over a notebook is enough in this instance to indicate the significance of what will happen later); we would need to show how the incredible inventiveness of gesture he manages to draw from his actors enriches the relationships between Sandro, his two brothers, his sister and his mother, obliterating any suggestion of theorizing; to indicate how the 'transports' of *bel canto* announce and prepare us for the final spasm when the horrific stillness of death supplants its lyrical simulation, and how the idea of sacrilege and profanation is precisely formulated in 'scandalous' images that are for once stripped of any puerile desire to provoke (the mother's funeral, the destruction of the family's possessions, etc.).

In bolstering the rigorousness of a revolutionary ideology with a form that is worthy of it, Bellocchio isn't simply being innovatory; he has achieved the ambition of every young film-maker – he holds up a mirror in which his own generation can recognize the conditions of its own existence. But he is neither a prophet nor a physician, and he knows that each of us has to live alone with our falling sickness. Once the demons have been exorcized, other films will perhaps show how we can actually be delivered. They too will be political films.

Translated by Norman King

Notes

1 Georges Bataille, novelist and essayist, 1897–1962; among the major preoccupations of his fiction, including *Histoire de l'oeil*, 1928 (translated as *A Tale of Satisfied Desire*, 1953), and *L'Abbé C*, 1950, are religion, blindness and eroticism.
2 François Mauriac, French novelist and poet, 1885–1970, whose best known novels are *Le Désert de l'amour*, 1925, *Thérèse Desqueyroux*, 1927, *Le Noeud de*

vipères, 1932; a Catholic, his novels are marked by anti-bourgeois themes and a concern with individual isolation. Hervé Bazin, French novelist and poet, b. 1911, among whose novels are *La Tête contre les murs*, 1949 (filmed by Georges Franju in 1959), about mental illness, and *Lève-toi et marche*, 1952, which describes the life of a paralysed woman determined to overcome her disease.

3 Michel Foucault: radical analyst, post-Freudian and post-Marxist and broadly 'structuralist' in method, of areas of social practice and the discourses of history, and of the constitution of the subject in historical writing. His translated works include *Madness and Civilisation*, London, Tavistock, 1968; *The Order of Things*, London, Tavistock, 1977; *The Archaeology of Knowledge*, London, Tavistock, 1977; *Language, Counter-Memory, Practice*, Oxford, Basil Blackwell, 1977. John Caughie places Foucault's work and its influence on film theory in *Theories of Authorship*.

30 | Jean-Louis Comolli: 'A Morality of Economics'

('Une morale de la dépense', *Cahiers du Cinéma* 190, May 1967)

It is just ten years ago that we had the *nouvelle vague* here. In other words, it has taken less than ten years for the 'new cinema', everywhere now, to appear and begin to take hold, despite all the dictates of aesthetics, economics and politics. (And how blind and deaf of Rossellini to announce the death of cinema – like some belated call for the death of Socrates. Dead it is – or not too far from it – if what is meant is the cinema of *profits*, which Rossellini's films hardly did much to swell in any case, and which he even contributed not a little to undermining.)

Given this kind of spontaneous and united generation, the important thing is to define what is unequivocally new (and the 'novelty' that needs analysing eludes us even as it emerges because it is too much of our time for us to be both its witnesses and its prophets, we who are its semi-initiators, semi-apprentices). Everything, or virtually everything, has changed or is changing, from conditions of production to the conditions governing the way a film is received and consumed, by way of aesthetic ambitions. But within that general transformation, all kinds of variations and contradictions are still sustained. The new cinema seems to be able to assimilate or invent every conceivable style, to have a limitless range, from the individual voice to the collective discourse, and to mix all kinds of ideas. What is the common factor of its works, since this does not lie in either their contents or the forms which contain them?

When what is at issue through all the technical, stylistic and economic upheavals has ceased to be just those precise categories and instead becomes the effect of their conjunction – a reformulation and therefore a redefinition of cinema, a new formulation of its status in society – we are entitled to talk of a *revolution*. And there can be no doubt that this is the first revolution the art has experienced, because the succession of technical advances and stylistic transformations which constitute the fabric of its history have in every instance changed only the modes of expression and not, as now, the very conditions of its existence and practice. What has been transformed is the way of envisaging cinema; our new film-makers have realized the need to re-evaluate the relation of cinema to society in its twofold role of producer and consumer.

Because more than any other art form it is involved in the real world (through the mechanical and material conditions of its existence, whether at the stage of manufacture or dissemination, through its need for funds as well as the profits it makes from them, through the influence it can exert and the pressures to which it is subject as a result), the cinema is totally implicated with the society to which it belongs. It is both the product and the victim of that society, both its expression and its means of exerting pressure, its witness but its judge; in other words, both its accomplice and its betrayer. The arrival of the talkie which marked the beginning of intensive commercialization of the cinema, ushered in the familiar era of its artistic/industrial double status. But far from setting up house together and even less fusing into the happy harmony dreamt of by some of its visionaries, art and industry are undergoing two different evolutions, equally ambitious in scale, but opposed in goals and results. The more the cinema asserts itself as an art, the more it acknowledges itself to be in the opposite camp to the industry, the less the art is going to make money and the less bothered the industry will be with safe-guarding artistic standards. The original double status has become decep-tion, confusion and trickery, all the more so because in the last few decades the development of cinema has been irrevocably linked to the development of the capitalist economy (the reign of the highest bid, growing investment in and impact of publicity, the exception made the rule, etc.).

It is against this gloomy background of crisis (aesthetic and moral as well as economic since everything, art and business alike, is a matter of 'arithmetic', a gamble, and very soon a compromise) that a hitherto ignored idea has emerged, in the wake of the *nouvelle vague* and above all the example of Godard; namely, the notion of responsibility. For young film-makers, their producers and their distributors (if they have them) the aim is no longer on one side to get through the biggest sums possible and on the other to channel them towards profits for themselves. Both sides are now doing their sums *a bit more realistically* so that from now on there is a real and vital balance between the cost of a film (necessarily moderate) and its takings (generally moderate) in place of the previous system of 'losses' and 'offsets' against them.

The introduction of the notion of responsibility in the face of an industry characterized by immaturity and the absence of professional conscience as much as of professional expertise immediately implies – and this changes a great deal – a certain honesty: financial, moral and artistic. For example, the archetypal 'new film-maker' making his first film runs up against the conditions of the archetypal system: no money without a trade of ideas, the system usually refusing (miracles and misunderstandings apart, i.e. compromises on both sides excepted) to take any risk without all kinds of guarantees, and not just financial ones. He therefore has to adopt 'pirate' techniques to produce the goods. In other words he has to cut the costs of the film (and if the sums are done right the reduction can be as much as 50 per cent) via a series of chain-reaction expedients: reducing the crew and the equipment, reducing the shooting time, improvising, limiting the takes to two only, filming in 'actual locations', etc. Such stylistic options begin as economic imperatives but in the end they become moral decisions. All of which means that the film-maker is bound to become conscious, infinitely more than in the past, of the very conditions of existence of cinema.

The obstacles appear again in the case of the film made on the 'fringe' of the system. The system refuses to distribute it or put money into it, whether from a fear of financial risk or quite simply the wish to subdue the unruly. After the film has been produced our 'young film-maker' has to confront the harsh realities of distribution and exhibition, and this is a quite new process of reflection in cinematographic practice – the clearest manifestation of the revolution. The solution again is to have reduced the cost of the film sufficiently for the expenditure to be recovered through a kind of pirate, para-commercial and marginal distribution system; in France that means the 'Art et Essai' circuits,[1] the film societies and other venues fixed from one day to the next.

To sum up, as far as both the making and the distribution of film is concerned, the industry/commerce system, with its obstructions and demands, its profits policy and its corollary lack of real concern, the total bankruptcy one cannot help but see in it, in the end forces the film-maker to turn against it, to fight, to think clearly and responsibly enough to take on a revolution in habits, customs and techniques – a revolution which eventually opens out into a questioning of the whole system itself and through it of the whole of the society that governs it. Like it or not, making a film today is making a film which is politically committed. Because it's not just a matter of thinking about all that you would like to express through film, it's just as much a matter of thinking about all that works against that will to express. Equally, it is a political choice to stop seeing the audience as an inert, amorphous mass open to all sorts of manipulation by publicity, but on the contrary to bank on the existence of an audience that is lucid, demanding, capable of taking its risks, as responsible and, ultimately, as creative as the film-maker.[2]

For all these reasons, the cinema is today the instrument of social reform at both the production and consumption stage; it is even, apart from direct political or revolutionary action, one of the rare and perhaps the only effective means of reform, and that is why in relation to the 'new cinema' it is appropriate to talk politics and not just art. The film is no longer the idealizing or realist mirror of the world, no longer the image or model of a reality or the fiction of that reality serving to preserve them both. It is the shattering of the mirror itself, revealing the reflection for what it is and rejecting reassuring likenesses and resemblances: the obverse side of the film-set, as yet only a puny scarecrow but already a dangerous and ever-watchful public prosecutor.

Translated by Diana Matias

Notes

1 'Art et Essai': a circuit of cinemas subsidized to promote the exhibition of 'minority interest', 'quality' films, in effect 'art houses'.
2 Cf. Comolli's comments in 'Notes sur le nouveau spectateur', *Cahiers* 177, April 1966, translated as 'Notes on the New Spectator' in this volume, Ch. 21, where he talks at greater length about the new audience.

31 | Jean-Luc Godard: 'Struggling on Two Fronts': Godard in interview with Jacques Bontemps, Jean-Louis Comolli, Michel Delahaye, Jean Narboni (extracts)[1]

('Lutter sur deux fronts: conversation avec Jean-Luc Godard', *Cahiers du Cinéma* 194, October 1967)

In La Chinoise *cinema takes on many aspects and they could even be contradictory . . .*
The thing is, I once had lots of ideas about cinema, now I have none at all. I stopped knowing what cinema was as soon as I made my second film. The more you make films the more you realize that you're either working along with received ideas, or you're working against them – which almost comes to the same. That's why I think it's criminal that someone like Moullet isn't given *Les Aventuriers* or *Deux billets pour Mexico*[2] to make. It's criminal too that Rivette, like a lot of people before him (all victims of the gestapo run by the economic-aesthetic structures which the Holy Alliance of producers-distributors-exhibitors has set up) is cutting a five-hour film down to the sacrosanct hour and a half.[3]
[. . .]
But you're saying that it's necessary to go on making films all the same.
Yes, of course, and that's where all the tension is. You want to make films that are different, and you have to make them with people you despise, people you don't even want to see, instead of making them with the people you like and spend your time with. The whole infrastructure is rotten – from the lab stage to the point where the film, if it's lucky, reaches the audience. Of course, there are times when something happens. Hyères for instance is preferable to Cannes – not ideal, but still better. And Montreal is better than Venice.[4] You have to keep pushing ahead. The Canadian cinema is interesting as an example. The National Film Board is an impressive film factory, more so than Hollywood today. It's a great set-up. But what's the pay-off? Zero. There's nothing to see for it. The films just aren't coming out. What Daniel Johnson[5] ought to do is nationalize all the cinemas in Quebec. But he won't do it. The best he's capable of is seeing that De Gaulle gets a welcome on the Metro screens. So, over there as well, cinema is subject to a special brand of imperialism, just like everywhere else. Those of us who are trying to make films in a different way ought to be the fifth column trying to bring the system down.

But there is already a particular cinema operating outside the system . . .
Yes, of course. Bertolucci isn't making American cinema, neither are Resnais, Straub, Rossellini or Jerry Lewis. But that other cinema, whether good or bad, represents one ten-thousandth, or even one hundred-thousandth of what's being made.
But is there still really an American cinema?
No. There isn't an American cinema any more. There's a phoney cinema calling itself American, but it's only a poor shadow of what American cinema was once.
Are you going to work for an American company again?
If that's the way I get to make films, I don't ask for anything better. Or if it gives me the chance to shoot an expensive film, *Mickie the Circus Dog*, say, where more money goes into the image than into the pockets of the stars. But that in no way contradicts my views on America and the imperialist policies of the major companies. First, because there are Americans and Americans. Then, because America also needs a fifth column and the American companies need to be given the idea of making a different kind of cinema, and the will to make it. Given one success, for example, you can change the system gradually. But it's hard work and you run up against imperialism physically, at every level of production and distribution. All the same, you have to stay optimistic. People can change. And something's begun to move in America. You see it in the Blacks, and in the opposition to the Vietnam war. Where cinema is concerned, the universities are beginning to distribute films and their circuits are fantastic. New companies are being formed. I sold *La Chinoise* to Leacock.[6] But anyway, there's more to the world than America, and I would lump the Americans and the Russians together because their systems are more or less identical. In both places young film-makers are victimized. In America it's got to the point where there *are* no young film-makers. All the American film-makers we admire came into the cinema young. Now they're old but no one's taking their place. When Hawks started out he was the same age as Goldman[7] and Goldman is alone. Of course Hollywood still gets the young coming in but they aren't bringing with them the equivalent in ideas that, let's say, Hawks did once. They're shaped by structures which have become decadent and they haven't dared to blow them up. They aren't born free into cinema. Nor are they born into poverty, aesthetic or otherwise. They're neither the explorers nor the poets of the cinematic enterprise any more. Whereas all those who made Hollywood what it was were poets, brigands almost, who took over Hollywood by force and made it accept their own poetic laws. The bravest at the moment, the only one who's come out of it, is Jerry Lewis. He's the only one in Hollywood doing something different, the only one who isn't falling in with the established categories, the norms, the principles. That's exactly how Hitchcock was for a long time. Lewis is the only one today who's making courageous films. And I think he's perfectly well aware of it. He's been able to do it because of his personal genius. But who else is there? Nicholas

Ray is absolutely typical of the situation American cinema is in. The really sad thing is that all those film-makers who couldn't hold out, who've stuffed themselves silly with the good things, are now bumming their way round the world at large. The better part of the American cinema has become what Nicholas Ray has become. As for the New Yorkers, they're hardly more encouraging. They've buried themselves already and they want to burrow down even further with their 'underground' cinema, for no good reason. If the Russians aren't helping Hanoi bombard New York, what's the point in going underground?

There will be other great American film-makers (there's already Goldman, [Shirley] Clarke and Cassavetes). We have to wait for that, and to help and encourage them. I mentioned the universities a minute ago – there you've got, or you're beginning to get, cinema in a place which had none at all before. That's the important thing. The cinema has to go everywhere. What we need to do is draw up a list of places where it doesn't exist yet and tell ourselves – that's where we have to go. If it isn't in the factories, we have to take it there. If it isn't in the universities, we have to go into the universities. If it isn't in the brothels, we have to go into the brothels. Cinema has to leave the places where it does exist and go into places where it doesn't.

You mean that from the outset, in its very existence, cinema has a political dimension . . .

Always. In earlier days that political dimension was unconscious, now it is tending to become conscious, or let's say that people are trying to discover the language of that unconscious.

[. . .]

Your short film Anticipation *conveys the impression of a desire to destroy the image itself as a prop of realism . . .*[8]

The annoying thing is that the actors are so recognizable. But at the start I had no ideas of this kind. Then I got the idea of giving the film what you might call a 'biological' side, turning it into something like a flow of plasma, but plasma that said something.

In doing that you touched something virtually sacred – the precise, clear and full cinematographic image.

But the image is always an image from the moment it's screened. In fact I didn't destroy anything at all. Or rather, I only destroyed a particular idea of the image, a particular way of envisaging what it ought to be. But I never thought that through in terms of destruction. . . . What I wanted was to pass across to the *inside* of the image, since most films are made on the *outside* of the image. What is the image itself supposed to be? A reflection. Does the reflection in a pane of glass have a depth of some kind? Usually in cinema you remain outside the reflection, external to it. What I wanted was to see the other side of the image, like being behind the screen rather than in front of it. Instead of being behind the real screen you were behind the image and in front of the screen. Or rather, inside the image. Just as certain paintings give you the sense that you're inside them, or that as long as you are on the outside you don't understand them. In *The Red Desert* I had the sense that the colours were *inside* the camera, not in front of it. With *Le Mépris*, on the contrary, I had the sense that the colours were in front of the camera. You really do get the feeling with *The Red Desert* that it's the camera which has manufactured the film. With *Le Mépris* there was on the one hand the instrument, and on the other the objects outside it. But I don't think I know how to *manufacture* a film like that [like *The Red Desert*]. Except that maybe I am beginning to be tempted to try something of the sort. *Made in USA* was the first sign of that temptation. That's why it wasn't understood; the audience watched it as if it were a representational film, whereas it was something else. Of course they lost out because they were trying to follow a representation, they tried to understand what was going on. Actually they did understand without any trouble, but without knowing that they did and thinking on the contrary that they were failing to understand. What struck me for example is that Demy likes *Made in USA* a lot, and I've always thought of it as a film that's 'sung' by comparison with *La Chinoise* which is a 'talkie'. *Made in USA* most resembles *Les Parapluies de Cherbourg* as a film. The people in it may not sing, but the film does.[9]

While on the subject of cross-references, do you not see some link between Persona *and your most recent films?*

No, I don't think so. Anyway, I don't think Bergman likes my films very much. I don't believe he takes the smallest thing from me or anyone else. And after *Through a Glass Darkly*, *Winter Light* and *The Silence*, *Persona* was really the only film he could make.

Persona *does have more stylistically bold features by comparison with his previous films – like the duplication of the speech, for instance.*

I don't think so. I think the narrative level is the aesthetic sequel or deepening of the long take of Ingrid Thulin in *Winter Light* when she makes her confession. But it's more striking in *Persona*, almost an assault at the formal level. It hits you as a process, to the point where you're tempted to say, 'That's fantastic, I've got to use it in one of my films'.

That's how I got the idea for the first shot of my next film, after re-seeing *Persona*. I said to myself: what's needed is a static shot of people talking about their sexuality. But in a sense for me that relates back to the first shot of *Vivre sa vie* where I stayed behind the couple, whereas I could have overtaken them to view them from the front. It's also more or less what corresponds to the interviews in my films. In Bergman it's very different, but what you come back to in the end is always the desire to convey a dialogue. And with that you also get back to Beckett. I once intended to make a film of *Happy Days*. I never did because they wanted me to take on Madeleine Renaud whereas I wanted to use young actors. I'd have liked to do it because I had a text and all I needed to do was film it. I'd have had just a single tracking shot beginning in long shot and ending in close-up. It would have started at precisely the distance necessary to bring me into close shot in an hour and a half, to end on the last sentence. It was just a matter of elementary arithmetic, a simple calculation of speed in relation to time.

But how do you see all the things in Persona *which remind you of the fact that you are watching a film?*

I didn't understand anything in *Persona*. Absolutely anything. I watched it carefully and this is how I saw things: Bibi Andersson is the one who is ill and the other woman is her nurse. In the end I always believe in 'realism'. So when the husband thinks he recognizes his wife, as far as I am concerned, since he's recognized her, it really is her. I mean if you didn't base yourself on realism you wouldn't be able to do anything any more, you couldn't even step into a taxi in the street, always assuming you dared to go out in the first place. But I believe everything. It isn't about two separate things – one 'real' and the other a 'dream'. It's all just one thing. *Belle de jour* is fantastic. And at certain points it's the same as with *Persona*. You say to yourself, 'Right, from here on I'm really going to concentrate so I know exactly what's going on'. And then suddenly . . . you say, 'Shit! There you go! . . .' and you realize you've gone back again.

It's like trying to force yourself to stay awake so as to be in on the moment when you drop off to sleep.

For a long time now Bergman has been at the stage where the film is created by the camera, suppressing anything that's not the image. That should be one of the axioms you start out from for the editing, instead of some rule that says the pieces have to be joined correctly according to this or that. What you ought to say is: everything that can be said should be suppressed, but at the same time leaving room for the axiom to be reversed so that the opposite principle applies, keeping only what is said, as Straub does. In *La Chinoise* I leaned to the side of what is said. But the result is fundamentally different from Straub because it's not the same things that are being said. Buñuel suppressed everything that was said, because even what is said is seen. And the film has an extraordinary freedom. You get the impression that Buñuel is 'playing' at cinema in the way that Bach must have played at the organ towards the end of his life.

Translated by Diana Matias

Notes

1 These extracts from the interview can be supplemented by further extracts, largely related to discussion of *La Chinoise*, translated as 'Interview on *La Chinoise*' in Jean Collet, *Jean-Luc Godard*, New York, Crown, 1970.

2 *Les Aventuriers* and *Deux billets pour Mexico*, directed by Robert Enrico and Christian-Jaque, 1966 and 1967, respectively, both large-budget adventure movies. Luc Moullet (see Ch. 13, note 3), meanwhile, was making interesting movies on minuscule budgets. In his 'Notes sur le nouveau spectateur', *Cahiers* 177, April 1966, translated as 'Notes on the New Spectator' in this volume, Ch. 21, Comolli refers to Moullet as a 'precursor' of the 'new cinema', while Godard, in a passage from this interview omitted here, calls Moullet's 1966 film *Brigitte*

et Brigitte 'a revolutionary film – otherwise I don't rightly see what a revolutionary film could be'. Moullet's 1967 *Les Contrebandières* was voted by *Cahiers* tenth best film shown in 1968.

3 The reference seems to be to Rivette's *L'Amour fou*, released in 1968.

4 The 'new cinema' gravitated towards film festivals other than those associated with the market-place, like Cannes, or quality and prestige, like Venice: Hyères called itself the 'Festival du jeune cinéma' and Montreal specialized in 16mm independent production.

5 Daniel Johnson, Premier of Quebec 1966–8.

6 Godard's relationship with Leacock, mentioned optimistically here, did not last very long. During 1968 Godard worked with Leacock and D. A. Pennebaker on a 16mm picture, *One American Movie*, or *1 A.M.* Godard abandoned the project in March 1970 but some of the footage, plus some footage of the shooting itself, was put together by Pennebaker to make *One P.M.* (i.e. One Pennebaker Movie), released in 1971.

7 Peter Emmanuel Goldman, whose 1966 film *Echoes of Silence* won the Special Directors Award at the Pesaro Festival 1966 and was widely shown at subsequent festivals. Jean-Claude Biette's article, 'Sur *Echoes of Silence*', *Cahiers* 188, March 1967, is translated in *Cahiers du Cinéma in English*, no. 11, September 1967.

8 Jean-Louis Comolli addresses the question of the 'destruction of the image' in his *Cahiers* 191, June 1967, review of Godard's sketch *Anticipation*, translated in Royal Brown, *Focus on Godard*, Englewood Cliffs, N.J., Prentice-Hall, 1972; and these points are pursued further in relation to *La Chinoise* in Comolli's 'Le point sur l'image', *Cahiers* 194, October 1967, translated as '*La Chinoise*' in Ian Cameron, ed., *The Films of Jean-Luc Godard*, London, Studio Vista, second ed., revised and enlarged, 1969.

9 Jacques Demy's *Les Parapluies de Cherbourg*, 1964, in which all the dialogue is sung, was promoted as a film '*en-chanté*', i.e. both 'in song' and 'magic', and it is this that Godard is referring to here; there are interesting similarities between the two films in relation to their stylized use of colour.

32 | Jean Narboni: 'Towards Impertinence'

('Vers l'impertinence', *Cahiers du Cinéma* 196, December 1967)

It is often said – and quite correctly – that it is difficult for cinema to escape from its vocation for realism, since the cinematographic image corresponds perfectly to its object. This absence of arbitrariness in its signs, this ability to replicate the real world, this resemblance, motivation or, as linguists say, pertinence, has usually been seen as its major privilege. But if we consider the clutter of references to the 'real world' made by people whose analyses in other fields are so punctilious, must we not recognize that its powers are now being directed against itself? Just as painting was liberated by photography from the need to be life-like, should cinema not now itself be challenging its too notorious pertinence? It is not without a legitimate feeling of irritation that this or that lucid theorist of the novel expresses his surprise that after several centuries of literature it is still necessary to repeat that you can't go to sleep in the word *bed*, but how many of them go on trying harder and harder to climb up the image *tree*?

This kind of preoccupation is of course not new. Ever since cinema has existed, schools and *auteurs* have been trying to challenge the subjection of the image to the thing shown, to rescue it from the clutches of the all-too-present referent. Just for the record, we should first of all mention the aesthetic movements which wore themselves out in the process without achieving greatness or leaving a posterity.[1] Although more coherent, various forms of expressionism failed too; unable to provide solutions other than plastic ones, they proposed a *look* at a deformed reality, using all kinds of optical distortions, and not a new *reading*.[2] Only Eisenstein, by mapping out a space and a time that were rigorously and exclusively filmic, constituted his work both as a model and as a perfect simulation of the world.

His lineage is now coming to the fore, with films that apparently have nothing in common except an ordering of structures, a rigorous narrative, a tight articulation of the various segments and the careful matching of filmic elements, with the result – since the gap between image and object, signifier and signified is made as wide as it could possibly be – that any attempt to read *through* the film or to take a segment in isolation must fail in its attempt to find reference points outside the film. I am thinking here, among a few others, of *Belle de jour* in which we learn about the mutations of a formal object caught between two strands of the narrative, of *La Chinoise*, the *writing of a spectacle* that imposes its own time and space (what can one say about the events in it except that they last . . . for an hour and a half?), and of *Persona*, the sufferings of a narrative that is about its own logic, a film that devours itself.[3]

Since they constitute film as an autonomous and irreducible object, these examples will certainly lead to a host of frivolous efforts. An old myth – that of total cinema – has only ever aspired to one thing: to raise the status of film to that of absolute structure, accountable only to itself for all its excesses and arbitrariness. Is it necessary to add that these attempts will (as they always have done) lack coherence and *validity* which are, in this instance, the only measures of efficiency and effectiveness? It is one thing to make a meaning obscure, it is another to kill it off slowly.[4] As self-avowed reflections on cinema's specific mode of operation, the films I have referred to and those I would wish to see being made can only collect up as they go along the soil of lived experience and the struggles of the world, integrating them into their substance (rather than reproducing them) in order to bear witness to them. The reference to Eisenstein and, at this late stage, to *Nicht versöhnt* should be enough to clear them of any suspicion of gratuitousness.

Translated by Norman King

Notes

1 Narboni has in mind primarily the 1920s French avant-garde and film-makers like L'Herbier, Epstein, Dulac, Delluc, Kirsanoff, perhaps Gance. Two different, but both influential, views of film history have conspired, until recently, to undervalue the importance of this avant-garde, for both its films and its theoretical work – André Bazin's (see Ch. 3, note 2), and the Surrealists' (see, for example, The French Surrealist Group's 'Some Surrealist Advice', *L'Age du cinéma*, no. 4–5, August–November 1951, translated in Paul Hammond, *The Shadow and Its Shadow: Surrealist Writings on Cinema*, London, British Film Institute, 1978). Very soon after Narboni's piece, *Cahiers* itself (no. 202, June–July 1968) published a special issue which revalued '*La première vague*' (The First Wave), as the lead article by Noël Burch and Jean-André Fieschi put it. Of this issue, only André S. Labarthe's short article, 'Epstein à l'état naissant', has been translated, as 'The Emergence of Epstein', *Afterimage*, no. 10, which also included a selection of Epstein's writings. However, Richard Roud's *Cinema: A Critical Dictionary*, London, Secker & Warburg, 1980, contains a number of entries by *Cahiers* writers of this period which can give a sense of the way these 1920s film-makers were revalued. See, for example, Fieschi on Delluc and on Epstein, Burch on L'Herbier, Bernard Eisenschitz on Gance (and, from a very different perspective, P. Adams Sitney on Kirsanoff).

2 It is quite clear that the reading you can make of a film today derives at least

in part from the responsibility of the *auteur*, and that a concern of this order must be the founding principle of the film, to which is delegated the task of authorizing – and especially of forbidding – this or that interpretation. Films do not suffer today from a lack of comprehension (quite the contrary) but from a failure to read (and to listen). (Author's note.)

3 Since the notion of gaps in the narration, of lacks or lacunae in the story is what *Persona* is based on, is the moment in the middle when the celluloid catches fire really a heavily symbolic reference to the disintegration of the characters? Isn't it rather the burning itself that is illustrated in a metaphorical kind of way by the events and the fiction the film recounts? (Author's note.)

4 I am referring to a large proportion of *essais* and experimental films made in Europe and New York. At the other extreme, McLaren's technique takes a cinema stripped as far as possible of any referent outside the film to a limit that is exemplary – but which is all the same a limit. It goes without saying that the cinema I am trying to sketch out here differs radically from both of these approaches. (Author's note.)

('Lecture à plusieurs voies', *Cahiers du Cinéma* 197, Christmas 1967–January 1968)

1 There are some films (for instance, *Les Carabiniers*, *Les Contrabandières*) which are difficult to approach and which present the naked eye with surfaces as slippery as the celluloid they are made of. The nature of these films has already been discussed and explained in these pages and so, by a process of deduction, has the effort they demand of the spectator.

Makavejev's second film is far from making any imperious demand for alertness of that kind on the part of the spectator. From the very beginning the way the film functions demonstrates a power few could match. At first the power seems to come from a technique calculated with scientific precision, an arrangement by a master of audiovisual counterpoint, and a tension generated by the exemplary construction of the narration; gentle habituation has to that extent ensured an art film audience agreeably tickled by films so manifestly 'intellectual'.

The diegetic line of *Switchboard Operator*[1] has been described well enough (to be precise, here in *Cahiers* by Makavejev[2]) for any lengthy discussion to be unnecessary. The plot is situated on three principal levels: (1) the story of the Isabela-Ahmed affair; (2) the discovery of Isabela's body and the autopsy; (3) the discussions of sexuality (and crime), which set the first two, initially parallel, levels on a head-on collision course at increasing speed until their final impact inscribes them as symbol and example of the third.

Whether the Eisensteinian theory of 'montage of attractions' is here a matter of conscious application or unconscious recall, the magnificent simplicity and effectiveness of the film's construction is in itself already sufficient guarantee of innovation and modernity. It may not be revolutionary to begin a narrative with a preview of the tragic end (it's been done by others many times before, from *Le Crime de Monsieur Lange* to *Joszef Katus*, and from *The Quiet American* to *Terra em Transe*), and the editing technique Makavejev illustrates does not lack celebrated examples elsewhere. But the installation of a critical level within the actual fiction

303

of the film here functions in a completely new way (which owes nothing to the Godard of *Deux ou trois choses que je sais d'elle*, in particular); integrated and at the same time separate, it is like the facade of a fine piece of architecture.

2 But so far there is nothing about all this that does not run smoothly in the end, nothing that does not give satisfaction in a beautiful piece of art whose crafting is original but not alarming – a work easy to accept and digest. Fiendish perfection and formal mastery of this sort can take one's breath away, but it also runs the risk of seeming merely clever, even if the cleverness (like that of Preminger's *Bonjour Tristesse*, for example) pays off in being both moving and impressive. To put it in a nutshell, *Switchboard Operator* is a perfectly closed fiction which from the outset supplies the complete bunch of keys to itself. However, were we to end on this observation of semi-failure – after a critique which is itself self-fulfilling and quite closed – we would be ignoring the fact that a film is not reducible to its plot. By inducing from the preceding argument that we are dealing with a closed and perfectly decipherable work we would also undoubtedly be missing the essential modernity of Makavejev's film.

What in fact constitutes the profound modernity of this film is unarguably its openness at the level of the narration (which makes it, if you like, the contrary of *L'Immortelle* where a desire to open up the fiction fails to compensate for extreme closure, coupled moreover with much that is paltry, at the level of the *écriture*). This film belongs with those which offer in an exemplary manner several ways into a reading of one and the same narrative. Thus, without attempting the impossible and trying to say the last word on a film, I should like to propose a concurrent set of equally evident and equally possible routes to a reading.

The first of these is the 'documentary' route, which is defined not by the innumerable ways things are observed and noted (already listed by J.-L. Comolli[3]) and which run from a cooking recipe to a formal deposition (and roughly mark out a didactic route), but rather, by the way Makavejev has of using the camera as if he were engaged in news reporting. He looks at and shows his characters 'live', i.e. in the course of their daily activities (pest extermination, work at the post office, hanging out washing, etc.) and in the actual places where they carry them out.

Then there is the 'taxonomic' route, about which it is perhaps possible to be more precise. This allows us to see *Switchboard Operator* as a vast survey of all the ways there are of talking about sex – from the scientific-historical (the sexologist), to the metaphorical (the mattress comber and his song), and the symbolic, either precise (the list here would be a long one – we might mention just the installing of the geyser which combines a good half-dozen such), or imprecise (Isabela's fingers rubbing egg whites into flour). This dimension of the film is moreover underscored and summed up 'in the margins' by the parallel procedure adopted in the sequence of the criminologist's lecture (panoply of weapons, enumeration of various kinds of clues leading to the capture of a criminal), which inevitably refers to those great taxonomists, Freud and de Sade.

Finally, there is the 'critical' route (the film itself is surely a 'critical path' in the data-processor's sense). This is not so much a matter of the distanciation effect in relation to the fiction (although that comes into play in at least one scene, the one of the Mayakovsky song, where revolutionary romanticism gets its come-uppance). It shows itself rather in an extraordinary critical detachment in relation to the other two routes mentioned. It is worth remembering the very consciously ironical value (cf. numerous interviews with Makavejev) placed on all the interventions of the sexologist and the criminologist.

3 In proposing this kind of non-univocal reading, and in broadening the field of action for current film-makers who have been producing their 'complete works' from film to film for some time now, Makavejev bears witness above all to the existence of a 'new cinema' and the *écriture* which marks and defines it.

The *écriture* in question is one of pure narration, in which the diegesis seems to be becoming less and less important as such and through which modern cinema seems to be casting off the shackles of Representation. It would be superfluous to paraphrase here the pertinent observations on this subject made by Jean Narboni last month.[4] I will content myself with a quote from a theoretician of the *nouveau roman*: 'There is of course a plot. But its nature is very curious: at its best it is the integral outcome of developments in an *écriture*; it is least likely of all to render itself up completely to those (psychological, philosophical, political) techniques whose field of action is the everyday world. It can only be understood through an integral literary reading which follows exactly the fluctuations of the creative process at every instant' (Jean Ricardou). It is thus possible to distinguish the weaving together of works in other ways quite distant from each other (in style, theme, etc.), a close network of diagonal lines which make up something like a thematic backdrop for the *écriture* of the 'new cinema': these are scriptural themes (an inadequate term, used for want of a better one) whose systematic inventory is still to be made, and which blossom in *Switchboard Operator* as they do in nearly all the recent great films.

Thus we have the sequence which begins – right after the sexologist's digression on the subject of the egg – with Isabela hanging out the washing in the yard, continues with the revolutionary song, then with the nuts and honey episode, and ends with Isabela preventing Ahmed from concentrating by singing him a Hungarian song. Admirable here are: 1) the concern with an elaborated musical construction (*Persona*, *La Religieuse*, *L'Authentique Procès de Carl Emmanuel Jung* . . .); 2) the usage of the 'open' metaphor (*Barrier*, *Three on a Couch*, Chytilova's short *Pearls of the Deep* . . .); the documentary eye (*Pop Game*, *Deux ou trois choses que je sais d'elle*, *About Something Else*); 4) the sharp critical distance in relation to the plot and the narrative (*Daisies*, *Le Départ*).

4 So far as the narrative construction of *Switchboard Operator* is concerned, the preceding discussion has only given an account, and in a fragmentary way at that, of this film's ethical relation to society – in other words, its *écriture*. To put it precisely, our concern has been with the film's emblematic value for a particular 'new cinema'. Nothing could be more valid as an exercise, given that the cinema being made today is bringing us more and more important films and fewer and fewer *auteurs*.

It would nevertheless be unfair to Makavejev not to note at least the degree to which his second film ensures the organic existence of a style: in reasserting that 'man is not a bird'[5] (or as it is so admirably put by Isabela, 'We're not made of wood, for God's sake!'), *Switchboard Operator* is a fine defence and illustration of a stylistic process which ensures maximum contact with the earth – a style that is 'plantigrade' in the primary sense of the word. Makavejev's first two films are firmly earthbound; around 'man's' relations to society and the world, they develop a rhetoric whose shadings are almost 'peasant' in character and which allows them to go with confidence straight to first truths.

Translated by Diana Matias

Notes

1 *Switchboard Operator* accumulated a large number of alternate titles: in Britain its main title was *Switchboard Operator* but it was also known as *The Tragedy of a Switchboard Operator*; in the USA, its main title was *Love Affair*, but it was also known as *The Case of the Missing Switchboard Operator* and as *An Affair of the Heart*.
2 Dusan Makavejev, 'Une affaire de coeur: entretien', *Cahiers* 191, June 1967, pp. 38–41.
3 'Commentaires: Semaine de la Critique': Jean-Louis Comolli on *Switchboard Operator*, *Cahiers* 191, June 1967, p. 49.
4 Jean Narboni, 'Vers l'impertinence', *Cahiers* 196, December 1967, translated as 'Towards Impertinence', in this volume, Ch. 32.
5 Makavejev's first feature was *Man is not a Bird*, 1966.

34 | *Cahiers du Cinéma*: 'Editorial: The Langlois Affair'

('Editorial', *Cahiers du Cinéma* 200–1, April–May 1968)

Langlois finally reinstated, his authority strengthened,[1] our Cinémathèque free at last – and this comes not just after more than two months of struggle, but after long years of interference and misdirected intervention by the state. So, and undoubtedly for the first time, we have the whole of cinema, from cinephile to film-maker, winning a victory (and not the habitual Pyrrhic victory) over those who, whether they are agents of the state or not, traitors or not, have more or less made it their business to oppose or weaken the cinema. For all that, the fate of the Cinémathèque, its future, is not settled, since more than ever it depends on all those who fought for it and who must not now rest on their laurels. More than ever there is – there must be – a symbiosis between cinema and Cinémathèque. The truth is – to speak only of ourselves – that without Langlois there would have been no *Cahiers du Cinéma* and no *nouvelle vague*, and we shall therefore endeavour to ensure that the converse is no less true. But should we leave it there? Should not the battle of the Cinémathèque be regarded as the first of those battles – all of them – which are still to be fought to ensure that after so many years of growing up, of crisis and tutelage, the cinema in France will acquire a genuine status, a status justified by its maturity and its freedom (the former a reality, the latter unfortunately still only potential)? This is the concern which, in our 200th issue, we address in the form of an inquiry to French film-makers regarding their ideas about and experience of relations between Cinema and State. The first replies we publish show both that these relations are necessary and that their reform is essential. They show also something that may still need to be proved: that as of now the film-makers of France are not only in a position to define the nature of this reform, but are the only ones who can bring it about.

Translated by David Wilson

Note

1 'The Langlois Affair': Sylvia Harvey, *May '68 and Film Culture*, London, British Film Institute, 1978, offers a brief account of the events surrounding the dismissal and reinstatement of Langlois, pp. 14–16. A fuller account is given in Richard Roud, *A Passion for Films: Henri Langlois and the Cinémathèque Française*, London, Secker & Warburg; New York, Viking Press, 1983. Roud's account usefully includes the wider background of problems through the 1960s (Chapter 8: 'The State vs. Henri Langlois') and the details of the 'affair' itself (Chapter 9: 'The Battle for the Cinémathèque'). See also François Truffaut's foreword to Roud's book.

35 | *Cahiers du Cinéma*: 'Editorial: The Estates General of the French Cinema'

('Editorial', *Cahiers du Cinéma* 202,
June-July 1968)

The 17th May saw the opening, at the School of Photography and Cinema in the Rue de Vaugirard, of the Estates General of French Cinema.[1] Some 1,500 people connected with the cinema, both professionally and semi-professionally, met there (many of them for the first time) and came back nearly every evening for a whole month: a first and by no means negligible revolution in the habits of the cinema in France. For our part, we have for a long time (and again recently, in our 200th issue[2]) been urging those involved in the cinema to bring together their efforts and ideas, to criticize and to act in order to secure the future of the cinema. It is in answer to this that the Estates General have here and now demonstrated (though, here too, the fight goes on) that in every one of the cinema's professional categories – and also among those many people for whom the 'profession' has remained closed – there is one supreme desire: to transform the 'system', the state of affairs in which the cinema in France has been so self-enclosed, so cut off from any social or political reality. The Estates General have not only started to tackle the problems of the cinema; they have also shown, in the strike of the technicians and production workers, in their involvement in the marches and demonstrations, that their action was at one with that of the students and the workers, that it was an act of solidarity.

At a time when, in the cinema as elsewhere, the purveyors of easy solutions are mustering their forces of reaction (there is talk of setting up a Civil Action Committee for the cinema!), the existence of the Estates General becomes all the more necessary, as a challenge to every abuse, privilege or red-tape routine. All this we will take up in our next issue.[3]

Translated by David Wilson

Notes

1 The Estates General: see Sylvia Harvey, *May '68 and Film Culture*, London, British Film Institute, 1978 (reprinted 1980), for an overview, pp. 16–27. Documents from the Estates General are reproduced in Harvey and in *Screen*, vol. 13, no. 4, Winter 1972–3 (see Appendix 2, under *Cahiers*, for details).
2 See Editorial to *Cahiers* 200, in this volume, Ch. 34.
3 *Cahiers* 203, August 1968, included much documentation on the Estates General; see note 1, above.

36 | *Cahiers du Cinéma*: 'Editorial: Changes in *Cahiers*'

('Editorial', *Cahiers du Cinéma* 203, August 1968)

Readers will notice two important changes in this issue: the 'Conseil des Dix'[1] has gone, and there are fewer critical notes in the list of films released in Paris. In forthcoming issues, the format of the 'Petit Journal'[2] and of the review section will also be changed. These four sections are by their nature tied to what is referred to as 'current cinema' – which, being wholly dependent on what films are released in Paris, has less and less to do with what we regard as cinema now. Indeed, given that the policy of distributors, programmers and exhibitors is to make a profit, most of the important films are regularly held back, when they are not simply blocked or even sabotaged (by being mutilated or because of thoughtless programming). Cinema has increasingly less resemblance to the image created by the kinds of films shown on the Champs Elysées or even in the Latin Quarter. So it is no longer a question of defending a 'parallel cinema', forever the poor relation of 'official' cinema: to a greater or lesser extent it is this latter category of cinema that now seems to us to be marginal. Marginal is just what this 'official' cinema has been for some time in our round-up of films, which has been divided between films which could no longer be seen except in *cinémathèques* and film clubs, and new films which were by no means widely available and which risk being even less so given that political censorship has now been added to commercial censorship. These two categories nevertheless make up what is essential in cinema, which it is our function to talk about with our readers, everything else being merely auxiliary or anecdotal. In this perspective the 'Conseil des Dix', fatally compromised by the arbitrary way in which films are released in Paris, no longer has any *raison d'être*. Of the films released in Paris we intend to discuss only those which merit attention – or stricture. In the same vein, the purpose of the 'Petit Journal' and the review section will be to speed up awareness and circulation of what is genuinely the cinema of today. This is also why, by continuing and expanding the programme of the 'Semaines des *Cahiers*',[3] we ourselves intend to take and support every initiative which will result in the showing of films which have not been shown and ought to be. A task which, it goes without saying, cannot be done properly without the active support of our readers.

Translated by David Wilson

Notes

1 'Conseil des Dix': see Ch. 13, note 5.
2 'Petit Journal': this had always been the diary and odds and ends section *Cahiers* used for news, reviews of Cinémathèque screenings, short accounts of films seen abroad, etc.
3 'Semaines des *Cahiers*': *Cahiers* had programmed and sponsored, since 1966, week-long seasons of 'new cinema' films, in association with the 'Festival du jeune cinéma' at Hyères, in an active effort to get the films seen and distributed publicly. In 1966 the programme included Bertolucci's *Prima della Rivoluzione*, Bellocchio's *I Pugni in Tasca*, Skolimowski's *Rysopis* (*Identification Marks: None*), Luc Moullet's *Brigitte et Brigitte*, Straub's *Nicht versöhnt* (*Not Reconciled*). In 1967 the programme was: Pasolini's *Uccellacci e Uccellini*, Skolimowski's *Barrier*, Glauber Rocha's *Terra em Transe*, Francis Leroi's *Pop Game*, Juleen Compton's *Stranded*, Adrian Ditvoorst's *Paranoïa*, James Ivory's *Shakespeare Wallah*. 1968's programme was: Philippe Garrel's *La Concentration*, Luc Moullet's *Les Contreband-ières*, Michel Soutter's *Haschich*, Jean-Pierre Lefèbvre's *Jusqu'au coeur*, Bertolucci's *Partner*, Werner Herzog's *Signs of Life*, Matjaz Klopcic's *On Paper Planes* (*Na Papirnatih Avionih*). Due in part to the efforts of *Cahiers* many of these films were taken into distribution in France.

37 | Jean-Louis Comolli: 'Postscript: *Hour of the Wolf*'

('Postface', *Cahiers du Cinéma* 203, August 1968)

Behind the credits of *Hour of the Wolf* we hear the noise of a set being made ready for a shot – a black frame on which is written the title, *Vargtimmen*. A black screen in fact, an image (if one can so describe it) of total darkness before the first real, luminous images. But in this night before the film, soon to be driven out by the light of the film, nothing sleeps. Noises off, and we quickly realize that the preparations are complete, so that finally, at a given moment, when the order to shoot is given, film and light together occupy the entire space, the *only* space there is, the space of the frame, of the screen. A voice can be heard giving this order. Roll camera: the darkness vanishes from the screen, and in the twilight there appears the weary face of Liv Ullmann.

All this – night passing into day, darkness into an image, the innermost mystery of a film being made turning into the brilliant light which is the evidence of the film itself, cinema becoming the shot filmed and projected – all this lasts for ten seconds or so. Long enough to anchor the narrative in a kind of primordial night; long enough to make us feel, as the light and the first images appear, that we are waking out of a confused dream – waking into another dream?

Nights without night. Such a shadowy opening first of all matches, corresponds with the theme of twilight which the film develops. Elsewhere in this issue[1] Bergman defines 'the hour of the wolf' as the hour which in legend belongs to all those transformations into vampires and animal forms that are associated with the transformation of night into day and day into night: the moment when waking and sleeping merge into one, when there is no difference between them because nightmares make no distinction between one state or the other. These dawns without end (which extend into twilights) which keep appearing in the film had to be preceded, however briefly, by a real night.

Before light comes. However, beyond the thematic significance of this correspondence, the dark night of this beginning encompasses nothing more

313

(that we are aware of) than the preparations for a shot. And not just any shot; indeed, this is the *first* shot of the film, the one we see as the film starts rolling.

The work on the set which leads to, produces (or at least we assume produces) and directly precedes this first shot is not shown to us (except for a few sounds picked up at random). As though it were in the nature of what prepares and indicates the making (and reproduction) of images by light that it should be and remain impervious to light. The concealment of that which allows something to be seen.

What we have, then, is the banal reality of any film (of any piece of exposed film), that it is all that remains to be seen from the work which leads up to its being seen.

Counterflow. If, however, Bergman decides to begin his film by reminding us that it came out of the making of a film, and if he identifies this period of gestation as a night from which, at a given moment, there issues forth a whole sequence of images, as something from within the process of representation which in one movement tilts into spectacle, it may be that this relationship of the film to its source is not so simple, nor devoid of mystery. Is this not confirmation that the film, even if it seems to flow naturally from its making, in fact not only completely obliterates it, but in a way chases it out, frees itself from it, somewhat in the way that a dream breaks free of the night which contrives it by giving it a light of its own, or of the impressions which shape it by creating a private logic and leading it down a road far from the beaten track?

The film unfolds like a dream in progress, in itself a kind of dream, resisting a predetermined course, switching direction at will. Which gives credence to the idea of the film as an independent object, freed at last from the constraints of narrative and form which, powerlessly, its 'author' would wish to impose on it: the film as a living organism; a fabrication, of course, but also something which in a sense fabricates itself.

Breaking point. One recalls that the interweaving narrative of *Persona* was framed by its beginning and its end – as in its fragmented centre – by the incongruous image of a reel of film passing through a projector and breaking up as it did so. The impression is that the film is 'in pain', cracking under the strain of the story, reacting against it. In *Hour of the Wolf* the impression is that the film, no sooner set in motion by the word 'Roll', follows its own independent course; and by going back to the credit titles two-thirds of the way through, the film implies not that the dramatic continuity has been broken and the viewer awakened from his reverie, but rather that the film itself is imposing its own whims or its own secret logic on the ritual chronology of the projection process: rolled up in a loop, like dreams, the film begins a new cycle. But Bergman says[2] that when he was shooting *Hour of the Wolf* he had the same idea as with *Persona*: to give the film a framing 'prologue' and 'epilogue' in which one would see Liv Ullmann confessing to Bergman's camera on the set of *Hour of the Wolf*. He adds at once that the film's power, its very nature, *prevented*

314

him from following this plan.[3] From which the only conclusion is that once it is set in motion, the film exists independently of Bergman's will, that it can resist such aesthetic considerations.

Dream dreamt. In this respect, *Hour of the Wolf* is the cinema in revolt, as was also the case in *Persona*. In both films everything happens as if from the very first shot the film has a life and a force of its own. At one moment fracturing its fiction (while simultaneously being fractured by it), at another giving it free rein, the chance to proliferate.

The structure of *Hour of the Wolf* is witness to the fact that at any point the film is stronger than its 'author', in that it is in a position to follow a logic, a sequence of events, which *nobody* could have *determined*, so inexplicable are they – nobody except perhaps the dream *within* the film.

The narrative proceeds along a very devious route of *misconnections*, starting from the passage of night into day as described above. Liv Ullmann is revealed, making her confession, confiding the story of her adventure as though she had reached the end of it. She talks about her husband's diary. This first narration (actually the second in relation to the introductory darkness) is soon 'illustrated' – a second narrative, this time peopled with 'characters', following on from the confession. This narrative proceeds up to the point when Liv Ullmann discovers her husband's diary and starts to read it. So there is a third narrative superimposed on the first two. Liv takes over from the images which have illustrated – going far beyond it – her initial confession. But her reading is in turn illustrated by scenes and paintings: a fourth narrative is grafted on to its predecessors. Phantasms of extreme violence are unleashed by this new proliferation of the unfolding narrative. Up to the moment when Liv confesses to her husband that she has read his diary. Now begins a long night, in which the couple's phantasms, hitherto convergent and complementary (we don't know *who* is dreaming them), begin to develop in common. After the night in the castle, the climax of this eruption of dreams, the house of cards begins piece by piece to collapse. The characters evaporate, melt into the night. The painter takes refuge in a forest, and dies – if he is not already dead, already a phantom conjured up in his companion's dreams. Alone now (though not without the diary), Liv resumes her confession at the point where we left her at the start, in the same close-up, as if only a fraction of a second had elapsed between two close-ups of the same face and all remained to be said anew. How can this fraction of a second, which lasts a whole film, be expanded except in dream time? The film (if one assumes the film as being this first shot following the blacked out scene of the film being made, with Liv Ullmann talking to the camera which we know is there) has set about dreaming. In between two identical shots which ought to follow each other a whole dream is interpolated, with its cyclical returns to the same reference points (the diary, the castle), its feeding off itself, its reincarnations and metamorphoses of the dead into the living and of men into beasts. The film has become a dream;

and when we wake from it, it is as if nothing had moved, except the dream.

Translated by David Wilson

Notes

1 'Entretien avec Ingmar Bergman sur *L'Heure du loup*'; it is to this interview that Comolli intends his own piece as a 'postscript'.
2 *Ibid*.
3 Bergman discusses these points, in a rather more down to earth way, in *Bergman on Bergman*, London, Secker & Warburg, 1973, pp. 215–22.

38 | Jacques Rivette: 'Time Overflowing': Rivette in interview with Jacques Aumont, Jean-Louis Comolli, Jean Narboni, Sylvie Pierre (extracts)[1]

('Le temps déborde: entretien avec Jacques Rivette', *Cahiers du Cinéma* 204, September 1968)

[. . .] *How do you now see* Paris nous appartient?
I haven't seen it again for a long time and I'm very much afraid of seeing it again. I wanted too much to film it to be able to disown it, but with perspective on it I am very unhappy about the dialogue, which I find atrocious. I still like the idea of the film, including the naïve aspects of it; I like the way it's constructed, the way the characters go from one décor to another and the way they move among themselves. I don't even mind the fact that the plot is rather unpolished, but the style of the dialogue and the resulting style of acting bother me prodigiously. I thought when I was writing it that it was counter to Aurenche and Bost,[2] but I realize that it's the same thing – dialogue for effects, in the worst sense of the term. The lines are saved by certain of the actors; some make them worse – but they are terribly pleased with themselves, and I can't stand that any more. Even the theatre scenes are conventional and that's what made me want to show the theatre in another way.

In any case, that's nothing special. All films are about the theatre, there is no other subject. That's choosing the easy way, of course, but I am more and more convinced that one must do the easy things and leave the difficult things to pedants. If you take a subject which deals with the theatre to any extent at all, you're dealing with the truth of the cinema: you're carried along. It isn't by chance that so many of the films we love are first of all about that subject, and you realize afterwards that all the others – Bergman, Renoir, the good Cukors, Garrel,[3] Rouch, Cocteau, Godard, Mizoguchi – are also about that. Because that is the subject of truth and lies, and there is no other in the cinema: it is necessarily a questioning about truth, with means that are necessarily untruthful. Performance as the subject. Taking it as the subject of a film is being frank, so it must be done.
Isn't that a bit like taking the cinema directly as the subject of the cinema?
There have been many attempts in the cinema to make films on the

cinema and it doesn't work as well; it is more laborious and comes off as affectation. It doesn't have the same force, maybe because there is only one level. It's the cinema contemplating itself, while if it looks at the theatre, it is already contemplating something else: not itself but its elder brother. Of course, it's another way of looking at itself in a mirror, but the theatre is the 'polite' version of the cinema. It's the face it takes when it is communicating with the public; while a film crew is a conspiracy, completely closed in upon itself, and no one has yet managed to film the reality of the conspiracy. There is something infamous, something profoundly debauched about cinema work. Maybe it should be filmed in a more critical manner, or a more violent manner, the way Garrel films his 'scene of the crime'. In any case, it's very difficult. Even *8½* stops before the film is begun; the fact that Mastroianni may be about to start shooting his film forces Fellini to end his.

Independently of all that, don't you think that what modern film directors – or those who have always been modern, like Renoir – are more and more interested in is something in common between the theatrical setting and the setting as it comes into modern cinema? When you see Persona *or Garrel's films, you can't help asking yourself about the setting.*

Whether the setting is pre-existent? Whether the film is an exploration of the setting? All I can say, empirically, is that in *L'Amour fou*, if the décors had been different, everything would have been fundamentally different, and first of all there is an operation of taming and exploring these two décors. We tried to show the flat in different dramatic situations: familiar, strange, tidy, messy, demolished, welcoming, hostile; and on the contrary, to show the theatre décor as completely immobile, since it is totally artificial. We were quite comfortable in that décor, because it was very large and very cosy at the same time. You could feel the lines of force in that place, which I really liked; each time I went back there, I felt good. While in the flat, it completely depended on what you made of it.

At the first and the last shots, with the stage and the blank screen, one gets the impression that the setting is tending to absorb the film, that space is devouring . . .

Precisely: 'Nothing will have taken place but the place itself'. Besides that, this beginning and ending were done to tie up the parcel, to try to find a bit of an equivalent – a purely functional one, based on the theatre – to the beginning and ending of *Persona*.

That is also what I still like about *Paris nous appartient*, the labyrinth that the décors create among themselves, the idea that one brings away from the film, of a sort of series of settings with relationships between them – some cut off, others communicating, others that are optional itineraries – and people moving about like mice inside these labyrinths, ending up in culs-de-sac or caught nose to nose. Then at the end it all disappears and there's nothing left but this lake and some birds flying away . . . In that, the setting is very, very different from the setting of the beginning – unlike *L'Amour fou . . .*

318

[. . .]

Do you believe that the cinema is useful? Or that a revolutionary cinema can exist?

I think revolutionary cinema can only be a 'differential' cinema, a cinema which questions all the rest of cinema. But in France, in any case, in relation to a possible revolution, I don't believe in a revolutionary cinema of the first degree, which is satisfied with taking the revolution as its subject. A film like *Terra em Transe*[4] which does take the revolution as its subject is also really a revolutionary film; it's always stupid to make assumptions, but I don't think that could exist in France now. Films that content themselves with taking the revolution as a subject actually subordinate themselves to bourgeois ideas of content, message, expression. While the only way to make revolutionary cinema in France is to make sure that it escapes all the bourgeois aesthetic clichés: like the idea that there is an *auteur* of the film, expressing himself. The only thing we can do in France at the moment is to try to deny that a film is a personal creation. I think *Playtime* is a revolutionary film, in spite of Tati: the film completely overshadowed the creator. In films, what is important is the point where the film no longer has an *auteur*, where it has no more actors, no more story even, no more subject, nothing left but the film itself speaking and saying something that can't be translated: the point where it becomes the discourse of someone or something else, which cannot be said, precisely because it is beyond expression. And I think you can only get there by trying to be as passive as possible at all the various stages, never intervening on one's own behalf but rather on behalf of this something else which is nameless.

But that is something that very often happens, for example in Bergman, even though he is on the contrary very active, a real demiurge.

That's true, but I still get the impression that Bergman is someone who writes scripts without asking himself questions about the meaning of what he is writing. People have often talked about the commonplace elements in *Persona*, for example; but what is important in *Persona* is precisely that beyond all those elements which Bergman started off with, he hasn't kept that 'something else' coming through. Maybe it's precisely because he doesn't question what he feels like filming that he does film that way. In a sense, he accepts being only an intermediary; Bergman's films are something completely different from Bergman's vision of the world, which interests no one. What speaks in Bergman's films isn't Bergman but the film, and that's what is revolutionary, because that is what seems to me to question very deeply everything that justifies the world as it is and as it disgusts us.

But don't we then end up back with the idea of an auteur *strong enough to let the film speak for itself?*

Not necessarily – I think there are a lot of methods. Bergman's 'genius' is a method, but the absence of genius can also be just as effective a method. The fact of being a collective, for example . . .

Don't you think that's a myth?

No, I don't think so. Of course I know that the effect would have been completely different with Bulle and Jean-Pierre and a different director, apart from any question of talent or anything else. It has nothing to do with that; it's an aggregate of almost physical or biological reactions; it has nothing to do with intelligence.

Maybe there is one more point to mention about Bergman: the fact that he works with his 'family', with the same people, that he doesn't write his scripts in the abstract and then afterwards wonder: 'Who on earth could I use? Sophia Loren isn't free; I know, I'll take Liv Ullmann . . .' It's like Renoir, who only wrote scenarios for people he'd chosen beforehand. Maybe it's only at that level that a collective can exist. In any case, Renoir is the person who has understood the cinema best of all, even better than Rossellini, better than Godard, better than anyone.

What about Rouch?

Rouch is contained in Renoir. I don't know whether Renoir saw Rouch's films, but if he saw them, I'm sure that, first of all, he'd find them 'stunning', and that on the other hand he wouldn't find them stunning at all. Rouch is the force behind all French cinema of the past ten years, although few people realize it. Jean-Luc Godard came from Rouch. In a way, Rouch is more important than Godard in the evolution of the French cinema. Godard goes in a direction that is only valid for himself, which doesn't set an example, in my opinion. Whereas all Rouch's films are exemplary, even those where he failed, even *Les Veuves de quinze ans.* Jean-Luc doesn't set an example, he provokes. He provokes reactions, either of imitation or of contradiction or of rejection, but he can't strictly be taken as an example. While Rouch or Renoir can be.

Do you believe that a cinema which takes directly political elements for its theme has the power to mobilize people?

Less and less. I believe more and more that the role of the cinema is to destroy myths, to demobilize, to be pessimistic. Its role is to take people out of their cocoons and to plunge them into horror.

One can do that very well using the revolution as a theme.

Yes, but on the condition that the revolution is just a theme like any other. The only interesting film on the May 'events' (obviously, I haven't seen them all) is one about the return to the Wonder factories,[5] filmed by students at IDHEC – because it is a terrifying and painful film. It's the only film that was really revolutionary. Maybe because it's a moment when reality is transforming itself at such a rate that it starts to condense a whole political situation into ten minutes of wild dramatic intensity. It's a fascinating film, but one couldn't say that it mobilizes people at all, or if it does, it's by provoking a reflex reaction of horror and rejection. Really, I think that the only role of the cinema is to upset people, to contradict structures which pre-shadow those ideas: it must ensure that the cinema is no longer comfortable. More and more, I tend to divide films into two sorts: those that are comfortable and those that aren't. The former are all vile and the others positive to a greater or lesser degree. Some films I've seen, on Flins or Saint-Nazaire,[6] are pitifully comfortable; not only do they change nothing, but they also make the audience feel pleased with themselves. It's like *Humanité*[7] demonstrations.

Obviously, it's difficult to believe in political films which think that by showing 'reality' it will denounce itself.

I think that what counts isn't whether it is fiction or non-fiction, it's the attitude that the person takes at the moment when he is filming; for example, whether or not he accepts direct sound. In any case, the fiction is actually direct sound, because there is still the point when you are filming. And with direct sound, ninety times out of a hundred, since people know they are being filmed, they probably start to base their reactions on that fact, and so it becomes almost super-fiction. All the more so because the director then has complete freedom to use the material that's been filmed: to tighten up, to keep the long bits, to choose, not to choose, with the sound faked or not. And that is the real political moment.

Do you think the film-maker takes a moral position with regard to what he is filming?

Without any doubt, that's all there is. First, with regard to the people he is filming, and then again with regard to the audience, in the way he chooses to communicate to them what he has filmed. But all films are political. In any case, I maintain that *L'Amour fou* is a deeply political film. It is political because the attitude we all had during the filming and then during the editing corresponds to moral choices, to ideas of human relationships, and therefore to political choices.

Which are communicated to the audience?

I hope so. The will to make a scene last in one way and not in another – I find that a political choice.

So it's a very general idea of politics . . .

But politics *is* extremely general. It's what corresponds to the widest-ranging point of view one can have regarding existence. *La Marseillaise* is a film that is directly political, but so very different from a film like *Toni*, which is indirectly political, and even from *Boudu*, which doesn't seem to be political at all. While actually *Boudu* is a completely political film: it is a great film of the left. Almost all Renoir's films are more or less directly political, even those that are the least explicitly political, like *Madame Bovary* and *Le Testament du Docteur Cordelier*. I think what is most important *politically* is the attitude the film-maker takes with regard to all the aesthetic – or rather, so-called aesthetic – criteria which govern art in general and cinematic expression, in triple inverted commas, in particular. One can refine down afterwards, within the choices one has made, but that is what counts first of all. And what counted first of all for us, for Jean-Pierre and myself, him for *Andromaque*, me for the film, was the rejection of the idea of entertainment, and on the contrary the idea of an ordeal either imposed on or at least proposed to the viewer – who is no longer the comfortable viewer, but someone who participates in common work – long, difficult, responsible work something like delivering a baby. But it's a sort of work that always has to be done again, this work of denying entertainment. There is a perpetual co-opting taking place or which always might take place, of the preceding stage, which is immediately taken up from an aesthetic point of view or a contemplative point of view: the prudent distance of people who won't let themselves be caught twice, which is the basic attitude of all Western audiences.

And it is precisely the fear of always being co-opted which makes this desire to deny entertainment limitless. Films like Bergman's or like Godard's are actually only superficially co-opted by this sort of Parisian habit which makes it possible to take films in by saying 'Oh, yes, of course, the theme of the absence of God', and various other stupid remarks like that. This superficial co-opting does oblige the director to go further in the following film, to try once and for all to show that it isn't a question of the absence of God or anything else, but of being suddenly confronted with everything one rejects, by will or by force.

What do you think of Garrel's films, from that point of view?

In my opinion, they correspond exactly to what one should expect of the cinema today. That is, that a film must be, if not an ordeal, at least an experience, something which makes the film transform the viewer, who has undergone something through the film, who is no longer the same after having seen the film. In the same way that the people who made the film really offered up troubling personal things, the viewer must be upset by seeing the film; the film must make his habits of thought go off their beaten tracks: so that it can't be seen with impunity.

But, precisely, intelligent people who don't like Garrel accuse him of having a conception of art as a 'primal scream' and of making films which aren't very far from Hitchcock's, a cinema of fascination, a hypnotic cinema which, in the end, seems very old-fashioned.

I wondered quite a bit whether one could create a 'distanciated' cinema, and basically I don't think so. The cinema is necessarily fascination and rape, that is how it acts on people; it is something pretty unclear, something one sees shrouded in darkness, where you project the same things as in dreams: that is where the cliché becomes true.

What about Straub?

That's another sort of fascination, which is not contradicted by the intellectual tension he requires, but on the contrary is connected to it – actually very similar to the great amount of work we sometimes do in a dream in order to follow it. But fantasy is not necessarily fascination; it can have lots of dimensions.

What's certain is that we are attacking a whole conception of the cinema based on communication and ease of communication.

Which is actually theatre. It is admirable, but I believe it's incompatible with what the cinema is becoming; literally, in any case.

But in American cinema there's an abundance of examples – Lubitsch, the Chaplin

of Verdoux – *based on the fact that you could tell people things while seeming to tell them something else.*
Maybe it's everything which, for the time being, seems to be impossible, not because it was harmful or bad in itself, but because it has been co-opted; it's become docile. [. . .]

Translated by Amy Gateff

Notes

1 The whole of the interview is translated in Jonathan Rosenbaum, *Rivette: Texts and Interviews*, London, British Film Institute, 1977, from which these extracts are taken.
2 Jean Aurenche and Pierre Bost, French scriptwriters, now perhaps better known for Truffaut's attack on them in 'Une Certaine Tendance du cinéma français', *Cahiers* 31, January 1954, translated as 'A Certain Tendency of the French Cinema' in Nichols, *Movies and Methods*. Among the scripts they collaborated on were *La Symphonie pastorale* (Delannoy, 1946), *Le Diable au corps* (Autant-Lara, 1947), *Au-delà des grilles* (Clément, 1949), *L'Auberge rouge* (Autant-Lara, 1951), *Jeux interdits* (Clément, 1952), *Le Rouge et le noir* (Autant-Lara, 1954), *Le Blé en herbe* (Autant-Lara, 1954), *Gervaise* (Clément, 1956), *La Traversée de Paris* (Autant-Lara, 1956), *En cas de malheur* (Autant-Lara, 1958).
3 Philippe Garrel: young, avant-garde French film-maker, much valued by *Cahiers* at this time; Garrel was one of the four French film-makers featured in the special issue of *Cahiers*, no. 204, September 1968, devoted to 'Quatre cinéastes français', along with Rivette (this is the issue containing the present interview), Jean-Daniel Pollet and Marc'O.
4 *Terra em Transe*, directed by Glauber Rocha, 1967.
5 *La Rentrée des usines Wonder*, 1968, is discussed by Jean-Louis Comolli in his article on the influence of *direct* cinema, 'Le détour par le direct' I & II, *Cahiers* 209, 211, February and April 1969, extracts of which are translated in Williams, *Realism and the Cinema*; additionally, Comolli and Jean Narboni cite the film as one belonging to category (g) – 'live cinema' but one which 'attacks the basic problem of depiction by giving an active role to the concrete stuff of (the) film' – in their editorial 'Cinéma/Idéologie/Critique (1)', *Cahiers* 216, October 1969, translated as 'Cinema/Ideology/Criticism (1)' in *Screen*, vol. 12, no. 1, Spring 1971, reprinted in *Screen Reader 1* and Nichols, *Movies and Methods*.
6 Flins and Saint-Nazaire: two major factories where there were strikes and sit-ins in May 1968.
7 *L'Humanité*: the daily newspaper published by the French Communist Party.

39 | Sylvie Pierre, Jean-Louis Comolli: 'Two Faces of *Faces*'

('Deux visages de *Faces*', *Cahiers du Cinéma* 205, October 1968)

1 Around the void

Faces is about the faces which are constantly being scanned by the probings of a hyper-attentive camera. Faces which make faces when they set into ridiculous or unhappy expressions. We know very little about the characters behind the faces – the investigation is only concerned, precisely, with what their faces betray: excitement, desire, fatigue. Nuances of mood or fine psychological distinctions do not enter into it (which is perhaps why it is hard to think of the film in any other format than blown up 16mm).

Which is also why the film gives the impression of being a thorough investigation which, however, uncovers nothing at all; the film's subtle probings proceed apace, but the frequent irruptions of violence (divorce, suicide) are left unexplained. It seems such a scandal that the spectator begins to think that whole scenes are missing, in particular that of the suicide – how did it happen? and why?

What, in our view, is so fine about Cassavetes' film is that it makes us aware of one of the weaknesses of the cinema: its right and proper inability to explain the inner world, since all it can literally grasp are external signs, as being not unrelated to inner turmoil. As if the silence to which the inner world has been relegated by any self-respecting cinema were the background against which a cry, silent in the echo of its own emptiness, could issue forth.

Like films by Godard, Straub and Lefèbvre, *Faces* is one of the great films of emptiness, heart-rending, as for all its dizzy emphasis on the external it gets drawn into the most unsettling of inner worlds. Which could be defined, in this case, as the total loss of direction experienced by the individual American. The various bouts of vertigo, nausea, depression or madness, leading up to or following on from drunkenness that we see in this film might well be regarded as discreet metaphors for this malaise. Except that there is nothing to literally authorize such generalizations

324

about the film's symbolic meaning. What we most admire about the film is that it has borrowed from the effects of alcohol – heightened awareness and lucidity, moments of emotion and flashes of insight – the very form, unsteady and rigorous, of its poetry.

Sylvie Pierre

2 Back to back

A project – that of *Faces* – which involves the same team and the same community for three years, which is the interlocking point of so many lives and adventures, which becomes, if we are to believe one of the team, Cassavetes, as much a part of, as necessary to each of the participants as the air he breathes, such a project distinguishes itself immediately as being radically different from the models which normally regulate the conception and elaboration of films. Indeed, the cinema offers few examples (Rouch, Perrault, Rivette) of an approach which follows the rhythms of daily life so very closely that it soon becomes impossible to draw the line (if indeed such a line still exists) between film and non-film.

For the same reasons, a change of some importance comes about in the very nature of the work: the preparation and the shooting of the film no longer define, as is usually the case, a *reserved area* in space-time, a privileged enclave, protected and as it were disinfected, at all events more or less successfully kept away from possible contamination by the real world and the laws of society; the film is no longer that *representation* of itself which society not only authorizes but encourages, not innocently either, even when it seems to be putting obstacles in the way and showing disapproval; that critical examination of which the cinema is capable is no longer being conducted from the 'correct' vantage point, from the 'right' distance, as defined in the rules – hence, all too often, an illusory distance and criticism, non-existent and ineffective.

On the contrary, in a film like *Faces*, where film time and lived time merge, where the actors/authors (character-making characters) are making the film and leading their lives all at once, the rules of this *society game* which is what the cinema is nine times out of ten are broken from the word go. Also violated by this new breed of film poacher are the frontiers, barriers and prohibitions which seek to make the cinema into some kind of isolated area dominated by the false idea that 'everything is possible', a miniature version of the 'real' world, a private hunting ground where, according to convention, only blank shots are fired. Let us say that *Faces* no longer lends itself to the role traditionally assigned to the cinema by the 'spectator society', that of a mirror declared to be 'impartial' – that is to say, in reality, completely determined by the object it reflects. What the film sends back to society is no longer a more or less faithful image of itself, but something quite different: a partial and biased view.

Faces might have been, like so many other American films, a more or less complacent reflection of American lower middle-class life: by virtue, however, of its narrative principles, themselves linked to the principles which underlie the shooting, it rejects the descriptive function habitually allotted to the cinema. The lows and occasional highs of four ordinary Americans, city-based men and women, are not described in so far as they are not the fictional reproduction of actions or gestures which have or might have already taken place in an elsewhere supposed to be more 'real' than the film, and on which the film would attempt to model its realism. In a number of ways, through the time involved in the making of the film, the use of amateur actors and the disorienting effect, both cinematographic and economic, of the 16 mm format, it is the movement of the film itself which *produces* the behaviour patterns, the relationships, the fiction and the characters. The latter, as they get worked up, shout, laugh and above all talk on the screen, are not pretending to replicate the sound and fury of an existence or story which exists outside the film, they are not miming anything for the purposes of the spectacle; nor are they small-scale models of their contemporaries and fellows, and nor is the film a parable or a fable.

Caught in the film as in the very trap of their existence and subject to its rhythm, the characters in *Faces* are not stock characters; they are not predetermined, or put there once and for all, arbitrarily, at the beginning of the film; rather, they define themselves gesture by gesture and word by word as the film proceeds. That is to say that they are self-creating – the shooting is the means whereby they are revealed, each step forward in the film allowing them a new development in their behaviour, their time span coinciding exactly with that of the film. Once that is the case, cinematographic realism is out of the question: called into being by film, moulded by the peculiarities of the shooting and of the project in general, the characters – who are the one and only source of the fiction – no longer refer to some plausible real-life situation, of which they would be the more or less respectful representation; they are coherent and plausible only in relation to themselves, and in the context of the film itself. Certainly, there is nothing we see on the screen which has not also happened 'in real life', but 'in real life', in this case, means in front of the camera and through the camera. Cassavetes and his friends do not use the cinema as a way of reproducing actions, gestures, faces or ideas, but as a way of *producing* them. We start from scratch, they say: the cinema is the motor, the film is what causes each event to happen and to be remembered.

This kind of *spontaneous writing* in film is based, in *Faces*, on the extreme mobility of the cameras and framings on the one hand, and of speech on the other. The use of two cameras, which does away with the notion of 'linking up', immediately creates the impression of a natural continuity in space and time, a space-time in perpetual expansion, such that you have the sensation not only of fluidity but also of speed: the variations in scale of the shots, the changes of angle do not break up the movements of the characters but emphasize them, add to their mobility and variety, keep the momentum going and increase it, so that through the combination and multiplication of these two mobilities (within and between frames) a general movement of the film is created which gives the impression of itself creating, through its own means, the individual movements which make it up. It is as if the rhythm of the film were self-generating, once the initial thrust is given and the momentum established. In this way, as far as the development of the fiction is concerned, a purely formal logic (relating to sequences of movements) is substituted for the psychological scheme which the characters' behaviour would otherwise not have failed to introduce into the film.

The other thing that flows continually in *Faces* and brings the film to life is speech. Here again, the film works in terms of escalation and chain effects, in this case a never-ending stream of phrases, a free-wheeling mode of discourse which soon robs words of their points of reference, which makes the *meaning* of words less important than the way in which they are spoken and the patterns they create, so that what might have been a film about faces and gestures is also in the end a film about the wanderings of speech, about a time span occupied by speech and movement, that is to say, a cinematographic time.

Translated by Annwyl Williams

Note

1 Comolli pursues his thinking about *Faces* and other films in which he sees 'a certain tendency of modern cinema . . . an increasingly apparent recourse – in the "fiction" film – to the modes of *direct cinema*', in 'Le détour par le direct', I & II, *Cahiers* 209, 211, February and April 1969, extracts of which are translated in Williams, *Realism and the Cinema*, pp. 225–43.

Appendix 1

Cahiers du Cinéma Annual Best Films Listings 1960–8

Do annual best films lists serve any useful critical purpose? For *Cahiers du Cinéma* they often had a polemical edge, designed to express particular tastes and priorities and to generate debate. The composite listings reproduced here can function as a useful indicator of broadly shared tastes and values at *Cahiers*, although they inevitably even out some areas of dispute, particularly in the early 1960s. As the listings show, nevertheless, tastes and values changed markedly between 1960 and 1968. The most obvious change from the annual lists in the 1950s, published in Volume 1, is the prominence given to American cinema: mainstream American films become very scarce in the lists by 1967–8, and the commitment of *Cahiers* to 'new cinema' is correspondingly clear.

The lists reproduced here were arrived at by compiling individual ten best lists. Individual lists were contributed by regular *Cahiers* critics of the time, not a consistent group in the 1960–8 period but one including at different times, for example, Jacques Bontemps, Jean-Louis Comolli, Serge Daney, Michel Delahaye, Jean Domarchi, Jean Douchet, Jean-André Fieschi, Gérard Guégan, Fereydoun Hoveyda, André S. Labarthe, Louis Marcorelles, Michel Mardore, Luc Moullet, Jean Narboni, Claude Ollier, Jacques Rivette, Eric Rohmer, André Téchiné, François Weyergans. Lists from regular critics like these were supplemented by lists from former *Cahiers* critics, now mostly film-makers but still occasional contributors to *Cahiers* and strongly associated with it, for example, Alexandre Astruc, Claude Chabrol, Jacques Doniol-Valcroze, Jean-Luc Godard, Pierre Kast, François Truffaut, and later, of course, Rivette, Rohmer, Moullet. In addition individual listings would represent film theoreticians and historians who contributed occasionally to *Cahiers* (for example, Henri Agel, Raymond Bellour, Noël Burch, Christian Metz, Jean Mitry, Georges Sadoul), critics from other journals (for example, Robert Benayoun, Michel Ciment, Roger Tailleur, Bertrand Tavernier, all associated with *Positif*, or Pierre Marcabru, Henry Chapier, and others) and sympathetic film-makers – a shifting group which included at various times, for example, René Allio, Bernardo Bertolucci, Mag Bodard, Pierre Braunberger, Jacques Demy, Jean Eustache, Marcel Hanoun, Alain Jessua, Jean-Pierre Melville, Jean-Daniel Pollet, Alain Resnais, Jacques Rozier, Agnès Varda. The principle on which lists were solicited seems to have remained essentially as explained in *Cahiers* 67, January

1957: these were not exactly '*Cahiers* lists', nor lists representative of all critics; the choice of contributors corresponded to 'the desire to reach a certain objectivity by including in it several tendencies but excluding those which were frankly anti-*Cahiers*. A list of friends, then, but often disagreeing with us . . . and among themselves'.

The lists are reproduced as published in *Cahiers* each year, of varying lengths. The titles used for non-English language films are those in most common use in Britain and the USA.

1960 (Cahiers 117, March 1961)
1 *Sansho Dayu* (Kenji Mizoguchi, Japan, 1954)
2 *L'Avventura* (Michelangelo Antonioni, Italy, 1960)
3 *A bout de souffle* (Jean-Luc Godard, France, 1960)
4 *Tirez sur le pianiste* (François Truffaut, France, 1960)
5 *Poem of the Sea* (Alexander Dovzhenko/Julia Solntseva, USSR, 1958)
6 *Les Bonnes femmes* (Claude Chabrol, France, 1960)
  Nazarin (Luis Buñuel, Mexico, 1959)
8 *Moonfleet* (Fritz Lang, USA, 1955)
9 *Psycho* (Alfred Hitchcock, USA, 1960)
10 *Le Trou* (Jacques Becker, France, 1960)
11 *Zazie dans le métro* (Louis Malle, France, 1960)
12 *Party Girl* (Nicholas Ray, USA, 1959)
13 *Le Testament d'Orphée* (Jean Cocteau, France, 1960)
14 *Pather Panchali* (Satyajit Ray, India, 1955)
15 *Time Without Pity* (Joseph Losey, GB, 1956)
  Les Yeux sans visage (Georges Franju, France, 1960)
17 *La Dolce Vita* (Federico Fellini, Italy, 1960)
18 *Heller in Pink Tights* (George Cukor, USA, 1960)
  The Bells Are Ringing (Vincente Minnelli, USA, 1960)
  Suddenly, Last Summer (Joseph L. Mankiewicz, USA, 1959)

1961 (Cahiers 129, March 1962)
1 *Lola* (Jacques Demy, France, 1961)
2 *Une Femme est une femme* (Jean-Luc Godard, France, 1961)
3 *Paris nous appartient* (Jacques Rivette, France, 1960)
4 *Rocco and his Brothers* (Luchino Visconti, Italy, 1960)
5 *Shin Heike Monogatari* (Kenji Mizoguchi, Japan, 1955)
6 *At Great Cost/The Horse that Cried* (Mark Donskoi, USSR, 1957)
7 *La Notte* (Michelangelo Antonioni, Italy, 1961)
8 *L'Année dernière à Marienbad* (Alain Resnais, France, 1961)
9 *Elmer Gantry* (Richard Brooks, USA, 1960)
10 *Two Rode Together* (John Ford, USA, 1962)
11 *Le Testament du Dr Cordelier* (Jean Renoir, France, 1961)
12 *Exodus* (Otto Preminger, USA, 1960)
13 *The Criminal* (USA: *Concrete Jungle*) (Joseph Losey, GB, 1960)
14 *La Pyramide humaine* (Jean Rouch, France, 1959)
15 *Shadows* (John Cassavetes, USA, 1961)
16 *Die Tausend Augen des Dr Mabuse* (Fritz Lang, West Germany-France-Italy, 1960)
17 *The Young One/Island of Shame* (Luis Buñuel, Mexico, 1961)
18 *Saturday Night and Sunday Morning* (Karel Reisz, GB, 1960)

19 *Une aussi longue absence* (Henri Colpi, France, 1961)
20 *The Lady with the Little Dog* (Josef Heifitz, USSR, 1960)
21 *The Island* (Kaneto Shindo, Japan, 1961)
22 *Les Godelureaux* (Claude Chabrol, France, 1961)
23 *The Bellboy* (Jerry Lewis, USA, 1960)
24 *Léon Morin, prêtre* (Jean-Pierre Melville, France, 1961)
25 *Blind Date* (USA: *Chance Meeting*) (Joseph Losey, GB, 1959)
26 *Pickup on South Street* (Samuel Fuller, USA, 1953)
27 *Description d'un combat* (Chris Marker, France-Israel, 1960)
28 *Mother Joan of the Angels* (Jerzy Kawalerowicz, Poland, 1960)
29 *La Maschera del demonio/Black Sunday* (Mario Bava, Italy, 1961)
30 *Era notte a Roma* (Roberto Rossellini, Italy, 1960)
31 *Dov'è la libertà?* (Roberto Rossellini, Italy, 1953)
32 *Underworld USA* (Samuel Fuller, USA, 1961)
33 *Judgment at Nuremberg* (Stanley Kramer, USA, 1961)
34 *L'Enclos* (Armand Gatti, France-Yugoslavia, 1961)
35 *Chronique d'un été* (Jean Rouch-Edgar Morin, France, 1961)

1962 (Cahiers 141, March 1963)
 1 *Vivre sa vie* (Jean-Luc Godard, France, 1962)
 2 *Jules et Jim* (François Truffaut, France, 1961)
 3 *Hatari!* (Howard Hawks, USA, 1962)
 4 *Viridiana* (Luis Buñuel, Spain, 1961)
 5 *Le Signe du Lion* (Eric Rohmer, France, 1959)
 6 *Wild River* (Elia Kazan, USA, 1960)
 7 *The Trial* (Orson Welles, France-Italy-West Germany, 1962)
 8 *Through a Glass Darkly* (Ingmar Bergman, Sweden, 1961)
 9 *Le Caporal épinglé* (Jean Renoir, France, 1962)
10 *Vanina Vanini* (Roberto Rossellini, Italy, 1961)
11 *Advise and Consent* (Otto Preminger, USA, 1962)
12 *Cléo de 5 à 7* (Agnès Varda, France, 1962)
13 *Ride the High Country* (UK: *Guns in the Afternoon*) (Sam Peckinpah, USA, 1962)
14 *Education sentimentale* (Alexandre Astruc, France, 1962)
15 *The Ladies' Man* (Jerry Lewis, USA, 1961)
   The Man Who Shot Liberty Valance (John Ford, USA, 1962)
17 *West Side Story* (Robert Wise/Jerome Robbins, USA, 1961)
18 *L'Eclisse* (Michelangelo Antonioni, Italy, 1962)
19 *Splendor in the Grass* (Elia Kazan, USA, 1961)
20 *The Flaming Years* (Julia Solntseva, USSR, 1961)
21 *Merrill's Marauders* (Samuel Fuller, USA, 1962)
22 *Boccaccio '70*: episode *Il Lavoro* (*The Job*) (Luchino Visconti, Italy, 1962)
23 *The Miracle Worker* (Arthur Penn, USA, 1962)
24 *Adorable menteuse* (Michel Deville, France, 1961)
25 *The Four Horsemen of the Apocalypse* (Vincente Minnelli, USA, 1962)
26 *Un coeur gros comme ça* (François Reichenbach, France, 1961)
27 *Le Rendez-vous de minuit* (Roger Leenhardt, France, 1962)
28 *Primary* (Richard Leacock/Don Pennebaker, USA, 1960)
29 *Les Honneurs de la guerre* (Jean Dewever, France, 1960)
30 *Too Late Blues* (John Cassavetes, USA, 1962)

1963 (Cahiers 153, March 1964)
1 *Le Mépris* (Jean-Luc Godard, France, 1963)
2 *The Birds* (Alfred Hitchcock, USA, 1963)
3 *The Exterminating Angel* (Luis Buñuel, Mexico, 1962)
4 *Adieu Philippine* (Jacques Rozier, France, 1963)
5 *Le Procès de Jeanne d'Arc* (Robert Bresson, France, 1962)
6 *Muriel* (Alain Resnais, France, 1963)
7 *The Nutty Professor* (Jerry Lewis, USA, 1963)
8 *Les Carabiniers* (Jean-Luc Godard, France, 1963)
9 *Salvatore Giuliano* (Francesco Rosi, Italy, 1962)
10 *8½* (Federico Fellini, Italy, 1963)
11 *Banditi a Orgosolo* (Vittorio de Seta, Italy, 1961)
Il Gattopardo/The Leopard (Luchino Visconti, Italy, 1963)
13 *Donovan's Reef* (John Ford, USA, 1963)
14 *The Chapman Report* (George Cukor, USA, 1962)
15 *Harakiri* (Masaka Kobayashi, Japan, 1962)
16 *The World of Apu* (Satyajit Ray, India, 1959)
17 *Cronaca familiare* (Valerio Zurlini, Italy, 1962)
18 *Le Mani sulla città/Hands Over the City* (Francesco Rosi, Italy, 1963)
19 *Cleopatra* (Joseph L. Mankiewicz, USA, 1963)
20 *The Cardinal* (Otto Preminger, USA, 1963)
21 *Two Weeks in Another Town* (Vincente Minnelli, USA, 1962)
Le Petit soldat (Jean-Luc Godard, France, 1963)
23 *Le Feu follet* (Louis Malle, France, 1963)
Nine Days of One Year (Mikhail Romm, USSR, 1962)
25 *Les Abysses* (Nico Papatakis, France, 1963)
Il Posto (Ermanno Olmi, Italy, 1961)
27 *This Sporting Life* (Lindsay Anderson, GB, 1963)
28 *La Baie des Anges* (Jacques Demy, France, 1963)
Tom Jones (Tony Richardson, GB, 1963)
30 *Irma la Douce* (Billy Wilder, USA, 1963)
31 *Knife in the Water* (Roman Polanski, Poland, 1962)
32 *Il Sorpasso* (Dino Risi, Italy, 1962)
33 *The Errand Boy* (Jerry Lewis, USA, 1961)
34 *Le Joli Mai* (Chris Marker, France, 1963)
35 *Vacances portugaises* (Pierre Kast, France, 1963)

1964 (Cahiers 165, April 1965)
1 *Bande à part* (Jean-Luc Godard, France, 1964)
2 *Gertrud* (Carl T. Dreyer, Denmark, 1964)
3 *Marnie* (Alfred Hitchcock, USA, 1964)
4 *Une Femme mariée* (Jean-Luc Godard, France, 1964)
5 *Man's Favorite Sport?* (Howard Hawks, USA, 1964)
6 *Il Deserto Rosso* (Michelangelo Antonioni, Italy, 1964)
7 *America, America* (UK: *The Anatolian Smile*) (Elia Kazan, USA, 1963)
8 *The Silence* (Ingmar Bergman, Sweden, 1963)
9 *Now About these Women* (Ingmar Bergman, Sweden, 1964)
10 *The Servant* (Joseph Losey, GB, 1963)
11 *Les Parapluies de Cherbourg* (Jacques Demy, France, 1964)
12 *La Peau douce* (François Truffaut, France, 1964)

13 *Wagonmaster* (John Ford, USA, 1950)
14 *Passenger* (Andrzej Munk, Poland, 1963)
15 *The Patsy* (Jerry Lewis, USA, 1964)
16 *A Distant Trumpet* (Raoul Walsh, USA, 1964)
17 *I Fidanzati* (Ermanno Olmi, Italy, 1963)
18 *Thomas Gordeyev* (Mark Donskoi, USSR, 1959)
19 *Dr Strangelove, or How I Learned to Stop Worrying and Love the Bomb* (Stanley Kubrick, USA, 1964)
20 *The Damned* (Joseph Losey, GB, 1961)
21 *Pour la suite du monde* (Pierre Perrault, Michel Brault, Canada, 1962)
22 *La Jetée* (Chris Marker, France, 1962)
23 *My Fair Lady* (George Cukor, USA, 1964)
24 *Il Terrorista* (Gianfranco de Bosio, Italy, 1963)
25 *David and Lisa* (Frank Perry, USA, 1962)
26 *La Punition* (Jean Rouch, France, 1963)
27 *Le Journal d'une femme de chambre* (Luis Buñuel, France-Italy, 1964)
28 *Il Tempo si è fermato/Time Stood Still* (Ermanno Olmi, Italy, 1959)
29 *The Cool World* (Shirley Clarke, USA, 1963)
30 *La Bataille de France* (Jean Aurel, France, 1964)
31 *Woman of the Dunes* (Hiroshi Teshigahara, Japan, 1964)
32 *Cheyenne Autumn* (John Ford, USA, 1964)
33 *Cyrano et d'Artagnan* (Abel Gance, France, 1963)
34 *A Hard Day's Night* (Richard Lester, GB, 1964)
35 *The Hidden Fortress* (Akira Kurosawa, Japan, 1958)

1965 (Cahiers 175, February 1966)
 1 *Pierrot le fou* (Jean-Luc Godard, France, 1965)
 2 *Vaghe stelle dell'Orsa/Sandra/Of a Thousand Delights* (Luchino Visconti, Italy, 1965)
 3 *Winter Light/The Communicants* (Ingmar Bergman, Sweden, 1963)
 4 *Paris vu par . . .* (*Gare du Nord* episode) (Jean Rouch, France, 1965)
 5 *Alphaville* (Jean-Luc Godard, France, 1965)
 6 *Lilith* (Robert Rossen, USA, 1964)
 7 *Shock Corridor* (Samuel Fuller, USA, 1963)
 8 *The Family Jewels* (Jerry Lewis, USA, 1965)
 9 *The Gospel According to St Matthew* (Pier Paolo Pasolini, Italy, 1964)
10 *Le Bonheur* (Agnès Varda, France, 1965)
11 *L'Amour à la chaîne* (Claude de Givray, France, 1964)
12 *Peter and Pavla/Black Peter* (Milos Forman, Czechoslovakia, 1964)
13 *The Enchanted Desna* (Julia Solntseva, USSR, 1965)
14 *La Vieille Dame indigne* (René Allio, France, 1964)
15 *Kiss Me Stupid* (Billy Wilder, USA, 1964)
16 *Paris vu par . . .* (*Place de l'Etoile* episode) (Eric Rohmer, France, 1965)
17 *A High Wind in Jamaica* (Alexander Mackendrick, GB, 1965)
18 *La 317e Section* (Pierre Schoendorffer, France, 1964)
19 *Young Cassidy* (John Ford/Jack Cardiff, USA, 1965)
20 *The Disorderly Orderly* (Frank Tashlin, USA, 1964)
21 *Paris vu par . . .* (*La Muette* episode) (Claude Chabrol, France, 1965)
22 *In Harm's Way* (Otto Preminger, USA, 1965)
23 *Giulietta degli Spiriti/Juliet of the Spirits* (Federico Fellini, Italy, 1965)
24 *Memetih/The Blizzard* (Vladimir Bassov, USSR, 1964)

25 *Vidas Secas* (Nelson Pereira Dos Santos, Brazil, 1964)
26 *The Sandpiper* (Vincente Minnelli, USA, 1965)
27 *King and Country* (Joseph Losey, GB, 1964)
28 *Paris vu par . . .* (*Montparnasse-Levallois* episode) (Jean-Luc Godard, France, 1965)
29 *Le Journal d'une femme en blanc* (Claude Autant-Lara, France, 1965)
30 *A Shot in the Dark* (Blake Edwards, USA, 1964)

1966 (Cahiers 187, February 1967)
 1 *Au hasard Balthazar* (Robert Bresson, France, 1966)
 2 *Walkover* (Jerzy Skolimowski, Poland, 1965)
 3 *Nicht versöhnt/Not Reconciled* (Jean-Marie Straub, West Germany, 1965)
 4 *Masculin féminin* (Jean-Luc Godard, France, 1966)
 5 *L'Homme au crâne rasé/The Man Who Had His Hair Cut Short* (André Delvaux, Belgium, 1966)
 6 *Seven Women* (John Ford, USA, 1966)
 7 *La Prise de pouvoir par Louis XIV* (Roberto Rossellini, France, 1966)
 8 *Torn Curtain* (Alfred Hitchcock, USA, 1966)
 9 *Red Line 7000* (Howard Hawks, USA, 1965)
10 *I Pugni in Tasca/Fists in the Pocket* (Marco Bellocchio, Italy, 1966)
11 *Chimes at Midnight* (Orson Welles, Spain-Switzerland, 1966)
12 *La Guerre est finie* (Alain Resnais, France, 1966)
13 *The Naked Kiss* (Samuel Fuller, USA, 1965)
14 *Fahrenheit 451* (François Truffaut, GB, 1966)
15 *Le Père Noël a les yeux bleus* (Jean Eustache, France, 1965)
16 *Marie Soleil* (Antoine Bourseiller, France, 1966)
17 *About Something Else/Something Different* (Vera Chytilova, Czechoslovakia, 1962)
18 *A Blonde in Love/Loves of a Blonde* (Milos Forman, Czechoslovakia, 1965)
19 *Le Chat dans le sac* (Gilles Groulx, Canada, 1964)
20 *Brigitte et Brigitte* (Luc Moullet, France, 1966)

1967 (Cahiers 199, March 1968)
 1 *Persona* (Ingmar Bergman, Sweden, 1966)
 2 *Belle de jour* (Luis Buñuel, France, 1967)
 3 *Week-End* (Jean-Luc Godard, France, 1967)
 4 *La Chasse au lion à l'arc* (Jean Rouch, France, 1965)
 5 *Playtime* (Jacques Tati, France, 1967)
 6 *The Big Mouth* (Jerry Lewis, USA, 1967)
 7 *Daisies* (Vera Chytilova, Czechoslovakia, 1966)
   La Religieuse (Jacques Rivette, France, 1965)
 9 *Deux ou trois choses que je suis d'elle* (Jean-Luc Godard, France, 1967)
10 *La Chinoise* (Jean-Luc Godard, France, 1967)
11 *Made in USA* (Jean-Luc Godard, France, 1967)
12 *Shakespeare Wallah* (James Ivory, India, 1965)
13 *Oz Fuzis/The Guns* (Ruy Guerra, Brazil, 1964)
14 *Méditerranée* (Jean-Daniel Pollet, France, 1963)
15 *The Countess from Hong Kong* (Charles Chaplin, GB, 1967)
16 *The First Teacher* (Andrei Mikhalov-Konchalovsky, USSR, 1965)
17 *Le Départ* (Jerzy Skolimowski, Belgium, 1967)
18 *La Collectionneuse* (Eric Rohmer, France, 1967)

19 *Blow-Up* (Michelangelo Antonioni, GB/Italy, 1966)
   Les Demoiselles de Rochefort (Jacques Demy, France, 1967)

1968 (Cahiers 211, April 1969)
 1 *Chronik der Anna Magdalena Bach* (Jean-Marie Straub, West Germany, 1968)
 2 *Prima della Rivoluzione/Before the Revolution* (Bernardo Bertolucci, Italy, 1964)
 3 *The Edge* (Robert Kramer, USA, 1968)
 4 *Histoires extraordinaires/Spirits of the Dead* (episode *Toby Dammit/Never Bet the Devil Your Head*) (Federico Fellini, France-Italy, 1968)
 5 *Il ne faut pas mourir pour ça/Don't Let it Kill You* (Jean-Pierre Lefèbvre, Canada, 1966)
 6 *Le Règne du jour* (Pierre Perrault, Canada, 1967)
 7 *Barrier* (Jerzy Skolimowski, Poland, 1966)
 8 *Baisers volés* (François Truffaut, France, 1968)
 9 *Ride in the Whirlwind* (Monte Hellman, USA, 1966)
10 *La Mariée était en noir* (François Truffaut, France, 1968)
   Les Contrebandières (Luc Moullet, France, 1967)
12 *Oedipus Rex* (Pier Paolo Pasolini, Italy, 1967)
13 *2001: A Space Odyssey* (Stanley Kubrick, USA, 1968)
14 *Hour of the Wolf* (Ingmar Bergman, Sweden, 1968)
15 *Rosemary's Baby* (Roman Polanski, USA, 1968)
16 *Point Blank* (John Boorman, USA, 1967)
   Les Idoles (Marc 'O, France, 1967)
18 *Un soir un train* (André Delvaux, Belgium, 1968)
19 *Reflections in a Golden Eye* (John Huston, USA, 1967)
20 *Bonnie and Clyde* (Arthur Penn, USA, 1967)

Appendix 2

Guide to *Cahiers du Cinéma* Nos 103–207, January 1960–December 1968, in English translation

There is no comprehensive record of material from *Cahiers du Cinéma* which has been translated into English. This appendix offers, both for further reading and as a research resource, a tentative listing of such material which is nevertheless as comprehensive as it has been possible to make it. The editor would welcome additional entries from readers.

The material listed here is rather different from the translated material in the period 1951–9 (in Volume 1), which was scattered over many different publications. A large amount of the translated material in the period 1960–8 comes from the two years 1966–7 and was published in *Cahiers du Cinéma in English* (published in New York, with Andrew Sarris as editor). *Cahiers du Cinéma in English* (which folded after twelve issues) published some retrospective *Cahiers* material from the 1950s (see, for example, entries in Appendix 2 in Volume 1 under Astruc, Bazin, Chabrol, Leenhardt, Ophuls, Truffaut), including one example of pre-*Cahiers* writing from *La Revue du Cinéma* (Jean-George Auriol's 'Chez Ernst', on Lubitsch, from *La Revue du Cinéma*, September 1948), but the concentration was on fairly current *Cahiers* material in 1966–7. This has the value of giving the flavour, in English, of what a typical issue of *Cahiers* in 1966–7 looked like, including examples of minor news items (from the regular 'Petit Journal du Cinéma' section, rendered in English as 'Odds and Ends'), the monthly film release guide ('Le Conseil des Dix', rendered as 'The Council of Ten'). This flavour is somewhat marred by the overall quality of translation, which leaves much to be desired: material often quite difficult in the original becomes too often much more difficult to understand (and considerably less elegant) in these English translations.

Book and journal references are given in full in each entry except for a few books which are cited frequently and are therefore given in abbreviated form. Details of these are:

Godard on Godard:
Godard, Jean-Luc, *Godard on Godard* (edited and translated by Tom Milne), London, Secker & Warburg, 1972; New York, Viking, 1972.
Caughie, *Theories of Authorship*:

Caughie, John (ed.) *Theories of Authorship: A Reader*, London and Boston, Routledge & Kegan Paul, 1981.
Sarris, *Interviews with Film Directors*:
Sarris, Andrew (ed.), *Interviews with Film Directors*, New York, Bobbs-Merrill, 1967.

ALLIO, René
'Deux arts en un: René Allio et Antoine Bourseiller répondent à Jean-Luc Godard et Michel Delahaye' (interview/discussion) in *Cahiers* 177 (April 1966)
trans. as 'Allio-Bourseiller-Godard-Delahaye: Two Arts in One' in *Cahiers du Cinéma in English*, no. 6, December 1966.

ANTONIONI, Michelangelo
'La nuit, l'eclipse, l'aurore: entretien avec Michelangelo Antonioni par Jean-Luc Godard' in *Cahiers* 160 (November 1964)
trans. as 'Jean-Luc Godard interviews Michelangelo Antonioni' in *Movie*, no. 12, Spring 1965; as 'Night, Eclipse, Dawn . . .: an interview with Michelangelo Antonioni, by Jean-Luc Godard' in *Cahiers du Cinéma in English*, no. 1, January 1966, reprinted in Sarris, *Interviews with Film Directors*.

'Antonioni à la mode anglaise' (report and interview by Stig Björkman) (in 'Petit Journal') in *Cahiers* 186 (January 1967)
trans. as 'Stig Björkman: interview with Antonioni – English Style' in Antonioni, M., *Blow-Up*, London, Lorrimer Books, 1971; also in Huss, R. (ed.), *Focus on Blow-Up*, Englewood Cliffs, New Jersey, Prentice-Hall, 1971.

AUMONT, Jacques
'Petit lexique des termes lewisiens' (with Jean-Louis Comolli, André S. Labarthe, Jean Narboni, Sylvie Pierre) in *Cahiers* 197 (January 1968)
trans. as 'A Concise Lexicon of Lewisian Terms' in Johnston, C. and Willemen, P. (eds), *Frank Tashlin*, Edinburgh, Edinburgh Film Festival in association with *Screen*, 1973.

'Entretien avec Jacques Rivette' (Aumont with Jean-Louis Comolli, Jean Narboni, Sylvie Pierre) in *Cahiers* 204 (September 1968)
trans. as 'Time Overflowing: Interview with Jacques Rivette' in Rosenbaum, J. (ed.), *Rivette: Texts and Interviews*, London, British Film Institute, 1977; extract reprinted in this volume.

BELLOCCHIO, Marco
'La stérilité de la provocation' in *Cahiers* 177 (April 1966)
trans. as 'The Sterility of Provocation' in *Cahiers du Cinéma in English*, no. 7, January 1967.

BERGMAN, Ingmar
'La peau du serpent' in *Cahiers* 188 (March 1967)
trans. as 'The Serpent's Skin', in *Cahiers du Cinéma in English*, no. 11, September 1967.

BERKELEY, Busby
'Entretien, par Patrick Brion et René Gilson' in *Cahiers* 174 (January 1966)
trans. as 'Interview' in *Cahiers du Cinéma in English*, no. 2, 1966.

BERTOLUCCI, Bernardo
'Versus Godard' in *Cahiers* 186 (January 1967)
trans. as 'Versus Godard' in *Cahiers du Cinéma in English*, no. 10, May 1967.

BEYLIE, Claude
'Un testament olographe' in *Cahiers* 123 (September 1961)
trans. (extract) as 'On Le Testament du Dr Cordelier' in Leprohon, P., *Jean Renoir*,
New York, Crown, 1971.

BIETTE, Jean-Claude
'Situation du nouveau cinéma: sur "Echoes of Silence"' in *Cahiers* 188 (March 1967)
trans. as 'Echoes of Silence' in *Cahiers du Cinéma in English*, no. 11, September
1967.

BJÖRKMAN, Stig
See under Antonioni (*Cahiers* 186)

BLUE, James
See under Forman (*Cahiers* 174)

BONTEMPS, Jacques
'Le cahier des autres' in *Cahiers* 174 (January 1966)
trans. as 'Jottings from Other Publications' in *Cahiers du Cinéma in English*, no. 3,
1966.

'Du paradoxe au lieu commun' (on Polanski's *When Angels Fall*) in *Cahiers* 176
(March 1966)
trans. as 'Quand les anges tombent' in *Cahiers du Cinéma in English*, no. 4, 1966.

'Reminiscences' (on Robert Rossen) in *Cahiers* 177 (April 1966)
trans. as 'Reminiscences' in *Cahiers du Cinéma in English*, no. 7, January 1967.

'L'heure la plus jaune' (on Bourseiller's *Marie Soleil*) in *Cahiers* 177 (April 1966)
trans. as 'Marie Soleil' in *Cahiers du Cinéma in English*, no. 6, December 1966.

See under Mankiewicz (*Cahiers* 178)

'En marge de "Forty Guns"' in *Cahiers* 193 (September 1967)
trans. as 'Forty Guns' in Will, D. and Wollen, P. (eds), *Samuel Fuller*, Edinburgh,
Edinburgh Film Festival in association with *Scottish International Review*, 1969.

See under Godard (*Cahiers* 194)

'Une libre variation imaginative de certains faits' (on Godard's *La Chinoise*) in
Cahiers 194 (October 1967)
trans. as 'La Chinoise' in Cameron, I. (ed.), *The Films of Jean-Luc Godard*, London,
Studio Vista, 2nd ed. 1969.

BOURSEILLER, Antoine
'Deux arts en un: René Allio et Antoine Bourseiller répondent à Jean-Luc Godard
et Michel Delahaye' (interview/discussion) in *Cahiers* 177 (April 1966)
trans. as 'Allio-Bourseiller-Godard-Delahaye: Two Arts in One' in *Cahiers du Cinéma
in English*, no. 6, December 1966.

BRAULT, Michel
'Dix questions à cinq cinéastes canadiens' in *Cahiers* 176 (March 1976)
trans. as 'Ten Questions to Five Canadian Film Makers' in *Cahiers du Cinéma in English*, no. 4, 1966.

BRESSON, Robert
'Le testament de Balthazar: propos recueillis par M. Merleau-Ponty et Jean-Luc Godard' in *Cahiers* 177 (April 1966)
trans. as 'Testament of Balthazar' in *Cahiers du Cinéma in English*, no. 6, December 1966.

'La Question: entretien avec Robert Bresson par Jean-Luc Godard et Michel Delahaye' in *Cahiers* 178 (May 1966)
trans. as 'The Question: Interview with Bresson' in *Cahiers du Cinéma in English*, no. 8, February 1967.

BRION, Patrick
See under Berkeley (*Cahiers* 174)

Comden and Green: filmographie in *Cahiers* 174 (January 1966)
pub. in *Cahiers du Cinéma in English*, no. 2, 1966.

Robert Rossen: filmographie in *Cahiers* 177 (April 1966)
pub. in *Cahiers du Cinéma in English*, no. 7, January 1967.

Joseph L. Mankiewicz: biofilmographie in *Cahiers* 178 (May 1966)
pub. in *Cahiers du Cinéma in English*, no. 8, February 1967.

Elia Kazan: biofilmographie in *Cahiers* 184 (November 1966)
pub. in *Cahiers du Cinéma in English*, no. 9, March 1967.

Anthony Mann: biofilmographie (with Olivier Eyquem) in *Cahiers* 190 (May 1967)
pub. in *Cahiers du Cinéma in English*, no. 12, December 1967.

BUÑUEL, Luis
'Entretien avec Luis Buñuel' (1965) by Juan Cobos and Gonzalo S. J. de Erice and 'Post-scriptum' (interview, 1967) by M. Torres, Vicente Molina Foix, M. P. Estremara and C. R. Sanz, in *Cahiers* 191 (June 1967)
trans. as 'Two Interviews with Luis Buñuel' in Buñuel, L., *Belle de Jour*, London, Lorrimer Books, 1971.

BURCH, Noël
Series of 10 articles under the rubric 'Esthétique' in *Cahiers* 188–97 (March 1967–Christmas 1967/January 1968) collected into a book, *Praxis du cinéma* (Paris, Gallimard, 1969), trans. as *Theory of Film Practice*, London, Secker & Warburg, 1973;
Articles originally published as below (English translation designates chapter titles in *Theory of Film Practice*):
'Comment s'articule l'espace-temps' (*Cahiers* 188) ('Spatial and Temporal Articulations')
'"Nana" ou les deux espaces' (*Cahiers* 189) ('*Nana*, or the Two Kinds of Space')
'Plastique du montage' (*Cahiers* 190) ('Editing as a Plastic Art')
'Vers un cinéma dialectique (1): Répertoire des structures simples' (*Cahiers* 191) ('The Repertory of Simple Structures')

'Vers un cinéma dialectique (2): Absence de dialectique – Dialectiques complexes' (*Cahiers* 192) ('Absence of Dialectic and Complex Dialectics')
'Vers un cinéma dialectique (3): De l'usage structural du son' (*Cahiers* 193) ('On the Structural Use of Sound')
'Fonctions de l'aléa' (*Cahiers* 194) ('Chance and its Functions')
'Structures d'agression' (*Cahiers* 195) ('Structures of Aggression')
'Réflexions sur le sujet (1): Sujets de fiction' (*Cahiers* 196) ('Fictional Subjects')
'Réflexions sur le sujet (2): Sujets de non-fiction' (*Cahiers* 197) ('Nonfictional Subjects')

CAEN, Michel
'L'oeil du cyclone' (on Godard's *Pierrot le fou*) in *Cahiers* 174 (January 1966)
trans. as 'Pierrot le Fou' in *Cahiers du Cinéma in English*, no. 2, 1966.

'Victime et bourreau' (on Polanksi's *Repulsion*) in *Cahiers* 176 (March 1966)
trans. as 'Repulsion' in *Cahiers du Cinéma in English*, no. 4, 1966.

'Les temps changent' (on Resnais's *La Guerre est finie*) in *Cahiers* 179 (June 1966)
trans. as 'The Times Change' in *Cahiers du Cinéma in English*, no. 8, February 1967.

CAHIERS DU CINÉMA
'Les Etats Généraux du Cinéma Français I: Historique' in *Cahiers* 203 (August 1968)
trans. as 'The History' in Harvey, S., *May 68 and Film Culture*, London, British Film Institute, 1978.

'Les Etats Généraux du Cinéma Français II: Projets de Nouvelles Structures: L'ancien et le nouveau, projet 16; Projet 13; Projet 4; Projet 19; Projet de synthèse; Motion finale des Etats Généraux' in *Cahiers* 203 (August 1968)
trans. as 'Projects for New Structures: The General Line (The Old and the New), Project 16; Project 13; Project 4; Project 19; The "Synthesis" Project' in *Screen*, vol. 13, no. 4, Winter 1972–3.

COBOS, Juan
See Welles (*Cahiers* 165)

See Welles (*Cahiers* 179)

See Buñuel (*Cahiers* 191)

COLLET, Jean
'Les absences de Sandra' (on Visconti's *Vaghe stelle dell'Orsa/Of A Thousand Delights/ Sandra*) in *Cahiers* 174 (January 1966)
trans. as 'The Absences of Sandra' in *Cahiers du Cinéma in English*, no. 2, 1966.

'Le Cahier des Ciné-clubs' in *Cahiers* 174 (January 1966)
trans. as 'Notes on French Film Societies' in *Cahiers du Cinéma in English*, no. 3, 1966.

'Indiscrétions' (on Forman's *A Blonde in Love*) in *Cahiers* 176 (March 1966)
trans. as 'Indiscretions' in *Cahiers du Cinéma in English*, no. 8, February 1967.

COMDEN, Betty
'Comden et Green: Entretien par Jean-François Hauduroy' in *Cahiers* 174 (January 1966)
trans. as 'Interview' in *Cahiers du Cinéma in English*, no. 2, 1966.

COMOLLI, Jean-Louis
'Signes de piste' (on Ford's *Cheyenne Autumn*) in *Cahiers* 164 (March 1965)
trans. as 'Signposts on the trail' in Caughie, J., *Theories of Authorship*.

'A rebours?' (on Godard's *Alphaville*) in *Cahiers* 168 (July 1965)
trans. as 'Alphaville' in *Cahiers du Cinéma in English*, no. 3, 1966.

'Kaleidoscopie de Busby Berkeley' in *Cahiers* 174 (January 1966)
trans. as 'Dancing Images' in *Cahiers du Cinéma in English*, no. 2, 1966.

'Notes sur le nouveau spectateur' in *Cahiers* 177 (April 1966)
trans. as 'Notes on the New Spectator' in *Cahiers du Cinéma in English*, no. 7, January 1967; also in this volume (new translation).

'Une tempête au fond des yeux' (on Pollet's *Une balle au coeur*) in *Cahiers* 177 (April 1966)
trans. as 'Une balle au coeur' in *Cahiers du Cinéma in English*, no. 6, December 1966.

'Tous dans le même cul-de-sac' (on Malle's *Viva Maria* and Enrico's *Les Grandes gueules*) in *Cahiers* 177 (April 1966)
trans. as 'Viva Maria and Les Grandes Gueules' in *Cahiers du Cinéma in English*, no. 6, December 1966.

'Jack le Fataliste' (on Welles's *Chimes at Midnight*) in *Cahiers* 181 (August 1966)
trans. as 'Jack le Fataliste' in *Cahiers du Cinéma in English*, no. 11, September 1967.

'L'auteur, les masques, l'autre' (on Truffaut's *Fahrenheit 451*) in *Cahiers* 184 (November 1966)
trans. as 'The Auteur, the Masks, the Other' in *Cahiers du Cinéma in English*, no. 9, March 1967.

'Le Rideau soulevé, retombé' (on Hitchcock's *Torn Curtain*) in *Cahiers* 186 (January 1967)
trans. as 'The Curtain Lifted, Fallen Again' in *Cahiers du Cinéma in English*, no. 10, May 1967.

'Le médecin malgré lui' (on Lewis's *Three on a Couch*) in *Cahiers* 186 (January 1967)
trans. as 'Three on a Couch' in *Cahiers du Cinéma in English*, no. 11, September 1967.

'Le Fantôme de Personne' (on Bergman's *Persona*) in *Cahiers* 188 (March 1967)
trans. as 'The Phantom of Personality' in *Cahiers du Cinéma in English*, no. 11, September 1967.

'A l'assaut de l'image' (on *Le plus vieux métier du monde* and Godard's episode *Anticipation*) in *Cahiers* 191 (June 1967)
trans. as 'Anticipation' in Brown, R. (ed.), *Focus on Jean-Luc Godard*, Englewood Cliffs, N.J., Prentice-Hall, 1972.

'Le point sur l'image' (on Godard's *La Chinoise*) in *Cahiers* 194 (October 1967)
trans. as 'La Chinoise' in Cameron, I. (ed.), *The Films of Jean-Luc Godard*, London, Studio Vista, 2nd ed., 1969.

See under Penn (*Cahiers* 196)

'Petit lexique des termes lewisiens' (with Jacques Aumont, André S. Labarthe, Jean Narboni, Sylvie Pierre) in *Cahiers* 197 (January 1968)
trans. as 'A Concise Lexicon of Lewisian Terms' in Johnston, C. and Willemen, P. (eds), *Frank Tashlin*, Edinburgh, Edinburgh Film Festival in association with *Screen*, 1973.

See under Rivette (*Cahiers* 204)

DANEY, Serge
See under McCarey (*Cahiers* 163)

'Un rien sur fond de musique douce' (on Lewis's *The Family Jewels*) in *Cahiers* 175 (February 1966)
trans. as 'The Family Jewels' in *Cahiers du Cinéma in English*, no. 4, 1966.

'Les corps étrangers' (on Edwards's *The Great Race*) in *Cahiers* 175 (February 1966)
trans. as 'The Great Race' in *Cahiers du Cinéma in English*, no. 3, 1966.

'Welles au pouvoir' (on Welles's *Chimes at Midnight*) in *Cahiers* 181 (August 1966)
trans. as 'Welles in Power' in *Cahiers du Cinéma in English*, no. 11, September 1967.

DE BOSIO, Gianfranco
See under Forman (*Cahiers* 174)

DELAHAYE, Michel
'Tout droit' (on Pasolini's *Il vangelo secondo Matteo*) in *Cahiers* 166–7 (May–June 1965)
trans. as 'The Gospel According to Matthew' in *Cahiers du Cinéma in English*, no. 3, 1966.

See under Dreyer (*Cahiers* 170)

See under Polanski (*Cahiers* 175)

'Double Kiss' (on Fuller's *The Naked Kiss*) in *Cahiers* 176 (March 1966)
trans. as 'The Naked Kiss' in *Cahiers du Cinéma in English*, no. 4, 1966.

'Deux arts en un: René Allio et Antoine Bourseiller répondent à Jean-Luc Godard et Michel Delahaye' (interview/discussion) in *Cahiers* 177 (April 1966)
trans. as 'Allio-Bourseiller-Godard-Delahaye: Two Arts in One' in *Cahiers du Cinéma in English*, no. 6, December 1966.

'Les portes du sens' (on Straub's *Nicht versöhnt*) in *Cahiers* 177 (April 1966)
trans. as 'The Gates of Meaning' in *Cahiers du Cinéma in English*, no. 7, January 1967.

'Remplir sa case' (on Zetterling's *Loving Couples*) in *Cahiers* 177 (April 1966)
trans. as 'Loving Couples' in *Cahiers du Cinéma in English*, no. 6, December 1966.

'Harold fait du yoga' (on Donner's *The Caretaker*) in *Cahiers* 177 (April 1966)
trans. as 'The Caretaker' in *Cahiers du Cinéma in English*, no. 6, December 1966.

See under Bresson (*Cahiers* 178)

'Jean-Luc Godard ou l'enfance de l'art' in *Cahiers* 179 (June 1966)
trans. as 'Jean-Luc Godard and the Childhood of Art' in *Cahiers du Cinéma in English*, no. 10, May 1967.

See under Jean Renoir (*Cahiers* 180)

'Elia Kazan: préface à un entretien' in *Cahiers* 183 (October 1966)
trans. as 'Elia Kazan: Preface to an Interview' in *Cahiers du Cinéma in English*, no. 9, March 1967.

See under Kazan (*Cahiers* 184)

'La chute au plafond' (on Truffaut's *Fahrenheit 451*) in *Cahiers* 184 (November 1966)
trans. as 'The Fall to the Ceiling' in *Cahiers du Cinéma in English*, no. 9, March 1967.

'Jean-Luc Godard ou l'urgence de l'art' in *Cahiers* 187 (February 1967)
trans. as 'Jean-Luc Godard or the Urgency of Art' in *Cahiers du Cinéma in English*, no. 10, May 1967.

See under Jessua (*Cahiers* 188)

See under Skolimowski (*Cahiers* 192)

DONIOL-VALCROZE, Jacques
'Le facteur rhésus et le nouveau cinéma' (on Antonioni's *L'Avventura*) in *Cahiers* 113 (November 1960)
trans. as 'The RH Factor and the New Cinema' in *New York Film Bulletin*, series 2, no. 5 (31); also trans. in *Cahiers du Cinéma in English*, no. 2, 1966.

DOUCHET, Jean
'Hitch et son public' in *Cahiers* 113 (November 1960)
trans. as 'Hitch and his public' in *New York Film Bulletin*, series 2, no. 7 (33); in new translation in this volume.

'Naissance d'un soleil' (on Renoir's *Le Caporal épinglé*) in *Cahiers* 133 (July 1962)
trans. (shortened version) in Filmography in Bazin, A., *Jean Renoir*, New York, Simon & Schuster, 1973; London, W. H. Allen, 1974.

DREYER, Carl T.
'Entretien, par Michel Delahaye' in *Cahiers* 170 (September 1965)
trans. as 'Interview' in *Cahiers du Cinéma in English*, no. 4, 1966; reprinted in Sarris, *Interviews with Film Directors*.

DUBOEUF, Pierre
'L'autre face' (on Welles's *Chimes at Midnight*) in *Cahiers* 181 (August 1966)
trans. as 'The Other Side' in *Cahiers du Cinéma in English*, no. 11, September 1967.

EDWARDS, Blake
'Entretien, par Jean-François Hauduroy' in *Cahiers* 175 (February 1966)
trans. as 'Interview' in *Cahiers du Cinéma in English*, no. 3, 1966.

EYQUEM, Olivier
Anthony Mann: biofilmographie (with Patrick Brion) in *Cahiers* 190 (May 1967)
pub. in *Cahiers du Cinéma in English*, no. 12, December 1967.

342

FELLINI, Federico
'Visites et entretiens, par Pierre Kast' in *Cahiers* 164 (March 1965)
trans. as 'Visits with Fellini' in *Cahiers du Cinéma in English*, no. 5, 1966; reprinted in Sarris, *Interviews with Film Directors*.

FIESCHI, Jean-André
'La difficulté d'être de Jean-Luc Godard' in *Cahiers* 137 (November 1962)
trans. as 'The Difficulty of Being Jean-Luc Godard' in *Cahiers du Cinéma in English*, no. 12, December 1967; reprinted in Mussman, T. (ed.), *Jean-Luc Godard*, New York, E. P. Dutton, 1968.

'Après' (on Godard's *Alphaville*) in *Cahiers* 168 (July 1965)
trans. as 'Alphaville' in *Cahiers du Cinéma in English*, no. 3, 1966.

'La satire prisonnière' (on Donner's *Nothing But the Best*) in *Cahiers* 174 (January 1966)
trans. as 'Nothing but the Best' in *Cahiers du Cinéma in English*, no. 2, 1966.

'Cabiria trépanée' (on Fellini's *Giulietta degli spiriti*) in *Cahiers* 174 (January 1966)
trans. as 'Juliet of the Spirits' in *Cahiers du Cinéma in English*, no. 2, 1966.

See under Polanski (*Cahiers* 175).

'Luis Buñuel: l'ange et la bête' in *Cahiers* 176 (March 1966)
trans. as 'The Angel and the Beast' in *Cahiers du Cinéma in English*, no. 4, 1966.

'Le règne des archetypes' (on Jewison's *The Cincinnati Kid*) in *Cahiers* 176 (March 1966)
trans. as 'The Cincinnati Kid' in *Cahiers du Cinéma in English*, no. 4, 1966.

'Robert Rossen: le film unique' (on *Lilith*) in *Cahiers* 177 (April 1966)
trans. as 'The Unique Film' in *Cahiers du Cinéma in English*, no. 7, January 1967.

'Le cahier des lecteurs' in *Cahiers* 177 (April 1966)
trans. as 'Readers on *La Religieuse*' in *Cahiers du Cinéma in English*, no. 7, January 1967.

See under Renoir (*Cahiers* 180).

FORMAN, Milos
'Entretien, par James Blue et Gianfranco De Bosio' in *Cahiers* 174 (January 1966)
trans. as 'Interview' in *Cahiers du Cinéma in English*, no. 8, February 1967.

'Plus près des choses' in *Cahiers* 177 (April 1966)
trans. as 'Closer to things' in *Cahiers du Cinéma in English*, no. 7, January 1967.

FRANJU, Georges
'Petit journal du cinéma' (Franju interviewed by François Truffaut) in *Cahiers* 104 (February 1960)
trans. as 'Interview with Georges Franju' in Denby, D. (ed.), *The 400 Blows*, New York, Grove Press, 1969.

GILSON, René
See under Berkeley (*Cahiers* 174).

' "Mon Dieu, me quitterez-vous?" ' (on Bresson's *Au hasard Balthazar* . . .) in *Cahiers* 182 (September 1966)
trans. as 'Balthazar' in *Cahiers du Cinéma in English*, no. 11, September 1967.

GODARD, Jean-Luc
'Frère Jacques' (on Jacques Becker) in *Cahiers* 106 (April 1960)
trans. as 'Frère Jacques' in *Godard on Godard*.

'Petit journal du cinéma' in *Cahiers* 109 (July 1960)
trans. as 'Le Petit Soldat' in *Godard on Godard*.

'Les dix meilleurs films de l'année' in *Cahiers* 116 (February 1961)
pub. as 'Ten Best 1960' in *Godard on Godard*.

'Les dix meilleurs films de l'année' in *Cahiers* 128 (February 1962)
pub. as 'The Ten Best Films of 1961' in *Godard on Godard*.

'Entretien avec Jean-Luc Godard' in *Cahiers* 138 (December 1962)
trans. as 'An Interview with Jean-Luc Godard' in Mussman, T. (ed.), *Jean-Luc Godard*, New York, E. P. Dutton, 1968; extract trans. in Collet, J., *Jean-Luc Godard*, New York, Crown, 1970; also trans. in *Godard on Godard*: extracts from this trans. in this volume; also trans. in *New York Film Bulletin*, no. 46, reprinted in Sarris, *Interviews with Film Directors*.

'Les dix meilleurs films de l'année' in *Cahiers* 140 (February 1963)
pub. as 'The Ten Best Films of 1962' in *Godard on Godard*.

'Feu sur les Carabiniers' in *Cahiers* 146 (August 1963)
trans. as 'Taking Pot Shots at the Riflemen' in *New York Film Bulletin*, no. 46, reprinted in Mussman, T. (ed.), *Jean-Luc Godard*, New York, E. P. Dutton, 1968; trans. as 'Les Carabiniers under Fire' in *Godard on Godard*.

'Cinq à la zéro: Le Mépris' in *Cahiers* 146 (August 1963)
trans. as 'Le Mépris' in *Godard on Godard*.

'Dictionnaire de 121 metteurs en scène' in *Cahiers* 150–1 (December 1963–January 1964)
trans. as 'Dictionary of American Film-makers' (Richard Brooks, Charlie Chaplin, Stanley Kubrick, Richard Leacock, Jonas Mekas, Orson Welles, Billy Wilder) in *Godard on Godard*.

'Les meilleurs films américains du parlant' in *Cahiers* 150–1 (December 1963–January 1964)
pub. as 'The Ten Best American Sound Films' in *Godard on Godard*.

'Orphée' in *Cahiers* 152 (February 1964)
trans. as 'Orphée' in *Godard on Godard*.

'Les dix meilleurs films de l'année' in *Cahiers* 152 (February 1964)
pub. as 'The Ten Best Films of 1963' in *Godard on Godard*.

'La Femme mariée' in *Cahiers* 159 (October 1964)
trans. as 'La Femme Mariée' in *Godard on Godard*.

'La nuit, l'eclipse, l'aurore: entretien avec Michelangelo Antonioni par Jean-Luc Godard' in *Cahiers* 160 (November 1964)
trans. as 'Jean-Luc Godard interviews Michelangelo Antonioni' in *Movie*, no. 12,

Spring 1965; as 'Night, Eclipse, Dawn . . .: an interview with Michelangelo Antonioni, by Jean-Luc Godard' in *Cahiers du Cinéma in English*, no. 1, January 1966, reprinted in Sarris, *Interviews with Film Directors*.

'Sept questions aux cinéastes' plus 'réponses' (special issue on French cinema) in *Cahiers* 161–2 (January 1965)
trans. as 'Questionnaire to French Film-makers' in *Godard on Godard*.

'Les meilleurs films français depuis la Libération' in *Cahiers* 161–2 (January 1965)
pub. as 'The Six Best French Films since the Liberation' in *Godard on Godard*.

'Les dix meilleurs films de 1964' in *Cahiers* 165 (April 1965)
pub. as 'The Ten Best Films of 1964' in *Godard on Godard*.

'Six Paris contés – Jean-Luc Godard: Montparnasse-Levallois' in *Cahiers* 171 (October 1965)
trans. as 'Montparnasse-Levallois' in *Godard on Godard*.

'Pierrot mon ami' in *Cahiers* 171 (October 1965)
trans. as 'Pierrot my friend' in *Godard on Godard*; as 'Pierrot Mon Ami' in Mussman, T. (ed.), *Jean-Luc Godard*, New York, E. P. Dutton, 1968.

'Parlons de Pierrot: nouvel entretien avec Jean-Luc Godard', in *Cahiers* 171 (October 1965)
trans. as 'Let's Talk about Pierrot' in *Godard on Godard*; also trans. in Godard, J-L., *Pierrot le Fou*, London, Lorrimer Publishing, 1969.

'Les dix meilleurs films de l'année 1965' in *Cahiers* 174 (January 1966)
pub. as 'The Ten Best Films of 1965' in *Godard on Godard*.

'Deux arts en un: René Allio et Antoine Bourseiller répondent à Jean-Luc Godard et Michel Delahaye' (interview/discussion) in *Cahiers* 177 (April 1966)
trans. as 'Allio-Bourseiller-Godard-Delahaye: Two Arts in One' in *Cahiers du Cinéma in English*, no. 6, December 1966.

See under Bresson (*Cahiers* 177, 178)

'Trois mille heures de cinéma' in *Cahiers* 184 (November 1966)
trans. as 'Three Thousand Hours of Cinema' in *Cahiers du Cinéma in English*, no. 10, May 1967, extracts reprinted in Mussman, T. (ed.), *Jean-Luc Godard*, New York, E. P. Dutton, 1968.

'A propos de *Méditerranée*: Impressions anciennes' in *Cahiers* 187 (February 1967) (originally written in 1964)
trans. as 'Méditerranée' in *Godard on Godard*.

'Lutter sur deux fronts: entretien avec Jean-Luc Godard, par J. Bontemps, J-L. Comolli, M. Delahaye, J. Narboni' in *Cahiers* 194 (October 1967)
trans. as 'Interview on *La Chinoise*' (extract) in Collet, J., *Jean-Luc Godard*, New York, Crown, 1970; further extracts trans. in this volume.

Closely related material: see contemporaneous but non-*Cahiers* interview and other material in *Godard on Godard*; Mussman, *Jean-Luc Godard*; Collet, *Jean-Luc Godard*.

GODET, Sylvain
'Petite divagation' (on Lewis's *The Family Jewels*) in *Cahiers* 175 (February 1966)
trans. as 'The Family Jewels' in *Cahiers du Cinéma in English*, no. 4, 1966.

'Angoisse derrière la vitre' (on Hitchcock's *Torn Curtain*) in *Cahiers* 186 (January 1967)
trans. as 'Anxiety Behind the Window Pane' in *Cahiers du Cinéma in English*, no. 10, May 1967.

GREEN, Adolph
'Comden et Green: Entretien par Jean-François Hauduroy' in *Cahiers* 174 (January 1966)
trans. as 'Interview' in *Cahiers du Cinéma in English*, no. 2, 1966.

GROULX, Gilles
'Dix questions à cinq cinéastes canadiens' plus 'Réponses'
and
'L'expression de l'homme québecois' both in *Cahiers* 176 (March 1966)
trans. as 'Ten Questions to Five Canadian Film Makers' plus 'Responses'
and
'The Expression of Quebecois Man' both in *Cahiers du Cinéma in English*, no. 4, 1966.

GUEGAN, Gérard
'Décollages' (on Godard's *Une Femme mariée*) in *Cahiers* 163 (February 1965)
trans. as 'A Married Woman' in *Cahiers du Cinéma in English*, no. 3, 1966.

HAUDUROY, Jean-François
See under Comden and Green (*Cahiers* 174).

See under Edwards (*Cahiers* 175).

HOVEYDA, Fereydoun
'La réponse de Nicholas Ray' in *Cahiers* 107 (May 1960)
trans. as 'Nicholas Ray's Reply' (extract) in Caughie, J., *Theories of Authorship*; trans. in full in this volume.

'Autocritique' in *Cahiers* 126 (December 1961)
trans. as 'Autocritique' (extract) in Caughie, J., *Theories of Authorship*; trans. in full in this volume, as 'Self-Criticism'.

INOBRAN, Jean
See Narboni (?) (*Cahiers* 166–7).

JESSUA, Alain
'Entretien avec Alain Jessua, par Michel Delahaye' in *Cahiers* 188 (March 1967)
trans. as 'Meeting with Alain Jessua' in *Cahiers du Cinéma in English*, no. 11, September 1967.

JUTRA, Claude
'Dix questions à cinq cinéastes canadiens' plus 'Réponses' in *Cahiers* 176 (March 1966)
trans. as 'Ten Questions to Five Canadian Film Makers' plus 'Responses' in *Cahiers du Cinéma in English*, no. 4, 1966.

KAST, Pierre
'L'âme du canon' (on Truffaut's *Tirez sur le pianiste*) in *Cahiers* 115 (January 1961)
trans. in 'Reviews' (as Pierre Kas) in Braudy, L. (ed.), *Focus on Shoot the Piano Player*, Englewood Cliffs, New Jersey, Prentice-Hall, 1972.

See under Fellini (*Cahiers* 164)

KAZAN, Elia
'Entretien avec Elia Kazan, par Michel Delahaye' in *Cahiers* 184 (November 1966)
trans. as 'A Natural Phenomenon, Interview by Michel Delahaye' in *Cahiers du Cinéma in English*, no. 9, March 1967.

LABARTHE, André S.
See under Resnais/Robbe-Grillet (*Cahiers* 123).

'La chance d'être femme' (on Godard's *Une Femme est une femme*) in *Cahiers* 125 (November 1961)
trans. as 'Une Femme est une femme' in Collet, J., *Jean-Luc Godard*, New York, Crown, 1970.

See under Penn (*Cahiers* 196)

'Petit lexique des termes lewisiens' (with Jacques Aumont, Jean-Louis Comolli, Jean Narboni, Sylvie Pierre) in *Cahiers* 197 (January 1968)
trans. as 'A Concise Lexicon of Lewisian Terms' in Johnston, C. and Willemen, P. (eds), *Frank Tashlin*, Edinburgh, Edinburgh Film Festival in association with *Screen*, 1973.

LAMOTHE, Arthur
'Dix questions à cinq cinéastes canadiens' plus 'Réponses' in *Cahiers* 176
and
'Adieu Philippines' both in *Cahiers* 176 (March 1966)
trans. as 'Ten Questions to Five Canadian Film Makers' plus 'Responses'
and
'Adieu Philippines' in *Cahiers du Cinéma in English*, no. 4, 1966.

LEFEBVRE, Jean-Pierre
'Dix questions à cinq cinéastes canadiens' plus 'Réponses'
and
'La mèche et la bombe' both in *Cahiers* 176 (March 1966)
trans. as 'Ten Questions to Five Canadian Film Makers' plus 'Responses'
and 'The Fuse and the Bomb' in *Cahiers du Cinéma in English*, no. 4, 1966.

LEVY, Jacques
'Brisées' (on Groulx's *Le Chat dans le sac*) in *Cahiers* 187 (February 1967)
trans. as 'Cat in the Sack' in *Cahiers du Cinéma in English*, no. 11, September 1967.

LEWIS, Jerry
'Entretien, par Axel Madsen' in *Cahiers* 175 (February 1966)
trans. as 'Interview' in *Cahiers du Cinéma in English*, no. 4, 1966.

MADSEN, Axel
See under Lewis (*Cahiers* 175)

McCAREY, Leo
'Entretien, par Serge Daney et Jean-Louis Noames' in *Cahiers* 163 (February 1965)
trans. as 'Taking Chances, Interview' in *Cahiers du Cinéma in English*, no. 7, January 1967.

MANKIEWICZ, Joseph L.
'Entretien, par Jacques Bontemps et Richard Overstreet' in *Cahiers* 178 (May 1966)
trans. as 'Measure for Measure, Interview' in *Cahiers du Cinéma in English*, no. 8, February 1967.

MANN, Anthony
'Entretien, par. J.-C. Missiaen' in *Cahiers* 190 (May 1967)
trans. as 'A Lesson in Cinema, Interview' in *Cahiers du Cinéma in English*, no. 12, December 1967.

MARCORELLES, Louis
'Nouveau cinéma à Pézénas' (in 'Petit Journal') in *Cahiers* 177 (April 1966)
trans. as '"New Cinema" at Pézénas' in *Cahiers du Cinéma in English*, no. 6, December 1966.

MARDORE, Michel
'L'Enfer, sourire aux lèvres' (on Donner's *What's New Pussycat?* and *Nothing But the Best*) in *Cahiers* 174 (January 1966)
trans. as 'What's New Pussycat?' and 'Nothing But the Best' in *Cahiers du Cinéma in English*, no. 2, 1966.

'Age d'or, âge du fer: notes sur la politique et le cinéma' in *Cahiers* 175 (February 1966)
trans. as 'Cinema and Politics: Age of Gold, Age of Iron', in *Cahiers du Cinéma in English*, no. 3, 1966.

MARTIN, Paul-Louis
'Sérieux trop sérieux' (on Owen's *Nobody Waved Goodbye*) in *Cahiers* 179 (June 1966)
trans. as 'Serious, Too Serious' in *Cahiers du Cinéma in English*, no. 10, May 1967.

'Le paradoxe de la communication' (on Truffaut's *Fahrenheit 451*) in *Cahiers* 184 (November 1966)
trans. as 'The Paradox of Communication' in *Cahiers du Cinéma in English*, no. 9, March 1967.

MERLEAU-PONTY, Maurice
See under Bresson (*Cahiers* 177)

METZ, Christian
'Débat: A propos de l'impression de réalité au cinéma' in *Cahiers* 166–7 (May–June 1965)
trans. as 'On the Impression of Reality in the Cinema', chapter 1 of Metz, C., *Film Language*, New York, Oxford University Press, 1974.

'Le cinéma moderne et la narrativité' in *Cahiers* 185 (December 1966)
trans. as 'The Modern Cinema and Narrativity', chapter 8 of Metz, C., *Film Language*, New York, Oxford University Press, 1974.

MISSIAEN, Jean-Claude
See under Mann (*Cahiers* 190)

MOULLET, Luc
'Jean-Luc Godard' in *Cahiers* 106 (April 1960)
trans. as 'Jean-Luc Godard' in *Cahiers du Cinéma in English*, no. 12, December 1967,
reprinted in Mussman, T. (ed.), *Jean-Luc Godard*, New York, E. P. Dutton, 1968;
also trans. in this volume (new translation).

NARBONI, Jean
'Condamné au silence' (on Losey's *King and Country*) (as Jean Inobran?) in *Cahiers*
166–7 (May–June 1965)
trans. as 'King and Country' in *Cahiers du Cinéma in English*, no. 3, 1966.

'Sacher et Masoch' (on Welles's *Chimes at Midnight*) in *Cahiers* 181 (August 1966)
trans. as 'Sacher and Masoch' in *Cahiers du Cinéma in English*, no. 11, September
1967.

'La preuve par huit' (on Ford's *Seven Women*) in *Cahiers* 182 (September 1966)
trans. as 'Casting Out the Eights' in Caughie, J., *Theories of Authorship*.

'Notes sur *Deux ou trois choses que je sais d'elle*' in *Cahiers* 186 (January 1967)
trans. as 'Notes on *Two or Three Things* . . .' in *Cahiers du Cinéma in English*, no.
10, May 1967.

'La machine infernale' (on Hitchcock's *Torn Curtain*) in *Cahiers* 186 (January 1967)
trans. as 'The Infernal Machine' in *Cahiers du Cinéma in English*, no. 10, May 1967.

'Petit lexique des termes lewisiens' (with Jacques Aumont, Jean-Louis Comolli,
André S. Labarthe, Sylvie Pierre) in *Cahiers* 197 (January 1968)
trans. as 'A Concise Lexicon of Lewisian Terms' in Johnston, C. and Willemen, P.
(eds), *Frank Tashlin*, Edinburgh, Edinburgh Film Festival in association with *Screen*,
1973.

See under Rivette (*Cahiers* 204).

NOAMES, Jean-Louis
'Trois Tourneur' (on *Wichita, Appointment in Honduras, Anne of the Indies*) in 'Petit
Journal du Cinéma' in *Cahiers* 155 (May 1964)
trans. as 'Three Tourneurs' in Johnston, C. and Willemen, P. (eds), *Jacques
Tourneur*, Edinburgh, Edinburgh Film Festival, 1975.

See under McCarey (*Cahiers* 163).

See under Rossen (*Cahiers* 177).

OLLIER, Claude
'Un roi à New York: King Kong' in *Cahiers* 166–7 (May–June 1965)
trans. as 'A King in New York' in Huss, R. and Ross, T. J. (eds), *Focus on the
Horror Film*, Englewood Cliffs, N.J., Prentice-Hall, 1972; also trans. in this volume
(new translation).

OVERSTREET, Richard
See under Mankiewicz (*Cahiers* 178).

PASOLINI, Pier Paolo
'Le "cinéma de poésie"' in *Cahiers* 171 (October 1965)
trans. as 'Pier Paolo Pasolini at Pesaro: The Cinema of Poetry' in *Cahiers du Cinéma in English*, no. 6, December 1966, reprinted in Nichols, B. (ed.), *Movies and Methods*, Berkeley, Los Angeles and London, University of California Press, 1976.

PENN, Arthur
'Off-Hollywood: entretien avec Arthur Penn, par Jean-Louis Comolli et André S. Labarthe' in *Cahiers* 196 (December 1967)
trans. as (extract) 'Bonnie and Clyde: An Interview with Arthur Penn' in Cawelti, J. G. (ed.), *Focus on Bonnie and Clyde*, Englewood Cliffs, N.J., Prentice-Hall, 1973.

PHILIPPE, Claude-Jean
'L'indifférence et la terreur' (on Lewis's *The Family Jewels*) in *Cahiers* 175 (February 1966)
trans. as 'The Family Jewels' in *Cahiers du Cinéma in English*, no. 4, 1966.

PIERRE, Sylvie
'La beauté de la mer' (on Tourneur's *I Walked with a Zombie*) in *Cahiers* 195 (November 1967)
trans. as 'The Beauty of the Sea' in Johnston, C. and Willemen, P. (eds), *Jacques Tourneur*, Edinburgh, Edinburgh Film Festival, 1975.

'Petit lexique des termes lewisiens' (with Jacques Aumont, Jean-Louis Comolli, André S. Labarthe, Jean Narboni) in *Cahiers* 197 (January 1968)
trans. as 'A Concise Lexicon of Lewisian Terms' in Johnston, C. and Willemen, P. (eds), *Frank Tashlin*, Edinburgh, Edinburgh Film Festival in association with *Screen*, 1973.

See under Rivette (*Cahiers* 204).

POLANSKI, Roman
'Paysage d'un cerveau: entretien avec Roman Polanski, par Michel Delahaye et Jean-André Fieschi' in *Cahiers* 175 (February 1966)
trans. as 'Interview' in *Cahiers du Cinéma in English*, no. 3, 1966.

PRUNEDA, Juan Antonio
See under Welles (*Cahiers* 165).

RAY, Satyajit
'De film en film' in *Cahiers* 175 (February 1966)
trans. as 'From Film to Film' in *Cahiers du Cinéma in English*, no. 3, 1966.

RENOIR, Jean
'Mes prochains films: entretien avec Jean Renoir, par Michel Delahaye et Jean-André Fieschi' in *Cahiers* 180 (July 1966)
trans. as 'My Next Films: Interview' in *Cahiers du Cinéma in English*, no. 9, March 1967.

RESNAIS, Alain
'Entretien avec Alain Resnais et Alain Robbe-Grillet par André S. Labarthe et Jacques Rivette' in *Cahiers* 123 (September 1961)

trans. as 'André S. Labarthe and Jacques Rivette in conversation with Alain Resnais and Alain Robbe-Grillet' in *New York Film Bulletin*, no. 2, vol. 3, March 1962, reprinted in Sarris, *Interviews with Film Directors*.

RIEFENSTAHL, Leni
'Leni et le loup: entretien avec Leni Riefenstahl, par Michel Delahaye' in *Cahiers* 170 (September 1965)
trans. as 'Leni and the Wolf' in *Cahiers du Cinéma in English*, no. 5, 1966, reprinted in Sarris, *Interviews with Film Directors*.

RIVETTE, Jacques
'La Mort aux trousses' (on Cocteau's *Le Testament d'Orphée*) in *Cahiers* 106 (April 1960)
trans. as 'Death Taken Seriously: *Le Testament d'Orphée*' in Gilson, R., *Jean Cocteau*, New York, Crown, 1969.

See under Resnais (*Cahiers* 123).

'Entretien avec Jacques Rivette, par Jacques Aumont, Jean-Louis Comolli, Jean Narboni et Sylvie Pierre' in *Cahiers* 204 (September 1968)
trans. as 'Time Overflowing: Interview with Jacques Rivette' in Rosenbaum, J. (ed.), *Rivette: Texts and Interviews*, London, British Film Institute, 1977; extract reprinted in this volume.

ROBBE-GRILLET, Alain
See under Resnais (*Cahiers* 123)

ROSSEN, Robert
'Leçons d'un combat: entretien avec Robert Rossen' by Jean-Louis Noames in *Cahiers* 177 (April 1966)
trans. as 'Lessons Learned in Combat, Interview' in *Cahiers du Cinéma in English*, no. 7, January 1967.

RUBIO, Miguel
See under Welles (*Cahiers* 165, 179).

SEBERG, Jean
'Lilith et moi' in *Cahiers* 177 (April 1966)
trans. as 'Lilith and I' in *Cahiers du Cinéma in English*, no. 7, January 1967.

SKOLIMOWSKI, Jerzy
'Le vingt-et-unième' in *Cahiers* 177 (April 1966)
trans. as 'The Twenty-First' in *Cahiers du Cinéma in English*, no. 7, January 1967.

'Passages et niveaux: entretien avec Jerzy Skolimowski par Michel Delahaye' in *Cahiers* 192 (July–August 1967)
trans. as 'Passages and Levels, Interview' in *Cahiers du Cinéma in English*, no. 12, December 1967.

STRARAM, Patrick
'Dossier canadien: L'amour avec des si' in *Cahiers* 176 (March 1966)
trans. as 'Love With Hopes' in *Cahiers du Cinéma in English*, no. 4, 1966.

STRAUB, Jean-Marie
'Frustration de la violence' in *Cahiers* 177 (April 1966)
trans. as 'Frustration of Violence' in *Cahiers du Cinéma in English*, no. 7, January 1967.

TECHINE, André
'Le sourire de Prague' (on Milos Forman) in *Cahiers* 174 (January 1966)
trans. as 'The Smile of Prague' in *Cahiers du Cinéma in English*, no. 8, February 1967.

'Les joues en feu' (on Lewis's *The Family Jewels*) in *Cahiers* 175 (February 1966)
trans. as 'The Family Jewels' in *Cahiers du Cinéma in English*, no. 4, 1966.

'L'air du large' (on Kaufman and Manaster's *Goldstein*) in *Cahiers* 177 (April 1966)
trans. as 'Goldstein' in *Cahiers du Cinéma in English*, no. 6, December 1966.

'Les naufragés de l'autocar' (on Hitchcock's *Torn Curtain*) in *Cahiers* 186 (January 1967)
trans. as 'The Castaways of the Bus' in *Cahiers du Cinéma in English*, no. 10, May 1967.

THEVOZ, Michel
'Collages' (on Godard's *Une Femme mariée*) in *Cahiers* 163 (February 1965)
trans. as 'A Married Woman' in *Cahiers du Cinéma in English*, no. 3, 1966.

TRUFFAUT, François
'Petit journal du cinéma' (Franju interviewed by François Truffaut) in *Cahiers* 104 (February 1960)
trans. as 'Interview with Georges Franju' in Denby, D. (ed.), *The 400 Blows*, New York, Grove Press, 1969.

'Entretien avec François Truffaut' in *Cahiers* 138 (December 1962)
trans. as (extracts) 'Interview with François Truffaut' in Graham, P. (ed.), *The New Wave*, London, Secker & Warburg; New York, Doubleday, 1968; extract also trans. in Braudy, L. (ed.), *Focus on Shoot the Piano Player*, Englewood Cliffs, N.J., Prentice-Hall, 1972.

'Le Testament d'Orphée' in *Cahiers* 152 (February 1964)
trans. (original plus additional material) as 'Le Testament d'Orphée' in Truffaut, F., *The Films in my Life*, New York, Simon & Schuster, 1978; London, Allen Lane, 1980.

'Journal de *Fahrenheit 451*' in *Cahiers* 175–80 (February–July 1966)
trans. as 'The Journal of *Fahrenheit 451*' in *Cahiers du Cinéma in English*, nos. 5–7, 1966–January 1967; extracts reprinted in Johnson, W. (ed.), *Focus on the Science-Fiction Film*, Englewood Cliffs, N.J., Prentice-Hall, 1972.

VISCONTI, Luchino
'Un drame du non-être' (on *Vaghe stelle dell'orsa/Of a Thousand Delights/Sandra*) in *Cahiers* 174 (January 1966)
trans. as 'Drama of Non-Existence' in *Cahiers du Cinéma in English*, no. 2, 1966.

WELLES, Orson
'Voyage au pays de Don Quichotte: conversations avec Orson Welles par Juan Cobos, Miguel Rubio et J. A. Pruneda' in *Cahiers* 165 (April 1965)
trans. as 'A Voyage to Don Quixoteland' in *Cahiers du Cinéma in English*, no. 5, 1966, reprinted in Sarris, *Interviews with Film Directors*, extracts reprinted in Bessy, M., *Orson Welles*, New York, Crown, 1971; in Welles, O., *The Trial*, New York, Simon & Schuster; London, Lorrimer, 1970, in Gottesman, R. (ed.), *Focus on Citizen Kane*, Englewood Cliffs, N.J., Prentice-Hall, 1971.

'Orson Welles: *Chimes at Midnight*' (interview by Juan Cobos, Miguel Rubio) in *Cahiers* 179 (June 1966)
trans. as 'Welles on Falstaff' in *Cahiers du Cinéma in English*, no. 11, September 1967.

ZETTERLING, Mai
'Rencontre avec Mai Zetterling' (in 'Petit Journal du Cinéma') in *Cahiers* 177 (April 1966)
trans. as 'Meeting with Mai Zetterling' in *Cahiers du Cinéma in English*, no. 6, December 1966.

Appendix 3

Cahiers du Cinéma in the 1950s and the 1970s

This volume of material from *Cahiers du Cinéma* covers the period 1960–68. Volume 1, published in 1985, covered the period 1951–9; Volumes 3 and 4 will cover the periods 1969–72 and the later 1970s respectively.

Volume 1: 1951–9
When *Cahiers* was founded in 1951 it inherited many of its critics (André Bazin, Eric Rohmer, Jacques Doniol-Valcroze, Pierre Kast, for example) and many of its critical concerns (and even its cover design) from the earlier journal *La Revue du Cinéma*. It was here in the 1940s that Bazin and Rohmer had developed much of their thinking about realism and the evolution of film language, and it was here that American cinema had been championed. These were both crucial components in *Cahiers* in the 1950s: attitudes to Italian cinema – neo-realism and Roberto Rossellini in particular – and to American cinema as a whole are strongly represented in Volume 1. To the *Cahiers* critics – both the older critics and the soon distinctive 'young Turks' François Truffaut, Jean-Luc Godard, Jacques Rivette and Claude Chabrol – Italian cinema and American cinema offered much that was found to be lacking in contemporary French cinema, particularly an engagement with social reality and an inventive freedom of form. Throughout the 1950s, as *Cahiers* increasingly established its own identity and importance as a journal, its critics engaged in fierce polemics over French cinema, as well as making short films themselves and criticising cinema very much from the standpoint of future film-makers. Volume 1 thus traces the development, in reviews and discussions, of the *Cahiers* critics to their acclaim in 1958–9 as directors of the so-called *nouvelle vague* or 'new wave'.

The international impact of the 'new wave' films drew much attention to *Cahiers* and in particular to its controversial positions on popular American cinema. These positions – centred around the contentious concept of the *politique des auteurs* (the 'auteur policy', which became known later in Britain and the USA as the 'auteur theory') and around associated ideas about *mise en scène* – were to initiate intense critical debate in Britain and the USA, ultimately producing radically changed critical assumptions. As well as general articles on the nature of American cinema, on authorship, on genre and on technological aspects such as CinemaScope, Volume 1 offers a range of *Cahiers* writing on *auteurs* such as Howard Hawks,

Alfred Hitchcock, Fritz Lang, Samuel Fuller, with a short critical dossier on Nicholas Ray, one of the American film-makers most revered by *Cahiers*.

Volume 1 seeks to reflect the broad range of critical interests and polemics which characterised *Cahiers* in the 1950s, perhaps its best known and most influential period.

Volume 3: 1969–72

In the later 1960s, represented in Volume 2, *Cahiers* was marked by the development of a polemic for a 'new cinema' and for a conscious politicization of film criticism. These new emphases involved a reassessment of the stance *Cahiers* had taken towards American cinema in the past and a recognition of important ways in which film-making itself had been changing. Thus, in the latter half of the 1960s *Cahiers* was already evolving towards the more rigorously political and theoretical positions usually associated with the journal in the period after the political and cultural upheavals of May 1968. Paradoxically, *Cahiers* changed owner-publisher in the mid-1960s and was redesigned to look more 'popular', just at the time it was beginning to become less 'popular' in the areas of cinema it valued and hence less 'popular' in appeal. During the short but very intense period covered by Volume 3, *Cahiers* lost readers and went through ownership crises, ending the period with a very austere cover design and a new financial structure.

If the critical identity of *Cahiers* had been clear and influential in the late 1950s, then less distinct in the 1960s, it now became, in the post-1968 period, once again polemical and a source of enormous influence and controversy. This time, however, the polemics – more political, more theoretical – had less widespread appeal: whereas the critical controversies around authorship and American cinema and *mise en scène* in the late 1950s subsequently entered, in however crude or partial a form, writing about film generally – in newspaper reviewing, for example – the theoretical work of *Cahiers* in the 1969–72 period had its effects in the narrower field of serious film writing and film teaching.

Those effects were, however, very radical. They had to do, essentially, with the elaboration of a 'politics of cinema' in the wake of the events of May 1968[1] and the upheaval they caused within left-wing politics in France and, within those politics, radical thinking about the function of culture and cultural work. The crucial areas of debate became those embodied in the title of a celebrated 1969 *Cahiers* editorial: 'Cinema/Ideology/Criticism'.[2] Central to this debate was the concept of 'dominant ideology', formulated by philosopher Louis Althusser in his re-reading of Marx, and the manner in which such a dominant ideology was carried in cinema. As Volume 3 puts it, part of what was involved was a definitive break with the 'idealist' representational aesthetic of realism associated with André Bazin, so central to *Cahiers'* past, and its replacement with an aesthetic based on 'montage' and its association with dialectical materialism, in particular its relationship to Eisenstein and the Soviet cinema of the 1920s, which became a major area for 'rediscovery' by *Cahiers* in this period.

The nature and function of criticism itself also became central: what was the status of the 'scientific' criticism *Cahiers* wished to practise, with its borrowings from the post-Freudian psychoanalytic work of Jacques Lacan, in relation to the spectator as 'subject', and from grammatologist Jacques Derrida, in relation to the process of 'reading'? As well as a rediscovery of Soviet cinema, this period also produced sustained work in the 're-reading' of French and American cinema of the past, in analysis of the new cinema of film-makers such as Miklos Jancsó and

355

Jean-Marie Straub and Danièle Huillet, and in systematic ideological analysis of contemporary 'political' films, such as those by Costa-Gavras.

Volume 4: The Later 1970s
The *Cahiers* project in the later 1970s very much continues and extends the political and theoretical positions elaborated in the post-1968 period, in particular questions around the place of the spectator, from the psychoanalytic work of Lacan, and questions around politics and history arising out of the work of Michel Foucault. The continuing overall commitment to understanding the operation of bourgeois cinema, through systematic re-reading of both films and film history, criticism and theory, was complemented by a commitment to exploring alternatives to bourgeois cinema, whether the deconstructed European cinema of Godard, Straub-Huillet and others or, increasingly important in this period, the 'anti-imperialist' cinema in, for example, Algeria, Palestine, China, Chile. To some extent there was also a re-focusing on French cinema, as *Cahiers* had done in the 1950s, prior to the New Wave, and on the way in which a genuinely 'national' French cinema needed to be understood and generated. In these senses, questions about cinema and cultural struggle remained at the head of the *Cahiers* agenda: what could a radical film journal contribute to political struggle on the cultural front?

Notes

1 For an account of the events of May 1968, see Sylvia Harvey, *May 68 and Film Culture*, London, British Film Institute, 1978
2 Jean-Louis Comolli and Jean Narboni, 'Cinema/Ideology/Criticism', *Cahiers* 216, October 1969; trans. in *Screen*, vol. 12, no. 1, Spring 1971, reprinted in Bill Nichols (ed.), *Movies and Methods*, Berkeley, University of California Press, 1976, and in *Screen Reader 1*, London, Society for Education in Film and Television, 1977.

Index of Names and Film Titles

357

361

Index of Names and Film Titles